GIAMBATTISTA TIEPOLO

HIS LIFE AND ART

Michael Levey

TIEPOLO
GIAMBATTISTA

HIS LIFE AND ART

Yale University Press · *New Haven and London*

Designed by Gillian Malpass
Set in Monophoto Bembo by
SX Composing Ltd, Rayleigh, Essex
Printed in Italy by
Amilcare Pizzi S.p.A., Milan

Library of Congress Cataloging-in-Publication Data

Levey, Michael.
  Giambattista Tiepolo: his life and art.

  Bibliography: p.
  Includes index.
  1. Tiepolo, Giovanni Battista, 1696–1770.
2. Painters—Italy—Biography.   3. Tiepolo, Giovanni
Battista, 1696–1770—Criticism and interpretation.
I. Title.
ND623.T5L58   1986   759.5 [B]   86-7730
ISBN 0-300-03018-5

Frontispiece: Detail of Pl. 26 showing self-portrait of Tiepolo.

To

HELEN AND ALLAN BRAHAM

with affectionate gratitude

ACKNOWLEDGMENTS

MY FIRST, fundamental acknowledgment must be to my wife, Brigid Brophy, whose constant interest in and encouragement of my project of writing at length on Tiepolo sustained me in the task.

Over the years I have benefited much from exchanging ideas with colleagues and friends, as well as being the grateful recipient of articles and photographs. To list them all would not be possible but I should like to single out my colleague at the National Gallery, Michael Helston, who has been especially kind and helpful. Several students of Tiepolo have borne my interest in mind, keeping me in touch with their own research and publications; and I must mention appreciatively Professor George Knox.

In Venice I am particularly grateful to Dr Filippo Pedrocco who undertook research on my behalf, checked numerous Tiepolo documents and supplied valuable transcripts. Specific results of his research are acknowledged in the notes. And while mentioning Venice, I must refer gratefully to another scholar, Professor Terisio Pignatti, with whom I first looked at some of Tiepolo's great works in the Veneto, and who has never failed to respond to appeals for information and help. I also want to mention gratefully Professor Alessandro Bettagno for his ever-generous interest and kind assistance. My gratitude goes also to Mrs Grace L. Ginnis, for once again typing from a tangled manuscript with such care and skill.

To my publisher, John Nicoll, and my editor, Gillian Malpass, I owe much: his early enthusiasm for the concept of this book fostered its growth, while Gillian Malpass's acute attention to the resulting text has improved it. To her I am also indebted for a lay-out conceived not only handsomely but intelligently.

Finally, I must express my thanks to Helen and Allan Braham. My good fortune has been to enjoy absorbing opportunities to study and discuss with them works by Tiepolo in England, Italy and Spain; and I ask them to accept the dedication of this book as some token of my indebtedness.

M.L.
London, 1986

1. Detail of Pl. 42.

Each Change of many-colour'd Life he drew,
Exhausted Worlds, and then imagin'd new:

Johnson, *Prologue at the Opening of the*
Drury Lane Theatre

'Al presente sono alla fine del modello della Gran Opera, che tanto è vasto . . . fatica
grande ma per tal Opera ci vuol coraggio.'

Tiepolo, Letter of 1762

CONTENTS

1 BACKGROUND, BIRTH AND EARLY YEARS

GIAMBATTISTA TIEPOLO was an artist born and bred Venetian. Behind such a banal-seeming statement lies a surprising proliferation of facts and implications that offer useful ways of approaching him and his art.

He was born in Venice of parents with an ancient, noble Venetian name. He was baptised in the ancient cathedral of Venice. He grew up absorbing and embodying a great native artistic tradition; and it is hard to envisage him originating in any other Italian centre, so deeply imbued is his art with those qualities of brilliant colour, exuberant invention and virtuoso handling of paint that are most often singled out as characteristic of the Venetian School.

In temperament too, Tiepolo seems the typical Venetian artist: a hard-working practitioner, absorbed by his art to the exclusion of other activities, with no theoretical views to propound on aesthetics, no ambition to shine in polite, literary society and no eagerness to claim particular status for the artist as such. His goals in life seem to have been simple, though strongly adhered to: a happy family existence, reasonable prosperity and, above all, constant employment. He achieved all three. He was to enjoy a career of ceaseless, successful activity which lasted for more than half a century. Until the end, he was at work, with a fresh major project materialising when he was unexpectedly taken ill and abruptly died.

He died far away from his wife, his city and his country, but that was because of his compulsion to seek work, never to remain unemployed; even in old age, and when comfortably off, he sought new challenges. He and his art had travelled far, he to Germany and Spain, and his work to Sweden and Russia as well. In Venice he was not forgotten. When news of his death in Madrid reached Venice, a local diarist noted it with almost elegiac phrases, mentioning the 'bitter loss', recalling the place Tiepolo held and not unaware perhaps that with his death an artistic era had ended: 'the most famous Venetian painter, truly the most renowned . . . well known in Europe and the most highly praised in his native land'.[1]

Tiepolo had been heir to Titian and Tintoretto, as well as to Veronese. He was, in his way, a Renaissance artist, for all that he lived in 'the age of reason'. Certainly he was the last of the race in Venice. He left no successor, and, though some gifted painters (like his brother-in-law Francesco Guardi) lived on, with Tiepolo there effectively closed the strongest traditions of Venetian painting.

There are yet other aspects of the Venetian-ness of Tiepolo. Born in a city that was still the capital of an empire, a European attraction if no longer a European power, and conscious of its proud history as the 'most serene', unconquered republic, Tiepolo was subtly fostered, as well as patronised, by an intensely conservative society. Imaginatively, at least, he reflected its standards and its assumptions. Church and state were elsewhere undergoing sharp scrutiny, if not open attack, and even in Venice there were tremors of unrest under the bland public appearance of firm, unchanged, unalterable government. Tiepolo's art is far from bland and by no means without its flavour of irony. Nor was he exactly an official artist, in a city which by his day found little state employment for artists.

2. Detail of Pl. 42.

But his imagination could not fail to respond excitedly to high-sounding traditional and essentially aristocratic concepts embodied in an élite of human and divine persons: saints, heroes and heroines, gods and goddesses, Venus and the Virgin Mary, and God himself. Politically, Venice was indulging in a dangerous day-dream, in order to keep out cold facts, wrapping around itself all the mingled glamorous associations of its past under supernatural guidance. To make the past an artistic reality, to set a hero acting heroically along the wall of a palace, and bring all heaven on to the ceiling of a church, was Tiepolo's particular gift, whatever his personal beliefs. Thus he comes to be a symbol of that rigid, *ancien-régime* Venice that the *ancien régime* of the rest of Europe already saw as out-dated and probably doomed. In retrospect, there might subjectively seem something hectic and extreme in his art, as if its very splendours are sunset ones; and as if, in reflecting eighteenth-century Venice, it fortells the decline of the Republic, which was to expire within twenty-five years of the artist's own death.

Tiepolo was not born to overturn things, either in artistic terms or otherwise. He was quite devoid of the prickly, 'difficult' characteristics often supposed typical of later, Romantic artists but manifested in his Venice by such contemporaries as Canaletto and Piazzetta. Tiepolo seems always to have been amiably responsive to his patrons, adaptable when necessary, unawed by even the greatest and never over-taxed by their requirements. His imagination was at the service of those who could afford him, and the more ambitious their concepts, the more contented doubtless he was. To apotheosise a family's ancestor or bring down to earth a celestial vision presented him with no problem. Secular or sacred, myths became visual actuality.

Yet there is nothing airy or insubstantial, in the sense of vague, about the resulting work. Tiepolo's images are incisive, in concept and in execution, realised with the greatest clarity and assuredness, pungently physical and 'real'. He is so effective in conveying the supernatural exactly because of his instinctively powerful grasp on the natural and actual. Dizzily rising or falling through space—itself vividly realised pictorially as a concept—the bodies of his figures are astonishing in their trajectory because they possess such weight and corporeal solidity. And in his typical heaven there are usually clouds, but there is no cloudiness.

A further indication perhaps of Tiepolo's truly Venetian character is that there should be not only the grasp on physical reality but frequently with it a vein of earthy, half-mocking humour. It can obtrude with possibly disconcerting effect even into elevated scenes of religious subject-matter—just as Tiepolo's own features can look out quizzically, sometimes from under bizarre headgear, from among the attendants in some grandiose composition, inviting a smile at the extravagant spectacle of which he is the deviser (see Pl. 2).

It is less of a paradox than it might at first appear that Tiepolo, the creator of cloud-capped towers and gorgeous palaces, was an artist whose feet were so resolutely on the ground. His vision began with observation of life around him: from contemporary faces (not least his own) to farm buildings, including the shape of a naked shoulder, a brooch, the folds of some drapery, a bird's wing, a broken column, a dog's snout and the foliage of a pine tree.

Life itself, he might have claimed, had he been sententious, has in it nothing alien to his art. The naked shoulder would become that of a demon or a river-god, and the bird's wing the pinions of an angelic messenger. A pine tree would serve for Tiepolo's Greece or Egypt—or indeed for anywhere else, including the gardens of Armida. What he saw in terms of contemporary costume and personality could rarely be fitted into the 'high' style of his serious commissions but it found expression in his caricature drawings. He could have been a painter of genre scenes or land-scapes, view-pictures too, or of portraits, all as practised by specialists in eighteenth-century Venice. He chose the most traditional and respected category of art, becoming not merely a history painter but a decorative history painter, thus linking himself directly with the style created two centuries earlier in Venice by Veronese. It was in that mode that from the first he obviously saw his imagination as having its greatest scope.

Veronese had defended his art before the Inquisition, when criticised for his introduction of profane, incongruous-seeming elements into sacred subjects, by claiming 'the same licence' as was given to poets and jesters. It was a defence of artistic liberty that Tiepolo was not called on to make, partly because the very mixture of gravity and light-heartedness, of the aristocratic and plebeian, of religious and secular—all assembled on a large scale, with opulent colour and decorative effect—had by the eighteenth century become accepted as typical of Venetian art. Until the last, Tiepolo was inescapably, and with far greater resonance than intended by the writer, the figure designated by the King of Spain's chief minister on his arrival in that country as the 'Professore Veneziano'. With moving pride, Tiepolo's eldest son, Domenico, was to etch his father's final painting after his death in 1770, and proclaim its author to be Giambattista Tiepolo, in the service of His Hispanic Majesty, 'Venetus Pictor'. Given the widest interpretation, it is the truest of epitaphs.

★   ★   ★

On 16 April 1696 the sixth child of Domenico and Orsetta Tiepolo was baptised in S. Pietro di Castello, then the cathedral of Venice, and given the names Giovanni Battista. His grandfather had been called Giovanni, as it happens, but the boy's names were chosen presumably in honour of his godfather, a Venetian nobleman, Giovanni Battista Donà.[2]

In the location of his baptism, as in his surname, traditional associations were stirred and indeed united. The Tiepolo were one of the oldest of all Venetian patrician families. Before 1300 they had given the republic two Doges. If the name of Baiamonte Tiepolo, who in 1310 led an abortive aristocratic revolt against the government, was execrated, subsequent members of the family, acting in roles such as ambassadors, had consistently proved good servants of the state. In 1619 Giovanni Tiepolo became Patriarch of Venice, and under him the interior of S. Pietro was remodelled into the Palladian form it retains. It may be that the coincidence of name is without significance, or there may have been some link, though no direct relationship, between the Patriarch and the family of the future painter.

The profession of Domenico Tiepolo was stated in his son's baptismal entry merely as 'merchant', but from entries for his other children, and references elsewhere, it appears he was captain and part-owner of a ship,[3] a 'merchant of Venice' comparable to Shakespeare's Antonio, if not on such a grand scale. Neither he nor his famous son seems to have claimed kinship with the noble family of the Tiepolo, but it is likely that somehow a member of it had adopted an ancestor of the painter's and permitted, or encouraged, use of the name. Converts from Judaism, for example, might take the name of their sponsor. It was thus that the future librettist Lorenzo da Ponte acquired his name, that of Monsignor Lorenzo da Ponte, Bishop of Ceneda in the Veneto, the patron under whom a whole Jewish family was converted. In some perhaps less dramatic way it is conceivable that the Patriarch Tiepolo had patronised a member of the merchant Domenico's family (arguably his father Giovanni) and allowed his distinguished surname to be adopted. That the noble family was not unfriendly in the eighteenth century to the great painter's own is shown by the fact that the Cavaliere Alvise Tiepolo accepted the dedication by the artist's son, another Domenico, of his etchings and stood sponsor at his marriage. Domenico also referred gratefully to the patronage Alvise Tiepolo had extended to his father.[4]

The seventeenth-century merchant Domenico obviously had good relations with several noble Venetian families. Apart from calling on Giovanni Donà, he had godfathers for some of his other children from the Mocenigo, Giovanelli and Dolfin (a

family from which were to come some of the painter's earliest and most faithful patrons). Other non-noble families now associated with artists found godparents among patricians. It is not surprising that Count Pietro Zenobio, the patron of Carlevaris, acted as godfather to Carlevaris's son, named after him Pietro. A member of the Contarini family stood as godfather to the sister of Rosalba Carriera. A procurator of St Mark's, Alvise Pisani, stood similarly to the twin sisters of Giambattista Pittoni. Nevertheless, Domenico Tiepolo, the painter's father, seems to have made a distinct speciality of the practice and to have enjoyed considerable acquaintance among the patrician class—possibly through his mercantile activities.

The Tiepolo family home was in the narrow Corte di S. Domenico in the poor but lively Castello district, in a house now destroyed. Quite close to the Arsenal and atmospherically far distant from the Piazza S. Marco, Castello has its own sense of being a little Venice within the greater one and has probably not vastly changed in that way since Tiepolo's birth. The area had its own traditions, one being confrontation annually with the Nicolotti (from the district of S. Niccolò dei Mendicoli) on the Ponte dei Pugni. The eve of St Peter's day, 29 July, was celebrated by one of the four popular night festivals in Venice, with bonfires and puppet-shows in the campo in front of S. Pietro di Castello, as depicted by Canaletto (Pl. 3). Tiepolo's birthplace was so-called after the nearby church of S. Domenico, also now destroyed, as are some other churches then existing in the vicinity. Custom may have dictated choice of S. Pietro, as the cathedral of Venice, for baptism; or Giambattista's father may have had reasons for a special personal attachment to it.

Certainly, in retrospect, its suitability for the baptism of Tiepolo is considerable, quite apart from associations, accidental or otherwise, with the Patriarch Tiepolo. Another noble family was partly commemorated there, that of Morosini, on the altar of whose chapel was a painting by one of the more attractive and stylistically colourful of seventeenth-century painters, Ruschi. The name of Morosini had acquired the greatest lustre in the years immediately before Tiepolo's birth, when the outstanding figure in Venice was Francesco Morosini, a heroic naval warrior who became Doge and who had died on campaign in 1694. He was the last great Venetian captain, perhaps the last truly great personality in the history of the Republic, and his achievements were to be specially celebrated in the Doge's Palace by a permanent triumphal arch, decorated with paintings by artists who included Tiepolo's future teacher, Gregorio Lazzarini.

In S. Pietro di Castello there were religious paintings by significant painters of the past—among them Veronese—but also contemporary large-scale paintings which had been executed following the canonisation in 1690 of the first Patriarch, St Lorenzo Giustinian, and which dealt with the saint's life. On one side of the high altar was thus the *Charity of St Lorenzo Giustinian* (Pl. 4), a highly elaborate composition, with clear echoes in it of motifs derived from Veronese, which was the work of Lazzarini. He lived locally, so it is not surprising that he had been commissioned for the cathedral and was to be chosen as master of the young Tiepolo. But he was a distinguished practitioner of the day, more accomplished than is sometimes realised. Since cleaning, the *Charity of St Lorenzo Giustinian* is seen to be richly coloured and far from timidly handled; and though it does not quite announce Tiepolo's genius, it acts as quite suitable artistic godfather to the style to be developed by the painter baptised in the same church.

Giambattista Tiepolo had been born on 5 March 1696.[5] He was never to know his father, who died just over a year later, aged about fifty.[6] The doctor then called in was a certain Dr Zanetti, conceivably Dr Girolamo Zanetti, who himself died in 1711. Dr Girolamo is of some artistic relevance since he was the father of Anton Maria Zanetti, a considerable amateur in eighteenth-century Venice, a witty draughtsman of caricatures and a collector, a friend of Rosalba and several other artists of that generation, as well as being acquainted with Tiepolo. It is therefore conceivable that the Tiepolo–Zanetti link went back to the death of Giambattista's father. No more is known about him, and still less is known of Giambattista's mother. Tiepolo was to give her first name, Orsola (Orsetta in Venetian), to his own youngest daughter, but the mother's maiden name is not as yet established. The family circumstances of the widow and her children—most of whom were under the age of ten in 1697—are not clear. They may possibly have moved from the Corte di S. Domenico, though remaining probably in the district of Castello. Of the painter's brothers and sisters not much has been traced. His brother Ambrogio seems later to have lived with or near him. His unmarried sister Eugenia (born 1691) made in her will in 1752 a tantalising reference to paintings she had presumably inherited, 'li quadri de parte de mio padre e mia madre', and which she bequeathed to her by then very famous brother, should he wish to have them.[7] That seems to be the sole reference connecting the family with an interest in painting before the emergence of the young Giambattista.

4. G. Lazzarini, *Charity of St Lorenzo Giustinian*, S. Pietro di Castello, Venice.

5. Salvator Rosa, *Seated soldier*, Gabinetto Nazionale delle Stampe, Rome.

6. Rembrandt, *Studies of men's heads*, Albertina, Vienna.

In the Castello district Lazzarini's would be the obvious choice of studio for a youthful artist to join, and probably around 1710 Tiepolo entered it. No records survive to confirm what seems most patent: Tiepolo's precociousness and the likelihood that it was early apparent that the boy had a remarkable gift—a gift for drawing. He began with none of the personal and artistic advantages of Piazzetta and Canaletto, whose fathers were already active in other areas of the visual arts, and without an uncle to train him, like Pittoni. He was talented—very soon it was to be clear that he was brilliantly talented, with an imagination daring and ardent—but he was alone. And in certain ways that is perhaps how he remained as far as his fellow-painters were concerned, detached from most of them not only by sheer genius but conceivably by temperament as well. He may even have had to work harder to help his widowed mother and at a very early age grown used to the concept of always working.

He entered the studio of Lazzarini to be trained as a painter. Yet at the core of his art was draughtsmanship, and he drew as instinctively as he breathed. From the first, drawing was for him much more therefore than a matter merely of preparatory studies for paintings. As a medium it was the obvious one for an artist of such fecund ideas, such spontaneity and bubbling energy—all the qualities that contemporaries were quick to discover in his art and sum up as 'fire'. Light too, posterity would add as a quality, for it was light in the sense of an illuminating power defining objects that Tiepolo set out to convey and which, with a few strokes of pen or crayon, or the slightest wash, he could indeed capture on a single sheet of paper.

In the medium of drawing lay the greatest freedom for the artist, and there again the medium suited Tiepolo from the first. It allowed his bizarre fancies to find immediate expression—and he had much to express of highly personal fantasy and caprice. His teachers in that area were to be artists very different from Lazzarini, chiefly seventeenth-century figues like Salvator Rosa (Pl. 5) and Castiglione and Callot and Rembrandt (Pl. 6) all of whose etched work was available to him. It is no accident that the graphic aspect of these artists appealed to him, for brilliant draughtsmanship would be the basis of his own art. And perhaps Castiglione, whose drawings were collected and prized in Venice, meant most to him. Their energy and their fantasy were not unlike his. As late as the *St Tecla* (Pls 196–7), he seems partly to be recalling Castiglione.

Yet none of this means that his training under Lazzarini was without its uses. Lazzarini had been born in 1655 and was to live until 1730, by which time Tiepolo's genius was brilliantly patent. He was a typical figure of his period, competent rather than thrilling as an artist but accomplished as a portraitist, as well as a history painter. He worked slowly—a contrast to his pupil—and was 'learned'; at home in mythological subject-matter and also in architecture and perspective, on which he wrote a treatise. For him, as for so many Venetian painters of the day, Veronese stood as the dominant influence from the past. As a young man, Lazzarini had copied the central group of musicians from Veronese's *Marriage Feast at Cana* (then in the refectory of SS Giovanni e Paolo), and his own *Charity of St Lorenzo Giustinian* borrowed architectural elements from the same painting.

Lazzarini had several pupils and probably took the training of them as seriously as he seems to have taken his art. He is recorded as of a retiring nature, studious rather than social in personality, but not the least significant factor of employment in his studio was the extensive patronage he enjoyed—in Venetian patrician circles but also beyond Italy altogether.

To the basic grounding Tiepolo gained from Lazzarini must first be added valuable awareness of mythology and history (which he would always be required to depict) and then perhaps some association with noble patrons. The Labia and the Donà were only two of the families who patronised Lazzarini. Tiepolo was to work for the former, and from the latter had come his godfather. It would have been easy for the young, still apprenticed painter to learn something of the ways—as well as the usefulness—of noble patrons. And perhaps the international demand for Lazzarini's paintings, which went from his studio to Amsterdam and Vienna and Spain, was also a stimulus for the future.

As Tiepolo grew up he must, however, have become increasingly aware that Lazzarini's artistic style belonged in the past, being 'safe' and even dull in terms of other developments going on in Venice. The most obvious of these is represented by Sebastiano Ricci, not Venetian by birth but working periodically in the city during Tiepolo's boyhood, and also by Giovanni Antonio Pellegrini who was, however, absent from Venice in the years Tiepolo was training as a painter.

Ricci was only four years younger than Lazzarini, and he too had been significantly influenced by Veronese, as well as by Pietro da Cortona and Giordano. But he was a far more vigorous painter, with greater gifts of colour and real fluency of style, a major figure in the new renaissance of the Venetian school of brilliant decorative painting which was attracting attention throughout Europe. Pellegrini's colouristic sense was perhaps more sheerly original and enchanting than Ricci's, and his handling of paint more spontaneous. If he had not much to 'say' in terms of serious art, he certainly said his little with maximum ease and gracefulness.

7. Federico Bencovich, *Blessed Pietro Gambacorti*, S. Sebastiano, Venice.

Yet this style, which might have been expected to interest Tiepolo of all the young painters of the period, seems at that date to have hardly affected him. Much more of an influence on his early work was a quite different style, black and white, as it were, rather than full of colour, rougher and 'realistic' rather than decorative, itself deriving from the past but with as its ultimate source not Veronese but Caravaggio. Two living artists especially exemplified it for Tiepolo.

One was the still somewhat mysterious Federico Bencovich, born in 1677, possibly in Venice, but trained in Bologna and influenced by the tradition of Lombard realism. He rarely settled for long in Venice and seems never to have found a contented niche there; and his art has an almost uncouth force and expressive originality, well shown in the altarpiece of the *Blessed Pietro Gambacorti* (Pl. 7), painted for a Venetian church. The types of the figures, their poses, and the drama of light and shade investing and agitating the whole composition, all have affinities with the work of the second artist, the greatest of Tiepolo's Venetian contemporaries, Giambattista Piazzetta.

Tiepolo and Piazzetta might be termed the Picasso and Matisse, or perhaps better the Turner and Constable, of their period. They were too different to be exactly rivals, contrasted in personality as in style but with careers that inevitably linked them together, just as they were linked by the possession of true genius. Psychologically, they were clearly of fascinatingly opposed temperaments; and whereas Tiepolo grew up fatherless, Piazzetta grew up motherless, having lost his mother when he was two. As their careers developed, so did the contrast between them, and the different artistic approach of each. Piazzetta was the older by fourteen years but he was the opposite of precocious. Not until 1711 was he inscribed in the Venetian painters' guild lists, after training in Bologna under Crespi, and his earliest public work in Venice as a painter virtually coincides with Tiepolo's own.

If in later years Piazzetta's art and that of Tiepolo came to stand for markedly different artistic ideals, there is no doubt that in the years of Tiepolo's formation Piazzetta profoundly affected and influenced the younger man. This is less surprising than it might at first seem and was based on more than a general recognition of Piazzetta's abilities. What Tiepolo was responding to was the forceful yet not coarse or exaggerated realism that Piazzetta conveyed, as much in his accomplished, admired drawings—by which he first became known—as in his paintings. Physical actuality, summed up in the body, was grasped with an originality that embraced idiosyncratic types of physiognomy, consciously ordinary, even plebeian, but exuding a challenging, pungent air of being 'true'.

Ricci and Pellegrini, and the older decorative or semi-decorative history painters, might well seem vapid and conventional, despite their competence, beside this novel realism, which in Piazzetta is beautifully disciplined and given its own authentic poetry. Ricci's altarpiece of the *Virgin and Child with saints* (Pl. 8), painted in 1708, is a sumptuous manifesto of new decorative achievement in Venice, prophetic of later achievements by Tiepolo, Pittoni and other fully eighteenth-century decorative painters, as well as great in its own right. It is one of Ricci's religious masterpieces. Yet when compared with a typical altarpiece by Piazzetta (Pl. 9), painted within Ricci's lifetime, it looks inert under its surface charm, a dressed-up charade of no particular significance beside the bold, fervent and profoundly engaged vision that is Piazzetta's. It is as if a muscular fist had knocked down a pasteboard palace or shaken some toy theatre.

The feathery angels and bright-coloured saints of Ricci's composition might be parakeets, fluttering and perching in a spacious aviary, and with scarcely more duties to perform than birds. But the solemn, sculpted figures of Piazzetta's imagining are intensely realised, brought into a relationship that is psychologically dramatic and artistically so, conveyed with conviction and concentration that not even Tiepolo could match. In altarpieces like this he may well have ruefully recognised Piazzetta as for ever the better artist—'il miglior fabro'.

He probably first encountered Piazzetta's work as a draughtsman and found appealing the types of figures depicted, in addition to the mastery of anatomy Piazzetta displayed (Pl. 10). Truth to appearances—an old man's gnarled hand, a half-squinting face or a sprawled naked body—mattered to both artists at this time, regardless of dignity and perhaps in reaction to the blandly dignified or simply

8

pretty figures that filled the average history painter's compositions. An interesting early drawing by Tiepolo (Pl. 11) documents the seriousness with which the nude was then being studied in Venice. Both Piazzetta and Tiepolo were anxious to look at life freshly, but Tiepolo was looking to some extent through spectacles borrowed from Piazzetta. If the effects were unexpected, disconcerting, faintly mocking at times, that was only part of his declaration of originality and probably also a testimony to youthful high spirits.

Tiepolo's career opens neatly enough in traditional telling—almost as if he were an artist of Vasari's period—with a record of his executing in some sort of competition and exhibiting, at the age of twenty, a *Crossing of the Red Sea*. He showed it at the annual display of paintings held on the saint's day, 16 August, at the Scuola di S. Rocco where it at once attracted attention. The painting seems early to have disappeared—adding to the effect of the story—though a canvas come to light in recent years may well be it or connected with it.[8]

In fact, Tiepolo's career is likely to have begun some years before and with less of a thunderclap. There exist paintings by him, often on quite a small scale, which could conceivably have been painted before he was twenty, and also drawings, though their dating is more problematical, which are certainly youthful and which pay homage to Piazzetta. Some confusion is understandable, since there are hardly any dated works from this immature period, and traditional statements—even when made in Tiepolo's lifetime—may be only approximations to the truth.

10. Piazzetta, *Seated nude from back*, Detroit Institute of Arts, H. T. Kneeland gift (55.283).

However, three aspects of Tiepolo's youthful activity helped to make the public in Venice aware of him and his talent. He painted at least one of the series of canvases in the arched spaces above the altars in the church of S. Maria dei Derelitti (the Ospedaletto), the *Sacrifice of Isaac* (Pl. 12). His *Crossing of the Red Sea* may have followed shortly afterwards. In any case, by being shown at S. Rocco in the annual event on St Roch's day (the nearest Venetian equivalent to a proper, regular exhibition of painting), it must have been seen by a considerable number of people. Altogether humbler was the task of making some drawings of sixteenth-century paint-

11. '*La scuola del nudo*', Katria Bellinger Collection, London.

9

12. *Sacrifice of Isaac*, Ospedaletto, Venice.

ings in churches and in the Doge's Palace, to be engraved in a large volume, *Il Gran Teatro di Venezia*, the first edition of which appeared in 1717. In that year Tiepolo was inscribed in the lists, the *Fraglia*, of Venetian painters. He must have set up on his own as an independent artist; and indeed by his mid-twenties he had some sort of semi-official position as a painter much patronised by the reigning Doge, Giovanni II Cornaro, a weak ruler though apparently a perspicuous patron, with the distinction of being the first in the long line of Tiepolo's high-born patrons.

On later occasions Tiepolo was to show himself perfectly prepared to execute drawings for publications. In drawing scenes painted in the Doge's Palace, he confronted works by Giuseppe Salviati and Francesco Bassano, probably more interesting for their subjects than their style as far as he was concerned. The Salviati was of the Gathering of Manna in the wilderness (a subject to be treated by Tiepolo much later, at Verolanuova). The Bassano depicted a defeat of German troops by Giorgio Cornaro and his fellow-general (Pl. 13). The print based on Tiepolo's drawing was specifically dedicated by the publisher to the Doge Cornaro—an understandable act in itself but given additional suitability if already at that date the young executant was enjoying the Doge's patronage.

For the Cornaro palace Tiepolo is recorded to have painted some over-doors, 'with portraits and fine paintings'. These must have dated from before the Doge's death in August 1722 and the effect of such decoration (dispersed and, in part at least, lost)[9] was probably much more baroque and backward-looking than Tiepolo's typical later work. The paintings were presumably all canvases, possibly inserted amid elaborate stucco decoration, and the general air may have been similar to the décor surviving in, for example, the Palazzo Barbaro.

Of Tiepolo's *Crossing of the Red Sea* little can be said definitely, but no doubt it was highly dramatic, forceful and baroque. What can be judged of the shape of the composition and the disposition of the main groups—with Moses on a rocky promontory at the left, and Pharaoh's host overwhelmed at the right—suggests that for this ambitious theme Tiepolo had glanced at the woodcut based on Titian's design of a not common subject (though it had been painted by Lazzarini). Such an echo, if one existed, would have been no more than homage to a great artist of the past. The theme, however, may have had its own associations with the present. Defeat by sea of a pagan enemy through God's aid would have a familiar sound for Venetians

13. Tiepolo after F. Bassano, *Defeat of the Germans*.

during the years around 1717 when the Republic was engaged in constant naval battles against the Turks. In 1716 Corfù held out successfully after forty-two days' siege; the Turkish fleet had to retire, effectively defeated. Other naval engagements followed, and a distinct Venetian victory by sea was gained in 1718, at the very time the congress of Passarowitz was settling a European peace in which Venice ceded the territory of the Morea to Turkey. From the treaty of Passarowitz is often dated the decline of Venice, but the heroic achievements of the Venetian naval commanders (and of Marshal Schulenburg in the service of Venice and as the defender of Corfù) were at the period matters of probably more moment to Venetians, stirring patriotic memories of Francesco Morosini and the long tradition of Christian fighting infidel which in Venice meant the Republic battling against the sea-power of the Ottoman empire. Even the fact that Tiepolo's painting was executed in some sort of competition with other painters is suggestive.

To turn to a surviving certain early painting by Tiepolo, the *Sacrifice of Isaac*, is to emerge from mists of conjecture on to reasonably firm ground. Even here, however, all is far from clear, beginning with the general obscurity in the church of the Ospedaletto and the height at which the painting is placed. The earliest reference apparently to it is annoyingly confused. The biographer of Lazzarini, Vincenzo da Canal, writing in or around 1732, goes out of his way to praise Lazzarini's pupil Tiepolo, 'now famous', and mentions his executing in the Ospedaletto, at the age of nineteen, some 'Apostles'. In fact, the *Sacrifice of Isaac* is only one of a series of canvases by different artists, all similarly shaped and placed above the altars, and of which the remainder depict Apostles and Fathers of the Church; so da Canal's slip, if it is a slip, is the more understandable. The *Sacrifice of Isaac* is uncontestably by Tiepolo, and a knowledgeable Venetian guidebook of 1733 gives the painting to him (and additionally a canvas of 'Two Prophets').[10]

Lazzarini executed a *Pool of Bethesda* for the Ospedaletto, under Tiepolo's *Sacrifice of Isaac*, and may well have had a hand in obtaining the commission for his youthful yet patently gifted pupil or ex-pupil. Tiepolo seems to have been the youngest painter employed on the series of shaped canvases. Hr alone received, or engineered, a commission which had a specific incident, indeed a dramatic narrative. Fitting that scene into the extremely awkward shape of the canvas was a challenge he perhaps relished. He found a highly ingenious solution to the problem of presenting the figures of Abraham and Isaac on the mountain specified in Genesis, along with the irruption of the angel who stays Abraham's hand at the moment of sacrifice.

The deep curve of the canvas serves to suggest the top of the mountain on which both Abraham and Isaac recline, Isaac collapsed on logs of wood poking up and Abraham a hunched figure turning at the angel's appearance but still grasping a knife close to his son's throat. To accommodate the angel in what space remained, Tiepolo chose to have him floating in backwards with legs up and a detached-seeming foot near Abraham's shoulder.

This is no perfunctory 'decoration'. Working alongside older men, Tiepolo is obviously determined to create a powerful, compressed drama from the scene. The real triumph of the painting is in the figure of Isaac, whose nearly nude body is modelled with tremendous virtuoso contrasts of light and shade, and keen response to bone and musculature under the skin. The effect is Piazzettesque but already more fluent, graceful for all its forcefulness. Tiepolo's Isaac cannot help composing his limbs, even at the point of imminent death, into a crisp, elegant arabesque. Yet his body is still a tribute to Piazzetta's influence, as indirect teacher perhaps more than as painter, in the sense of encouraging Tiepolo to study anatomy and the nude. Tiepolo was fortunate that such an early commission—arguably his first major one—allowed him an opportunity to display what he had learnt. And the subject is also oddly fortunate, even prophetic. Tiepolo was so often to paint visions of divine intervention on earth. Heavenly aid or comfort is never distant, it seems, in his art; and the

14. S. Ricci, *Liberation of St Peter*, S. Stae, Venice.

16 (facing page). *Martyrdom of St Bartholomew*, S. Stae, Venice.

15. Piazzetta, *St James led to martyrdom*, S. Stae, Venice.

career that may have publicly begun with this vision to Abraham was to end some fifty years later with an angel splendidly appearing to the humble Spanish Franciscan gardener, St Pascual Baylon (Pls 231 and 233).

Other church commissions in Venice began to come the way of the young painter, and when the Doge Cornaro died in 1722 Tiepolo was probably not without further noble, if less highly placed, patrons. Venice as a physical entity was very far from declining. Churches as well as palaces continued to be built; older foundations were often to receive, sometimes through pious bequests, modern improvements and adornments. More than once Tiepolo and Piazzetta, as well as Sebastiano Ricci, would find themselves in the persons of their work juxtaposed in a church. Some of the paintings attributed to Tiepolo in Venetian guidebooks well within his lifetime were probably not his but vaguely in his style—and yet the mistake itself testifies to a feeling of his growing fame, quite apart from his activity.

Twelve paintings of the Apostles were posthumously commissioned by the patrician Andrea Stazio, who died in May 1722, for 'my beloved parish church of S. Stae', and twelve painters were chosen by the agents he had designated in his will.[11] Once again, Tiepolo was the youngest of those selected, who included Ricci, then aged sixty-three, Pellegrini, Piazzetta and Giovan Battista Pittoni, born in 1687. In this fascinating assembly of local talent—including Lazzarini—Ricci produced a *Liberation of St Peter* (Pl. 14) that economically derived from one of his own earlier compositions, with the very faintest suggestion of a prison and imprisoned saint but decorated by an attractively coloured, air-borne angel, stylistically descended not from heaven but from Luca Giordano, in some tinted, misty space. In contrast to this rococo chamber-music, Piazzetta orchestrated a thundery, assertive, almost growling baroque cantata for bass voice and brass, in which the brawny figure of the aged St James is haled to martyrdom by an executioner bronzed and equally brawny (Pl. 15).

It was to the music and style—and even perhaps the actual composition—of this impressive painting that Tiepolo responded when he came to paint his contribution, the *Martyrdom of St Bartholomew* (Pl. 16). The saint was skinned to death, and though Tiepolo stops short of the grisly operation, he depicts the executioner with knife at the ready, a stolid, staring man in profile whose fingers horribly caress with connoisseur-like anticipation the tender skin under the saint's armpit. The mood is more desperate than in Piazzetta's painting, but the violent, clashing emotions, the fierce contrasts of light and dark, force and weakness, pale, holy flesh of victim and sunburnt flesh of brutal executioners, help to make the pair of paintings twins in their up-to-date assertive 'realism'. The figures are as close to the front of the picture plane as are Ricci's, and, similarly, little spatial recession is suggested; but what in his composition is light and airy is made by both Piazzetta and Tiepolo in theirs smoky and thick with foreboding, skies of stormy darkness against which sinewy limbs stand out.

Looking for additional vigour, Tiepolo has looked behind Piazzetta and borrowed —as rarely was he to do again—the pose of the executioner seen from the back, at the bottom right, from a harmless servant in a *Rebecca at the Well* painted by the famous Neapolitan Solimena.[12] That painting and its pendant of *Rachel and Jacob* hung in the Casa Baglioni at Venice. Other paintings by Solimena were in private houses in Venice in the early eighteenth century and certainly exercised some influence— though perhaps less fundamentally than some scholars have supposed. Piazzetta, for example, did not really reach his stature as an artist simply by swallowing a few magic pills concocted from other men's styles, and genius is often less in need than are scholars of evolving by stages of stylistic derivation.

What Tiepolo shared with Piazzetta was pursuit of expressive intensity, and that was far from being some youthful urge later lost amid decorative emphases. He

17 (right). (?) *Expulsion of Hagar*, Rasini Collection, Milan.

19 (bottom). *Seated male nude*, Staatsgalerie, Stuttgart.

18. *Three nude men*, Museo Civico, Udine.

sought to match mood to the subject he was painting, and as late as the *St Tecla* altarpiece for Este (see Pl. 197), he could revert to thundery, dramatic realism of a nearly shocking kind.

In the early 1720s he was, inevitably, still experimenting, perhaps attracted particularly to overtly dramatic subjects. His *Martyrdom of St Bartholomew* is, in some ways, wilder and more emotional than anything by Piazzetta, and subjects like the Rape of the Sabines and Tullia driving her chariot over her father's body—both of which he probably painted in this period[13]—offered every opportunity for heightened drama. The so-called *Expulsion of Hagar* (Pl. 17) has a haunting conviction and violence of contrasting emotions, echoed by the powerful contrasts of light and shade. At the base of a strange, huge drum-like structure (with its bas-relief, more classical-seeming than Biblical) a heavily draped, aged priest or sage gesticulates imperiously over the prostrate, imploring body of a woman, while two figures look on, one indifferently, the other as though anxious to intercede. Penitence, perhaps, is what the woman's pose suggests. Whatever the exact emotion, it has felled her to the ground by its force—and Tiepolo delights, artistically, in conveying the desolate pose of her collapsed body, utterly abased before the dominant old man. The originality of the treatment is striking, and that is only underlined if the subject really *is* the Expulsion of Hagar.[14]

The moody, half-capricious atmosphere is like that of some of Tiepolo's early drawings, where the male nude, possibly studied by Tiepolo at first in some academic environment, is set out of doors, in a rather bleak Arcady (Pl. 18), and there is no ostensible 'subject'. In chalk studies he could capture a hunched body (Pl. 19) and give lugubrious individuality to the face. In drawing a conventional subject like the Annunciation (Pl. 20), he could invest it with dazzlingly vivid originality; vibrant pen strokes depict a lanky angel, convey a sense of light bursting out overhead and add—like a grace-note—two playful, air-borne putti. Here the true Tiepolo, speedy, brilliant, superbly, even insolently, confident, has emerged.

Although there is still some homage to Piazzetta in aspects of the *Madonna of*

joannij Baptista Tiepolo inectographum.

20. *The Annunciation*, Fogg Art Museum, Cambridge, Mass., Bequest—Charles A. Loeser.

Mount Carmel (Pl. 21), a major large-scale painting from these years, executed for a side chapel in S. Aponal in Venice, the Christ Child standing on a cushion beside the Madonna is entirely of a Tiepolo type, individualised in his art in a way that would suggest portrayal of a real child, conceivably one of his nephews. The handling of paint here is also unmistakably his, rich yet luminous. There is an unforced majesty about the Madonna, standing as unaffectedly straight as the giant, fluted pillar rising behind her. The group around the Madonna and Child was carefully planned by Tiepolo not to be central but to be seen at the right of the long composition,

21. *Madonna of Mount Carmel*, Brera, Milan.

leaving to the left a drama of half-naked bodies (in a further display of anatomy), in which an angel rescues souls from purgatory. The painting was cut after leaving the church and only much later was this portion reunited to the main group of the Madonna with the Child and saints, which is sometimes still reproduced by itself, falsifying the deliberately asymetrical effect Tiepolo intended. A hint for this effect (as for the poses of the Madonna and the Child, supported by a column) he probably got from Titian's Pesaro altarpiece (not far away in the church of the Frari). In Tiepolo's composition—the most ambitious and impressive of his early religious paintings—the sacred figures form a bastion of faith, an almost literal rock of salvation, amid the uncertainties of this sinful world and the dramatically illustrated threat of punishment in the next.

Such religious commissions represent only one aspect, though an important one, of Tiepolo's activity as an oil painter in Venice during the years he was becoming known. Patrons had a taste also for mythological pictures, sometimes mildly erotic in content, which could be traced back to the Venice of the sixteenth century. In the subsequent century a painter like Pietro Liberi had made something of a speciality of the female nude, in a rather milk-and-water manner which yet was probably meant to provide titillation, if only of a discreet sort. In Tiepolo's day the softly coloured, slightly boneless mythologies of Amigoni (Pl. 22), in a gentle rococo style, catered for rather similar tastes and seem to have been popular as paintings to hang in the rooms of Venetian palaces. But in eighteenth-century Venice the subject of the female nude was seldom to be treated with the abandon associated with Paris at the same period; and though Tiepolo created his own brand of bare-breasted heroine, divine or mortal, with a magnificent display of opulent flesh, his women tend to be too aloof, too indifferent, too sheerly magnificent perhaps, for carnality. Besides, every so often, he adds a dissolving touch of salt humour that breaks any sexual spell.

Already, in one of his very earliest surviving mythological paintings, the *Rape of Europa* (Pl. 23), which must date from no later than his and the century's mid-twenties, he approaches the subject tongue in cheek, though not without throwing over it both charm and personal application. The painting is one of four similarly sized mythologies, of varying subject-matter, not necessarily all done for the same patron, though homogeneous in handling and scale of figures in relation to the landscape.[15] In tackling such themes Tiepolo was moving out of Piazzetta's orbit and closer to that of Sebastiano Ricci. For all four paintings the source was Ovid's *Metamorphoses*, and it is notable that Tiepolo follows the poet's text quite carefully. The result is highly sophisticated art, presumably for a sophisticated client or

22. J. Amigoni, *Zephyr and Flora*, Museo Correr, Venice.

clientèle, seen at its most Ovidian in the *Rape of Europa* where impudent humour brings Tiepolo close to sending up the subject. He must have been well aware of the popularity of it in Venetian painting, and to tackle it once again was a challenge—made more topical by the presence in the Doge's Palace, from 1713 onwards, of Veronese's famous composition of the subject, bequeathed to the state by Bertucci Contarini (Pl. 24). There are also some unexpected similarities in terms of composition between Tiepolo's treatment and that of the same subject by Watteau (in a lost painting, not engraved until 1730). Whatever the explanation, it is certainly not a simple matter of both borrowing from Veronese.

In an enchanted coastal landscape—one of the first landscapes in Tiepolo's art—where steep mountains slide imperceptibly into the sea, a solemn and very youthful Europa stares out, demurely seated on the bull that is Jupiter disguised, while girls attend to her toilet. Tiepolo adds a negro page-boy to her entourage, less for flippant effect perhaps than as a personal allusion. The additional cattle in the painting illustrate Ovid's words that the disguised Jupiter mingled with the herd, and the bull's munching of flowers is also directly based on what Ovid writes. In this quiet pastoral there is no 'rape' as such, but there is a witty allusion to Jupiter's presence in

23. *Rape of Europa*, Accademia, Venice.

24. Veronese, *Rape of Europa*, Doge's Palace, Venice.

his eagle on a cloud floating above Europa, accompanied by a cheeky putto who graphically conveys to two other putti attempting to land on this particular cloud the message 'piss off'.

In the fair, girlishly plump features of Europa can be recognised a face that occurs often in Tiepolo's later work and is seen most obviously in a painting not far in date from the *Europa*, in the likeness of Campaspe in *Apelles painting Campaspe before Alexander* (Pl. 26). There the Apelles is Tiepolo himself—in the first of so many self-portraits of this kind—and the Campaspe, and thus the Europa, is almost certainly his wife, Cecilia Guardi. The studio of Apelles contains canvases that are highly Tiepolesque, and the negro page-boy again appears, suggesting that he may well have been a domestic servant of the young married couple.

Tiepolo had married Cecilia, sister of Francesco and Gian Antonio Guardi, on 21 November 1719, after a curious episode that has only recently become known. In an undated letter addressed to the Curia Patriarcale at Venice, Tiepolo, stating that he was already virtually engaged, asked for permission to marry in secret, because if it became known that he was marrying Cecilia Guardi obstacles would be put in his way by members of his family.[16] What the Tiepolo family's objections were is not apparent; they may have been based on the lowly status of the Guardi rather than on the bride herself. Her father, Domenico Guardi, had been a painter of a fairly humble kind. He died at the age of thirty-eight in 1716, leaving a widow and several children, of whom the eldest, Gian Antonio, was then just seventeen. At the time of her marriage, Cecilia Guardi was only the same age—and she looks hardly more than twenty or so in the *Europa*. Perhaps it privately amused Tiepolo to depict her as a beautiful heroine of antiquity carried off by a god and a ruse—to a happy, fertile future. To that extent, the story of Cecilia Tiepolo, as she became, proved remarkably similar to Europa's.

Above all, Tiepolo pays tribute to her attractiveness for him, and in the *Apelles*—whatever the original commission may have been—he celebrates their life together in playfully affectionate terms. Painting Campaspe, the mistress of Alexander the Great, Apelles fell in love with her, and the generous monarch gave her to the artist. The theme had obvious appeal for painters, though primarily perhaps as an indication of the status of the artist. As an epithet, being the Apelles of his time had been applied in the sixteenth century to Titian in the patent granted him by Charles V. The only comparable service Tiepolo had so far enjoyed was that of the Doge Cornaro, which had ceased before the *Apelles* was painted. Yet there was possibly another application in choosing to paint himself as Apelles, for as well as being a court artist Apelles had been famous for his abilities as a draughtsman. Still, in the last analysis, it was the award of Campaspe to Apelles that perhaps meant most to Tiepolo. He was never to paint a straightforward portrait of his wife; the closest he came to it is the unfinished portrait on the easel here. According to the classical sources, Campaspe had posed naked for Apelles. Tiepolo does not care to go so far. His Campaspe, seen from the back in a pose derived from classical antique sculpture, is discreetly décolletée to the spectator—though not to the painter. It is with surely conscious wit that the pop-eyed painter turns to gaze at his model, leaving his brush poised on the breast of the figure he is painting, just above her nipple.

The story of Alexander's handing over of his mistress can hardly be taken seriously —at least, Tiepolo scarcely attempts to take it seriously beyond the personal meaning it has for him. His Alexander the Great is an uncouthly seated, plebeian-looking individual, dwarfed by the tall Campaspe and almost a parody figure, like a clown who has assumed an emperor's clothes. Mingling classical setting with further personal allusion, Tiepolo shows two large modern canvases in the painter's studio, one possibly of Venus appearing to Aeneas, the other certainly of Moses and the brazen serpent. Neither composition is known today among Tiepolo's *œuvre* and yet the style of these paintings, quite apart from their location, suggests they were

works by him—and probably not fantasy ones either. Just as the setting is a mixture, so are the costumes. It is remarkable that for himself as Apelles, Tiepolo creates a costume flagrantly unclassical and not even eighteenth century; his shako-like cap is of a type seen most often on heads in Piazzetta's work, sometimes worn by the artist himself.

The painting must date from a few years after the *Rape of Europa*, and the Palladian-style screen at the left, combined with the device of soldiers with pikes being set at a level imagined below the area of the main action, suggests that Tiepolo has become sharply aware of Veronese: of, in particular, the *Family of Darius before Alexander* (Pl. 25), then in the Palazzo Pisani-Moretta. In later years he would pay artistic tribute to the influence of that famous composition more obviously than in the *Apelles*. He would, in effect, exchange Piazzetta for Veronese as the dominant personality from whom he could learn; and in the *Apelles* his allegiance is already shifting. Its colouristic brilliance, like its high spirits and its vivacious handling of paint, belong, however, to Tiepolo alone. It seems suitable that he should assert his artistic individuality in a painting of a great painter at work and give that painter his own features and much of his own personal context.

In reality, the early 1720s were not all unalloyed joy for Tiepolo and his wife. Previously unpublished and unknown documents show that the family suffered sadly through an outbreak of smallpox in the autumn of 1723.[17] It has not previously been known that Tiepolo had a first child, a daughter, Elena, born as early as around 1720. Eventually ten children were born (not nine, as usually stated), though only seven seem to have survived into adulthood. A second daughter, Anna Maria, was born in 1722, and in August 1723 the first boy, Giandomenico (Domenico being the name of both his dead grandfathers).

When the smallpox broke out, Tiepolo was probably living close to or with his elder brother, Ambrogio, in the parish of S. Ternita (properly S. Trinita). On 15 October 1723 Ambrogio's small son, Domenico, aged two, died of the disease. Three days later Tiepolo's son, a baby of less than three months, died from it; and on 30 October, it killed the three-year-old Elena. Not until 1726, apparently, was another child born to Cecilia Tiepolo, a girl christened Elena. In the following year a boy was born and given the name Giandomenico; he was to survive and grow up to be a gifted artist and the deeply devoted assistant of his father for the rest of his father's life. The youngest of all the children was Lorenzo, born in 1736, also to become a painter, one of less ability than his brother though, like him, part of the family team. Tiepolo's four daughters (the other two were Angela and Orsetta) and his other son, Giuseppe, who became a priest, all find a place in the family's art, as

26. *Apelles painting Campaspe*, The Montreal Museum of Fine Arts, Adeline Van Horne Bequest (945.929).

well as in Tiepolo's life. Cecilia's own voice is heard eventually, two years before her death, in the will she made as a widow at the age of seventy-five, where a fondness for fine clothes seems to go hand in hand with real piety and family feeling, and where she proudly speaks of herself as a mother 'always loving and affectionate'.[18]

In the mid-1720s her husband was not yet more than wonderfully promising and artistically ambitious: an Apelles of the future. His drawings and his oil paintings revealed his talent, but already he had mastered another medium, where his gifts were to blaze forth supremely, outshining all competitors, to make him undisputed sovereign of that realm: fresco painting.

2 THE FIRST FRESCOES

THE EARLIEST source for Tiepolo's activity is Vincenzo da Canal, an amateur of the arts, born about 1680, who wrote an unpublished treatise, *Della maniera di dipingere moderno*, as well as the life of Lazzarini (also unpublished until many years after his death).[1] Da Canal enormously admired the industry and the diligent, natural and non-hectic style of Lazzarini ('naturale e non furiosa') and wrote, he declared, to persuade people that in Venice, 'in questa città', there was good, truthful and agreeable painting, embodied in Lazzarini's work.

Such a figure might have been expected to be reserved, at best, when confronted by the young Tiepolo. About Ricci, da Canal was definitely not enthusiastic, celebrated though Ricci was. But in his treatise, written about 1730, he spoke warmly of Tiepolo as a young artist who lacked nothing 'in boldness or colouring or novel inventiveness'. And on to his account, of a year or two later, of Lazzarini's career, he tacked a miniature 'life' of Tiepolo so far. In it he mentions several frescoes by Tiepolo no longer known, and though in some cases he may have been mistaken, it seems unlikely that every one of these now lost works was by some other artist. Fortunately, and in da Canal's favour, he makes one reference to an early fresco which does survive and is by Tiepolo: the ceiling of the Palazzo Sandi in Venice. By itself, that ceiling admirably exemplifies the qualities da Canal singled out in Tiepolo's art, and which were to go on being seen at their finest in his frescoes.

The tradition of fresco decoration was thoroughly established at Venice, as an activity which was, however, practised most extensively outside the city, with its damp, salt air and where the character of palace ceilings especially had been gilded wooden compartments inset with canvases, very much as in the Libreria and the Doge's Palace. When this type of ceiling gave way to something lighter in effect, offering scope for fresco, it still remained a tendency in Venice for the walls to be left unfrescoed and used rather for display of oil paintings. Thus rooms completely frescoed with a single coherent scheme were a rarity. In the villas of the Veneto, the climate—both physical and moral—was rather different, and the sixteenth century had already seen a number of villas splendidly frescoed. Veronese's frescoes at the Villa Barbaro may be the most famous, but there were other examples of complete rooms decorated, like the ground-floor sala at the Villa-Castello Da Porto Colleoni, frescoed by Fasolo and Zelotti with scenes of ancient history, including the Banquet of Cleopatra (Pl. 27).

If for the seventeenth century there are fewer examples to cite, those that were created tend to be highly elaborate in their simulated architectural settings, increasing the illusionistic effect and extending the appearance of the actual space. The scenes themselves are sometimes rather flat, even perfunctory, though often of a serious nature: the founding of Padua was frescoed at the Villa Selvatico, not far from Padua, and (more pertinent for Tiepolo a century later) fresco scenes relating to and taken from the *Iliad* and the *Aeneid*, as well as from the *Odyssey*, were executed by Ruschi in the Villa Venier Contarini at Mira (Pl. 28).

Few painters specialised in the medium of fresco, though any decorative painter might be expected to work in it on occasion. Sebastiano Ricci was so called on, but

27. Fasolo and Zelotti, *Banquet of Cleopatra*, Villa-Castello Da Porto Colleoni, Thiene.

28. Francesco Ruschi, *Rape of Helen*, Villa Venier Contarini, Mira.

21

not, as it happens, in Venice or the Veneto. Thus he signally failed to exercise any very direct influence on Tiepolo's frescoes. The medium was scarcely one for Piazzetta, with his dark palette and, even more, his laborious, slow-working creative processes. By its nature it called for a speedy brain and hand, for 'dash' and spontaneity and tremendous confidence. It was made for Tiepolo, and he probably needed the minimum of tuition before he recognised how perfectly it matched his most instinctive gifts. At its most basic, fresco might be described as drawing in colour on a large scale; and certainly the secret of Tiepolo's frescoes lies, from the first, in their keen, clean draughtsmanship, of a bracing quality and total sureness of touch that make for exhilaration in the spectator.

Tiepolo was not alone in mastering fresco and making it his speciality. Much older than he was Ludovico Dorigny, born in 1654 and living on into his eighties. Dorigny was French by birth but working in North Italy and active widely, executing frescoes in the Duomo at Udine and for Venetian villas, as well as for palaces in Venice itself. The very wealthy Manin family employed him to decorate their vast villa at Passariano, and he also worked for the 'new' nobility like the Widmann and the Baglioni families. There is perhaps a wall-to-wall element of dutiful, if agreeable, covering of surfaces in Dorigny's frescoes (Pl. 29). His doe-eyed people, embodied in slightly inflated forms, disport gracefully and are charmingly coloured, but the effect tends to be monotonous. More exciting and more mannered in style are the frescoes of Giambattista Crosato (1685/6–1758), easily the most accomplished fresco painter next to Tiepolo, who probably exercised some influence over his older contemporary. Crosato was to be drawn away, stylistically and physically, to Turin, one of the court centres where Tiepolo never worked, and to add Frenchified rococo graces to the complex blend of styles that lay behind his always sprightly frescoes.

29. L. Dorigny, fresco decoration of the walls of the north-east room, Villa Manin, Passariano.

In fact, the eighteenth century proved the great age of fresco decoration in North Italy, and especially in Venice and the Veneto, but the phenomenon is personified by—almost inspired by—Tiepolo to such an extent that even now it is hard to gauge what it was or would have been without him.

According to da Canal, his earliest fresco was done outside Venice, in the church of the Assumption at Biadene, near Treviso, built by, he says, the 'Procurator Pisani'. The reference has gone largely undiscussed, since until recently no fresco by Tiepolo was thought to survive there.[2] The Pisani owned a villa at Biadene, and two members of the family could be the Procurator in question, Carlo or Alvise, the latter of whom was to become Doge in 1735. Da Canal seems so specific in his reference that it is quite likely that he is correct about Tiepolo's commission. He makes other tantalising references to early frescoes by Tiepolo, one being to 'a room' decorated by him in Venice in the Casa Baglioni at S. Cassiano. The Baglioni, a family of publishers who had bought their way into the nobility, collected paintings widely, and Tiepolo's awareness of one of their paintings by Solimena is virtually documented by the *Martyrdom of St Bartholomew* in S. Stae.

Whatever the precise truth about these references, they suggest what the visual evidence would indicate: that the first ceiling fresco by Tiepolo which survives, along with its *modello*, cannot have been his first essay in the medium. This is the ceiling in the Palazzo Sandi at Venice, one of the most brilliant, well-preserved and yet least known of Tiepolo's surviving fresco output. In some senses it is the freshest of all.

The palace is a modest building, tucked away in a corner of the small Corte dell'Albero, close to the Grand Canal in the parish of S. Angelo. It was begun in 1721 for Tommaso Sandi by the architect Domenico Rossi, someone who had been slow to emerge on to the Venetian architectural scene. At Udine he had worked for the Manin family. In Venice he won the competition for the façade of S. Stae in 1709, when he was already over fifty, and was thenceforward involved in designing or altering several Venetian palaces.

The Sandi ranked as one more instance of recent nobility. The family was associated with the profession of law and had been ennobled in 1685. For the ceiling of the main salone of their palace an unusual theme was chosen, illustrated by a most unusual combination of subjects. Normally described as an 'Allegory of the Power of Eloquence', it is a little more *recherché* than that; and though it may well allude to the Sandi family's legal distinction, urging the triumph of mind over matter, verbal cunning over brute force, it extends to the power of sound not only through words but through music. At the centre of the scheme preside Minerva and Mercury as deities of Wisdom and Eloquence, but a place is also found, outside the fresco itself, for Apollo.

Four heroic episodes were selected for the sides of the ceiling: Orpheus leads Eurydice past Cerberus; Hercules 'Gallicus' enchains people by his tongue; Bellerophon on Pegasus slays the chimera; and Amphion, by the power of music, causes the walls of Thebes to build themselves.

The room to be frescoed was the salone on the second floor, a fairly large room, longer than wide, entered by a single doorway and with main windows overlooking a small side canal. No grandiose stucco cornice had been built, and no feigned architectural framework was apparently required for the fresco. The room was simple and sober, its walls relieved by lightly modelled pilasters and its sole ornament a stucco relief of a female figure above the doorway. Between the walls and ceiling now runs a frieze, painted in oil on, presumably, canvas, of animals, centaurs and men, of obscure significance, certainly not from Tiepolo's hand and arguably by a painter of an older generation.

Tiepolo prepared a *modello* spirited in handling yet obviously thought out with great care (Pl. 30). Partly because it is painted on a red ground, it lacks the luminosity that is so striking in the fresco itself; but it has its own brilliance and sparkle and audacity. And as Tiepolo's earliest surviving *modello* for a fresco, it has, if only accidentally, something of the nature of a manifesto by an emergent genius. Its flecks and flicks of hot vermilion paint come from the cauldron of a molten mind, stirred by the prospect of a challenging commission. The four episodes are conceived and sketched with the greatest energy, and only the pale, somewhat ineffective and confusedly linked figures of the two deities hint at Tiepolo's inexperience and uncertainty in aerial effects—not a failing of his later work.

Tiepolo designed the *modello* with most space given to the scene of Amphion causing Thebes to be built, with stones flying into place while its citizens gaze in astonishment. This occupies one of the long sides and was clearly planned as of special prominence, since on the ceiling it would be the first scene to confront anyone entering the room. Opposite it on the *modello* he placed Hercules 'Gallicus', dragging people along by a chain hanging from his neck, with, left and right, Orpheus and Bellerophon. When the ceiling came to be executed, however, the disposition of all three scenes was altered. Opposite Amphion with his lyre was placed Orpheus, brandishing not his more usual lute but a violin. Thus much greater emphasis was given to the theme of music's power. Hercules 'Gallicus' was moved to the short, right-hand wall and Bellerophon to that on the left. In these changes there is perhaps some influence from the intended use of the room, doubtless for receptions and feasts but possibly also for concerts and dancing. Music has a social role, for not only does it help Orpheus in Hades but, with a god's aid (and Amphion's instrument is that created by Mercury), it can construct the walls of a great city. 'In sweet music is such art...'

Each incident presented Tiepolo with a problem of illustration, even before he came to the problems—rare in his mature work—raised by the changes of position in the fresco. The groups of figures were contained in roughly triangular areas, kept fairly low and pinned close to the edges of the composition, leaving a very free expanse of sky for the comparatively tiny figures of Minerva and Mercury. In terms

30. *Allegory of the power of Eloquence*, Courtauld Institute Galleries, London (Princes Gate Collection).

31. Detail of Pl. 30 showing Bellerophon.

of illustration, the main subject—of Amphion—was certainly the most testing. For understandable reasons, his magic building of Thebes was a rare subject to be depicted at any period, and its prominent treatment in the Palazzo Sandi is probably unique.

Amphion positively whirls into action (Pl. 32), striking his lyre as he plants himself on a spur of rock, watching the effect of his music-making, while around there crouch and recline the amazed Thebans, young and old, male and female, accompanied by a refined though blasé-seeming hound. In these figures is collected a cast of Tiepolo's future favourite characters, his touring company, with the fat woman and the bearded man, assembled here for the first time, and all lovingly elaborated on in the actual fresco, with a baby, a small boy and a bird.

In the Hercules scene of the *modello*, the hero drags along enchained, nearly naked bodies whose poses recall those in some of Tiepolo's earliest known drawings, and two prominent figures are collapsed very similarly to Isaac in the Ospedaletto painting. Against a billowing, black cloud Orpheus clasps the desperate Eurydice, and the flailing legs of hellish demons add to the horror. Most vividly conveyed of all is the ardour of Bellerophon on an upreared Pegasus, charging to attack a passive, stuffed-toy chimera and armed only with a branch he has broken from a tatty, bare tree conveniently at hand (Pl. 32).

This motif is an interesting one. Tiepolo seems to have intended by it to indicate

24

32. Detail of Pl. 30 showing Amphion.

the hero's ingenuity, and in this he follows, by chance or otherwise, illustrations of the subject in non-Italian, sixteenth-century editions of Alciati's *Emblems*.[3] That too was to be changed for the fresco.

The rather subdued tonality of the *modello*, with hot flesh tones and passages of dark blue for Amphion's cloak and of scarlet for Bellerophon's, enhances its vigour and its artistic seriousness. There is nothing playful or flippant about it, though in the figure types and in its handling of paint it has clear analogies with the four mythologies of which the *Rape of Europa* (Pl. 23) is one. They are finished paintings, whereas the *modello* is very much a prepatatory sketch. Nevertheless, the style is comparable, suggesting that a convincing date for the *modello* could be around 1722—not long after building of the palace had begun.

The fresco itself can scarcely, it would seem, be so early. Tiepolo had a good deal of thinking to do, making some changes which were doubtless at the patron's instigation and, as a result, needing to expand the Orpheus and Eurydice group, as well as turn his whole spirited yet essentially miniature and short-hand sketch—a rehearsal outline, at best—into the full-scale, fully realised performance on the ceiling (Pl. 33). It seems already typical of him that most probably he did not produce an intermediate new sketch or even make preparatory drawings, though that is less certain. Yet at every point, and often in details that only he can have demanded of himself in the sheer delight of inventing, he enriched and improved as he worked on the actual fresco. He added to the scene in Hades Pluto and Proserpina, accompanied by female figures who include an aged crone stretching her withered neck, and a younger one fingering a distaff in ominous fashion, the Fate Atropos perhaps, about

26

to snap the destiny of Orpheus and Eurydice (Pl. 34). Above the lovers Tiepolo now introduced Cupid, flying blindfold, mutely protesting, it may be, at what is to come. The faces of the two lovers have a familiar look, despite the tilted angle of them, and are likely to be portraits once again of the painter and his wife.

Although no greater space was allowed to it, the Bellerophon group significantly changed (Pl. 36). Tiepolo brought the chimera to life; it was invested with terrier-like aggressive stance, plus the supernatural addition of fiery breath. Pegasus took on a nobler form, becoming a poetic steed, white and rampant. The bare tree was suppressed, and with it the illustration of Bellerophon's quick-wittedness. Equipped with a shield along one arm, he holds an immensely long, pointed lance which seems bound, without much subtlety, to dispose of the chimera at first impact.

There are considerable changes also to the Hercules group, but for quite different reasons. How Tiepolo originally executed it can no longer be judged since it was to be extensively reworked by him at least some ten to fifteen years later. The evidence for this is stylistic but unmistakable. It must be supposed that damage had occurred, possibly through damp, to that portion of the ceiling, and that Tiepolo agreed to re-fresco the area. He did so conscientiously, though inevitably in a style that had evolved markedly; only in the bare back of the left-hand male figure does his original handling survive.

It was of course the Amphion group (Pl. 37) that was intended to be the *tour de force* of a forceful ceiling. Not only the gesticulating figures but the very walls of Thebes had to be drawn in perspective to suggest—with no aid from any fictive architectural framework—a sense of space up and into the heaven of the ceiling where Minerva gazes directly down. Fewer obvious changes were introduced into this portion of the fresco as compared to its treatment in the *modello*, but Tiepolo sharpened acutely the city walls and related Minerva, seated atop a drift of cloud, much more closely to what was happening on earth. When increasing the Theban onlookers Tiepolo added the boy at Amphion's feet and had him—alone of the figures on the ceiling—look out and down, away from the action, as though seeking to engage the eye of the spectator in the room.

There remains the greatest change of all between *modello* and fresco, a matter of technique, it might seem simply, but more than technique. The *modello* is no pre-paration for the flooding light and freshness of colour that make the ceiling an absolute revelation. Against an expanse of deep-mauve sky the pale, honey-coloured stones of Thebes fly into place like so many pieces of obedient jig-saw puzzle. Amphion is still wearing blue but, as with so many of the garments depicted, his has suffered a sea-change into something now richer and more luminously blue, while his own appearance has altered from that of dark, crop-haired thug to a blonde, Apolline minstrel, twin in likeness to Orpheus opposite. Elsewhere on the ceiling there are passages of pale green and brickish red, and striped draperies put in with that felicity of touch that Tiepolo never lost in forty years of fresco painting.

But the real, novel achievement of the Palazzo Sandi ceiling goes beyond the merely colourful and decorative, enchanting as it is in those ways. What Tiepolo has conjured up is profoundly imaginative 'theatre', peopling the ceiling with intensely realised beings involved in intensely realised incidents, so that remote mythology and allegory take on palpable shape and dramatic actuality. The scale of the ceiling seems only to have given him a greater sense of freedom to create a whole cosmos where light as much as harmony triumphs. To parallel its achievement it is necessary to look outside Venetian painting altogether and back to Roman seventeenth-century decoration and to Rubens.

Nothing else by Tiepolo exactly like this survives in Venice, but the brilliant, piquant colouring and the controlled yet patent exuberance of mastery anticipate or recall his frescoes in the Archbishop's Palace at Udine, and it is hard to think that much of an interval separates the two achievements.

33. *Allegory of Eloquence*, Palazzo Sandi, Venice.

The Palazzo Sandi scheme did not stop with the ceiling. Three canvases were also required for the room, though unfortunately no longer there today, and they too continued the themes of ingenuity and music. Tiepolo might have preferred to execute these as wall frescoes, but the convention of large-scale oil paintings to decorate the walls of a room continued. Two narrow, upright canvases depict *Apollo flaying Marsyas* and *Hercules killing Antaeus*.[4] The god cruelly punishes the satyr's presumption in challenging him to a musical competition. Hercules displays not force but cunning, since he outwitted Antaeus by lifting him up, removing his contact with the source of his strength, his mother, the earth. The largest canvas is a horizontal one, almost certainly to occupy the left-hand wall, showing a classic scene of ingenuity, *Ulysses discovering Achilles among the daughters of Lycomedes* (Pl. 35). In these paintings there is little sense of artistic advance. The *Apollo and Marsyas* partly echoes the composition, as well as the theme of the *Martyrdom of St Bartholomew*. The *Ulysses* is more ambitious, yet not entirely successful in combining the requisite drama of the central incident with pageant-like tendencies, anticipating the *Finding of Moses* (Pl. 80) of some years later. For all the artist's delight in individual details, not least the extensive landscape, the composition fails to cohere. The big scale of the long canvas seems to present difficulties—in contrast to the ease felt on the ceiling—and, not for the last time, Tiepolo seems less at home with the more prosaic task of painting in oil, breathing less happily as he comes down from heaven to earth and is out of his natural medium of fresco.

★   ★   ★

Whenever the Palazzo Sandi ceiling was finished, it was almost certainly by 1726. In the June of that year, the Confraternity of the Most Holy Sacrament in Udine chose as the artist to decorate their chapel in the Duomo there Tiepolo, designated in

34. Detail of Pl. 33 showing Orpheus and Eurydice.

35. *Ulysses discovering Achilles among the daughters of Lycomedes*, Da Schio Collection, Castelgomberto, Vicenza.

36. Detail of Pl. 33 showing Bellerophon.

37. Detail of Pl. 33 showing Amphion building Thebes.

the minute of their meeting as 'the celebrated painter'.[5] The work that Tiepolo carried out in the chapel is, for all its attractiveness, quite modest, and in itself the commission was not much of one for a 'celebrated' figure. However, he may already have had links with the city, and in choosing him the Confraternity may have been doing the obvious thing.

The Patriarch of Aquileia had his seat and palace at Udine, and the then Patriarch was Dionisio Dolfin, a member of the highly distinguished Venetian family which was to employ Tiepolo in the 1720s in the family palace at S. Pantalon in Venice. Giovanni Dolfin, of the same family and probably the Patriarch's brother, had been godfather to one of Tiepolo's brothers, Giovanni Francesco, born in 1693. The oil paintings done by Tiepolo for the Dolfin palace are dispersed (and discussed in the following chapter), and some frescoes he apparently executed in the Dolfin villa on the Venice-Treviso road are destroyed.

Fortunately, his frescoes carried out for Dionisio Dolfin in what was then the patriarchal palace survive intact and, indeed, beautifully preserved. It is reasonable to suppose that work on some of them had started by June 1726. On the façade of the palace is a date, 1718, referring to the wing of it built by Rossi for the Patriarch Dolfin, then in the nineteenth year of his patriarchate. As late as July 1725, however, there is a reference which shows that work inside was still proceeding: a staircase, which would not have 'its equal in all Italy', was being constructed.[6] The grand staircase of the palace, rising through three floors and decorated with elaborate, allusive stucco ornaments at each level, is clearly the one referred to. In the planning the uppermost area seems to have been intended from the first for a fresco. From the ground there is apparent a large rectangular space, framed by stucco mouldings that include in their decoration a mitre and an archiepiscopal cross, as well as a crozier, and as the staircase is climbed to the top, the whole ceiling (rarely well photographed and perhaps seldom inspected) is revealed as filled not only by a central fresco composition but by eight subsidiary compartments, all the work of Tiepolo.

For the arresting central composition, the subject of St Michael throwing the rebel angels out of heaven was selected (Pl. 38). It was, for obvious reasons, a long-

38. *Fall of the Rebel Angels*, staircase, Arcivescovado, Udine.

popular subject for ceiling paintings, though usually those of churches not palaces.

By Tiepolo's standards, the fresco is not entirely successful. St Michael is an oddly undynamic figure, with a faint Ricciesque air of the languid. The remarkably small band of rebel angels seems in no haste to fall, and the most effective is the virtuoso one seen from the back, with an arm modelled in stucco to grip the frame of the fresco from which he is tumbling. The composition is rather too small for the site, and from the ground its effect is distinctly muted. Illusionism for its own sake is not a hallmark of Tiepolo's style at any date. Nor is war in heaven perhaps the ideal subject for his imagination, but it may have had significance for episcopal rulers. He was to paint it only once again, a quarter of a century or so later, for the chapel of the Prince-Bishop's Residenz at Würzburg. Around the central scene at Udine are mauvish-monochrome episodes, elegantly illustrating the story of Adam and Eve, and a further hint of admonition comes from a painted sword and scales, symbolising justice and punishment. Elsewhere in the palace Tiepolo was to fresco the Judgment of Solomon.

It is the book of Genesis that provides the source of the subjects frescoed in the narrow gallery at the front of the palace, a room reached through the throne-room where portraits of the saints and patriarchs of Udine filled the walls. For the gallery (Pl. 39), lit by five windows and leading nowhere, frescoes had possibly been intended from the time of its construction. Here the patriarchate was commemorated by illustrating scenes from the lives of the first patriarchs of all, Abraham, Isaac and Jacob. There was probably a significance beyond the individual Patriarch Dolfin in this emphasis, for the patriarchate was a vexed political matter and although it was titularly of Aquileia it had for long been settled at Udine, the capital of Friuli and a city hailed as 'Nuova Aquileia'. The existence of the patriarchate was a source of pride to Venice but of annoyance to the Holy Roman Emperors whose Austrian subjects were positively forbidden to obey the Patriarch. A judgment of Solomon was eventually required of the Pope, who split the territory into two archbishoprics and suppressed the patriarchate in the reign of Dolfin's successor and nephew, Daniele. If Dionisio Dolfin could scarcely see so far, he must have known very well the history and the emotions connected with his high office, and God's promise to Abraham and Jacob's journeyings and his rights of primogeniture could find their application in the story of the patriarchate. The office itself was virtually a prerogative of certain noble Venetian families, as if to bear out the words of Genesis: 'Unto thy seed have I given this land. . .' Dionisio Dolfin was the second Patriarch from his own family and probably looked to being succeeded by his nephew.

To Tiepolo the assignment of the room was no less significant. Here, most likely for the first time, he and his collaborator were allotted every inch of space, of wall as well as ceiling, and set free to decorate it. Rarely again would such total freedom be his, and rarely again could even he respond with such energy and fertility, such bubbling spontaneity. The gallery at Udine deserves to be appreciated in its own right, not as a mere prologue to later achievements that were certainly to be grander, even more glamorous, though seldom so sheerly lyrical.

The setting was a patriarch's palace and the theme Biblical. As a reminder of the former, the room is closed at each end by boldly painted simulated archways, created out of great twisted columns and topped by the Dolfin scutcheon crowned by the Patriarch's hat, shaped and tasselled like a cardinal's but in green. As for the Biblical theme, Tiepolo approached it in a mood of light-heartedness that may have surprised the commissioner and his advisers, or perhaps went unnoticed in the effective total treatment of the room. What Tiepolo seized on was the pastoral element in the stories he had to depict, and also perhaps the comparative licence they offered for fantasy, being neither strictly historical nor sacred in the sense of the New Testament. The result is a sort of pictorial *Midsummer Night's Dream*, where mortal and immortal beings meet and part in a world in which everything seems suffused

by magic. Not the least delight of the room is its near-perfect preservation. Its windows are normally, prudently, shuttered, and only on the opening of them does the whole scheme spring into dazzling life.

Its effectiveness owes much, more than at first perhaps appears, to the ingenious and gracefully inventive painted architectural framework that by itself transforms the bare, tunnel-like room. For this Tiepolo was indebted, according to tradition, to the gifted *quadratura* specialist Girolamo Mengozzi Colonna, who was certainly his collaborator on several important subsequent commissions (e.g. at the Scalzi, the Palazzo Labia and the Villa Valmarana). He was a few years older than Tiepolo, having been born around 1688 in Ferrara, and had not trained in Venice. Specialists of his kind were far from uncommon in North Italy, though often little is known about their careers, but Mengozzi Colonna was clearly one of the most talented.

The seeds of what he devised at Udine go back to the ceiling of the galleria of the Palazzo Farnese. But instead of allowing only the corners of the ceiling to reveal sky imagined beyond, Mengozzi opens up three shaped roundels in the fantastic, lace-like structure feigned across the ceiling, all open to the simulated sky. Within the room is created a pavilion, spun out of icing-sugar in its curves and whorls, and in its tonality. Down the left-hand windowed wall there are feigned niches occupied by feigned statues. On the right-hand wall, where the majority of Tiepolo's frescoes were to be, the illusionism is at its most playfully complex. An architectural screen almost writhing in its scrolls and shells and undulating lines is pierced at each end for tall open-air scenes, then provides a pair of feigned niches and a pair of panels, executed by Tiepolo as bas-reliefs of ivory-white figures on a golden ground. At the centre, like a great scene on stage revealed when the curtain rises, there is the largest space of all, occupied by the fresco of *Rachel hiding the idols from her father, Laban* (Pl. 42).

33

This uncommon subject is only one uncommon aspect of the complete scheme. For all that may be argued about patriarchy, the room seems to lay stress on matriarchy and on women generally. Each of the painted statues is of a Prophetess, some (like Huldah) of considerable obscurity. While the subject of the angels appearing to Abraham is a familiar one in painting of all periods up to 1800, the angelic appearance to his wife Sarah is extremely seldom found. At Udine the two scenes complement each other, and though Sarah is visited to be told she shall bear a son, Isaac, the second patriarch, she is exalted—thanks to Tiepolo's imagining—into a memorable image. Hagar too, the bond-woman, finds a place on the ceiling.

A fairly recondite programme may be supposed to have been drawn up at the Patriarch's instigation, and probably from among his entourage, for Tiepolo to follow. Follow it he obediently did, but he invested it with qualities of humour and wit, and private allusion, as well as refined elegance, which the 'programme' is unlikely to have called for.

It would be wrong to declare that Tiepolo was not serious in his attitude, but undoubtedly he was not solemn. He had to invent an idiom, clothe his figures and give them a setting. For the costumes he looked back deliberately to the sixteenth century, specifically to Veronese. For the settings, he seems to have been inspired partly by the countryside around Udine, which in its mountainous character may have struck him as novel after an upbringing in Venice. A glimpse of what seems locally based landscape occurs in the background of the fresco where the kneeling Abraham is visited by angels (Pl. 40). The scene is set in Genesis as 'in the heat of the day', and Tiepolo seems to echo that in his own terms, with suggestions of siesta in a dusty-dry, Friulian summer landscape, where vision merges with mirage in a haze of heat. With his aged, gnarled hands clasped in almost tremulous ecstasy, Abraham is rapt before a vision, borne up on a soft snowball of cloud, of three slim angels, exquisitely clad, in olive-green, white and blue, interlinked sexless beings of almost Ariel-like insubstantiality, yet full of shimmering vitality, from their electrically curling tendrils of hair to their elegantly articulated toes and gleaming, bejewelled anklets.

More rustic still is the setting for Sarah (Pl. 41). Her advanced age is conveyed to the point of near-caricature—the withered throat, the missing teeth revealed by her smile, which is also part of the story: 'Therefore Sarah laughed . . . shall I of surety bear a child which am old?' Even her place in the admittedly ruined-seeming hut has its basis in Genesis, for she 'heard it [the promise of a child] in the tent door which was behind' Abraham. From those words Tiepolo creates a miniature drama that could almost be a scene from opera buffa and might, in its enchanted blend of observation and imagination, have made the Patriarch Dolfin smile too. Although planted in a rough shed of gaping planks, where the amenities are restricted to a piece of rope and a gourd suspended, by a bit of cloth, from a nail, Sarah is dressed in handsome, sixteenth-century costume and upstanding sweep of ruff, an exotic figure in such countrified surroundings though not as exotic as the pointing, blonde angel whose beautifully patterned black and white robe is hitched up in angelically negligent fashion to reveal a thigh. This is artifice, certainly, but the effect is far from artificial. Nature is also present, not only in the sinuous, bare tree-trunk (oddly affecting, as though a symbol of the barren state of Sarah, soon to change), but in the poppies blooming at its base, scrupulously studied, even down to the fat buds and the silvery green of the leaves. Such blending is Tiepolo's own, and the very individual flavour has been skilfully contrived to create a fairytale atmosphere of unexpected intensity.

It is experienced most strongly in the large central fresco of Rachel hiding the household idols from her father and thus expressing loyal devotion to her husband Jacob. Whatever the significance of the subject for the patriarchate of Aquileia, Tiepolo was—with almost impudent assurance—to give it personal significance for himself. And here the countryside and country life quietly assert a more prominent

41 (preceding page). *Angel appearing to Sarah*, Arcivescovado, Udine (detail).

36

place, justified by the pastoral context of the incident, and once again Tiepolo makes it dreamily topical and localised, despite the presence of some camels.

Mengozzi Colonna signalled the importance of the fresco to come by making a great stage setting, virtually an architectural drama in itself, with a proscenium arch breaking above the cornice line of the room like a wave-borne shell, with a skeletal mask below and fringed by dipping swags of gilded leaves and flowers. He curved the base of the area as well and contrived a central focus of fantasy, almost a mock coat-of-arms, with a semi-cartouche of white and gold supported by harpy-like creatures, all set against a feigned slab of inlaid, bluish marble.

It was as if he challenged Tiepolo to match and fill this capricious, inventive framework with something equally capricious and inventive. And Tiepolo rose to the challenge implied. He disposed his composition so ingeniously that the spectator forgets the oddity of shape—or, rather, the undulating lines with which he builds his composition seem to eddy outward and dictate the architectural framing. To increase the theatrical effect, he looped up a vast, dark, dun-coloured curtain at the right within his fresco, giving a sense of its having been pulled aside to reveal, inside her tent, the foreground Rachel seated on the household gods stolen from her father.

There is revealed not only a dialogue of love and duty, as Laban expostulates and Jacob quizzically looks on, but an airy panorama of pale, tinted sky and pale, distant mountain peaks hardly more solid than the pastel clouds. A whole pastoral world surrounds the protagonists, and the life of the countryside drifts on (Pl. 45). A moony-looking youth affectionately drapes his arm over a pale-washed, nearly colourless cow and behind is seen a flock of pure white sheep. A peasant girl has paused, holding a pitcher, in a stance of balletic grace, undisturbed by a child clutching at her skirt. Although there may be no specific 'debt' as such, the concept of setting a Biblical scene in such strongly rustic surroundings recalls several of Castiglione's Old-Testament paintings (not least his versions of Jacob's journey and his drawings, much esteemed in eighteenth-century Venice. Nomadic life is conveyed by the fawn camels being tended, the big, mysterious bundles, the cooking pots and jar, the women accompanied by children of all ages, begotten doubtless by Jacob. One boy clasps a pear; another sits self-confidently at Rachel's knee; an older girl stares uncertainly at a friendly brown and white hound. Here a fur-capped, fur-cloaked figure seems too warmly clad for such limpid weather; there a man largely stripped of his shirt has perhaps gone too far, though Tiepolo models his back with sensuous pleasure. At the right a solemn-eyed, turbaned woman, dressed in olive and violet, looks on at the central confrontation with eloquent, anxious doubt; she is probably intended for Rachel's sister Leah, in which case Tiepolo seems again to recall Genesis: 'Leah was tender-eyed; but Rachel was beautiful and well-favoured.'

Beside the urgently gesticulating Laban, Jacob seems a withdrawn figure, more concerned to catch the spectator's attention. Something of his detachment indicates that he is outside as well as of the composition, central though his position in it is. In a Veronese-style cap striped in blue and gold and a ruff-topped, green tunic tied by a blue-tasselled girdle, Tiepolo portrays himself, with no flattery of his slightly over-prominent nose, pop eyes and typical, rather worried expression.

As for Rachel, seen in profile, with her pervasive blondeness of complexion and hair and her sparkling, liquid-blue eye, she too is a portrait: of, once again, Cecilia Tiepolo. Husband and wife in the Old Testament and in reality, the pair do not exchange glances, and Tiepolo seems to stand back, almost literally, as he lavishes on the figure of his wife as Rachel as much art as love (Pl. 44). Flowers and jewels—pearls and sapphires—adorn her hair. A single string of pearls is round her neck, and to enhance that blonde tonality of skin which extends to her fluent hands he frescoed a dress of the most vivid, shimmering blue, with watery gleaming highlights on its puffed sleeve, seeming to capture an icy brilliance of surface as he laid on and hatched

42 (following pages). *Rachel hiding the idols from her father, Laban,* Arcivescovado, Udine.

37

the pigment now with rapid touches and now with deeper strokes of darker blue, creating the voluminous skirt, from under which falls another, in colour russet. Although there is the 'reality' of a portrait about this Rachel, she turns under Tiepolo's treatment into one of his ideal heroines. Heightened by his art, she assumes the costume and air of a princess, as much as a heroine, despite being seated on a bale of straw in a tent in the middle of the countryside. Such elevation of rank is not granted indiscriminately by the painter to his women. The figure who is probably Leah is not only more simply dressed but dressed in timeless, conventionally 'Biblical' garments. By contrast, Rachel's clothes and jewellery have been borrowed from the property box labelled 'Veronese', but re-arranged, improved and given new touches of fantasy so that there is nothing of pastiche in the result. It is a conscious caprice, at once familiar from sixteenth-century art, and yet made more exotic. Veils and scarves and jewels are added by Tiepolo to adorn and also to emphasise the mystique of womanhood. Rachel is only among the first of these heroines whose beauty and allure, including the allure of clothes, he finds it fascinating to create: enchantress women who are the real focus of his paintings, whether Cleopatra in antiquity or the obscure medieval Beatrice of Burgundy whose wedding at Würzburg becomes, artistically, a triumph of bride over groom, though that groom is the German Emperor (see Pl. 171).

A fresh detail seems to occur to Tiepolo to add to the costume of Rachel even when it might appear that hardly any space was left for further refinement. Where her striped veil falls over her shoulders there is a minute area which could be enlivened; there he pins a small brooch, with a single pendant pearl that casts its tiny patch of shadow on the swelling expanse of silky blue sleeve. Plate 44 allows us to see not merely this achievement in all its detail but also something of Tiepolo's method for creating such an achievement. Excitingly confident drawing, as if in coloured chalks, gives form to every springy ringlet of hair, fold of drapery and articulation of each half-fluttering finger. In all the area there is no space not enlivened by a sort of artistic 'furia'.

In description, Rachel's costume—indeed, the whole fresco—might sound fussy and over-rich, but Tiepolo is never undisciplined or unalert. If his frescoes are like vast irridescent bubbles, he knows exactly when the moment of maximum tension is reached, and the blowing has to stop. The fabric is stretched to its uttermost, always buoyant and light-filled, never overloaded, and yet in no danger of bursting. One secret lies in his recondite colour harmonies, which were certainly not borrowed from Veronese, or any other painter, with alternations of warm and cool tones which are as instinctive to him as his sense of when to introduce pattern, when to elaborate a passage, working up an effect for density, and when to hold back, allowing air to circulate. In almost musical ways, he varied his effects across a composition. The fresco of Rachel has calm, lyrical areas, like the pastoral scene at the left, exquisitely yet softly, quietly, tinted, fading into the atmosphere as though barely breathed onto the wall; and then sharper-focused, noisier, 'jazzy' areas amid the crowded group at the right, where he suddenly breaks out with a brilliant piece of blue ribbon or—in a well-loved device—dazzles by striping a sleeve or edging a robe with rapid, vibrant assault. On Tiepolo's inventive use of striped materials alone, a thesis could be written.

Already in this fresco he shows his instinctive understanding—though it may have been stimulated by Veronese's constant example—that profusion can best be depicted by economy. Half a leg and half a shoulder, a head partly hidden behind another, will suffice to suggest a gathering of people and leave to the imagination what is not shown, the feeling of teeming life beyond. For the fresco painter—for, anyway, Tiepolo as a fresco painter—the lesson was especially important as a way of avoiding heaviness and prosaicness. It is part of Tiepolo's economic concentration on what he sees as essential that nothing should mar the ultimate illusion of all: that a

solid wall has been—not decorated but dissolved. Tall fictive statues and the pair of simulated bas-reliefs of white on gold flank the central scene in the gallery at Udine, playing up the idea of opaque solidity and indeed mural decoration of the richest kind.

That illusion of the impenetrable serves to enhance the great sweep of light and air that breaks out in the fresco of Rachel, opening up the space in wave upon wave of luminosity. It is echoed explosively on the ceiling in the extraordinary aerial drama of heaven's intervention at the sacrifice of Isaac (Pl. 43). Through stormy clouds fierce shafts of celestial radiance suddenly stream down, bringing an angel like a visual thunderclap to arrest Abraham's uplifted hand. The fresco is a measure of how far Tiepolo had come from the days of the Ospedaletto canvas (Pl. 12), but it also shows how deeply he associated the opportunities of fresco with creation of the most precious and elusive of all effects: infinite light.

No dates have yet been established for Tiepolo's work in the patriarchal palace, but it must have been the product of several visits, for he was also to fresco the ceiling of the room now usually called merely the Sala Rossa but in fact the Sala del Tribunale. There can only be supposition based on the style of the main composition here, the *Judgment of Solomon* (Pl. 46), but it seems markedly later in date than the gallery frescoes, possibly not much before 1730 (nor long afterwards, since its

43. *Sacrifice of Isaac*, Arcivescovado, Udine.

44 (following page). Detail of Pl. 42.

41

46. *Judgment of Solomon*, Sala Rossa, Arcivescovado, Udine.

existence is referred to by da Canal). Four subsidiary frescoes portray the prophets Isaiah, Jeremiah, Ezekiel and Daniel (itself a popular name in the Dolfin family), steeply foreshortened in airy, almost windswept landscape settings, conveyed with great economy against glowing, pastel skies.

In these figures there seems less obvious drawing with pigment, less sheer dash in execution but a calmer mastery compared with the exuberance of the gallery, and altogether a more elevated mood. The *Judgment of Solomon* shows all this, together with a demonstration of new virtuosity and frank delight in splendour. The composition, placing the monarch enthroned at the right, seems to derive from Veronese's *Ahasuerus crowning Esther* on the ceiling of S. Sebastiano at Venice, though Tiepolo tilts his composition even further, with positively vertiginous effect. Other echoes of Veronese are detectable, some perhaps reaching Tiepolo via Ricci. Out of them he now blends a sumptuous pageant of brocades and banners, page-boys, statues and soldiery which unveils—arguably for the first time—the authentic atmosphere of his most imperial scenes, to become familiar in later commissions. Set in the bright open air, Solomon's court is alive with colour and characters (Pl. 49), somewhat distracting in its glittering panoply from the incident of the two mothers contesting the living and the dead baby. A famous court and a famous monarch from the distant, faintly oriental past set Tiepolo's imagination tingling. White statues support a vast, warmly golden brocade to form Solomon's throne—and only with difficulty can one of the lions, traditionally its supporters, be distinguished. A curving colonnade, equally white, and statue-crowned, runs the length of the composi-

45 (preceding page). Detail of Pl. 42.

47. *Angel musicians*, Cappella del Sacramento, Duomo, Udine.

48. *Angel musicians*, Städelsches Kunstinstitut, Frankfurt.

tion, adding Palladian overtones to the scene. Over it all, from the blonde page-boy in blue who stares down into the room with a portrait-like sense, as it might be Tiepolo's son, Domenico, to the dwarf with his dog, whose paws familiarly trample on him (Pl. 50), the youthful Solomon serenely presides. Dressed in robes ermine-trimmed and with giant, nut-shaped gilt buttons, wearing a turban, fez and a spiky crown, he is half doge and half eastern potentate, a symbol of the ruler as not only wise and just but glamorous. Tiepolo included himself, in profile, at Solomon's court, and, on one of the steps below, fully signed the fresco with a calligraphic flourish.

Just as he may have returned to Udine to fresco this scene and its companion ones, and certainly he was to fit in on a visit some overdoors in the castle there, so he had at

49 (following page). Detail of Pl. 46.

45

50 (preceding page). Detail of Pl. 46.

some point to execute the Holy Sacrament chapel frescoes in the Duomo. Modest though the commission might seem, he responded with enchanting verve, solving the awkward problems of a very restricted area, further interrupted by a window.

For a similarly dedicated but far bigger chapel in S. Giustina at Padua, Sebastiano Ricci had, around 1700, created grandiose illusionistic effects, which Tiepolo might envy but not emulate in the cramped confines at Udine.[7] All he had space for was a band of angel musicians descending from heaven, as it were through a roof (Pl. 47). He carefully planned the scheme, and an unusually detailed preparatory drawing exists (Pl. 48), taking note of the intrusive window.

Although oddly described in at least two modern Italian monographs as executed in monochrome, the frescoes in the upper portion, where the angels flutter as they sing, are in fact piquantly coloured. The monochrome areas are two obscure panels of fresco, not easy to see or examine. At the top of the vault Tiepolo created a feigned oculus (echo, conscious or not, of Mantegna's Camera degli Sposi) open to a celestial sky from which baby angels peer down. Even on the holy site Tiepolo could not restrain his exuberant spirits, and a sheet of heavenly music can be noticed, slipped from angelic hands and floating earthwards, casting a shadow as it falls.

Udine had given Tiepolo his first major commissions outside Venice, thanks primarily to the patronage of Dionisio Dolfin. He had been allowed scope to demonstrate—in church and palace—how perfectly attuned to his gifts was the medium of fresco. By 1730 his fame must have been significantly increasing, and soon other cities, sometimes larger than Udine and beyond Venetian territory, were seeking to employ him. When da Canal was writing of him in his life of Lazzarini, he noted that Tiepolo was 'now' aged thirty-five and was 'now' at work in Milan.[8]

Yet though Tiepolo had achieved so much and was by then poised to undertake commissions which represented new challenges, he had not been idle in Venice itself. There too he had benefited from Dolfin patronage; and the artist who was shortly to be referred to in print at Milan as 'the celebrated Venetian' had gone there only after further achievements in his native city.

3 'THE CELEBRATED VENETIAN': AT HOME AND AWAY

NEW COMMISSIONS 'abroad' might promise Tiepolo new scope, and all his life he was impelled by a personal interpretation of 'per ardua ad astra' that was to lead him eventually a long way from home.

He probably detected little changing at Venice, politically or artistically, in the decade ending in 1730 during which he himself came to prominence. Whatever the gradual decline of Venice as a power, in Europe and as a trading centre—and its more acute crises lay ahead—the city can scarcely have given any sense of running down. Heaven still seemed to afford it special protection, and in 1730 the Doge Alvise Mocenigo went in solemn procession to S. Maria della Salute to express gratitude for a century of the city's freedom from the plague. The Venetian state still continued to issue a stream of regulations, major and minor, concerned with life in the city and ranging from lighting of the streets and restoration of well-heads to the sale of newly invented iced drinks. Parish priests had to be reminded of their duty to register deaths. Over-luxurious fans were disapproved of, if not positively forbidden.[1]

The early years of the eighteenth century saw a succession of physical improvements and additions to Venice. Tirali's pavement was laid in the Piazza. New and partly new palaces continued to be erected. The Labia, Dolfin, Zenobio and Cornaro families were only some of those who built or re-built, often on a sumptuous scale. The churches offer perhaps even more striking evidence, and the financing of these extended on occasion beyond individual merchant or patrician resources, involving what would now be called public appeals. The churches of S. Rocco, S. Geremia and S. Vidal were re-built. Entirely new churches like S. Simeone Piccolo (Pl. 51), designed by Scalfarotto, came into prominent existence on the Grand Canal. Giorgio Massari seems to have edged out Scalfarotto from one of the most significant of church commissions, the construction by the Dominicans on the Zattere of the Gesuati, solemnly dedicated to the Madonna of the Rosary by the Patriarch of Venice, Marco Gradenigo, on 17 May 1726. For the cool, luminous interior of that church work was to be sought from Ricci and Piazzetta, as well as from Tiepolo— and all three painters were to respond memorably.

51. Canaletto, *Grand Canal with S. Simeone Piccolo*, National Gallery, London.

New theatres, hospitals and buildings connected with the Confraternities, the Scuole, were also added to the scene, often providing further opportunities for decoration by both painters and sculptors. Decade by decade, and with allowance made for the often uncertain dating of the buildings in question, it is the years 1719–1728 which have been computed to show the maximum building activity at Venice between 1709 and 1798, though the decade of 1759–1768 follows closely behind. After that comes a drastic fall.[2]

In painting, the opening years of the century had witnessed an efflorescence of talent that in its variety at least had no parallel in the history of Venetian art, and which was not to be repeated. Older ideals, as well as older practitioners, were dying out. Painters had a new clientèle in addition to new aims; and by 1730 Tiepolo's closest contemporary, Canaletto, was established as a view painter of a novel-seem-

52. P. Longhi, *The Hairdresser*, Ca' Rezzonico, Venice.

53. P. Monaco after Tiepolo, *St Francis receiving the stigmata*, British Museum, London.

ing kind, superior to Carlevaris (who died that year) because in Canaletto's pictures 'si vede', another painter wrote enthusiastically at the time, 'Lucer entro il Sole'.[3] Such praise of light-filled paintings might, in different guise, have been bestowed on Tiepolo.

Another emerging artist was Pietro Longhi, born in 1702, a phenomenon as much fostered by Venetian patrician patronage as Canaletto was by foreign, increasingly English patronage. Longhi's small genre scenes (Pl. 52) give a certain flavour of life in Venice behind the façades depicted by Canaletto, though they are highly selective and tend to shrink from the busy, variegated crowds—vendors, Orientals, workers and loungers—who populate so vividly Canaletto's views. Longhi's world was to seem to some Venetians of the period not merely topical and down-to-earth but 'true' in a way that Tiepolo's was not, and the comparison hinted at a reserve before the spectacle of Tiepolo's achievements which foreign visitors, including artists and connoisseurs, were to express more openly. Even foreign residents in Venice who collected contemporary paintings—like the future British Consul, Joseph Smith, and the defender of Corfù, Marshal Schulenburg—seem to have made no effort to patronise Tiepolo, though the Marshal owned some of Piazzetta's finest genre scenes and gave numerous commissions to Tiepolo's brother-in-law, Gian Antonio Guardi. It is also noteworthy that a scheme devised in the 1720s by Owen McSwiney, a bankrupt, Irish impresario, for a series of paintings of imaginary monuments to famous English figures, the *Tombeaux des Princes*, involved a number of leading Venetian painters—Sebastiano and Marco Ricci, Canaletto, Piazzetta and Pittoni—but omitted Tiepolo.

Da Canal speaks of Tiepolo's drawings as being much sought after; so Smith, for instance, could, had he wished, have been an early collector of these, if he thought Tiepolo's paintings were too colourful—or too expensive. It is perhaps a rhetorical touch in da Canal's attractive enthusiasm that he should claim that Tiepolo's drawings are despatched to 'più lontani paesi'. Certainly England, and almost certainly France, were not among the distant countries where examples of Tiepolo's art were sought at all.

At that date Tiepolo's activity as a draughtsman had its more 'finished' commissioned aspects. When the antiquarian scholar Scipione Maffei published his *Verona Illustrata* in 1732, the engraved illustrations included a dozen based on Tiepolo's careful drawings of Roman statues and busts, and Maffei praised the 'learned' result.[4] Other drawings engraved after Tiepolo at least allowed him freedom of invention, though with engraving in mind the compositions had indeed to be composed carefully, and the results lack some of the obvious 'fire' of execution characteristic of the artist. Yet through these engravings too his art became more widely known. A group of such drawings, chiefly of saints and all of sacred subjects, was owned by Pietro Monaco, an engraver born in Belluno in 1707 and settled in Venice around 1732. He included engravings of them in his *Raccolta . . . di pitture di storia sacra*, published at various times, first probably in 1739, and some, such as the *St Francis receiving the stigmata* (Pl. 53) record drawings that appear not to survive.[5] The mood and style are clearly close to Tiepolo's work at Udine, and this composition possesses all the elaboration that might be expected of a painting. The subject has its special interest, for Tiepolo painted it pre-1733 in a composition now lost and was to return to it in Spain in his last completed commission. The dramatically posed, ecstatic saint of the drawing, bathed in rays of light from heaven and accompanied by somewhat distracting, youthful angels, was to be re-interpreted far more calmly and simply by Tiepolo at the close of his career, by which time 'invention' of a more subtle kind was his goal.

To several of the Venetian palaces altered and improved in the early part of the century Tiepolo contributed his share in decorations now dispersed when not lost. He was called on for large-scale secular oil paintings which continued a taste of the

54. *Triumph of Marius*, Metropolitan Museum of Art, New York, Rogers Fund, 1965 (65.183.1).

55. *Brutus and Aruns*, Kunsthistorisches Museum, Vienna.

previous century's and which do not occur, in style or subject-matter, in his later output. Heroic, antique Roman subject-matter, with perhaps some flattering if obscure reference to the family of the patron, seems to have been preferred, giving a military emphasis very different from, say, the languorous air of the Cleopatra and Antony frescoes on the walls of the Palazzo Labia. The idea of eighteenth-century Venice as the inheritor of ancient Rome may seem to border on the ludicrous, but there was a strong tradition of the great modern republic descending from the great one of the past. The 'Senate and the Venetian people', S.P.Q.V., was a rather fanciful abstraction, yet since the fifteenth century, when a Florentine ambassador had complained about it to Pope Pius II, it was a Venetian boast that the Venetians were the successors of the Romans. Several noble families liked to trace their descent from famous Roman ancestors, with the ingenious derivation of their names. The Contarini assumed they descended from the Cotta 'of the Rhine'. The Cornaro claimed a distinguished ancestor in Publius Cornelius Scipio, and so on.

Quite possibly it was for Ca' Zenobio, where da Canal records he had worked, that Tiepolo painted the *Triumph of Aurelian* (now at Turin), a very large lateral canvas that depicts specifically the Emperor's capture of Queen Zenobia.[6] However interpreted, whether as showing her stoicism as a prisoner or Aurelian's implied magnanimity (for he spared her life), the subject's high Roman associations would have made it a suitable palace decoration, and it is even conceivable that the Zenobio liked to see in the heroine, who did die in Italy, some sort of ancestress. The painting's style, as much as its subject-matter, relates it loosely to the probably slightly earlier series of ten large and even sterner canvases, in a forceful, thundery and yet brilliant idiom, a personal 'baroque', that Tiepolo painted in the late 1720s for the Dolfin palace at S. Pantalon.

The source of these is basically Livy's History of Rome, as interpreted much later in the rhetorical version of Annaeus Florus. An imperial and inflated account of republican Rome made an ideal source (one from which extracts were to be written on the paintings) for the essentially grand manner of these stormy, martial and often bloody canvases. There was no place in them for touches of flippant humour, or for charm, feminine or otherwise. The state and its demands on the individual form the theme. Rome conquers—especially its traditional enemy Carthage (for which might be read Venice versus the Ottoman Empire). Two of the Dolfin brothers were patriots and heroic figures in the old style: one had fought under Morosini, and the other in his will expressed a wish to shed his blood to heal the wounds of the state. Blood flows in Tiepolo's paintings. Hannibal contemplates with horror the severed head of Hasdrubal, his brother, flung at his feet. In the most sensational of all the compositions, Brutus and Aruns pierce each other's bodies fatally and simultaneously (Pl. 55). Brutus' body slumps sickeningly forward; the shaft of Aruns' hefty lance has penetrated his shield and armour and is running thick with his blood. Such a depiction stirs associations with the story of an earlier heroic Dolfin who had fought in hand-to-hand combat with an enemy.[7]

In one of the biggest and most impressive of the series, the Moorish king Jugurtha is shown captive and chained, prominently displayed in the triumph of Marius (Pl. 54). That painting bears the date 1729, which provides a good enough indication of the period during which the series was produced. It probably occupied Tiepolo for some time and may have been worked on in the winter months of the very years whose summers were spent at Udine. Such a general pattern of work, dictated by the necessity of executing frescoes in the climatically favourable seasons of the year, was certainly to become typical of Tiepolo's activity. In the Palazzo Dolfin room he faced a task very different from anything he had faced at Udine. It is true that the taste he had to satisfy was partly an old-fashioned one. Vast canvases of Scipio, Junius Brutus and Cincinnatus had been painted by Ricci to decorate some palace, and in Venice itself there are similar paintings of Roman subjects in the Palazzo

Vendramin-Calergi, sometimes attributed to Bambini (1651–1736). Yet Tiepolo was to go on being commissioned for vast oil paintings, usually of religious subject-matter, and his ability to organise massed figures and to create intense drama continued to be called on—at least as late as the painting of *St Tecla* for Este (see Pl. 197).

Now that it is dispersed, the Dolfin palace series cannot be judged together or *in situ*, but there are distinct variations of quality between the paintings in terms of composition alone. When all hung in the same room, they doubtless made a consistently imposing, even perhaps somewhat overpowering, effect. The boldly moulded shadows, the heavy impasto and the areas of glittering, metallic colour, all suggest a lingering influence of Solimena. His large-scale *Aeneas before Dido* (in the National Gallery, London) may well have been in Venice at the period, and is exactly the type of painting Tiepolo could usefully have glanced at. What he did not adopt, however, was its frieze-like treatment of the figures across the composition. He aimed as always for much greater depth, with results that might be thought to recall Rubens's did they not go back to Veronese. In the *Triumph of Marius*, the pawing horses of the quadriga and the flying banners seem to go back in essence to S. Sebastiano again, to Veronese's *Triumph of Mordecai*.

In the *Marius* a tremendous procession, laden with spoils and trophies, and hailed by torch-bearers and trumpeters, with the Roman eagle held aloft, is advancing out of the canvas, almost threatening the spectator as it comes, proclaiming pitilessly the might of the conqueror and the subjection of the conquered. The Latin inscription at the top encourages the idea of the spectator as one with the applauding, grateful citizens witnessing the triumph: 'The Roman people behold Jugurtha laden with chains.' Tiepolo's ability to enter the ethos is remarkable; his response to this classical world has an intensity achieved by no other Italian painter except Mantegna.

The reverberating force of the *Marius* can be tested today in its present location in the Metropolitan Museum. It 'tells' across a far wider space than was ever originally envisaged, and its martial music is scarcely muffled. Patches of brilliant colour flash their message of excitement: a gleaming scarlet cloak is flung across and behind the chained Jugurtha, and against the strong blue sky Marius' victorious standard flutters in concertina-folds of pure brimstone-butterfly-yellow.

From the same years as the Palazzo Dolfin canvases must originate a further work for Venice, which, being a fresco, remains *in situ*: the *Apotheosis of St Teresa* (Pl. 56) in the chapel dedicated to the saint in the Scalzi. Da Canal mentions the fresco by Tiepolo, but he does not, as some scholars have stated, describe it as an early work. Its precise dating is undoubtedly a problem. In some ways it seems to renew Tiepolo's debt to Piazzetta, the Piazzetta who had, before August 1727, executed the ceiling of the *Glory of St Dominic* (Pl. 57) in SS Giovanni e Paolo. This is not a fresco but oil on canvas. Piazzetta's solution to depicting a heavenly vision to be seen from below was to suggest centripetal force, drawing up the saint and angels whirling all around towards the radiant Trinity and Virgin, placed like blanched statues at the emotional core of the composition. Between that distant sphere and earth, Piazzetta models on the rim of the scene a prominent group of Dominican friars whose position and solidity help to emphasise the visionary nature of what lies beyond.

Although it is true that Tiepolo's own treatment of a comparable theme—on a smaller scale—is different from Piazzetta's, the group of his angels bearing St Teresa to heaven (a far emptier heaven than that Piazzetta conceived) may well owe something to those in the *Glory of St Dominic*, as might also his feigned statues, especially the figure of Hope, which flank the central incident. The sophisticated, semi-architectural framework (traditionally the work of Mengozzi Colonna) is, however, typical of his preferred illusionism—and typical too, to be developed later, is the concept of this framework being broken by drifting cloud and air-borne figures. Although the saint herself is less successful, rising upwards in what seems a rather uncertain, even mildly apprehensive, state, the general style of the fresco suggests a

56. *Apotheosis of St Theresa*, Scalzi, Venice.

dating later rather than earlier in the 1720s, and arguably of around 1730. Udine, with all its enchantment, seems behind the artist. Ahead lie the opportunities—offered outside Venice—for him to develop as a painter particularly of ceiling frescoes.

Yet in Venice Tiepolo's outstanding virtuosity was becoming something of a legend. It is once again da Canal who refers to a work, now lost, executed by the artist in only ten hours: a *Communion of the Apostles*, in which the necessarily large group of figures were all half life-size. Even if the story has been enhanced in da Canal's admiring words, its emphasis is unmistakable. Speed, brilliance, uncomplicated readiness with brush or pen are the qualities that were henceforward to be associated with Tiepolo.

★   ★   ★

It was from Venice that Tiepolo wrote on 14 April 1731 to Count Giuseppe Casati in Milan.[8] This letter is the first documented occasion of Tiepolo speaking for himself, and it is entirely characteristic that he refers to work: the work he is already committed to finish in the Palazzo Archinto at Milan and the work he hopes he will manage to begin before the end of the season for Casati. It is also characteristic that this was no phrase-making, off-putting way of dealing with a patron. Tiepolo seems to have carried out his intentions and managed to execute both the heavy commission for the Archinto and that for Casati if not within the year then shortly afterwards.

Milan was a city under Austrian rule, though only recently had it become part of the Empire, following the War of Succession in 1714. At the time Tiepolo first worked there the Emperor was Charles VI, the father of Maria Theresa and the patron of Metastasio, who had settled in Vienna in 1730. In speed and virtuosity, the poet and the painter, close contemporaries in age, were well matched, and the decade that found Tiepolo expanding his career in a significant way was also that in which Metastasio produced some of his most famous works, including *La Clemenza di Tito*. That triumph of antique Roman virtue was conceived as a piece of imperial flattery—'per festeggiare il nome dell' Imperator Carlo'—only a year or two after Tiepolo had finished making his graceful painted allusions to princely merits through classical subject-matter.

Milan had its own distinguished noble families, though few perhaps as distinguished as the Borromeo, from whom had come a famous saint, S. Carlo Borromeo, and a famous near-saint, Cardinal Federico Borromeo. The marriage in 1731 of Giulia Borromeo to Filippo, eldest son of Carlo Archinto, who was a distinguished member of another eminent family, was probably the chief instigating factor in new rooms being added to the Archinto palace and the ceilings of some of those rooms being frescoed.[9] For that task Tiepolo was chosen.

Carlo Archinto was a scholar and author, interested in natural history and philosophy, in culture generally rather than in politics, though he had been a gentleman of the bedchamber to the Emperor Leopold I and received the Order of the Golden Fleece from the King of Spain. He, at least as much as his son or his son's wedding, was to be celebrated in the ceilings Tiepolo produced, especially the chief one, the *Triumph of the Arts and Sciences*, which bore the date 1731.

Tiepolo frescoed no less than four other, smaller ceilings in the palace, three with mythological subject-matter and the fourth with a personification of Nobility. Some at least of the ceiling paintings were set in extremely elaborate, presumably gilded mouldings, with the central scene surrounded by subsidiary ones in *grisaille*. The total effect must have been sumptuously rich and impressive. Tiepolo never received a commission for a private palace of comparable extent and rarely of such splendour. In those rooms of the Palazzo Archinto there must have been a sense of a perpetual masque being performed, devised for a specially favoured family.

Tragically, all the ceilings were destroyed by bombing in the Second World War. Apart from one small, sad fragment of the *Triumph* fresco, they survive only in photographs. The *Triumph of the Arts and Sciences* ceiling is seldom even reproduced *in toto*, so that its complex painted architectural framing (perhaps the work of a Milanese expert in the style), into which Tiepolo inserted richly dressed, kingly figures, among others, is often forgotten (Pls 58 and 59).

What, however, is quite clear is that no painter could have executed the five ceilings in a single season. The date of 1731 can only be the terminal date of the scheme, which might have been begun as early as 1729. The marriage of Giulia Borromeo and Filippo Archinto was already taken as arranged by January 1730, when the Archinto family's librarian, Argelati, was planning a collection of poems to celebrate it. That Tiepolo was working on the frescoes in the August of the same year is proved by a letter from a publisher in Verona, sent that month to a correspondent in Milan, referring to the painter as 'mio Carissimo Amico'. Several journeys to Milan were probably involved, and Tiepolo may have owed the commission in the first place to friends or admirers in Verona, who included the erudite Scipione Maffei, passing on his name to Carlo Archinto when he decided on the extensive

57. Piazzetta, *Glory of St Dominic*, SS. Giovanni e Paolo, Venice.

58 and 59. Details of the *Triumph of the Arts and Sciences* (destroyed), Palazzo Archinto, Milan.

decoration of his palace. In turn, the Archinto commission may well have proved a good recommendation for Tiepolo a few years later when he was asked to work in the Palazzo Clerici. By then Carlo Archinto was dead, but his daughter Maria was the mother of Giorgio Antonio Clerici, the commissioner of Tiepolo's fresco of the *Rising of the Sun*.

The Milanese painters of the period were not of great quality, though a local artist, Andrea Lanzani, had executed frescoes a good many years before in the Archinto palace. The family's traditional interest in the arts was testified to by a famous collection of old-master paintings, including works reputedly by Titian, Parmigianino and Michelangelo; among more recent artists, Giordano was represented. A guidebook published in 1737 explains that visitors to the palace could admire not only these works but also the frescoes in the new suite of rooms, from the hand of the celebrated Venetian, Tiepolo.

Tiepolo had not previously enjoyed, nor perhaps would he earlier have been able to benefit from, the scope he was now given to create entire secular heavens on the ceilings. At the Palazzo Sandi the heavenly element was only one portion of the whole fresco, and by no means the happiest. At Udine the ceiling of the Patriarch's gallery contained airy scenes but of events that took place on earth. Leaving aside the *Fall of the Rebel Angels* on the staircase there, only the Scalzi fresco of *St Teresa* had tackled a complete heaven, and to some extent that seems timid in the light of the Palazzo Archinto achievements.

Although assessment of these is obviously hampered, there happen to exist for two of the destroyed ceilings *modelli* which confirm Tiepolo's new mastery as well as revealing his approach to the compositions. Of the whole series the weakest seems always to have been the ceiling featuring Nobility, which may well have been painted with the help of assistants. No *modello* or sketch for it exists, nor does one for the ceiling featuring Juno and Venus, which seems certainly to have been entirely by Tiepolo and which had the clearest allusions to the Archinto-Borromeo marriage. Juno appeared in her chariot as goddess of marriage and pointed down from the clouds at a zephyr-like figure holding up a wreathed pole from which hung scrolls with the arms of the two families. She comes to give nuptial benediction, with the implication that the occasion will prove fruitful: 'Honour, riches, marriage-blessing', as she proclaims in celebrating the Milanese-Neapolitan union of Miranda and Ferdinand in *The Tempest*.

The largest of all the frescoes, the *Triumph of the Arts and Sciences*, for the main salone, had been considerably damaged by damp and neglect long before its destruction. What has sometimes been accepted as the *modello* is a sketch at Lisbon which, although it has variations from the ceiling itself, must be some form of record rather than the true preliminary *modello*. When every allowance has been made, it still seems likely that the ceiling fresco was not totally successfully organised, perhaps in part because of the vast scale which Tiepolo was not yet sufficiently experienced to cope with. The composition showed the Sciences and the Arts disposed on clouds —with Painting given particular prominence—under the patronage of Minerva and Apollo, seated high in the heavens. Both deities were to appear again in the adjoining rooms.

A preliminary *modello* must have existed for the fresco of the main salone, but before that stage Tiepolo made preparatory pen-and-ink studies for some of the chief figures, studies that are spontaneous-seeming in execution, with faintest wash to convey shadow and deft use of the untouched paper for the highlights (Pl. 60). At this stage Sculpture held her own mallet in a large hand and turned away from the spectator, baring a brawny right arm. By the stage of execution of the fresco he had re-thought the pose entirely. Sculpture is now accompanied by a putto brandishing her mallet. Her face is visible as she gazes upwards; and her shoulder is covered by a puff of striped drapery.

60. *Study for the Triumph of the Arts and Sciences*, Museo Civico, Trieste.

For the other two ceilings *modelli* exist. That for the *Perseus and Andromeda* ceiling is of wonderful accomplishment (Pl. 61), and, perhaps significantly, needed little alteration for the fresco itself. No programme survives for the Palazzo Archinto frescoes, but the central scene of Perseus rescuing Andromeda, having fallen in love with her at first sight, has obvious connotations for a marriage. The story was familiar enough from Ovid's *Metamorphoses*. In the seventeenth century its dramatic possibilities had been exploited by a play, with music, by Calderòn and an opera *Androm-eda*, staged at Venice, of which a long, vivid description survives.[10]

With painters the subject had been popular from the Renaissance onwards, but the moment usually depicted was the hero's coming down to release Andromeda and kill the monster, whereas Tiepolo is concerned with the subsequent action: the

victorious ascent of the lovers on the back of Pegasus, into a sky peopled by the gods of Olympus and—to judge from the *modello*—alive also with great rifts of cloud, ochre and grey, melting in the upper portion, where Jove presides, into a blinding, cloudless radiance as of pure ether. Tiepolo's focus was on the flying, entwined, putti-supported group made up of winged horse, hero and heroine, whose nudity is enhanced by the sheet of white drapery flapping around, without adequately covering, her. Love lends them additional wings, and Cupid or a cupid peers out from behind the rock at the bottom right, where the wounded monster glares up. It is like a visual expression of Dryden's line: 'None but the brave deserves the fair.'

Everywhere there is evidence of Tiepolo's care for the story. It was Andromeda's mother who offended the Nereids by boasting of her daughter's beauty as greater than theirs. Neptune sent a sea-monster to ravage the land, and Andromeda was chained to a rock as a sacrifice to it. Perseus—son of Jove—foiled Neptune's revenge. At the left Tiepolo depicts the disconsolate Nereids, while on Olympus he shows in the *modello* a prominent female figure (accompanied in the final ceiling by a male figure, crowned) pleading with Jove, perhaps for Andromeda's life.

The drama is not finished, though a happy outcome is assured. And in the *modello* the sense of dramatic excitement is perhaps greater than the ceiling conveyed, not merely through its vivacity of touch but through the steep diagonals which cross and clash in the composition. One is formed by the central flying group, continued by the outline of the rock below. Another echoes it: the long line of cloud behind, itself intersected by a diagonal leading up to the figure of Jove. The movement is always upwards. Everything is aspiring and soaring, away from earth and its constraints—and, like a symbol of eternal release, Andromeda's broken fetters fly weightlessly in the rush of air caused as she rises towards the married happiness the painter promises her.

Less easily understood as relevant to the Archinto family but probably the most successful artistically was the fresco of Phaeton asking his father Apollo to be allowed to drive the Horses of the Sun (Pl. 62), an oval ceiling whose powerful, dramatic luminosity can now only be guessed at. The ceiling seems to have been the most complex in composition, as certainly in mood, and the steps towards its final form show that it clearly exercised Tiepolo.

The source was, again, Ovid's *Metamorphoses*, but again Tiepolo prefers to stress the less familiar aspect of a story familiar from earlier paintings. What had been popular was the Fall of Phaeton, the result of Apollo's rash promise and Phaeton's fatal failure to manage the Horses of the Sun in their fiery course across the heavens. That Fall made an excellent subject for ceiling paintings—a sort of secular version of the Fall of the Rebel Angels—from Giulio Romano's treatment in the Palazzo del Te up to Sebastiano Ricci's in a palace at Belluno. The earlier scene had occasionally also appeared on ceilings, though none is likely to have been known directly to Tiepolo, except the almost contemporaneous fresco by Pittoni in the Villa Baglioni near Padua.

From the first, Tiepolo seems to have wanted to convey the doom overhanging Phaeton, and in the fresco he isolated in the otherwise empty, luminous upper portion of the composition one darkly silhouetted figure, of winged Time with scythe displayed, hovering like a hawk above the foolhardy Phaeton, who kneels before an already regretful Apollo behind whom the sun has begun to rise. Day is breaking. In the sky the Hours are yoking the immortal mettlesome Horses, as mentioned by Ovid; Tiepolo adds winged putti to wheel out the Sun's chariot. In a middle region of the sky the Seasons float with almost smug serenity, but elsewhere there is a sense of bustle, of life stirring again, as on earth shadowy, winged figures slip away and sunflowers turn to respond to the first rays of morning light.

Tiepolo's cosmos is tightly organised, proliferating with detail yet not crowded. As far as can be judged, the fresco was rich in chiaroscuro, quite apart from its colour.

61. *Perseus and Andromeda*, Frick Collection, New York.

59

62. *Phaethon and Apollo* (destroyed), Palazzo Archinto, Milan.

To some extent it is about Apollo as much as his son — Apollo as light-giver, the source of energy, fertility and lucidity, whom Tiepolo was to go on hailing in ceilings elsewhere: at Milan, at Würzburg and finally at Madrid. The Horses and the god's chariot, the attendant Hours, and above all the god himself, beautiful, beneficent, radiant, indeed the essence of illumination and enlightenment in the world, became for Tiepolo more than myth. It is as though in Apollo he sees the source of his own power as an artist.

Related to the Palazzo Archinto composition are several drawings and surviving sketches claimed with varying degrees of probability to be preparatory ideas.[11] Two publicly owned oil sketches in particular (Pls 63 and 64) are uncontestably by Tiepolo and undoubtedly relate to his thinking around the theme, if not necessarily with a ceiling in mind. Neither is in any sense a *modello* of the kind that exists for the *Perseus and Andromeda* fresco.

The larger sketch is likely to be the earlier in terms of evolution. At this stage it is Phaeton who has the greatest prominence as he bids his father farewell and is hurried almost roughly by Time towards his fate. The foreground is occupied by a scene on earth which rather prosaically includes the Hours yoking the Horses of the Sun. The handling of this sketch—rapid and flickering and truly sketchy in an accomplished way—suggests a date of around 1731, possibly a little later. Closer to the concept of the ceiling is the smaller sketch, still lacking any *sotto in sù* effect, in which Phaeton is shown approaching Apollo, and Time, huge and menacing, looms close above

63. *Phaethon and Apollo*, The Bowes Museum, Barnard Castle.

64. *Phaethon and Apollo*, Akademie, Vienna.

them, his scythe at the ready. Although not fully evolved, the group of the Seasons appears much as in the fresco. The Horses of the Sun yoked by the Hours, and the chariot, are now seen as if advancing out of the composition, which is more satisfactory in itself and also for the effect on a ceiling. Nevertheless, Tiepolo had several further improvements to conceive in the general disposition of most of the figures, as well as in the zones they occupy, before the fresco itself could be executed. A more evolved *modello* is therefore likely to have existed, even though some of the most inspired passages in the ceiling may have been devised only while he was at work on it. Not the least part of the exciting sense it must have conveyed will have come from the subtle tilting of the plane of earth and the outcrop of rock on which the leading Horse paws impatiently as he bursts out from the edge of the composition, gazing up at Apollo and eager for the day's task to begin.

The commission Count Casati gave Tiepolo was more limited in scope and smaller in scale than the Palazzo Archinto work. At the same time, he provided the painter with the always attractive opportunity of frescoing a complete room, walls as well as ceiling. The room was the large, principal salone of the Casati palace, of squarish dimensions, and the theme returned Tiepolo to the world of ancient Roman history, concentrating on a single heroic figure, Scipio. For these frescoes no *modelli* exist, no related oil sketches and apparently no preparatory drawings.

However, this must be an accident, for the scheme is an elaborate one which includes *grisaille* overdoors and allegorical figures painted between the windows,

61

65. *Scipio orders the release of a captive*, Palazzo Dugnani, Milan.

apart from the big ceiling fresco and the three on the side walls. Damp has caused much damage to the ceiling, the composition of which is usually described as an 'Allegory of magnanimity'. It actually appears to show the apotheosis of Scipio, who is thus rewarded for being virtuous and is celebrated by Fame, visible in the upper part of the ceiling. If this identification is correct, the ceiling becomes the first of a typical kind in Tiepolo's *œuvre*, to culminate with the virtual apotheosis of the Pisani family on the ceiling of their own villa at Strà (see Pls 214 and 215).

For the wall frescoes (now transferred to canvas), Tiepolo had to fit his scenes into extremely elaborate, feigned stonework, very much designed to be seen from below and framing his compositions with a swaggering, somewhat heavy architecture which in no way disconcerted him. Indeed, he made his personages display their ease by having them lean or perch on the simulated framework, like actors amid scenery; and as they project forward they increase the total illusionism. Within the frescoes themselves he created architecture of his own, also in quite strongly foreshortened perspective, so that Scipio dominates from a high throne as he orders the release of a captive (Pl. 65). In two longer scenes Tiepolo equally elevates the central incident onto a platform, building a positive stage on which Scipio displays his continence by handing back a fiancée to her conquered betrothed, and Sophonisba

66. *Sophonisba receives the poison*, Palazzo Dugnani, Milan.

accepts the poison sent, at Scipio's instigation, by her husband Manissa (an incident rather more to her credit than to Scipio's) (Pl. 66). Scipio is a popular enough subject in eighteenth-century painting to need no special explanation as the subject of the frescoes, but Casati's ancestors included a fifteenth-century Scipione Casati.

Although the theme is an ancient Roman one, and the mood heroic, Tiepolo has moved away from the idiom and the tonalities—as well as the grim 'reality'—of the Palazzo Dolfin canvases of such a short time before. The medium of fresco is no doubt one reason for his much lighter, sweeter palette, with decorative tones of apricot and mauve and green that are nearer to the delicious colouristic effects of the Udine frescoes. But the Palazzo Casati frescoes are grander than the scenes in the patriarchal gallery, as 'Roman' in their fashion as the Dolfin paintings, yet made deliberately elevated, stylish and almost stylised, with a strong sense of theatre that recalls *opera seria* of the period. There is a conscious stateliness about the fiancée who sweeps before the victorious Scipio with all the regality of the Queen of Sheba appearing before Solomon. Sophonisba extends one hand for the poison with a confident gesture that expects service, and the poison itself comes with style: a Moorish page holds the salver on which it has arrived in a slim, elegant vessel. Veronese is the source for the women's costumes in particular, but in these splendid settings the costumes too take on additional splendour, with ruffs larger and skirts fuller and stiffer than Veronese's figures had worn. These people, Tiepolo seems to say, were great personages, moving in an aura of exotic grandeur which can be conveyed visibly and which enhances the idea of their remoteness, exciting a sense of wonder as the chief emotion stirred.

Although always dated precisely to the year 1731, the Palazzo Casati frescoes may not have been completed entirely in that year; it depends how fast Tiepolo moved and how late in the season he went on working in Milan. By the autumn other tasks were being envisaged for him. It was at Bergamo that the governors of the Luogo Pio agreed to have the cupola of the Colleoni chapel suitably painted by Tiepolo,[12] and in the autumn of 1732 he had been, or still was, working there. Further frescoes were commissioned from him in 1733. Again in 1734, so successful had he obviously been with the current governors, he was to be pressed to do additional work there, but this time he was engaged elsewhere and the commission went by default. He was in fact much occupied by a task that he described in a letter as 'un forte impegno', which had taken him to a new location, the villa of Conte Niccolò Loschi, near Vicenza.[13]

It can have been only by extreme discipline, as well as by dividing his activities seasonally, that in these busy years of becoming more widely known, Tiepolo kept up his activity as a painter of altarpieces and other paintings in oil when not employed in fresco. Thus he was able around 1730 to respond to the task of painting the altarpiece of the *Education of the Virgin* (Pl. 67) for the recently built Oratorian church of S. Maria della Consolazione (La Fava) at Venice. There his painting confronted indirectly across the nave Piazzetta's altarpiece of the Virgin appearing to the founder of the Oratorians, St Philip Neri (Pl. 9), which was finally paid for at the end of 1726. Even among Piazzetta's religious paintings, this is an outstanding superb work, at once grandiose and fervent, where the statuesque main figures seem almost carved out of tones of brown and white, interspersed with passages of vivid blue, as the gazes of Virgin and saint interlock. The tall format of the canvas was wonderfully exploited by Piazzetta, who filled the upper part with the elongated Virgin, whose dignity is subtly increased by the sweep of cloak borne even higher, like a canopy, above her.

Less rewarding was the subject assigned to Tiepolo for his altarpiece, of almost exactly the same size, causing him something of a problem over how to fill the upper area of the canvas. The subject, however, was highly suitable for an Oratorian church, given the order's traditional concern with education, and something more

67. *Education of the Virgin*, La Fava, Venice.

68. *St John the Baptist preaching*, Colleoni Chapel, Bergamo.

homely than Tiepolo's painting may have been expected. From the first Tiepolo felt perhaps the competition implied by the existence so close of Piazzetta's masterpiece, and something Piazzettesque crept back into his own treatment: in its tonality and even in the types and poses of his three chief figures (especially the Joachim). St Anne's aged, hooked profile is stressed to a point nearly grotesque, where she might be as much Anna the ancient prophetess and the Virgin the girl of the Temple. The setting too is scarcely a humble one. The Virgin, bathed in holy glow, demonstrates her precocity and is depicted as already signally honoured: though only a child, she is raised above St Anne, while her heavy book, doubtless the Bible, is supported on a cloud. Another cloud helps fill the background, and there Tiepolo seems to feel released from Piazzetta's influence and free to paint a trio of his own typical angel forms, elegant, colourful and slightly languorous, floating conveniently in to occupy the upper part of the composition. Piazzetta's painting asserts itself by sheer forcefulness, but though Tiepolo is far from unaware of the value of such effects, what ultimately triumphs in his painting is gracefulness.

Away from Venice, when employed first in the Colleoni chapel at Bergamo, his chief task was to fill the four pendentives of the ceiling vaulting with personifications of Justice, Faith, Charity and Prudence (often wrongly identified as Fortitude). Cloud-borne and richly costumed, these essentially decorative figures offered little scope for Tiepolo's imagination, but he placed each quite easily within its rather awkward triangular area and, with equal ease, realised allegory in convincing visual terms. In execution there may be some variation, either through a temporary drop in energy or through studio assistance (and from the early 1730s he was taking pupils); a certain heaviness of outline and a perfunctoriness in handling drapery are detectable in *Charity*, which may well be altogether the weakest of the four concepts.

Much more absorbing for the artist and in the resulting art was the work undertaken in the chapel in 1733, when he frescoed lunettes from the life of St John the Baptist. Each of the three subjects received spirited, even sub-witty treatment, with a response to landscape and rustic atmosphere that recalls the Udine frescoes. St John preaches to an attentive group of characters, old and young, who make up a cast of Tiepolo's favourite people and include a sleeping hound, a child in arms and a baby at the breast (Pl. 68). The baby's mother looks like a fresh portrayal of Cecilia

66

69. *Execution of St John the Baptist*, Colleoni Chapel, Bergamo.

Tiepolo, who had in fact given birth in October 1732 to a son, christened Francesco. It is not surprising if the figure of the saint, accompanied by his lamb, cannot compete for the spectator's attention with the exotically dressed, literally colourful crowd, seated in a grey-green North Italianate countryside whose contours seem disposed to make up the most charming, natural auditorium. Even in the more solemn scene of the *Baptism of Christ*, the countryside is charmingly present: poplars line the bank of the Jordan, and the warmth of the day seems indicated by the hound now lapping up blue water at the river's brim.

In the third scene, the *Execution of the Baptist* (Pl. 69), mood and setting abruptly change. The massive stone walls of a prison are the background to the shocking spectacle of the Baptist's headless trunk streaming with blood and thrust forward, with maximum visibility, towards the front of the composition. Tender-hearted young female attendants look away from the sight, but an older woman almost savagely fixes her gaze on the saint's severed head while grasping a salver on which to receive it. Salome, elegantly tall, calm and quite unperturbed might—from her gesture—be merely indicating the cut of joint she wanted at the butcher's. The presence of her pet, white dog, jumping up at her skirts to attract attention, adds a further, disconcerting touch that is not exactly flippant but mitigates the central horror.

Oil *modelli* survive for two of the frescoes, the *Execution* and the *Baptist preaching*, and that for the *Execution* (Pl. 70) shows that Tiepolo originally conceived the scene with much less of an assault on the spectator's emotions. That is indeed the chief alteration, apart from suppression in the fresco of a second dog—the black and white hound familiar from the two earlier frescoes—which appeared sniffing at the bars of the underground cell or cistern where presumably the saint was incarcerated. St John's lifeless body is shown in the *modello* clad in a simple skin and huddled in a pose that is uncouth but contrives to conceal totally his bleeding neck. Whether the change was the artist's or that of the governors of the Luogo Pio, the final effect is both more shocking and more sumptuous. A voluminous, scarlet mantle and a green, fur-lined tunic wrapped around the muscular corpse, whose hands are now displayed, strongly modelled but inert; and all this sense of what was powerful life is counteracted by the blood cascading from the cervicle and dripping down the

70. *Execution of St John the Baptist*, National Museum, Stockholm.

67

steps as though it might flow on out of the fresco and into the chapel below. Such intensity is not foreign to Tiepolo, especially at the period. In the Colleoni chapel he had also had to deal again with the subject of St Bartholomew, and there he did not hesitate to depict the agony of the saint with skin already stripped and hanging in sickening, bloody flaps from his arms.

Quite different in every way except seriousness of purpose were the frescoes Tiepolo went on to execute for Count Loschi in his villa at Biron de Monteviale, near Vicenza. In the late summer of 1734, it seems, Tiepolo was hard at work on these, 'day and night you could say,' he wrote in November of that year, from Venice, to a friendly patron, 'without drawing breath.'[14] Utilising the existing site, Loschi re-built or at least greatly enlarged the villa, on designs possibly by the Venetian architect Massari, and completed it in 1734.[15] He must have decided early on that he would employ Tiepolo to fresco the interior; in referring, in the same letter of November 1734, to his 'heavy task', Tiepolo states that it was one he had had for many years, 'da molti anni'.

Even after re-building, the Villa Loschi was severely plain in its exterior, apart from the flourish of the owner's arms displayed in a moulding over the central, balconied window, and not particularly large, though set in a huge area of parkland. Inside the villa a double staircase leads up from the entrance through archways to the main-floor salone. Both areas were decorated in handsome white stucco, leaving comparatively simply framed spaces on both walls and ceilings to be frescoed.

The Loschi frescoes are Tiepolo's first surviving work of the kind in a villa, though the artist was already thirty-eight years old. Nor is the result typical of his future schemes, even in terms of style and presentation. A certain simplicity, combined with moral earnestness, is apparent in a scheme which dispensed with any feigned architectural framing of the sort seen, for example, at the Palazzo Casati. Little display of Tiepolo's own brand of illusionism was required, and the subject-matter was entirely allegorical.

What was elaborately stressed was a high, didactic tone, implying that the villa was a home, a positive temple, of the cardinal virtues and honour, innocence, humility and conjugal fidelity. No pride in ancestry is celebrated here with scenes of heroic exploits, however noble and disinterested; nor was there any playful, amorous or merely decorative mythological scene. All this must have closely reflected Loschi's wishes, and though no 'programme' as such survives, it is clear that the source for the various personifications was Cesare Ripa's *Iconologia*, a popular handbook to the attributes and depiction of Beauty, Humility, Time, Wealth, etc. Tiepolo doubtless frequently consulted it, perhaps had been introduced to it already in Lazzarini's studio, and in connection with at least one of the Villa Loschi frescoes can be shown to have been using the edition of 1611.

No oil sketches exist for the frescoes, but there are numerous preliminary drawings which—possibly for reasons of haste—may well have served instead.[16] It is rather unlike Tiepolo to identify the subject on one of his own drawings, but several of those related to the Loschi frescoes are so identified and may therefore have been submitted to the patron for him to choose the personification he preferred. There is nothing laboured about the drawings themselves. Executed in pen and wash, they rapidly seize the essence of a composition, sometimes—though not always—with a dash and *élan* lost in translation to the relevant fresco. Tiepolo can create a miniature drama out of the unpromising-sounding subject of Humility disregarding Pride (Pl. 71) or make convincingly solid and splendid Virtue crowning Honour.

The scheme is announced at the villa entrance by flanking frescoes of *Merit* and *Nobility*, feigned monochrome statues, male and female, that are severe in comparison with the bright tints and extensive, blue skies of the rest of the frescoes. In Tiepolo's decorative idiom it is not easy to be sufficiently aware of the stern lessons inculcated on the staircase, where on either side minatory women gesticulate over

71. *Humility disregarding Pride*, Victoria & Albert Museum, London (D.1825.18–1885).

recumbent men: Innocence banishes Vice and Industry triumphs over Idleness (a young, exhausted drunk who might almost be sunbathing beside the patch of vine where two putti play (Pl. 73). The ceiling is conceived with hardly a trace of *sotto in sù*, to show Truth unveiled in a warm-toned heaven by her father Time, all rather undynamically portrayed by Tiepolo's standards.

In the salone the central panel of the ceiling is more brilliantly coloured and more excitingly composed, with far more sense of figures air borne, seated or flying in space and seen from below (Pl. 72). Glory, in shimmering gold drapery, seems welcoming the group of Cardinal Virtues, among which Prudence is most vividly personified; and Fame, acutely foreshortened, trumpets through the skies praise of no individual but the general message to mankind to be good. It is like the Spirit's conclusion at the end of *Comus*: 'Mortals that would follow me/Love Virtue; she alone is free.'

On the walls around, more specific lessons are taught, with Liberality distributing her gifts (Pl. 74), Marital Concord uniting lovers and winged Virtue crowning a rather sulky, temperamental-looking, boyish Honour, who has something of the air, accidentally, of one of the more unbridled Roman emperors. Not only are these subjects unusual in a villa or palace of the period in North Italy, but Tiepolo's presentation of them is markedly simple, direct, uncluttered, with a minimum of grace notes. It is a sort of classicism, not unsuited to the moral matter in hand. It is less beguiling and less openly dazzling in terms of art than he had been or would be— though he could not fail to create enchanting colour effects, here enhanced by an ambient otherwise of pure white, and on the ceiling of the salone he relaxed from adherence to Ripa into a vision characteristically luminous and graceful. That ceiling

72. *Allegory of the Virtues*, Villa Loschi, now Zileri Dal Verme, Biron di Monteviale, near Vicenza.

looks forward in its accomplishment, while the Villa Loschi scheme generally may seem, and is, an isolated incident in Tiepolo's career, leading nowhere. Yet what is most remarkable about it is the adaptability of the artist to a patron's desires, as well as his own desire, it may be assumed, not to repeat himself. In the 1740s he would be quite different when creating frescoes for the Villa Cordellina. In the 1750s he would create yet another totally different idiom for the frescoes at the Villa Valmarana.

If in places the figures in the Loschi frescoes are oddly tall in their proportions, this tendency is not untypical of Tiepolo's work in the 1730s and 1740s and need not be an indication of studio assistance. Some of the faces are rather inexpressive—and yet that too is not untypical. His people often have an *hauteur* that can verge on the bovine. That he had some assistance in executing the Villa Loschi frescoes has more than once been suggested and need not be impossible, though in contradiction his

74. *Liberality*, Villa Loschi, now Zileri Dal Verme, Biron di Monteviale, near Vicenza.

75. *Liberality*, Museo Civico, Trieste.

own emphasis on his breathless activity there would suggest that the burden of the work was his. In some of the frescoes there are changes from the pen-and-wash drawings which point directly to his re-thinking. In the fresco composition of *Liberality*, for example, he not only moved forward the page-boy of the drawing (Pl. 75) and closed the composition with his kneeling pose, but turned his face outward, making the features so distinctive that they take on the air of a portrait (conceivably of a young member of the Loschi family).

Back in Venice in the winter of 1734, Tiepolo can have had scarcely any sense of respite from work. He had commissions for large-scale paintings to consider, and a summons soon to return to Milan, to fresco in the basilica of S. Ambrogio.[17] He received his first commission from beyond Italy—from Germany. And he would shortly receive his first major commission for a ceiling fresco in a Venetian church. Amid all this he could yet find time to turn aside to less official work, to begin

paintings by the artist he required in Paris—and it makes an intriguing pendant, though somewhat bigger, to Tiepolo's mythology. Boucher is often said rather carelessly to have been influenced by Tiepolo, but in the *Jupiter appearing to Danaë* it might almost be supposed that Tiepolo had been influenced, if not by Boucher, at least by French eighteenth-century art generally. A closer look shows that Tiepolo's approach, while 'plein d'esprit' and colourful, is more satiric than erotic. If his *Rape of Europa* subtly counters the rich pastoral poetry of Veronese's version of the subject in the Doge's Palace, his *Jupiter appearing to Danaë* may, not without mild fun, glance at Titian's treatments of the theme. One of these versions, that engraved, includes the incident Tiepolo borrows of the old woman avariciously holding up a dish to catch the rain of gold coins, itself a piece of mordant humour by Titian.[19]

Tiepolo is openly humorous in devising a squabble between Jupiter's eagle and Danaë's pet spaniel (the animal itself previously seen jumping up at Salome's skirt in the *Execution of the Baptist* at Bergamo). That is the broadest touch of humour, but everywhere there are implicit jokes. Danaë is a lazy courtesan, ogling the spectator and hardly aware of her divine lover. It is Cupid who has to tug up her shift, revealing her plump bottom to, again, the spectator. Tiepolo certainly paints her bare flesh and the sumptuous surrounding draperies with a succulent brush (anticipating Boucher's 'bottoms-up' odalisques) and with a spark of sensuous, if not quite sexual, fire. But Jupiter is a leering old man, with the beginnings of an old man's sagging body, reduced to paying cash for a woman's favours. He comes in no munificent shower of gold but with the smallest possible expenditure: a mere handful of coins sprinkle the air.

From the love of Jupiter and Danaë was born Perseus—the hero to whom Tiepolo had heroically responded on one of the ceilings at the Palazzo Archinto. In very different mood he saw the union of god and mortal. A lecherous old man is buying the favours of a sly girl, abetted by a boy-pander and a greedy hag. Yet the effect is very far from the biting cynicism of Prud'hon's later painting of the subject. From Palladian courtyard (no tower, as the story actually requires) to carved and gilded bed, the appurtenances are splendid, and indeed the humour wrapped in such glittering shapes has usually passed unperceived. The brushwork is part of the spirited air, but this painting is full too of literal *esprit*: wit of a kind associated rather with Tiepolo's son, Domenico, but clearly an inherited trait.

The mood recalls not only the *Rape of Europa* but the *Apelles painting Campaspe*. After the mid-1730s Tiepolo seems to have stopped painting with such tongue-in-cheek humour (that might have shocked a patron like Count Loschi), but he did not cease to be spirited in his art. Bigger commissions—in scale and concept—lay before him; in them he would be very much the artist Tessin had on quite brief acquaintance so vividly and aptly characterised.

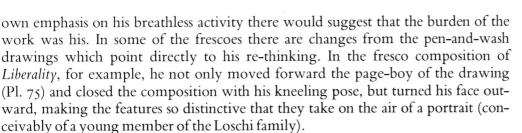

74. *Liberality*, Villa Loschi, now Zileri Dal Verme, Biron di Monteviale, near Vicenza.

75. *Liberality*, Museo Civico, Trieste.

own emphasis on his breathless activity there would suggest that the burden of the work was his. In some of the frescoes there are changes from the pen-and-wash drawings which point directly to his re-thinking. In the fresco composition of *Liberality*, for example, he not only moved forward the page-boy of the drawing (Pl. 75) and closed the composition with his kneeling pose, but turned his face outward, making the features so distinctive that they take on the air of a portrait (conceivably of a young member of the Loschi family).

Back in Venice in the winter of 1734, Tiepolo can have had scarcely any sense of respite from work. He had commissions for large-scale paintings to consider, and a summons soon to return to Milan, to fresco in the basilica of S. Ambrogio.[17] He received his first commission from beyond Italy—from Germany. And he would shortly receive his first major commission for a ceiling fresco in a Venetian church. Amid all this he could yet find time to turn aside to less official work, to begin

probably around the mid-1730s his first etchings. He also continued to produce small-scale paintings, of religious or profane subjects, for private collectors and cabinets—and sometimes perhaps for his own pleasure.

After the unremitting earnestness of the Villa Loschi scheme, it must have been a welcome diversion to turn to mythology in a comic, even satiric, spirit and produce the highly finished *jeu d'esprit* of *Jupiter appearing to Danaë* (Pl. 76). This small painting is playfully erotic as well as mildly ironic, all within a decorative convention. It was purchased in Venice by Count Carl Gustaf Tessin, a Swedish courtier and connoisseur, who came there briefly in May 1736, hoping to purchase the painter as well, with a view to his travelling to Stockholm and decorating the royal palace which Tessin's father had built. On discovering Tiepolo and his art, Tessin was enchanted: Tiepoletto, as he learnt he was called, seemed the ideal artist for the task. He was, Tessin wrote home, spirited and obliging ('plein d'esprit, accomodant . . .'), with fire and brilliant colour ('un feu infini, un coloris éclatant et d'une vitesse surprenante'.)[18] He finished a painting in less time than another artist took to grind his colours. Unfortunately Tiepolo knew—it emerged later—his own worth. The Swedish court could not meet his 'ultimatum' (as Tessin says Tiepolo himself described it) over the price he required to be paid, and the proposal collapsed, leaving Tessin complaining that the painter should in future be known as 'Tiepolazzo'.

During his fifteen-day stay in Venice, which he visited from Vienna, Tessin managed to buy the work of several local artists, including a view-picture by Canaletto, six drawings by Piazzetta and two small paintings by Tiepolo. One was the *modello* for the *Execution of the Baptist* which Tiepolo had painted in the Colleoni chapel at Bergamo three years earlier. The other was the *Jupiter appearing to Danaë*, which displayed another side of Tiepolo's art, though in style it appears close to the date of the *modello* and thus likely to have been painted well before 1736.

It must have appealed to Tessin not only for its fine quality but for its piquant subject and the humour with which Tiepolo had treated it. A few years afterwards Tessin went to France as Swedish ambassador and there he discovered Boucher. Boucher's *Jupiter and Leda* was a direct commission from Tessin—only one of several

4 FULL MATURITY: THE YEARS 1736–40

IN MARCH 1736, two months before Tessin arrived in Venice, Tiepolo celebrated his fortieth birthday. If he bothered to survey the artistic scene in his own city, a sense of his pre-eminence as a decorative painter must have been unavoidable. The older generation of artists was growing really old and out of date. Some of the greatest figures, like Sebastiano Ricci, were dead. Amigoni was far away, in the London of George II, whose wife Queen Caroline he painted. Pellegrini, now aged sixty-one, was no dominant figure. Closer in age and style to Tiepolo was Pittoni, an accomplished, successful artist whose art never achieved total individuality and never, for all its rococo charm, challenged Tiepolo's supremacy. Other decorative painters, older or younger than Tiepolo, offered still less challenge.

The leading painter in Venice was, however, probably acknowledged widely to be Piazzetta. It was he whom Tessin placed first in his survey of the local scene, though he also noted that Piazzetta was 'slow'. What Piazzetta could achieve at the end of his labours was demonstrated forcefully and publicly in 1736. In that year his vast *Assumption of the Virgin* (Pl. 78) was exhibited in the Piazza S. Marco before going off to Germany; it had been painted for the Archbishop-Elector of Cologne, younger brother of the Elector of Bavaria, who had earlier visited Venice and who had a private collection of pictures, as well as commissioning pictures for churches in which he was specially interested.

Piazzetta's composition gathers the Apostles around a characteristically worn stone tomb, presented in no exciting way, nor even with much suggestion of recession, but simply as an uncompromising, horizontal slab. His plainly clad, bare-foot Apostles are awkward, plebeian figures, burdened by the gamut of emotions they express, of which the chief is stupefaction. They peer upwards and downwards, their hands shooting out to gesticulate or grip the tomb as if to absorb the shock. One Apostle, meant perhaps for St Thomas, by his immense, hallucinatory height and the sweeping arc of his outstretched arms, dominates as though the conductor of this symphony of emotion. Far above them is the white, incandescent yet girlish Virgin, carried beyond their ken by angels whose heavy, feathered pinions seem to fan the intervening air between an earth of earthy, bewildered people and a heavenly zone of eternal luminosity. Stubbornly untheatrical, soberly actual, and chromatically restricted largely to tones of brown and black and white, the *Assumption* is yet visionary, ardent and exciting.

Tiepolo was also, about the same date of 1736, to be commissioned by the Archbishop-Elector to paint an altarpiece, and his composition also depicted heaven and earth (Pl. 77). Perhaps it was fortunate that the subject called for splendour—or at least justified it. A pope, Clement I, the Elector's namesake, kneels before a vision of the Trinity. Set in a church of tremendous, spacious splendour that billows out behind him in a vista of giant marble and stucco columns and a cupola (a baroque setting of a kind used by Rubens) all dissolving into celestial vapour, the pope kneels encased in a gold and scarlet cope of near-metallic lustre on red velvet-carpeted steps. A vision of the Trinity fills the upper air, exploding softly with slow flush of summer

78. Piazzetta, *Assumption of the Virgin*, Louvre, Paris.

77. *Vision of St Clement*, Alte Pinakothek, Munich.

75

lightning, above and around the banked clouds that drift into being the forms of child-angel heads or suddenly harden into the bright cerulean blue and crocus-yellow trailing garments of a pair of older angels, blonde and dark, themselves manifested as worshippers of the Trinity. And while God the Father looks down on the earnestly praying Pope, Christ reclines on the clouds nearby with an aloofness that seems chilling.

Nothing suggests that the Elector of Cologne preferred Tiepolo's concept to Piazzetta's—or vice-versa. Indeed, he spread his commissions beyond them and had altarpieces painted by Pittoni. All three painters met the patron's requirements, not least in being able to depict a miraculous, sacred subject in artistically miraculous ways. Yet in the case of Piazzetta and Tiepolo the results were becoming almost violently contrasted as the younger artist developed his own manner, and went on developing, while in stylistic terms Piazzetta scarcely advanced at all. A late painting by him looks little different from an early one. He was, artistically speaking, the exponent of concentration to achieve maximum power, husbanding his resources, suppressing and paring away so that the final composition should have in it only what is essential. A few people, simply dressed (in clothes always unpatterned), occupied in illustrating the barest bones of the subject in a natural way, and themselves creating as far as possible the setting (usually otherwise unlocalised): such are the preferred elements of a Piazzetta painting. A profound humanity breathes from the resulting work, sometimes troubling in its psychological urgency, sometimes poignant in mood as his people seem lost in private dreams, hugging the shadows and essentially private, unglamorous, 'ordinary' beings, fragile and evanescent for all their fervour.

The given elements of Tiepolo's altarpiece for the Elector were as simple as Piazzetta might have desired, and it is not hard to envisage how Piazzetta would have treated St Clement and the vision to him. For Tiepolo, the subject, involving great personages and a miracle, needs to be treated in a way that openly surpasses nature, though everything should have a naturalistic appearance. He begins by the assumption that the scene must be splendid and physically rich, even opulent. Poor or uncouth things and people did not stir his artistic imagination. As Tessin remarked shrewdly, 'everyone in his paintings is richly dressed, even the beggars'.[1] A pope required a suitably papal setting, and so around his kneeling saint Tiepolo built a personal St Peter's which yields nothing in grandeur to the basilica in Rome; and in kneeling a pope may expect to be saved contact with naked stone or wood, so a fringed carpet of velvety texture and warm, glowing tone half negligently falls— as if thrown by some hurried master-of-ceremonies—down the steps where St Clement prays. The insignia of tiara and triple cross might well be included to indicate his papal status, but Tiepolo enhances their presence by putting them into the hands of a large child angel, seated on the topmost step and disposing of them like liturgical toys. The tiara, itself resting on a cushion, is a vast bauble, a sort of jewelled beehive, far bigger than the Pope as depicted could possibly wear.

The luxury on earth is echoed less materially but still thrillingly in the heavenly vision which hovers like a tinted cloud of incense, vaporous and yet bearing on it strongly realised, corporeal figures. There is no mystery here, despite the rich, flooding light and smoky vapour. Indeed, the Holy Ghost is patently a dove of the kind Tiepolo later shows fluttering around Venus. God the Father is a vigorous, elderly man of semi-ducal dignity, while Christ barely deigns to acknowledge the existence of the Pope far below. Heaven is a frank aristocracy. The final effect may not be highly spiritual, but it is graceful, colourful and agreeable to look at. Tiepolo had already declared in the *modello* (in the National Gallery, London) that these were the emphases he would give to the altarpiece. The *modello* is smooth and highly finished in surface. There are no known preparatory drawings for it, but radiography reveals that little was changed as it was being executed. Tiepolo's assurance was manifest as he began, and so apparently was that other quality Tessin had remarked on, of 'vitesse surprenante'.

Yet the approach embodied in the *St Clement* altarpiece is only one of those Tiepolo displayed in these years. He could be sumptuous and perhaps a little lacking in emotional engagement—at least when directly contrasted with Piazzetta. But, as his major work at S. Alvise (Pl. 92) was to show, he could aim at very strong pathos, almost assaulting the spectator, shifting as it were from being Veronese *redivivus* to being re-born as Tintoretto. In such ways, he allowed the mood of his paintings to be coloured by the subject-matter. With Piazzetta it might be said that, whatever his subject-matter, it is shaped, as much as coloured, by his narrow yet powerful, unvarying imagination. And before the 1730s were over, Tiepolo and Piazzetta were to be brought together penultimately in a Venetian church commission in which each followed the bent of his own personal genius, with results that were as divergent as they were stunning.

In other altarpieces not far in date from the *St Clement*, Tiepolo revealed a different approach, less sumptuous, more direct, and more obviously devotional. It was the Trinity drastically revised that he presented in one of the paintings (Pl. 79) he executed for Cardinal Daniele Dolfin, nephew of his old patron at Udine who had died in 1734. The Cardinal paid Tiepolo for this altarpiece in 1738, having the previous year paid him for two other paintings.[2] The Trinity picture was for the chapel so dedicated in the Duomo at Udine and it remains *in situ*.

In terms of sheer application of paint it is at least as rich as the *St Clement*. Juicy, almost fatty handling of the pigment is especially apparent in Christ's strongly modelled anatomy, with his flesh gleaming livid against the thundery darkness of the overcast sky. This is an image of Christ crucified but not of the Crucifixion. Not only are the other Persons of the Trinity present but Christ's body is barely marked by wounds; a mystic rather than desolate air invests the depiction, increased by the background landscape which is localised and apt, no fanciful Jerusalem but the mountainous countryside of the Friuli, depicted with great sensitivity not just to the terrain but also atmospherically. Once again, Tiepolo's response to landscape is striking: he positively seizes an opportunity to insert it into a composition (in distinct contrast to Piazzetta, for whom the subject seems to have held no appeal) and in other paintings by him for Cardinal Daniele it is the landscape which, despite being mere 'background', seems to have had his chief attention and to be the most original aspect of otherwise rather conventional religious compositions.

For these semi-Alpine scenes Tiepolo was perhaps dependent on drawings he had made on earlier visits to Udine. He seems to have been travelling outside Venice rather less in the later 1730s, though he paid one visit to Milan to execute frescoes in S. Ambrogio (the ceiling one destroyed and the lateral ones much damaged). His paintings were certainly going out to churches elsewhere as well as to Udine, but much of his activity was apparently concentrated in his own studio. The family was now living in the parish of S. Ternita (that is, Trinita), and there Tiepolo presumably also had his studio.

From about this time, or possibly a little earlier, must date one of his larger and definitely one of his most richly coloured canvases, a sumptuous piece of decoration which can rank with his frescoes, the *Finding of Moses* (Pl. 80). Its original commissioner and destination are unknown, but both are likely to have been Venetian, and it must have been for a palatial setting that the painting was intended. A number of large lateral compositions of the subject had been painted by Veronese and his workshop, and one of these remained in the Palazzo Grimani at Venice until sold to Dresden in 1747. Tiepolo seems to have copied that on a small scale for Algarotti, but in any case he shows himself to have been aware well before of Veronese's treatment by his own composition. The Palazzo Grimani Veronese had also inspired one of Sebastiano Ricci's versions of the popular subject.[3]

79. *The Trinity with Christ Crucified*, Duomo, Udine.

80. *Finding of Moses*, National Gallery of Scotland, Edinburgh.

81. Detail of Pl. 80.

Perhaps the exoticness of the subject and setting was part of its continual appeal. The story was picturesque enough, and Veronese had already lavished on it the resources of his imagination in ways that both Ricci and Tiepolo instinctively respected and could only echo. Though God's hand might piously be seen in the saving of the infant Moses from the Nile, the attractive aspect pictorially lay in the 'daughter of Pharaoh' come down to wash herself, with her maidens. A simple-sounding world is evoked by the words of Exodus, where—as in the *Odyssey*—the ruler's daughter is just a girl who has to go outside her home to wash herself or some clothes. Veronese had changed all that. He suppressed any idea of Pharaoh's daughter washing. He made her an opulent, modern princess, with an entourage befitting her rank, of ladies, dwarves, dogs and sixteenth-century halbardiers, placing the focus of the scene on her reaction to being shown the infant Moses. And Veronese's Egypt was a charming pastoral location, the setting, it might, be for an *al fresco* meal, not far outside a handsome modern city.

For Veronese the scene was topical—or, at least, topically interpreted. For Tiepolo, as for Ricci, a double past was invoked by adhering to the costumes which brought to mind High-Renaissance Venice before Old-Testament Egypt; but in Tiepolo's echo of Veronese there is, typically, not pastiche but creative fantasy with variations on the earlier artist's theme of the Finding of Moses. Tiepolo not only varied it considerably but mildly poked fun at it, drew out the stately implications to almost exaggerated degree and then placed a bawling, red-faced baby prominently at the foot of the composition, an embarrassing lump of raw actuality for his tall, cool princess to confront.

In Veronese's own variations on the theme, a constant was the princess's gracious concern with the discovery. Swaying slightly and steadying herself with easy

familiarity on a youthful, favoured companion, she illustrated the words of Exodus with a gloss of sixteenth-century deportment, tender for all her rich jewels and brocades: 'she had compassion on him'. The infant Moses too, in Veronese's treatments, behaves almost equally well, as though recognising a benefactress. Without stiff etiquette, decorum reigns; and, as usual with Veronese, the scene becomes a triumph of good manners and good breeding.

Tiepolo is sharper as well as more splendid. His treatment is dreamlike in fits and starts, with reality breaking in here and there, like a dreamer's snores, adding touches of piquancy to obtain a highly individual flavour. Nothing is as broadly comic as in the *Jupiter and Danaë*, but the same creative mind is at work. It is part of not following convention that leads Tiepolo, unlike Ricci, to dispense with any townscape background, and to set the scene in pure landscape very much of his own devising. It has its own panoramic sweep and luxuriance to complement the figures. The eye is led down the glassy crags of mineral-like, blinding white rifts shading into greyish green, to where a few scattered palm trees fringe the sinuous line of the river receding into the distance. The full effect of the composition can be judged only in copies or composite photographs, since at some date a philistine cutting-down of the canvas reduced its length and made a fragment out of the halbardier and dog Tiepolo placed, after a measured interval, at the far right to close the design.

In shape and scale the original composition can be compared to the central wall painting of *Ulysses discovering Achilles* (Pl. 35) at the Palazzo Sandi, painted about a decade before. And probably the *Finding of Moses* was commissioned to occupy a somewhat similar position in the salone of some palace. Tiepolo has learnt to group his figures much more skilfully. The subject required less obvious action than did the discovery of the disguised Achilles—and Tiepolo has even reduced the action from Veronese's treatments of the subject, where the baby is positively presented to Pharaoh's daughter, to a largely static effect. The narrative element is subordinated to the richest possible pageant display, well centred on the person of the princess, as she certainly deserves to be called.

She herself is scarcely animated, scarcely seems to care what happens to the infant so unexpectedly discovered; and in her consciousness of her beauty and her fine clothes, there is something of Trollope's Griselda Grantley. Dress, it seems, will always take precedence in her thoughts over any emotion. Although dwarf and duenna compete for her attention, she is somehow apart, as untouched as untouchable, a woman the very opposite of maternal, but glamorous, exotic, even improbable in her languid *hauteur* (Pl. 81). Perhaps Tiepolo covertly hits at her aristocratic inability to cope with events: she is young and royal and set apart from ordinary humanity. The artist sets her apart further by the detailed opulence of her costume, contrasting it with the loose, Biblical-style garments of the inferior women, whose arms and legs are bare. An elaborate, ochre-coloured dress of sixteenth-century style is sewn and hung with pearls, looped with a cameo-like medallion and crossed by a buckled chain worn diagonally across the bodice; and an Egyptian princess dressed thus is already more than halfway to the full regality of Tiepolo's Cleopatra, Queen of Egypt. Almost a part of her costume, and a sign of her high rank, is the tiny lapdog, carried on the folds of her skirt, minute yet alert, its eye attracted by the doughnut ring the dwarf perhaps teasingly holds up. The dog, at least, is alive and lively, even if his mistress is not.

For Tiepolo, a princess brings a train of attendants, and hers are the soldiers with halberds, as well as the black-clad, aged duenna in a lacy ruff (with the exact physiognomy of the old woman in *Jupiter appearing to Danaë*) and—a confection spun by Tiepolo out of the air—a red-blonde page-boy in pink and white silk, who stands nearby holding a tasselled cushion. Whether the cushion is meant to bear a coronet or serve merely for the princess should she ever consent to sit down in the open air, it adds its silky, extravagant note to the colour and luxury of the central group. Like the page-boy, who might be modelled in Meissen or Dresden china, it has come from Tiepolo's imagination as a fresh touch of fantasy, not found in Veronese or in Ricci (both of whom, however, had included a dwarf in the princess's retinue). In its way, it is at least as much part of the scene as the infant Moses; it belongs in the atmosphere of rarefied, courtly elegance, whereas a naked, angry, kicking baby is at once alien and an embarrassment.

Yet the basic vitality of the painting stems from the fact that it is so positively *painted*. The rich tonality and the range of colour apparent in the small canvas of *Jupiter appearing to Danaë* are now exploited on a vast scale. And so is the succulent paint-handling of the *Trinity* at Udine, with medium and pigment flowing together to give a surface glossy without hardness, the velvety bloom of fruit rather than of anything metallic or wooden. The very soil on which stand Pharaoh's daughter and the other figures benefits from this vital sense. There is nothing perfunctory about the scoops and scallops of alternating sandy earth and grass modelled by the paint, and even more poetically animated are the creeper-clad tree-trunks, silver and brown, rising to the top of the composition, with one sudden wild spray of copper-coloured leaves breaking out before they vanish from sight, against the icy, greenish-white flank of the background mountain. In the extraordinary, abstract beauty of that shimmering slab of rock—almost a cataract of frozen foam—oil paint for oil paint's sake takes over with intensely sensuous effect.

If the first location of this thoroughly Venetian painting cannot be confirmed definitely as a Venetian palace, Tiepolo's activity for Venetian churches at around the same date is beyond doubt. And it was at Venice, rather than elsewhere, that he was to be in demand as a fresco painter for churches.

In May 1737 he signed the contract for frescoes on the ceiling of the church of S. Maria del Rosario (the Gesuati), the first major commission of this nature that he received. The church was an entirely new one, put up by the Dominicans in place of a church that had earlier belonged to the minor order of the Gesuati, suppressed in 1668. What seems to have started as a modest project became something altogether grander. The architect eventually chosen by the Dominicans was the gifted Giorgio Massari. The laying of the foundation stone by the Patriarch of Venice was a solemn occasion on 17 May 1726, during the reign of a Dominican pope, Benedict XIII; and the future church was dedicated to the Virgin of the Rosary.[4]

The history of Venice gave it particular associations with the cult of the rosary. The decisive battle of Lepanto in 1571 had been a victory over the Turks won by the united forces of the Papacy, Spain and the Venetian Republic. Members of the Rosary Confraternity had been praying for the success of the Christian arms while the battle was being fought, and the Pope (Pius V) created an annual commemoration of St Mary of Victory. The feast of the Virgin of the Rosary was first instituted by Pope Gregory XIII; after the defeat of the Turks in 1710, Pope Clement XI declared the feast one to be celebrated throughout the Church.

Massari's church occupied a handsome site on the Zattere (Pl. 82), facing towards the Giudecca with Palladio's church of the Redentore, and within view of Palladio's church of S. Giorgio Maggiore. Echoes of the two churches are apparent in both the façade and the interior designed by Massari. Giant Corinthian columns support a huge triangular pediment on the outside, creating a severe and truly temple-like exterior, with niches for four huge statues of the Cardinal Virtues.

For Tiepolo the interior was of more direct concern. Massari continued the motif of giant Corinthian columns along the nave, supporting a high, monumental and notably well-lit vault, all giving an effect of lucid grandeur to the cool, grey and white interior. Side chapels did not distract from the strong visual emphasis down the nave and up effortlessly towards the compartmentalised ceiling which was probably destined from the first for frescoes.

When the church and its decoration were finished, the impressive total result was

82. Façade of the church of the Gesuati, Venice by Massari.

83. Piazzetta. *Saints Vincent Ferrer, Hyacinth and Luis Beltran*, Gesuati, Venice.

84. *St Dominic distributing the rosary*, Gesuati, Venice.

85. Detail of Pl. 84.

warmly praised by contemporaries, impressed no doubt also by the cost and the successful fund-raising carried out by the Dominicans. A leading Venetian sculptor, Morlaiter, did much of the decorative work in stone: bas-reliefs and altars, as well as individual statues. Shortly before his death, Sebastiano Ricci contributed an altarpiece of the enthroned Pope Pius V (canonised in 1712), with St Thomas Aquinas and St Peter Martyr, which is not only one of his most majestic and robustly realised paintings but a pictorial boast by the Dominican order of its great figures: the supreme theologian, the 'crusading' Pope and a famous martyr who was a native of North Italy.[5] A trio of missionary Dominican saints formed the subject of an altarpiece commissioned from Piazzetta (Pl. 83). Meditating as it were at the extreme edge of the world, St Luis Beltran seems to enjoy a vision of St Vincent Ferrer and St Hyacinth, but the real triumph of the painting is in its memorably austere tonality. The three saints' habits, of black, white and grey, are more solid though scarcely more colourful than the clouds and shadows that surround them; and Piazzetta seems to have reached here almost an ecstasy of restriction, to have distilled his art into its purest and most concentrated form. Not even he could surpass this achievement, and it is understandable that the Dominican commissioners were sufficiently grateful to make the artist a gift of nearly 100 lire in January 1739, having seen the painting installed on its altar.[6]

Tiepolo's chief task in the church was to fresco the ceiling, with a complex series of decorations, including subsidiary *grisaille* scenes, which doubly celebrate St Dominic and the rosary. The central and most important fresco shows St Dominic distributing the rosary—distributing it to rich and poor, by implication throughout the world—while its supernatural origin is conveyed by the presence of celestial figures above, including the Virgin and Child who himself holds aloft a rosary.

Two smaller frescoes show St Dominic carried to heaven and the appearance of the Virgin to the saint.[7] By Tiepolo's standards the scene of the saint's assumption is not entirely successful—conceivably through some lingering inhibition caused by Piazzetta's full-scale treatment at SS Giovanni e Paolo. The angels bearing St Dominic upwards are a rather unco-ordinated group, something of a gallimaufry of limbs and drapery. So violently foreshortened is the saint's head that he ceases to have a face, while his dangling feet and the heavy folds of his thick-looking habit increase an unfortunate suggestion that raising him heavenwards is an effort, even for angels.

More gracefully accomplished is the scene of the saint kneeling before a vision of the Virgin, her cloak extended to embrace a range of presumably Dominican saints or saintly persons, including a bishop, a cardinal and at least one pope. The future glory and prestige of the order are thus revealed, and the theme of some of the additional altarpieces in the chapels below is in effect summed up by the ceiling fresco.

Yet this too is only an adjunct to the glory of the huge central fresco, where the airy, angel-filled sky and the splendid architectural setting and the chromatic brilliance of the scene all give an artistic emphasis to the doctrinal message (Pl. 84). Here in essence is the order's highest claim to aid salvation. And here Tiepolo contrives that instead of aspiration up and into heaven, as in the adjoining frescoes, there shall be a feeling of descent, with the visual thrust down to the spectator who joins the other recipients of St Dominic's sacred gift to mankind.

Although various payments for the frescoes were made to Tiepolo during 1738, it was probably not until the autumn of 1739 that they were completed, in time possibly for the feast of the Rosary on 7 October. By allocating some if not all the *grisaille* frescoes to assistants, Tiepolo must have been the more free to concentrate intently on the dominant central composition. Not only was the commission important in itself, but he must have felt the need to respond to a modern architectural setting that was real, not feigned, with a framework for his fresco that Massari may personally have devised. In the latest religious building to go up in Venice—one of

the most beautiful too—Tiepolo was to add, if not precisely the final decorative flourish, certainly the major pictorial contribution, on the ceiling, where everyone could see it—and in the medium most felicitous for him, of fresco.

For such a task he seems, consciously or not, to have prepared himself by recollecting some of the solutions Veronese had achieved in devising ceiling compositions, profane as well as sacred. At this period he may anyway have been giving fresh attention to Veronese. In itself the *Finding of Moses* will have appeared to his contemporaries as a homage, across the centuries, to all the associations evoked by Veronese's art.

It was probably from Veronese, rather than from Massari's actual architecture, that Tiepolo felt the inspiration to construct the splendid architectural setting of his central fresco, especially the device of the broad, steep staircase descending from where St Dominic stands and culminating in a cornice and arch projecting illusionistically outwards. The acutely foreshortened balustrade and corner of pillared building seen against the sky were also motifs used more than once by Veronese, to give an effect at once grandiose and thrilling. In his famous ceiling of the *Triumph of Venice* in the Doge's Palace, he had created an elaborate yet spacious building, indeed a gorgeous palace, of columns and balustrade all open to the sky. Elsewhere, as in the *Adoration of the Magi* originally the centre of the ceiling in S. Nicolò ai Frari (and now in SS Giovanni e Paolo), he had more lightly demonstrated how to devise comparable architectural elements in perspective, but the most striking analogy lay in the central canvas of the ceiling of S. Maria dell' Umiltà, a now suppressed church on the Zattere, where the setting for the *Assumption of the Virgin* was a curved balustrade and a flight of foreground steps.

What Veronese had always used discreetly was to be taken up, vastly magnified and made almost the subject in Fumiani's virtuoso ceiling in S. Pantalon. There he shows the martyrdom and apotheosis of the saint in a complex architectural setting of giant columns and archways, with a massive flight of stairs, crammed with figures, at the top of which is the saint imminently to be martyred. Fumiani died as late as 1710, and his ceiling must have remained something of a showpiece, or at least a talking-point, in eighteenth-century Venice. Executed in oil, and in a style that would have come to seem especially ponderous by the time Tiepolo was beginning to work in fresco, the ceiling may nevertheless have had its general influence on decorative painters. At the Gesuati, Tiepolo seems to show himself distinctly indebted to it, though typically he adapts and evolves motifs from it until he has recreated in his own idiom any borrowing.

It was and would continue to be unusual for him to make quite such prominent compositional use of architecture as he does in the central fresco of *St Dominic distributing the rosary*, with the device of the broad, foreground flight of steps seen in steep recession and rising from a colossal, arched cornice. At the Palazzo Labia and at Würzburg—to take two obvious later examples—he certainly made ingenious use of foreground flights of steps; but the effect there is far less obtrusive. At the Gesuati, the perspective is itself so sheer because the fresco is right overhead on the ceiling of the vault, but equally striking is the amount of space it occupies, as well of course as its use as a setting for subsidiary figures, all the way down to the allegorical ones tumbling out of the bottom of the composition. Between them Veronese and Fumiani seem, at the very least, to have stimulated Tiepolo's solution to a complex problem. In turn, Tiepolo's Gesuati composition was to be directly the inspiration for the setting of Giambattista Canal's ceiling of the *Glory of St Euphemia*, in the church of the same name in Venice.[8]

The central fresco's composition conflates two subjects: the institution of the rosary, which occurred when the Virgin appeared to St Dominic, handing the rosary to him as a new form of prayer, a pious weapon in overcoming heresy, and the saint's subsequent distribution of it. Both aspects—the sacred origin of the devotion and the dissemination of it to mankind—needed to be stressed. A third element followed quite naturally for Tiepolo: the overthrow of heresy, illustrated by writhing, falling bodies, sent literally flying at the sight of the rosary. Thus the subject is the institution and also the triumph of the rosary, but the focus of the composition is on the saint.

Not unusually with Tiepolo, there were two preliminary oil sketches for the fresco, the earlier (once in Berlin, now destroyed)[9] showing approximately the final disposition of figures and space. Yet there it was the Virgin who extended the rosary from the clouds above the scene on earth, and the saint was not raised on the second flight of steps that leads up from the broad flight seen frontally in the fresco itself. The pillared, thoroughly Venetian building that was to serve Tiepolo as a suggestion, presumably, of the original location of a church in Toulouse, was at first shown at the right, behind St Dominic, who eloquently gestured (probably in reference to his preaching the merits of the rosary) with his left hand as he held up the rosary in his right. The attendant figures at this stage were also rather differently posed, less evolved, less bold in concept and including a standing man at the left who was a compositional distraction.

In the second sketch there is much greater approximation to the fresco (Pl. 86). Rather remarkably, given the traditional legend, the Virgin has now ceased to hold the rosary, and merely watches while the Child becomes the holder of it and, by implication, its institutor. The building is moved to the left of the composition, the surrounding figures are re-thought and sketched in poses very close to those in the fresco and, in the most patent alteration, the saint is made far more prominent by being placed at the top of a second flight of steps now introduced to give the effect of a podium. The figures who kneel before him are subsidiary, very much supplicants. No longer gesticulating, St Dominic is accompanied by respectful angels. His left hand clasps a book, while his right hand and the rosary he extends are placed against a large space of sky, with strong definition and easily read visual emphasis, patently the emotional centre of the whole scene.

For Tiepolo, and doubtless for his patrons, it is really to the world that St Dominic distributes the rosary. From the first sketch onwards, a doge was prominently included among its recipients, kneeling with as much anxious awe as the more humble people around him. In the fresco Tiepolo made this figure still more prominent and more eager. With the pious women and children who stand for Christian laity, he mingled a bishop, a nun and even a pope (barely seen, apart from his tiara, behind the saint) as well as an Oriental. At the extreme right, visible over the curve of the bishop's cope, he found a place too for himself, half glancing down into the church.

What Piazzetta would have made of such a scene can be gauged somewhat from his sole ceiling, of St Dominic, in SS Giovanni e Paolo. His heavenly light always burns at a white heat, and his bystanders or worshippers would probably have been baked, brown and earthy.

Tiepolo, calculating on the light that filled the church and flooded the area of his fresco, gave the scene a prismatic brilliance of colour. A wide, shimmering, blue-grey sky is enlivened by rainbow-tinted angels, puffs of summer cloud and cherubs flitting like pairs of turtle-doves (Pl. 85). The solid-seeming, chalk-white and grey architecture is as splendid as anything surviving from sixteenth-century Venice and of an impossible, gleaming purity. As brilliantly clad as any angel are the poor in their draperies of green, tangerine and pale blue, in tone and texture hardly less refined than the turbans and striped stuffs, vestments and armour worn by the other figures in this glinting, cosmic pageant. St Dominic's habit of black and white is effectively contrasted with the colours around, yet seems scarcely austere in such an environment and amid such richness. It is not just a richness of colour but a richness of invention. There is a sense of artistic prodigality quite foreign to Piazzetta, whose stubborn

86. *Institution of the rosary*, Senator M. Crespi Collection, Milan.

refusal to be showy makes him eternally an artistic puritan in contrast to Tiepolo the cavalier.

The fresco is also thoroughly Venetian and of Venice, even to the point of conveying a suggestion that it was there that St Dominic instituted the rosary. It is more than a matter of mood. The kneeling doge, who is perhaps the recipient of the very rosary the saint holds out, is most unlikely to be a thoughtless anachronism by Tiepolo or introduced purposelessly. Conceivably he is intended for the doge of the period, Alvise Pisani, but he might better be meant for the early Doge Jacopo Tiepolo who had in the thirteenth century given the Dominicans a magnificent donation of land in Venice on which the basilica of SS Giovanni e Paolo was built.

A new mastery is apparent in the Gesuati ceiling—in, above all, the central fresco. It has an authority of design that immediately halts and compels anyone entering the church. Tiepolo has learnt how to order a huge area, to fill it without crowding—indeed, to emphasise celestial spaciousness, so that what lies along the ceiling is a vision which dissolves the roof into one endless vista of palpitating cloud and sky. More marvellous than the vision of heaven as such is the vision of that Venetian earth, which might almost be an architectural caprice, blended from elements of the Libreria and the Scala dei Giganti, suspended dizzily in the air. Nothing could better increase the illusion of architecture raised up over a great void than the ostentatiously easy pose of the halberdier seated on the cornice with one leg dangling negligently in space (Pl. 87). He exists perhaps for no other reason, though Tiepolo is careful to have the line of his pike lead straight up to the rosary in St Dominic's hand. Otherwise, the halberdier is there in homage to Veronese; and had Tiepolo ever faced the Inquisition on the topic of supposedly irrelevant figures in religious compositions ('was a halberdier present when St Dominic distributed the blessed rosary?'), he might have answered, paraphrasing Veronese's words, that he added such figures to his paintings for ornament and enrichment.

The Dominicans responsible for decorating the Gesuati seem to have understood very well the nature of the different talents they called on for different commissions. Piazzetta had created a masterpiece of tonal restraint in his altarpiece of three Dominican male saints. For a celebration of the central glory of their order—a type of scene more usually associated with baroque churches in Rome—they had chosen Tiepolo. And Tiepolo had responded as intensely as Piazzetta, though in his own manner. He had unveiled a kaleidoscope of brilliant, exciting shapes. He had not previously been called on for something as major in artistic emphasis as in its religious implications. On the ceiling he had to yoke the zones of heaven and earth and achieve an overall sense of divine purpose, spreading out from the small yet erect, commanding Christ Child aloft in the clouds, descending through St Dominic and down the massive steps and over the cornice to the evil group hurtling out of the bottom of the fresco, eternally banished and damned. The world is seen as wonderfully well ordered, thanks to God's providence and the existence of the rosary. And for Tiepolo the well-ordered world is one not static but in movement of a non-violent kind. Clouds drift and re-form; angels twist and spin in delicately tinted ether with the natural felicity of fish in water; human beings kneel and pray in a variety of emotions before the spectacle of St Dominic, who stands as if perpetually distributing—from an inexhaustible, heavenly supply—rosary after rosary to the generations and ranks who make up a stream of living people.

As it happens, Dominican thinking was very much in tune with Tiepolo's approach, resolutely anti-quietist, eager to stress such practical devotions as the rosary and to urge the need to contemplate sacred images. The triumph of the Gesuati as a church was that all its considerable cost had been met from alms, given often by quite humble trades in Venice. The campaign of alms-giving had been skilfully and widely organised, but to the resulting splendid edifice even the most modest donors might feel they had made a contribution. Among those who gave

87. Detail of Pl. 84.

88. *Three female saints*, recto, Museo Civico, Trieste.

89. *Three female saints*, verso, Museo Civico, Trieste.

more lavishly was Lorenzo Pezzana, a well-known publisher,[10] who was godfather to Tiepolo's youngest son, Lorenzo.

Tiepolo received a further commission for the Gesuati, for an altarpiece in the first chapel at the right. He had completed all the frescoes by September 1739, and in December the canvas for his altarpiece was prepared. The subject was three Dominican saints—female ones. It is difficult not to see this altarpiece (Pl. 90) as, whether or not consciously intended, something of a *paragone* with Piazzetta's altarpiece only two chapels away. Tiepolo certainly delayed producing the painting for years, in a manner reminiscent of Piazzetta. Although an over-eager Venetian guidebook of 1740 refers to it in place on its altar, the painting did not reach the church until 1748, when it seems to have arrived by boat in some style, brought by Tiepolo's own servants. They received not only tips and rosaries from the Dominican commissioners but also a meal[11]—all perhaps to mark relief as well as gratitude at the painting's eventual arrival.

It is not clear when precisely Tiepolo first started thinking about the composition, which required depiction of St Catherine of Siena, St Rose of Lima and the more obscure St Agnes of Montepulciano, historically the earliest of the three but the last to be canonised (in 1726). A fascinating sheet, with drawings on both sides (Pls 88 and 89), had been stylistically dated by some scholars to the mid-1740s, or even later, before the documentation of the altarpiece was known.[12] Whatever its exact period, it clearly relates to the commission and shows Tiepolo was thinking of making St Rose and the Christ Child more of a focal point in the composition. At arguably the second stage (the verso of the drawing), suggestions of the church setting were sketched in, and also a hovering angel contemplating the group. The parallel with Piazzetta's altarpiece would then have been strong, possibly too strong.

In the final painting it is the Virgin who appears, not an angel, adding a fourth female presence, introduced somewhat awkwardly above the trio of saints and very much detached from them, as they seem oblivious of her. Tiepolo's problem lay in the considerable height of the altarpiece required—on an altar framed by giant double columns and a heavy double pediment. Piazzetta had placed his three saints on a diagonal, supported by cloud. Once Tiepolo localised his group, and set them all on the same plane, he compounded the problem of the upper part of the composition. Even tonally, his solution is not very happy. The creamy-white, grey and black of his saints' habits—more choice than austere, elegant in their restraint—is a unity marred by the conventional red and blue of the Virgin's robes. There is something altogether perfunctory and unsatisfactory about her presence in the painting.

An old-fashioned view of the altarpiece used to detect in it a distinct 'odor di femmina', as da Ponte's Don Giovanni calls it, finding an almost disturbingly languid air about the two standing saints, with their full lips and melting glances. Yet Tiepolo probably meant to convey the very opposite of a worldly sense. His saints are as single-minded in their piety as Piazzetta's, softer perhaps in conveying it, as may traditionally be expected of female saints, but no less ardent. And the two altarpieces absorbingly relate to and, as it were, rebound off each other. Piazzetta's seated, contemplative, black-clad St Luis Beltran is half-echoed by Tiepolo's crouching, profoundly contemplative, black-clad St Agnes. In the arms of Piazzetta's upward-gazing St Hyacinth is cradled a small statue of the Virgin and Child. Tiepolo's upward-gazing St Rose carries the large, living Child, as rosy as the big rose he holds. In these ways Tiepolo probably seized and played with motifs in the earlier altarpiece, almost 'doing a Piazzetta' with his own group of saints, as though to demonstrate that he could change from being the artist of the myriad-coloured vision on the ceiling to create a mystic, contemplative work, sober-toned, tender and unflamboyant. Of the Tiepolo who demonstrated his range in the Gesuati, Piazzetta might have exclaimed, anticipating great English rival painters of the second half of the century: 'Damn him, how various he is.'

90. *Saints Catherine, Rose of Lima and Agnes of Montepul-ciano*, Gesuati, Venice.

And in the years particularly of the late 1730s, Tiepolo seems to have been eager to display a variety of moods in his religious work. He caught the mood of calm ecstasy in a sumptuous altarpiece of St Philip Neri enjoying a vision of the Virgin and Child accompanied by angels. A fiercer subject—the Martyrdom of St Sebastian—drew from him a far stronger sense of drama.[13] And in the triptych of Passion paintings for the somewhat obscure church of S. Alvise at Venice, he contrived a tremendous emotional assault on the spectator, dealing with subjects which so many famous artists before him had tackled. The commissioner of these paintings (Pl 92) was Alvise Cornaro (a member of the family of Doge Giovanni Cornaro, Tiepolo's first distinguished patron), whose name-saint the church commemorated. It was to Alvise Cornaro that Tiepolo's son, Domenico, was to dedicate his first etchings, whose theme was also the Passion.

Tiepolo's first comparable triptych had been of profane subject-matter, the classical series painted for the Palazzo Sandi, where brutal action had been reserved for the two narrow side canvases. Something similar is true of the S. Alvise paintings. The two side scenes depict the Flagellation and the Crowning with Thorns. For the large central composition the subject was not the Crucifixion, or even Christ being nailed to the Cross, but the Way to Calvary, with Christ falling under the weight of the Cross, after St Veronica had wiped his face.

Although a reference in a guidebook of 1740 mentions only the two side paintings as in the church, the date of execution for all three must be approximately the same. They show Tiepolo well aware of Titian and Tintoretto and Rembrandt (in his etchings) in treating of the Passion—and also perhaps, less expectedly, of Rubens. A sketch by him of Christ falling under the Cross was in a Venetian collection at the period and was later owned by Consul Smith;[14] an echo, however faint, of that composition seems detectable in Tiepolo's treatment, mingled with more patent echoes of Tintoretto.

The central composition offered Tiepolo greater scope in every way than the two lateral scenes. In the *Crowning with Thorns*, and to a lesser extent in the *Flagellation*, the figure of Christ is strangely tall, an image of suffering detached from the bizarre onlookers and even from his torturers. In both paintings Christ is placed high in the composition, and the architectural setting is given a prominence which seems to be a conscious echo—in the *Crowning with Thorns* particularly—of Titian's *Crowning with Thorns* (today in the Louvre), which Tiepolo could easily have seen on his visits to Milan since it hung, until Napoleon removed it, in S. Maria delle Grazie. Between the pathos of the suffering Christ and the emphatic brutality of his torturers, the bystanders Tiepolo imagines are more than somewhat discordant. They might have strayed, it seems, from another, much less emotive composition; and in fact, in their character as in their grouping, they are very close to the figures of Tiepolo's first published etchings, the *Capricci*.

At S. Alvise the scene of the *Way to Calvary* was the most openly dramatic in concept of the three paintings. It offered Tiepolo an opportunity to set a whole pageant around the isolated, fainting Christ, and the question remains as to whether the result is not more thrilling than moving, at least to modern eyes. The Romano-Oriental world that Tiepolo so effortlessly imagined—and which, as it happens, is a remarkably accurate reflection in art of historical fact—is sumptuous, exotic and exciting. Trumpets and banners, noble, prancing horses and gleaming, muscular bodies all add to the colourful and almost noisy effect, a crescendo which compositionally curves round and up to the cliff-like hill of Calvary, already bearing the thieves' crosses and busy with animated, gesticulating figures.

Amid all this action, the passive, vermilion-clad, prostrate Christ is appealing and touching, yet melodramatically so, in his utter exhaustion. His cross is gigantically long, fearful as a burden yet oddly lacking in real weight, a little too much a stage property. His very prostration and his gesture of painful collapse are suggestive of the stage; there is an overt call for sympathy which is dangerously near the rhetorical. Pathos in religious subjects was not outside Tiepolo's range (as his Spanish years would prove), but perhaps at the root of the *Way to Calvary* lies an ambiguity about the intention. The attempt to combine martial grandeur and human panoply with a moment of divine weakness was certainly ambitious enough for any artist. Tintoretto had succeeded in the tremendous *Crucifixion* in the Scuola di S. Rocco—and Tiepolo surely looked hard at the series of Passion scenes in the Sala dell' Albergo there—but such a masterpiece required not only a concentration of resources but ruthless subordination of everything to the central incident and its significance. Tiepolo is more easily distracted and led to elaborate or emotional effects. In the *modello* for the large-scale painting in Berlin[15] he had conceived a far simpler pose for Christ, bowed, face towards the ground, with all the unforced poignancy of being 'A Man of Sorrows and acquainted with grief.' That mood is typical of his later, Spanish-period work. In the 1730s, in a major church commission, Tiepolo went for the fullest possible onslaught on the spectator's feelings: Christ, bleeding and heavily crowned with thorns, must be shown acting out a swoon of agony that no one can miss. Through the final painting runs not too little but too much emotion.

Other religious commissions in Venice were coming Tiepolo's way before the decade ended. None was more important than that for the Confraternity of the Scuola di S. Maria del Carmelo. In December 1739 the Confraternity settled unanimously on Tiepolo, 'extolled as the most celebrated of artists', to decorate their building.[16] At the same time they recorded that the painter had not yet accepted, owing to the pressure on him of numerous tasks, including an undertaking to carry out work in—once again—Milan. By January the following year Tiepolo had, however, managed to submit two 'pensieri' to the Confraternity about the scheme of decoration. Even by his standards, a decade of hectic activity, centred on Venice, was about to begin.

First there was the task in Milan. It required, among other things, a return to the discipline-cum-freedom of fresco as a medium, and also a return to the world of mythology, mythology of a cosmic kind and on something of a celestial if not cosmic scale. Not Phaeton but Apollo himself was to be the central figure in a huge ceiling in the Palazzo Clerici, illustrating the Course of the Sun (Pl. 93).

The commissioner was the Marquis Don Giorgio Antonio Clerici who had inherited the family palace in 1736. He later became a marshal of the Empire under Maria Theresa, who in 1740 succeeded her father, the Emperor Charles VI, and fought on her behalf. Clerici was another example of an outstandingly rich Milanese patron who saw in Tiepolo the ideal artist for his purposes. Powerful, prodigal with money and determined to create a magnificent setting in the environment of his own palace, Clerici commissioned the largest and the grandest fresco Tiepolo had yet executed. His own impending marriage may have been a factor in the commission, and in 1741 he married Fulvia Visconti.[17]

The room selected was the very long gallery-like main salone, itself elaborately decorated with gilded stucco and set with mirrors, a type of room quite uncharacteristic of Venice and vaguely Frenchified in style (Pl. 91). The long tunnel of vaulted ceiling was not the easiest space to decorate with a single, coherent composition, and as experienced today the room and its scheme have a slightly disorienting effect, increased by the fact that the ceiling is comparatively low. It takes a moment or more to discover the thematic centre of the whole decoration, Apollo's chariot rising with the disc of the sun over the world, in a scene of literal enlightenment, illuminating as it advances, with the four immortal Horses pawing the sky as they gallop upwards. The coming of Apollo lights and stirs into life the worlds of heaven and earth: Olympus and the gods, and the Four Continents that lie along the cornice.

91. View of the salone, Palazzo Clerici, Milan.

92. *Christ crowned with thorns* and the *Way to Calvary*, S. Alvise, Venice.

93a–f. *Course of the Sun*, Palazzo Clerici, Milan.

Over the real twin doorways north and south arch huge, feigned vaults of architecture alive with perching, reclining figures—and those areas are among the most sheerly effective portions of the fresco (Pl. 94).

If the total effect is not entirely successful (and damp in places has robbed passages of their original brilliance), some of the allegorical groups are among Tiepolo's most poetic creations, endlessly inventive in detail, serious or playfully exuberant and always beautiful. A vast, cosmic ballet is being danced down the ceiling. It is not organised with the supreme coherence Tiepolo would achieve at Würzburg, and it lacks the physical setting to enhance such coherence, but the bubbling creativity of the artist is, if anything, even fresher. Less for Clerici than for himself, it seems, does Tiepolo devise the exotic animals, the bare-breasted Allegories, the sun-tanned Rivers, the tumbling putti, down to the last tendril of hair and plume of wing.

He had been given the whole world to depict, and it was not too much. Indeed, the impression is of someone who had only been waiting for the opportunity to realise—to release—his vision of Time and Venus, the gods in the air and the nymphs of the sea, America with its feathered archers, Africa with its negroes, and the Arts that seem to include among them smoking. Not the novelty of the images but their wonderfully detailed vivacity is the essence of Tiepolo's achievement. He could not skimp, any more than he could be clumsy or pedestrian.

For the Palazzo Clerici scheme there exists a related oil sketch that must represent a very early stage of evolution (Pl. 95). It has marked differences from the ceiling in numerous ways, though none is more striking than the fact that Apollo, minus his chariot, is placed there at the compositional centre. On the assumption that this

94

94. Detail of Pl. 93.

95. *Apollo and the Continents*, Kimbell Art Museum, Fort Worth, Texas.

97 (facing page). Detail of Pl. 93 showing Venus and Time.

96. *Seated faun*, Metropolitan Museum of Art, New York, Rogers Fund (37.165.38).

sketch is definitely for the ceiling, it might be thought to indicate that Tiepolo had not yet seen the actual room in the palace or appreciated the problems it raised for him by its extreme length. No second *modello* is known to exist. Arguably there was one, but in any case Tiepolo now preferred to make preliminary studies of certain figures and groups in drawings. Numerous pen-and-wash drawings of casual, airy grace and lightness relate either to the oil sketch or to the ceiling itself.[18] These drawings seem to have been executed first in scribbled chalk, and then invested with greater substance, though still in inspired haste, by the use of pen and light wash. Sometimes out of a few rapid strokes a single figure is conjured up, such as a grinning faun (Pl. 96); and this serves as basis for the painted figure seated on feigned architecture at the south end of the room. Other studies are of groups; a river-god, a woman and a boy are set down, and their compact relationship to each other is preserved in the fresco, while everything else seems changed, developed and invested with poetic concreteness. The old god—whose belly in the drawing is made wrinkled by some three pen strokes—in the fresco grasps a water-pot in a gnarled hand. Instead of gesticulating, the woman is eventually painted adjusting a fold of her peach-red draperies, and the boy who in the drawing supported himself so easily at her knee is shown older, though still insouciant, and from his bare arm are suspended a couple of fish on a loop or two of line. The pleasure of inventing and going on inventing is preserved, it seems, even up to the moment of execution on the ceiling itself, as though Tiepolo was determined to leave himself free to improvise when it came to the touch of his brush on the damp plaster.

The huge ceiling was effectively all sky, and though it is full of groups of figures they needed to be organised into one single, coherent scheme. When creating the *modello*, Tiepolo had thought to have the main groups placed prominently at the four corners; and though something of that concept remains in the ceiling, the groups have been thinned out, extended along the cornice, and the vast area of sky animated by other groups—most notably the superb one of Venus and Time. Tiepolo probably saw too that he needed more drama than could be obtained by Apollo merely hovering in the air. The rising of the sun not only meant a more exciting group, of the god driving his Horses and chariot up into and as it were across the heavens, but it gave thematic and visual coherence—as far as Tiepolo could contrive on the very long vault—to the whole scene. Light is returning to the world; light sets life in motion; and the coming of light is an effortless triumph of beneficence. There is here no struggle of rival powers. Nothing impedes the progress of Apollo, and the world rejoices at his appearance. On an Olympus of clouds, Venus and Time float tranquilly, he splendidly winged, his powerful sunburnt back contrasting with her blonde figure seen from the front (Pl. 97). He seems to lay aside his scythe; she lightly clasps a white rose. The prominence Tiepolo gives them may indicate that the ceiling is, among other things, a sort of epithalamium, but for the painter Time and Beauty are always seen as great powers. Perhaps he could never have explained in words his sense of their reality for him, but even in his very last years he brought them together with haunting effect (see Pl. 225). At the Palazzo Clerici they calmly await the coming of day. Dawn heralds Apollo's approach. The Continents are roused into homage; under Apollo grain ripens and the dew falls. And his light penetrates every portion of the globe: 'The huntsmen are up in America. . .', in the words of Sir Thomas Browne.

The entire mood is serene and optimistic. There is a perpetual *joie de vivre* that makes the white-marble fauns grin and swing on the over-ornate feigned archways, where enamel-like flowers blossom improbably amid scrolls that seem cut from gilt paper (*quadratura* work which a local Milanese artist perhaps supplied). A generative force seems to be running through the sportive cupids—one of whom clutches a dove of Venus' upside down—and the tipsy Bacchus, between whose legs protrudes a giant flask of wine with frankly phallic effect. The ancient river-gods press to their

published a series of etched views of Venice. But preceding Tiepolo's etchings and again perhaps exercising some influence on him, if only obliquely, was a volume of Marco Ricci's etchings which appeared in 1730, the year of Ricci's death.[3] In several of these compositions of vast, mouldering ruins of antiquity, where tiny figures of women and children, as well as men, wander, recline and gaze, there are anticipations of Piranesi and also Francesco Guardi. In some ways, Tiepolo is far less elaborate and far less concerned than Ricci with topography or the grandeur of the past. Yet here and there, Ricci's vision, with its romantic wildness of the countryside and the almost surreal association of figures amid fallen columns, half-buried urns and broken capitals, offers a distinct foretaste of the far stranger and more private kingdom created by Tiepolo in his etchings.

With his facility of invention and delight in improvising—as though letting his mind guide him as it would—Tiepolo can hardly have needed preparatory drawings as such for his etchings. Indeed, some of the appeal of the medium may well have lain for him in the prospect of spontaneity, akin to that of drawing, but which can be reproduced and disseminated. No longer was he executing drawings to be followed by engravers; in himself he united engraver and draughtsman.

There seems to be no single obvious theme underlying the *Capricci*, though they share—with one exception—a very similar vocabulary, style and mood. The exception is the 'Rider with his horse'. This composition is based on an earlier prototype, going back possibly to Van Dyck and certainly related to a drawing by Castiglione.[4] Such dependence is untypical of Tiepolo, in any medium, and may indicate that this etching was an early one, conceivably his earliest surviving attempt.

While great seventeenth-century exponents of etching clearly exercised some influence on him, it was once again his contemporary Piazzetta who seems to have inspired him directly, despite the fact that Piazzetta was barely active as an etcher. What of course he did do—far more than Tiepolo—was to execute whole series of drawings, in connection especially with illustrated books, for the use of engravers.

From Piazzetta Tiepolo borrowed such accessories as fur caps and also, it would seem, figure-types like the very youthful, so-called 'soldier' who in the 'Three Soldiers' etching stares out, clasping a home-made-looking banner, his head wrapped in a floppy twist of drapery (Pl. 98). Although his armour is real enough, the general effect is of a boy dressing up, recalling very much some of Piazzetta's effects. The mood of the etchings generally has something of the highly personal, mysterious and haunting atmosphere that invests Piazzetta's genre paintings—for example, the scene known as an 'Idyll on the Seashore'.[5]

In all but one of the ten etchings, at least one figure is to be found seated or lying on the ground, brooding often or pensive, in a countryside that is ageless yet has about it associations of antiquity. A vast pyramid rises, brushed by leafy foliage; an urn, a column, a statue—and even a pile of bones—all suggest not unpleasurably the passage of time. There is something elegiac about these landscapes, where limitless space extends behind the foreground figures and motifs. The mood is a lulling one, half-siesta and half-magical, an afternoon mood where strange shapes are descried and strange incidents occur, yet without any power to disturb. When Death himself is encountered in this Arcady of lapsed figures and mouldering classical fragments (Pl. 99), the feeling is one of curiosity rather than fear. The group of living people, young and old—the woman with her pitcher, the youth, the bent, half-incredulous magus—peers at the hooded skeleton that is Death with frank fascination. They seem unaware of confronting their own future. They face the riddle of life with no more comprehension than the rather starved-looking dog, only a little less bony than Death.

'Saporitissimo' was one of the adjectives Zanetti chose when, several years later, he wrote appreciatively of Tiepolo's etchings;[6] and something on the lines of 'most piquant' is an adequate translation, well conveying the highly spiced flavour of them.

5 'MOST EXCELLENT PAINTER OF OUR DAY . . .'

TIEPOLO HAD always managed, it seems, to find time to draw; and what at first must have been training and exercise became a habit—even, perhaps, a compulsion. He probably always made drawings for their own sake: not only for sale, nor as specific studies for work in hand, but thrown off by sheer creative energy. In that way his caricatures may have come into existence, and also his late, economical and evocative landscape drawings. Humour and fantasy and pointed observation could not necessarily—could not often as commissions grew heavier—find an outlet in his major paintings, whether in oil or fresco.

He was now solidly established, famous and fully employed. When, on 2 June 1743, the Venetian diarist Girolamo Zanetti noted that his painted compartments for the Scuola del Carmine had been made publicly visible, he described Tiepolo as 'most excellent painter of our day, above all others. . .'[1] It represented one more testimony, if a private one, to Tiepolo's success, and the Carmine decorations could only confirm it. Also in 1743 there appeared a novel aspect of Tiepolo's activity. Another Zanetti, the elder Anton Maria, published a volume (the second, in fact) of his chiaroscuro prints chiefly after Parmigianino. The volume contained in addition ten etchings by Tiepolo, the *Capricci*.

Although the medium was a new one for Tiepolo, the concept of capricious and bizarre scenes, compositions of a few figures juxtaposed and placed in partly fantasy landscapes, already existed in some of his earliest known drawings. There might be found some nude men with a shield and two vases, strangely lit in an almost lunar light. When da Canal had, a decade or more before Zanetti's publication, written of engravers eager to possess 'le invenzioni e le bizzarrie di pensieri' produced by Tiepolo, he had given a quite apt description of the *Capricci*; and in them Tiepolo acted as disseminator of his own inventions. Besides, Tiepolo must have accumulated in his studio a mass of isolated studies—heads and torsos, pieces of armour and tree-trunks—which when leafed through would suggest piquantly capricious effects.

And then there was the example of great, earlier artists, both Italian and foreign, who had produced etchings. Not only Rembrandt but Castiglione, Stefano della Bella and Salvator Rosa were obvious examples.[2] Zanetti himself, producing prints after Parmigianino, may also have had some influence on Tiepolo. He probably knew Zanetti's fine collection of prints, and by the 1730s may have started his own collection which eventually, as left by Domenico Tiepolo, was impressively wide-ranging. Rosa and Callot had used the word *capricci* to describe their etchings, but compositions of 'capricious' subject-matter, with women and soldiers and obscure magus-like figures meditating in landscapes, had a thoroughly Venetian source in paintings associated with Giorgione and engravings by Campagnola.

Zanetti's first volume of woodcuts after Parmigianino appeared in 1731, and Tiepolo probably did not do any serious etching until much later in that decade. Other painters were to follow him in the production and publication of etchings. Around 1740 Canaletto began to be active as an etcher, creating a vein of moody fantasy that is not paralleled in his paintings of the same date. In 1741 Marieschi published a series of etched views of Venice. But preceding Tiepolo's etchings and again perhaps exercising some influence on him, if only obliquely, was a volume of Marco Ricci's etchings which appeared in 1730, the year of Ricci's death.[3] In several of these compositions of vast, mouldering ruins of antiquity, where tiny figures of women and children, as well as men, wander, recline and gaze, there are anticipations of Piranesi and also Francesco Guardi. In some ways, Tiepolo is far less elaborate and far less concerned than Ricci with topography or the grandeur of the past. Yet here and there, Ricci's vision, with its romantic wildness of the countryside and the almost surreal association of figures amid fallen columns, half-buried urns and broken capitals, offers a distinct foretaste of the far stranger and more private kingdom created by Tiepolo in his etchings.

With his facility of invention and delight in improvising—as though letting his mind guide him as it would—Tiepolo can hardly have needed preparatory drawings as such for his etchings. Indeed, some of the appeal of the medium may well have lain for him in the prospect of spontaneity, akin to that of drawing, but which can be reproduced and disseminated. No longer was he executing drawings to be followed by engravers; in himself he united engraver and draughtsman.

There seems to be no single obvious theme underlying the *Capricci*, though they share—with one exception—a very similar vocabulary, style and mood. The exception is the 'Rider with his horse'. This composition is based on an earlier prototype, going back possibly to Van Dyck and certainly related to a drawing by Castiglione.[4] Such dependence is untypical of Tiepolo, in any medium, and may indicate that this etching was an early one, conceivably his earliest surviving attempt.

While great seventeenth-century exponents of etching clearly exercised some influence on him, it was once again his contemporary Piazzetta who seems to have inspired him directly, despite the fact that Piazzetta was barely active as an etcher. What of course he did do—far more than Tiepolo—was to execute whole series of drawings, in connection especially with illustrated books, for the use of engravers.

From Piazzetta Tiepolo borrowed such accessories as fur caps and also, it would seem, figure-types like the very youthful, so-called 'soldier' who in the 'Three Soldiers' etching stares out, clasping a home-made-looking banner, his head wrapped in a floppy twist of drapery (Pl. 98). Although his armour is real enough, the general effect is of a boy dressing up, recalling very much some of Piazzetta's effects. The mood of the etchings generally has something of the highly personal, mysterious and haunting atmosphere that invests Piazzetta's genre paintings—for example, the scene known as an 'Idyll on the Seashore'.[5]

In all but one of the ten etchings, at least one figure is to be found seated or lying on the ground, brooding often or pensive, in a countryside that is ageless yet has about it associations of antiquity. A vast pyramid rises, brushed by leafy foliage; an urn, a column, a statue—and even a pile of bones—all suggest not unpleasurably the passage of time. There is something elegiac about these landscapes, where limitless space extends behind the foreground figures and motifs. The mood is a lulling one, half-siesta and half-magical, an afternoon mood where strange shapes are descried and strange incidents occur, yet without any power to disturb. When Death himself is encountered in this Arcady of lapsed figures and mouldering classical fragments (Pl. 99), the feeling is one of curiosity rather than fear. The group of living people, young and old—the woman with her pitcher, the youth, the bent, half-incredulous magus—peers at the hooded skeleton that is Death with frank fascination. They seem unaware of confronting their own future. They face the riddle of life with no more comprehension than the rather starved-looking dog, only a little less bony than Death.

'Saporitissimo' was one of the adjectives Zanetti chose when, several years later, he wrote appreciatively of Tiepolo's etchings;[6] and something on the lines of 'most piquant' is an adequate translation, well conveying the highly spiced flavour of them.

tanned bodies naked nymphs and naiads who seem very far from reluctant. Along the cornice there is a rustle and stir of life: an elephant's trunk twists up enquiringly; a negro page holds a hound on a leash; and the shapes of marvellous marine creatures, human and animal, appear activated by the warmth of the sun.

When one looks ahead to the staircase at Würzburg, it may seem that the effects—especially those characterising the Continents—are less developed, tentative, here and there, for all their vivacity. But looking back to the Villa Loschi or to the ceilings of the Palazzo Archinto is more useful and relevant. And Tiepolo's confidence at the Palazzo Clerici is far greater. His own poetry of invention is now more audacious. The mythological world he had to present was far more extensive than any he would be called on to create in Venice. Playful without being flippant, serious yet not overtly didactic or moralistic, the Palazzo Clerici ceiling is extraordinarily natural, concerned less with human beings than with natural energy: a pantheistic hymn in paint to nature at its purest and certainly at its most beneficent. And more openly than ever before did Tiepolo assert the beauty and the wonder of his imagined world. His Oceans and Winds, his Olympian deities, even his fishy monsters are summoned up with deep conviction and with an intensity that extends to the pencilling-in of their very contours, to make them more vivid and more glamorous than any reality.

Perhaps it was easy for him to believe in what he was painting, for the theme of the ceiling went beyond light to enlightenment, though it may have been enlightenment, in the patron's eyes, with a political tinge. 'Già fra l'ombre il sol prevale', Metastasio versified in a birthday cantata for the Emperor Francis I, the husband of Maria Theresa, making the sun emerge from out of shadow. It is perhaps the sun of Austria that is rising to illumine the world at the Palazzo Clerici, but Apollo is present also as protector of the arts. Mercury too is prominent on the ceiling, suggesting that intellectual light is another aspect of the theme.

The Marchese Don Giorgio Clerici did not ask Tiepolo to portray him on the ceiling, but he probably seemed to the painter a truly enlightened patron. He had, after all, given Tiepolo a most remarkable commission. And he had added to his own palace a gallery as effectively frescoed in its idiom as those famous ones of Apollo and Aurora in Rome by Reni and Guercino, but with a semi-monarchical grandeur more akin to the Salon d'Apollon at Versailles. As it happens, the fresco at the Palazzo Clerici was to be Tiepolo's last work in Milan. Something of what it meant for him—in terms of status as much as art—is shown by its being the subject at the time of verses by an anonymous Milanese poet, *Poesie dedicate al merito singolarissimo del Sig. Gio. Battista Tiepolo celebre pittore veneto imitatore di Paolo Veronese...*

The days of Tiepolo being an 'imitatore' of anyone were over, but the compliment was doubtless intended to be fulsome. It was a further testimony to Tiepolo's fame, itself by then as firmly established as his art.

98. *Three soldiers and a youth*, National Gallery of Art, Washington, Rosenwald Collection (B-19, 893).

99. *Death giving audience*, National Gallery of Art, Washington, Rosenwald Collection (B-19, 886).

They are sophisticated assemblages of partly incongruous elements which have yet been fused together without dissonance or triviality. To press too hard the question of what they mean, in the sense of telling any particular narrative, is to miss the essential aspect of their capricious nature; but, subtly distilled in the artist's mind, they take on meaning and carry a remarkable degree of conviction.

Some of the figures have drifted, consciously or not, from Tiepolo's own painted compositions, going back to the early 1730s, if not before. The tall woman who stands gracefully in profile holding an urn at the foot of a mysterious obelisk seems taken in reverse from the Salome of the *Execution of the Baptist* fresco in the Colleoni chapel at Bergamo, though both may be vaguely indebted, if only in terms of proportion, to Parmigianino. The groups of figures witnessing Christ's baptism or listening to St John preaching in the other frescoes there may less patently be related to figure-groups in the *Capricci*, but they already hint towards them, and out of studies for such figures may have evolved some of the inspiration for the more openly bizarre juxtapositions expressed in the etchings.

For Tiepolo there must have been a sense in which the *Capricci* allowed him to escape from the requirements of the average commission, with its specific subject-matter and related demands. In etching he satisfied primarily himself. Only at Zanetti's instigation, it may be, did he subsequently agree to publication. The etchings are certainly an outlet for fancy and free imagination for which commissions to Tiepolo by the early 1740s did not allow much scope. Unmistakable though the etchings are as Tiepolo's work, they are an unforeseen aspect of his activity and development; in them he goes outside and beyond the world of his paintings—further than Canaletto goes in his etchings and probably further than any other Venetian artist of the period. They represent a distinct 'break' in a heavily occupied career. Only Fontebasso was to follow suit with his group of eight etchings, published in 1744, *Varii Baccanali et Istorie*, themselves in part an obvious homage to Tiepolo and otherwise showing a mildly capricious approach to definite historical subjects like Sophonisba taking the poison[7]—the very themes Tiepolo had avoided in his etchings. It was left to Tiepolo to take up the medium again, in the subsequent decade, developing in technique and deepening the magic, irrational elements in ways that presage the atmosphere of some of Goya's *Caprichos*, though without the satire.

Publication of the *Capricci* in 1743 must virtually have coincided with work on two of Tiepolo's largest canvases, quite apart from his absorption in the decorative scheme for the Scuola del Carmine in Venice. It was the Confraternity of the Most Holy Sacrament at Verolanuova, situated between Cremona and Brescia, who commissioned from Tiepolo two huge paintings for the parish church, both concerned with illustrating Old-Testament prefigurations of the institution of Communion by Christ: the *Gathering of the Manna* and the *Sacrifice of Melchizedek* (Pls 100 and 101).

Pairing of the two subjects was by no means uncommon. Several painters had executed such pairs, and the *Gathering of the Manna* was painted by Cignaroli for the chapel of the Sacrament in the Duomo at Vicenza. The scale Tiepolo was working on for Verolanuova might suggest Tintoretto's giant canvases in S. Maria dell' Orto, while Tintoretto's late *Gathering of the Manna*, in S. Giorgio Maggiore, executed as a pair to the *Last Supper*, is relevant for the theme.

In fact, Tiepolo seems to have been very little influenced by earlier treatments—and an influence detected from a huge though horizontal composition by Ricci of *Moses striking the Rock*, painted for the church of SS Cosma e Damiano at Venice, seems, at best, faint. Not scale alone is responsible for the impressive effect of Tiepolo's two canvases, for they are tremendously effective pieces of painting. There is, however, a discrepancy between them which study makes only more marked in terms of quality, recognised—if unwittingly—by the tendency of scholars to give more space to reproduction and discussion of the *Gathering of the Manna*. On every

count, it is indeed the better painting. It could also well be the earlier one, the one Tiepolo composed more skilfully, took longer perhaps to complete. To call the *Sacrifice of Melchizedek* perfunctory may be harsh but the painting is unsatisfactory, especially by the standards set by its pendant.

Even the trees are powerfully realised in the *Gathering of the Manna*. Not merely is it the rugged sinuosity of their giant trunks, leading the eye up from the base of the composition to the very top, where an angel lets fall the manna, but equally effective are the patches of broken bark alternating with fronds of adhering creeper. It is those

100. *Gathering of the Manna*, parish church, Verolanuova, Brescia.

101. *Sacrifice of Melchizedek*, parish church, Verolanuova, Brescia.

102 (following page). Detail of Pl. 100.

trees that serve to integrate the disparate yet fully animated zones of heaven and earth: one remote and cloud-filled, the other packed with the bodies of the Israelites, men, women and children, eagerly scrambling for the miraculous substance raining down and around them. Between the two areas Moses occupies a middle zone, silhouetted against the sky, strikingly posed on an outcrop of rock, his eyes and arms raised to invoke the miracle that is already taking place. The height of the canvas is here skilfully exploited. A vast distance exists between earth and heaven. The manna drops from remote heights, beyond mankind's ken: mysterious snowflakes that speckle the sky as they fall and become as solid and palpable as pebbles as they reach the ground. Depth too is exploited by Tiepolo. There is a strong suggestion of the Israelite camp stretching away far behind Moses and the swarm of foreground figures, in winding lines of tents interspersed with linked, praying, grateful crowds that seem unending.

The hot reds and yellowish fawn of the costumes and the many areas of boldly modelled, muscular, bare flesh are painted with real gusto, to 'carry' from far away but equally satisfactory close to. The effect is grander than at S. Alvise, and ultimately more convincing; as drama the scene has all the action lacking in the *Finding of Moses*. Those are paintings that can reasonably be compared, however, in terms of handling. The stylistic indications accord broadly with what is known about the date of commissioning, which was around 1740 or slightly earlier.[8] It seems clear that even as late as September 1742 the two paintings had not reached Verolanuova, where they were anxiously awaited, and Tiepolo may have hastened work on the *Sacrifice of Melchizedek* so as to get the commission completed.

In the *Gathering of the Manna*, the urge to create a drama of varied human emotions is unusually powerful. It finds little explanation in the rather unemphatic text of Exodus, where Jehovah assures Moses, without any special appeal, 'I will rain bread from heaven for you', and the manna is discovered each morning lying 'like hoar frost on the ground'. Thus it was that Tintoretto—hardly neglectful of dramatic opportunities in painting—had shown the Israelites quietly collecting the fallen manna as simply one more of their workaday, semi-domestic tasks.

Tiepolo begins with the idea of its miraculous nature. His Moses summons it as commandingly as if he were striking the rock to cause water to flow, and gathering of it starts even while it is still falling. The actual process of the gathering is conveyed by a gamut of differing reactions, expressed in a favourite Tiepolo gamut of the generations: the young mother and child, the aged woman and bearded old men, and brawny youths handling massive vases (Pl. 103). Some cram the manna into their mouths as they crouch over it. One woman holds up her skirt to catch it as it falls. An exotically dressed old man peers at the substance he has clasped in his hands. In the distance a graceful girl walks delicately back to the tents, balancing a full pitcher on her head with all the self-conscious elegance of a model on the cat-walk (Pl. 102). Tiepolo's *invenzione* flows on, into the very variety of receptacles—jugs, dishes, baskets, as well as vases and pitchers—in which the manna is being collected. Not content with this busy assemblage, he devises the incursion of a Roman-style soldier gesticulating beside a noble, white steed. The echo of the heavenly horse and rider from Raphael's *Expulsion of Heliodorus* may be quite accidental, but the motif was splendid enough for Tiepolo to continue to introduce it, with or without rider, into a number of paintings, varying in subject from the *Crowning with Thorns* to the *Arrival of Cleopatra*. There are echoes also from his own work in several of the types and poses, and probably at least one study from the life, in the blonde boy standing right of centre in the painting, very much in every way a Tiepolo child and quite likely to be his youngest son Lorenzo at the age of about six.

Typically, Tiepolo does not let the manna just fall vaguely or inexplicably from heaven. He organises an angelic team to distribute it. While a child angel scatters it like confetti, in playful mood, a more earnest, older angel tilts a heavy, well-wrought

metal urn from which streams down manna inexhaustibly. For the miracle, and adding to its miraculous air, there must be visual logic.

It is Tiepolo's pondered thought that has produced an effect unusual in his work, a composition without its individual heroine and hero (for not even Moses is more vivid than the foreground Israelites) but where—in musical phraseology—the chorus are the protagonists; and the result is less opera than Old-Testament oratorio.

To expect the painter to create two such scenes, on such a scale, would be too much. The celebration by Melchizedek of Abraham's victory over assorted kings of Sodom and so on, was an inevitably static subject, where the colossal height of the canvas was bound to be something of an embarrassment. Even allowing for that, there is a vacuous air to the composition. The maidens dancing down the hillside border on the absurd. Abraham's army is rather conventionally suggested, and perhaps only the uppermost portion of the painting, with Jehovah blessing and angels flying, is imagined with any great conviction. The fat, oriental figures who help to close the composition at the left are as bovine as the ox whose head obtrudes at their side. The handling is undoubtedly Tiepolo's own, but the lack of overall coherence—a lack almost of artistic concentration—is marked, as is the sense of strain. The trees that are such a pronounced feature of the *Gathering of the Manna* seem reproduced here to help relate the two compositions, though with none of the masterly vigour and artistic sap that made them flourish so memorably in the manna-strewn desert. Yet, to judge from photographs of a pair of sketches that are usually accepted as the *modelli*,[9] the two compositions may have evolved at the same time, in which case the large-scale *Gathering of the Manna* benefited from Tiepolo's giving more time—if not thought—to its execution.

The early 1740s made considerable demands on his stamina, physically as much as intellectually. Completion of the Verolanuova paintings—the largest oil paintings he ever made—was required. At the same period he had commissions in Venice itself which required all his powers. A price had to be paid for being the 'most excellent painter of our day'.

Girolamo Zanetti used the words in the summer of 1743, but Tiepolo's thinking about the Scuola del Carmine commission went back at least to January 1740. When the Confraternity first approached him about executing eight paintings for the ceiling of the main, upper-floor salone of their building, he had objected to the prospect of his pictures surrounding the already existing central picture, an *Assumption of the Virgin* by the seventeenth-century painter Padovanino. Not only would there be no relationship between his paintings and Padovanino's, but, as he pointed out shrewdly, the earlier picture lacked any allusion to the title of the Confraternity, the Madonna of Mount Carmel.[10] As he had doubtless hoped, the result was a decision to move the Padovanino to another room and entrust 'the whole ceiling' to Tiepolo.

In so doing, the Confraternity entrusted him also with the initiative for proposing the complete scheme of decoration—as perhaps he had again hoped—and he responded with *two* elaborate programmes between which the members responsible might choose. For the central scene, however, the subject would remain the same: the Virgin, escorted by the prophets Elias and Eliazer, and 'by many troops of angels' (Tiepolo can almost be heard savouring his own suggestion), would be shown descending from heaven to proffer the holy Carmelite scapular to St Simon Stock who would be in suppliant attitude, imploring some mark of the Virgin's special protection.

One scheme envisaged this scene surrounded by five paintings of angels, plus two showing respectively the succour given by the Confraternity and the chastity, 'virginal or matrimonial', of its members, with an eighth painting of souls in purgatory. The second scheme devoted the eight paintings to chiefly pairs of Virtues: Fortitude and Temperance, Purity and Modesty, etc. The iconography of each

103 (preceding page). Detail of Pl. 100.

106

Virtue was carefully indicated, on the lines established by Ripa: 'a woman dressed in white, with lowered eyes, holding a lamb . . . an armed woman in tawny robes, leaning on a column. . .' This programme is commended in introductory phrases as 'more attractive and more suitable', and among its advantages is said to be its acting as a mirror in which the Confraternity could see itself devoutly reflected.

Another, unmentioned advantage was that it obviously appealed more to Tiepolo. Not surprisingly, the Confraternity decided to adopt the second scheme. When it came to be executed, however, Tiepolo combined aspects of the two proposals by dropping some of the Virtues (Chastity and Poverty were among the casualties) and combining others to occupy only four compartments, while the other four were filled with angels in varying roles.

There is no better documented instance in his long career of the deep thought and care Tiepolo could bring to the task of 'decoration', devising a scheme in great detail and yet evolving beyond it when he came to the execution, as well as getting out of the way an obstacle—such as Padovanino's old ceiling painting—to his own concepts. And then, with the literary and intellectual aspect over, he could confidently conjure up in paint the image of 'a woman dressed in white . . .', as well as troops of angels and, finally, the image of the Virgin herself, descending from heaven in a vision to St Simon Stock.

The Carmine commission came at a time—fortunately one prolonged throughout the 1740s—of utter artistic balance and felicity in Tiepolo's career. His mastery of oil paint was now total. He now expressed himself in it with an accomplishment equal to that displayed in his frescoes; and the Carmine ceiling is the most sustained example of his decorative achievements in oil. In the subsequent years, especially after 1750, he rarely translated the vivacity and lightness of his *modelli* into the finished, large-scale oil paintings, and a certain heaviness and hardness of outline became apparent. Tiepolo never again painted a religious scheme comparable to the Carmine one. The division there of the ceiling into a number of shaped areas to be filled by canvas paintings was traditionally Venetian (the Scuola di S. Rocco is the most obvious example that comes to mind), though the rich carving of the wooden framework and the stucco angels at the Carmine are contemporary with Tiepolo's activity.

When the ceiling was unveiled in 1743, the central canvas was not yet completed or in position ('non è ancora messo in opera', noted Zanetti), but Tiepolo was judged to have served the Confraternity well and was voted a member of it. His figures of the Virtues were far more gracefully disposed than at the Villa Loschi, though they have to fill extremely awkward, curved shapes at the corners of the ceiling. There is nothing angular or strained about the Carmine Virtues (Pl. 104). More placid in mood perhaps than the allegorical figures on the Palazzo Clerici ceiling, they are otherwise directly related, with rounded limbs and softly falling draperies, and also sisters in their dreamy voluptuousness to Veronese's Virtues on the analogous though more elaborate ceiling of the Sala del Collegio in the Doge's Palace. Tiepolo had shapes more difficult to fill than Veronese had had, but he opted for the same solution of chiefly reclining figures—Faith alone stands, wrapped in voluminous folds of gleaming cream and white—with hints of cornice emerging amid clouds, tilted to convey recession and placed against serenely spacious sky. Unlike Veronese's, these figures are air-borne. Each group is a complete vision, floating in an element beyond the confines of the room.

In their quiet way these paintings are a quintessence of Tiepolo's mature style. Whatever influences he had undergone, they are here totally absorbed. The easy assurance of the foreshortened figures is typical of him, as is the gentle rhythm of their grouping. Their faces are his preferred types: plump, snub-nosed, with heavy-lidded eyes, often turned on the neck to give a sideways rather than direct glance. Drawing still underpins the painting, and everything is crisply detailed, down to the

104. *Humility and other figures,* Scuola del Carmine, Venice.

105. *The Virgin appearing to St Simon Stock,* Scuola del Carmine, Venice.

clasp of a sandal or the cameo adorning a belt. Folds of drapery are also crisply drawn, in the large volumes and firm contours suggestive of the silky-textured yet stiff material that Tiepolo is fond of. The mood is one where even the most severe Virtue appears relaxed. Frankly feminine, palpable and sensuous, the figures are mainly shown bare-limbed and bare-breasted, with a calm hedonism far from the

slyly erotic or the flippant. But they are women before they are personifications, and in their almost luxurious sense of well-being they seem part of a long Venetian tradition, leading back to the sleepy blondes painted by Palma Vecchio, as healthy as they are indolent.

Tiepolo commanded far greater variety of mood than Palma. In the two long, narrow areas running down the sides of the ceiling he turned from allegory to doctrine, illustrating with compressed drama the spiritual and physical salvation that the Carmelite scapular could bring. In the first project he had included the incident of angels raising souls from Purgatory and that of a guardian angel saving a youth who wore the scapular from falling to death. These two scenes he retained, exploiting skilfully the limits of space in the second one, interlacing the angelically fair and plebeianly dark bodies, almost as though they were wrestling, and giving a dizzying angle to the scaffolded building from which the young workman has tumbled.

Not until the central painting was installed, however, could the full pictorial logic of what Tiepolo had planned be appreciated. And its effectiveness is such that the rest of the scheme tends to be ignored. It seems not uncharacteristic of Tiepolo that he should have replaced a painting of the Virgin going up to heaven with one of her coming down to earth. The hall of the Confraternity is privileged to become by extension the site of the vision of St Simon Stock (definitely a saint to its members, even if his actual canonisation is not documented), a central Carmelite story, as much part of the order's claims on devotion as the origin of the rosary for the Dominicans. The Carmelite scapular brought by the Virgin to mankind is Tiepolo's dominant theme, but the real triumph of the composition lies in the Virgin herself, swept from heaven with all the visual excitement of Mozart's Queen of the Night in paint (Pl. 105).

The formal elements of the subject were broadly similar to those of the main fresco on the Gesuati ceiling: a visionary appearance of the Virgin combined with a scene on earth. But whereas in the former there were two series of actions (with the saint engaged in his own distribution of the rosary), at the Scuola del Carmine the vision and its saintly recipient make up a single action, bringing the scene closer to the subsidiary Gesuati fresco of the Virgin appearing to the kneeling St Dominic. Yet the tempo of that composition lacks the heightened impact of the Carmine ceiling, the instantaneous, pictorial roll of thunder which reveals the Virgin at the centre of a cloudburst of flying angels, borne along with such velocity that she needs to place one hand on an angel's head to steady herself in flight. Magically weightless and of hallucinatory tallness, she is poised superbly on the back of the angel to whom is delegated the holding of the lesser scapular, while she effortlessly raises aloft in one hand her Infant Son. This regal personage is Mary, Queen of Angels, as well as the Madonna of Mount Carmel.

Gone are the Prophets originally proposed for the composition. Tiepolo has realised how very much more effective the apparition will be by creating a tight knot or fireball—almost a meteor—compositionally bound up with and subordinated to the Virgin. Before this vision the figure of St Simon Stock is virtually annihilated as he crouches low before it, not daring to look upwards at what his prayer has invoked, hardly conscious of the favour he is being granted. He crouches on a slab of stone jutting up like a spar from the smoky wreck of gaping tombstones, skulls and other bones that litter the foreground. All is murky, unsure and painful, without heaven's aid. Heaven stands for certainty as well as salvation, and nothing could be more certain than Tiepolo's vision of the Virgin and her entourage. They seem to fill the sky with their presence, though in fact occupying comparatively little of it. In a daring manner untypical of, say, Roman baroque compositions, Tiepolo leaves great spaces of sky empty, as if to increase reverberations of the miraculous moment that breaks all natural laws.

The painting is fuelled perhaps by Tiepolo's faith, in addition to his art. As Tintoretto had professed his devotion to 'Messer S. Rocco' when urging the Confraternity of the Scuola di S. Rocco to accept his extensive proposals for decorating its building, so Tiepolo is mentioned as living devoted to the Virgin Mary of Carmel, in a minute of the Confraternity's discussions on 21 December 1739. Clearly he had friends among the leading members, including a certain Francesco Driuzzi, who is named in later minutes as his 'cordial amico'. The devotion of the Confraternity was probably shared by Tiepolo. He certainly appears knowledgeable about Carmelite practices and traditions in connection with the scapular, and in his first proposal had intended to depict Chastity, 'virginal or matrimonial', which was enjoined on members of the Confraternity who wished to gain the privileges of the scapular. What the Confraternity wanted was a work of art 'that ought to remain on display until the end of the world' ('. . . fino al terminar del mondo'), but it was Tiepolo who had shrewdly pointed out how the existing ceiling by Padovanino lacked any allusion to the title of the Confraternity.

Its members were not churchmen or theologians but laymen. However Tiepolo's concept was arrived at, it was a remarkably apt choice, selecting the fundamental scene of Carmelite privilege: the vision to the thirteenth-century English prior-general which traditionally established the scapular. For a Venetian church Tiepolo had painted the Virgin of Mount Carmel some twenty years before (Pl. 21), where both large and small scapular are handed by the Virgin and Child to respectively St Simon Stock and St Andrew Corsini, but the painting is not of St Simon's vision.

That vision and especially the precise guarantee that the Carmelite scapular provided were matters which were by the late seventeenth century causing some unease and even controversy in the Church. The Carmelite scapular was believed to offer release by the Virgin from purgatory of those who had worn it in their lifetime, as Tiepolo strongly implies. He concentrates the eye on the smaller scapular, though the larger one is in the hands of the angel behind St Simon Stock. In presumably its smaller form, the Carmelite scapular—a piece of cloth—was, it seems, the first of such objects to be worn by lay-persons such as composed the Confraternity at Venice. 'You wear it', Bossuet had declared in his *Sermon pour le Jour du Scapulaire*, 'as a visible token of being yourselves Mary's children. . .'[11]

By the 1740s doubts were also being expressed about extreme aspects of the cult of the Virgin, including the feast of the Virgin of Mount Carmel. The famous historian Muratori, a friend of Pope Benedict XIV (elected Pope in 1740), was a prominent critic, and the Pope himself denied the authenticity of a bull of John XXII, who had claimed to have had his own special vision of the Virgin when she singled out the Carmelites for release from purgatory. Benedict XIV accepted the apparition to St Simon Stock. The general pious usage of the scapular was not then or later discouraged, but Tiepolo is far from content with vague notions. He specifically asserts the power of the scapular, in those lateral scenes where a workman's life is saved by an angel bearing it and where souls in purgatory are rescued equally by an angel. Above all, his central composition treats the vision of St Simon Stock as if it were one of the great visions of the Christian faith. The Confraternity had long to wait before Tiepolo finished this painting; he was far less speedy than he had promised, but the wait was worthwhile. When the members were assembled in this chief room, they could look up and see, hovering close at hand, fixed in space, an angel coming earthwards, bearing the small scapular in obedience to the wishes of the Virgin, herself seen in the sky above, swept along on a rush of wings and billowing drapery, with the promise of benevolence as long-lasting as this painted vision: 'until the end of the world'.

During the decade of the 1740s, Tiepolo received some of his most important profane commissions in and around Venice. Important new elements also entered his artistic life in personal terms. Nevertheless, the logic of his creativity leads straight from the Scuola del Carmine commission to another Carmelite task, the

106. *Holy House of Loreto* (destroyed), formerly Scalzi (S. Maria di Nazareth), Venice.

decoration of the nave of S. Maria di Nazareth, the Venetian church of the discalced Carmelites, the Scalzi. There he had been employed, more humbly, on two earlier occasions. Now he was to fresco the sole remaining area undecorated in the handsome and grandiose church, with a further great statement celebrating the Virgin Mary, translated, along with her Child and St Joseph and the holy house they had occupied, from Nazareth to Loreto.[12]

An Austrian bomb destroyed the Scalzi ceiling in 1915. Photographs of it exist (Pl. 106), as does a painted copy, as well as fragments of subsidiary portions of it and two *modelli* for the chief scene itself. Its overwhelming effect, however, has to be guessed at; and its loss is the more to be deplored as the ceiling proved the last of Tiepolo's great religious frescoes on a huge scale and the most majestic of all in its effect.

The contract for the commission was signed on 13 September 1743, before the series of paintings for the Scuola del Carmine had been completed. Tiepolo was given two years in which to finish the Scalzi frescoes. He was responsible for the whole scheme, inclusive of the 'ornamenti e s'occorarà d'architettura', on condition he chose Girolamo Mengozzi Colonna as his collaborator on those portions. The contract laid down that such portions should correspond to the pillars and marbles existing in the church since harmony must prevail between the two.

S. Maria di Nazareth had been built on the Grand Canal in the mid-seventeenth century to the designs of Longhena. More remarkable than its spacious but not particularly exciting interior was the highly elaborate façade of paired columns and statues in niches built in 1672 by Giuseppe Sardi and largely paid for by one of his patrons, the newly ennobled Gerolamo Cavazza. The church was opulently decorated, to the point where its opulence, as the church of an order dedicated to poverty, had to be defended and justified. A complete chapel honoured St Teresa, one of the great Carmelite saints. Only the nave remained undecorated—as Tiepolo must himself have noticed when working previously in the church. On the pillared high altar stood a fifteenth-century panel of the Virgin and Child on the Tree of Jesse, inscribed to the Virgin of Nazareth, and the church had been dedicated on the feast day of the translation of the Holy House. The Carmelites in Venice, and the city generally, cultivated a devotion to the Holy House, though it was not situated on Venetian territory. The Pope elected in 1740, Benedict XIV, fostered further interest and devotion around the Holy House; and in retrospect it seems obvious that, as the nave of S. Maria del Rosario illustrated the church's title, so at S. Maria di Nazareth, the theme of the nave decoration should arise from that title, though it was to be depicted with greater splendour and resonance. Possibly the rapid fame and success of Tiepolo's frescoes in the Gesuati had played a part in the Carmelite decision to have him work comparably in the Scalzi.

For the Scalzi commission he prepared first an oval oil sketch (Pl. 107), in which he stated the basic components of the main fresco. Under the eye of God the Father, a whirling flock of angels accompanies and bears up the Holy House, with the Virgin perched on its roof, virtually filling the sky, while other angels at the right salute its progress with trumpets, and as it flies onward evil figures at the left are suitably crushed. The moment seized by Tiepolo is that of the actual translation of the House, the most miraculous moment of all, when Nazareth lies behind and Loreto is not yet reached. To set a house flying through the air was nothing for an artist who had already filled several heavens and was to do so even more spectacularly in the years ahead.

But this central scene was to be, for all its dominance, only the culmination visually of an extremely elaborate architectual framework, painted by Mengozzi Colonna, creating within his scheme smaller areas for Tiepolo to fresco with Old-Testament incidents related symbolically to the main fresco's theme. Thus the whole vault was decorated, with a variety of shapes and patterns, the central area being

112

delimited by a massive, feigned cornice, seen in the steepest perspective, and a balcony so steeply conveyed that it probably passed unnoticed by the average visitor to the church. This heavy moulding around the central scene of the opened heavens is undoubtedly more Roman than Venetian in style, though in the most obvious examples of Roman baroque ceilings the mouldings are solid and real, with inevitably fewer fantasy elements than Mengozzi Colonna introduced. Nevertheless, illusionism of a highly dramatic kind, with figures flying across and tumbling out of the framework, was achieved at the Scalzi, revealing a new 'baroque' boldness in Tiepolo as well as in his collaborator.

So determined were the Carmelites to provide adequate scope for the two artists that they decide to restructure the vault of the church. Work on it, and then Mengozzi Colonna's decoration, would seem to have occupied much of 1744. After the initial payment in September 1743, Tiepolo was not paid again until April 1745; he received the 'ultimo residuo' on 23 November that year, 'per la pitura [sic] fatta da me nel sofito [sic] della chiesa'.

It may have been partly the reconstructing of the vault, and the subsequent creation of a much longer, narrower shape for his central fresco, that prompted

107. *Holy House of Loreto*, Accademia, Venice.

108. *Holy House of Loreto*, British Rail Pension Fund, on loan to the National Gallery, London.

113

Tiepolo to considerable re-thinking of his first idea. He produced a fresh oil sketch (Pl. 108), of greater freedom and arguably of even greater *élan*, revising all the previous elements with a combination of speed and assurance that seems to vibrate from the canvas. In some areas he simply blocked in coloured shapes on the buff ground, going back to give greater definition by 'pencilling' in black or brown paint over the shapes. In other places, like the mass of writhing bodies at the lower right, he scribbled hastily to convey the effect and did not bother to be more specific. Above all, he clarified the placing of the main portions of the composition and realised that the Holy House, with its surrounding figures, must occupy the central position, upper left, for greater significance and impact. He gave this group greater coherence, shifting some music-making angels into the entourage of God the Father and putting the Infant Christ into the Virgin's embrace. He also tidied up the topmost area, making God the Father a commanding, if tiny, silhouette in the remotest heaven. Suppressed utterly was an angel with a palm who had appeared in the first sketch and who as a motif is interesting in terms of chronology. That figure is very similar to an angel who is shown, far more relevantly, in both the preliminary sketch and the final altarpiece of the *Martyrdom of St John, Bishop of Bergamo*, a commission for Bergamo which Tiepolo undertook in July 1743.

With the Holy House finally placed at the centre of the composition in the Scalzi, Tiepolo was free in his second thoughts to deal with the space released at the lower right. He conceived this as a third, distinct area, to be occupied by evil figures retreating and overthrown before the spectacle of the Holy House advancing, and thus the whole composition gained in force as well as clarity. There was now a strong sense of movement from left to right, with the Holy House triumphantly sweeping all before it as it rocketed through the skies, cheered on, it might almost appear, by God the Father's excited, declamatory gesture of upraised right arm.

No further oil sketch was necessary. The broad solution had been found, and Tiepolo needed only to refine and develop when he came to execute the fresco. This he did, with one area of striking amendment. In the second sketch, the Virgin and Child group might be criticised as insufficiently emphasised. The Virgin's upraised arm—taken over from the earlier sketch—is open to the objection that it duplicates the new pose evolved for God the Father. The fact also that she gazes leftwards, while the whole tug and thrust of the composition is towards the right, makes for a slackening of impetus where it most matters.

For reasons at least as much artistic as religious, Tiepolo created a vast silver disc of full moon which at once isolated and emphasised the profile of the Holy House and the Virgin and Child atop it. He had effectively drawn a circle around them, neatly excluding, it may be noticed, the subsidiary figure of St Joseph. By so doing he also created around them a space of serenity amid so much hectic celestial movement. As for the Virgin, he integrated her body and that of the Christ Child into one compact, tender, ungesturing form, and by a last, inspired touch had her gaze in the direction the Holy House is travelling and thus also down from the ceiling into the church below.

At the four curved corners of the ceiling, there were painted balconies, devised doubtless by Mengozzi Colonna, where worshippers in sixteenth-century costume were painted by Tiepolo, staring upwards in pious awe at the scene taking place overhead. They mediate between that vision and the living worshippers, and are something of a novelty in Tiepolo's work. As such, they have been linked to Bernini's sculpted 'boxes' of spectators of the *Vision of St Teresa*, in the Cornaro chapel at S. Maria della Vittoria in Rome, a sister church of the Scalzi.[13] Nearer at hand was a Venetian precedent in fresco, though of purely profane significance, in the figures on the simulated balcony painted by Veronese in the Sala dell' Olimpo at the Villa Barbaro. Other Venetian villa fresco schemes had echoed that effect: Celesti's frescoes, for example, in the Villa Rinaldi at Casella d'Asolo include a feigned bal-

cony and figures on it.[14] Tiepolo himself had used figures amid painted architecture to frame and lead up to the visionary portion of the *Triumph of the Arts and Sciences* ceiling at the Palazzo Archinto, more than a decade before he worked in the Scalzi. Altogether, it seems unnecessary to invoke Bernini for what was probably part of a typically North-Italian decorative tradition.

Although Roman baroque church ceilings may, in an art-historical context, be ancestors of Tiepolo's unusually elaborate and undoubtedly most magnificent statement of a religious myth, great differences of accent remain between the Roman language and his own, even at the Scalzi. The remarkable thing about Tiepolo's vision there, as elsewhere, is that he does not pack his heaven with serried rows of saints, angels and devils. He avoids centralised effects and likes to compose in clearly formulated, often detached units, with surprising areas of space left between them. The Scalzi ceiling was characterised by no *horror vacui* but quite the opposite. A real sense of aerial spaciousness and atmosphere must have been felt in it, and not the least daring facet of Tiepolo's art—adumbrated as early as the ceiling of the Palazzo Sandi and expressed on a grand scale for the ultimate time in the throne-room ceiling at Madrid—is its love of air and cloud and sky for their own sake.

110. *Continence of Scipio*, Villa Cordellina, Montecchio Maggiore, near Vicenza.

111. *Family of Darius before Alexander*, Villa Cordellina, Montecchio Maggiore, near Vicenza.

Tiepolo was engaged contractually on the Scalzi commission by the autumn of 1743, a year that brought into life a new friend and patron, Count Francesco Algarotti; and it is Algarotti who documented in the same year the first definite activity of 'Tiepolo le fils'—that is, the young Domenico, soon to become the devoted assistant to his father. A devoted assistant of some sort must have been overdue in Tiepolo's now desperately busy existence. It is no wonder that the central oil painting for the Scuola del Carmine was not ready when the rest of the ceiling was unveiled in June 1743. By July Tiepolo was engaged on a ceiling fresco in the Palazzo Pisani Moretta. For this a *modello* of beautiful quality survives, in which, in tones of golden-buff and fawn, against a blue sky, a hero (probably the great Vettor Pisani, a naval hero of the distant past) is conducted by Venus to Olympus.[15] Tiepolo had also commissions from Algarotti for oil paintings. He had the altarpiece of the *Martyrdom of St John, Bishop of Bergamo* to undertake. And in the autumn he was hard at work executing frescoes in the villa of Carlo Cordellina, near Vicenza.

Confident of his physical powers and undiminished energy, Tiepolo, as he approached fifty, seems to have been not merely unflustered by a plethora of commissions but voracious in seeking, or accepting, fresh ones. It is as though he hated to turn down any opportunity to paint. He was prepared to execute a canvas of the combined arms of the Sagredo and Barbaro families.[16] He was prepared to paint a portrait of someone he had never seen, the sixteenth-century scholar of Rovigo, Antonio Riccobono (Pl. 109), whose portrait was one of a series commissioned from various painters by the local Accademia dei Concordi. The result could scarcely rank as one of his finest works, but it is far from perfunctory. Fluent, fluid brushwork conveys the textures of skin, fur, linen and leather. The head itself, with its slightly anxious expression, is modelled with a keen response to the wrinkles and veins that makes it a convincingly human image, the more striking since it is presumably an imaginary portrayal. The pose, within a feigned oval, may derive from Rembrandt's etchings of scholars and preachers (the oval etching, for example, of Jan Uytenbogaert),[17] but Tiepolo makes a miniature drama out of Riccobono's confrontation with the spectator, recalling another Northern portrait, that of Lucas van Uffelen by Van Dyck (in the Metropolitan Museum, New York). There is also a drama of light and shade which points directly back to Rembrandt's influence.

The *Riccobono* fits very well with a marked tendency in Tiepolo's profane work of the mid-1740s to be concerned with history, often Roman history, rather than mythology. No doubt the tendency was caused by the accident of commissions, but the result was to establish a very distinct idiom. It reaches its highest point in Venice with the Cleopatra and Antony frescoes in the Palazzo Labia, and they are followed shortly afterwards by the summons to Würzburg, to fresco the German historical scenes in the Kaisersaal. The idiom found its first large-scale expression, however, in the frescoes for the central ground-floor salone of the newly built Villa Cordellina at Montecchio Maggiore.[18]

The villa is a compact building, placed in flat countryside, with a Palladian, classical façade, the frontispiece of Ionic columns, attributed to Massari, the architect of the Gesuati. Construction of the villa seems to have begun in or around 1735 and it continued long after Tiepolo's frescoes were finished. The owner was a distinguished lawyer, Carlo Cordellina, slightly younger than Tiepolo and destined to outlive him by over twenty years. He had moved into the villa and was entertaining there certainly by the autumn of 1743. By then Tiepolo was at work on the frescoes and was conscious—as he wrote to Algarotti—of the agreeable distractions provided by the villa. According to this letter, dated 26 October, he was well advanced on the ceiling fresco and hoped to finish it no later than 10 or 12 November.[19] Apart from that, there were two large lateral frescoes to execute, and it must be supposed that completion of them took place in 1744.

The scheme required two famous and comparable subjects from ancient history on the walls—the Continence of Scipio and the Family of Darius before Alexander—and a related allegorical composition occupying the main area of the ceiling. These two figures, of Virtue and probably Nobility, embrace, while their union is celebrated by trumpeting Fame and a hag symbolising Ignorance is vanquished. Thus the heroic aspects of Scipio and Alexander being celebrated are not their great deeds as soldiers but their behaviour as human beings. By suppressing baser qualities they conquer, in effect, themselves. In positions of supreme power they are generous and merciful to their enemies. Carlo Cordellini did not associate himself vain-gloriously with the past when he had Alexander and Scipio depicted in his villa. He probably intended to preach a moral lesson as patently as had Count Loschi in his villa, but to do it in terms less of allegory than of history. It is perhaps no accident, given Cordellina's profession, that both heroes are virtually judging cases, listening to evidence or hearing a plea.

The room at the Villa Cordellina is very high and decorated with light stucco pilasters, cartouches and scrolls, restrained yet elegant trills of ornament against expanses of plain wall, in an idiom that might be characterised as rococo classicism. And to some extent, that is also Tiepolo's idiom here. The two lateral frescoes are conceived very much as severely framed paintings on the wall, with no *quadratura* settings of the kind Mengozzi Colonna specialised in and with no daring perspectives. They might almost be two huge tapestries hanging there. The ceiling decoration has its own restraint. No attempt is made to link it compositionally to the frescoes below, and indeed it remains in every way remote and unarresting.

Like the frescoes on the walls, and to a far greater degree, it has suffered from damp, so that its somewhat pale presence today is an accident. Yet perhaps from the first it suffered as well from some perfunctoriness. Tiepolo may have found it hard to concentrate in a social environment and under pressure to finish before the coming of the winter. For once, what seems vivid and satisfactory in the *modello* failed to expand on the scale of the eventual fresco. The expanse of sky that he knew how to make so meaningful, without the aid of figures, is here just an expanse of emptiness. On the walls, however, his imagination was engaged with his subjects and with the style of the room. He was returning to themes of ancient history with quite new ideas for presentation of them, compared to his earlier treatments in both fresco and oil. Dignity was now to be stressed, and though eager as ever to create a sense of 'theatre', he seems to prefer static or at least very stately scenes, borrowing every device of grandeur from Veronese and almost stifling emotion under the sheer splendour of his slow-moving personages who appear fully aware of performing under public gaze.

Most unusually, there survive the three *modelli* for the three chief areas of fresco, though unfortunately in three different countries. They show close similarities in handling, typical of Tiepolo's vivacity and assurance in the 1740s. The compositions are established rapidly yet with total certitude.

In the brilliantly fresh ceiling sketch (Pl. 112) Tiepolo marked out the appropriate shape of the composition within the decorative framework. The dimensions of the wall frescoes were perhaps not settled so exactly at the date the sketches were done. The eventual frescoes are wider than they are high, but in the sketches there is a strong vertical emphasis. It may have mattered very little to Tiepolo by this stage of his career. He had grasped to his own satisfaction not only the general disposition of each scene—which would not alter—but also the elements that made it up. Expanding or retracting, but preferably expanding, presented no problem. Still nobler architecture, a higher throne, a longer train for a dress—such were the very embellishments of the original concept that he probably hoped to have the opportunity to introduce.

Suppression no less than expansion could aid an effect. One shift in particular at the Villa Cordellina is, though slight, revealing. In the sketch for the *Continence of*

112. *Fame celebrating the union of Virtue and Nobility,* Dulwich Picture Gallery, London

113 (following page). Detail of Pl. 111.

Scipio he placed prominently at the foot of Scipio's throne a black and white pet spaniel of the kind found in *Apelles painting Campaspe* (Pl. 26). This animal has been omitted from the fresco, possibly because it seemed on reflection incongruous and even rather trivial in such a scene of lofty emotion. But it has been introduced into the fresco of the *Family of Darius before Alexander*, developed from a mere hint in the preliminary sketch where *a* dog can just be glimpsed at the extreme left, distracting the sole boy in the sad group of the Persian royal family as they kneel at Alexander's feet. Wriggling its way back into the fresco composition of this subject, the dog becomes neither over-prominent or irrelevant. It helps to strengthen a minute piece of psychological drama. As the youngest person among the defeated, imploring Persians, the boy scarcely comprehends the grave adult world around him and reacts instead to the incursion of something animated, domestic and natural into a situation otherwise of stiff panoply and grief.

Neither of the two main scenes at the Villa Cordellina (Pls 110 and 111) was a novel one for depiction, especially in Venetian painting. One of the most famous paintings in eighteenth-century Venice was Veronese's great *Family of Darius before Alexander*, then in the Palazzo Pisani-Moretta, where Tiepolo frescoed a ceiling in the early 1740s. The Continence of Scipio had been the subject of sixteenth-century frescoes in North-Italian villas and, closer to Tiepolo's day, had been a popular subject in Sebastiano Ricci's *œuvre*, paired on one occasion with the scene of the family of Darius before Alexander.[20] In Ricci's treatments of the Scipio scene, of which some six exist, there is one constant: the betrothed girl is always shown respectfully and gratefully kneeling before the hero.

That is only one of the marked differences between Ricci's and Tiepolo's treatment of the theme. Tiepolo had of course depicted the subject at the Palazzo Casati in Milan. Another composition by him on the theme of Scipio, paired with a *Triumph of Julius Caesar* by Bambini (who had died in 1736), is recorded in 1760 in a private palace at Brescia.[21] For Tiepolo the betrothed girl is no passive figure. Both at the Palazzo Casati and at the Villa Cordellina, she effectively dominates the scene, not merely standing but, in the latter, advancing towards Scipio in the full consciousness of being a heroine and a very great personage, whose retinue of pages, women and warriors would scarcely suggest anyone conquered. Before her allure and her effortless air of superiority it is Scipio who yields, as much under her spell as is patently her fiancé.

At first glance, the Villa Cordellina fresco seems not radically different from that of the Palazzo Casati, and the two compositions are indeed broadly similar, with Scipio enthroned at the left and the pair of lovers posed at the right, and in both frescoes the setting is vaguely Palladian. Yet in terms of style and presentation there are considerable differences. If something endearing, idiosyncratic and almost eccentric has gone from the later treatment, where vivacity is more controlled, just as the composition is better organised, there is a powerful, compensating sense of the painter's art matured. The figures are less highly individualised: they have settled into being the types Tiepolo is most fond of, and they too have matured in the sense that they move at a slower tempo and adopt poses of greater dignity. Spring, metaphorically, has given place to high summer.

The volumes of the very clothes seem larger, suitably for the larger stage at the Villa Cordellina, where grandeur and ceremony make the scenes true *opera seria*, with no place for burlesque or ironic touches. The architectual elements are far grander too, developed well beyond the suggestions of the *modelli* (Pls 115 and 116), but with a calm grandeur—visually emphasised by the long horizontals of the screen-like background buildings. The painted architecture derives from Veronese, much as Massari's real architecture derives from Palladio. Both Massari and Tiepolo see the antique past through thoroughly sixteenth-century eyes (indeed, they here become, as it were, the Palladio and Veronese of their own period). In explaining his

114 (preceding page). Detail of Pl. 110.

use of the frontispiece for domestic architecture, Palladio had invoked ancient practice: it denoted the entrance to a house, but also it greatly added 'to the grandeur and magnificence of the work'. Massari clearly agreed, and in his own idiom Tiepolo is saying much the same.

For the *Family of Darius before Alexander* Tiepolo was indebted, in an unusually close way, to Veronese's great painting. Only the motif of the gigantic tent was a major variation (and even that might have come to him via the engraving of Lebrun's famous painting of the same subject). It may be that he could not shake off his awareness of what Veronese had achieved, but more likely he—and Carlo Cordellina as well perhaps—intended a conscious homage to the earlier masterpiece. How deeply it had permeated his thinking is indicated by the incident of the boy and the dog, which appears to go back obscurely in inspiration to the dwarf clutching a dog and apprehensive of the pet monkey, which Veronese introduced at the extreme left of his composition. There one of the pair of Persian slaves puts a reassuring hand round the dwarf—in a moment of instinctive humanity, away from the tension and public drama being played out by the chief figures—and the total effect is not dissimilar from that in Tiepolo's fresco, where a grandmotherly old lady has her hand round the lively boy (Pl. 113).

Where in both frescoes Tiepolo oddly failed, or failed to be much interested, was

123

in the figures of Scipio and Alexander. It is as if he felt they were too absurdly heroic for him. Given every advantage of splendid setting and costume, they still fail to hold their own in terms of conviction. Alexander especially, with his rigid bearing and distinctly unimpressive physique, might be the castrato of this *opera seria*: assertive, even arrogant but slightly ludicrous amid the firmly characterised, robust, bearded baritones and the impressive range of sopranos who yet all depend on him. Tiepolo's tendency to fail in presenting heroic men is paralleled in Boucher's art, and perhaps partly for the same reason. Women and the role of women seem to both painters far more attractive to deal with in paint; and that attitude was not drastically to be challenged by the eighteenth century until the arrival of David.

In the *Continence of Scipio*, it is not only the leading female figure who takes the eye as she sails proudly on, a galleon fully rigged in bravura style, but also her attendant women, curious and a little more gracefully animated than she, and no less beautiful (Pl. 114). They appear before Scipio in robes tinted mauvish pink and orange, but her own clothes are more exquisite still, in colour pale olive and greenish gold, with a standing collar of white to her cloak, its lining apricot and its buoyant exterior of balloon-like, silky folds palest lilac. For all its airiness, this cloak has to be borne by two negro pages in light-blue tunics, while her fiancé is beside her in pine-green, furred robes, his hand on his heart, his eyes turned lovingly towards her, enhancing the sense she conveys of feminine allure.

Before Alexander, in the opposite scene, there kneels a group of women, aged and youthful, bare-breasted or more decorously clad, but all richly dressed, exotic and royal. In sunny weather, in the aftermath of a battle that has left no wounds but just the picturesque paraphernalia of lances and lazily flapping banners of rose-pink and cream, these ladies—as they essentially are—appeal to the magnanimous conqueror as to the spectator. They occupy the centre of the composition, kneeling and pleading in a way that is not seriously distressing, nor humiliating, but ultimately fitting and triumphant. They touch Alexander's heart, and again the male is conquered by the female, as Tiepolo and much of his century believed men should be.

Tiepolo's vision of history has crystallised in the Villa Cordellina frescoes into something very firm and clear, from which all Piazzetta-style 'reality' has been banished. The past is seen as a world of frank beauty, as well as of nobility and great grandeur. Sometimes it is supposed that the Cordellina frescoes show a new seriousness in Tiepolo's attitude to classical antiquity and that for it he is indebted to the influence of his new friend, Count Francesco Algarotti. Algarotti certainly owned Tiepolo's *modello* for the *Family of Darius before Alexander* and at this period was closely involved with Tiepolo, using him in a variety of ways. But both men, both after all Venetian, admired the work of Veronese; and it is he who is in the ascendant in these frescoes. Tiepolo seems to have deepened his understanding of Veronese, and perhaps also his understanding of the nature of his own art.

Yet at the Villa Cordellina, for all Tiepolo's accomplishment, the task is not quite fulfilling enough. The matured style and mood of high glamour seem to ask for more ambitious expression, not with more learning but with more open sensuousness and even extravagance. Only a step away lie the frescoes for the Palazzo Labia, positively anticipated here and there in a pose or a device or the character of a head. Those frescoes are the summation of all that is adumbrated by the ones at the Villa Cordellina.

The period of working at Montecchio Maggiore was a significant one for Tiepolo in personal as well as artistic terms. The year 1743 was marked by his meeting Algarotti and by speedy establishment of their friendship. It is also the year in which there emerges—thanks in part to Algarotti—as active and at Tiepolo's side his eldest son, Domenico. Following faithfully in his father's footsteps, Algarotti noted of the sixteen-year-old, promising artist; and faithful Domenico would remain for the rest of his father's life.

6 THE FRIEND AND THE SON

TIEPOLO HAD enjoyed far greater patronage than Count Francesco Algarotti was ever able to offer him, either on his own behalf or as an intermediary. Yet rarely, if at all, had Tiepolo's patrons been his friends. Nor does it seem that he had much contact with the learned, literate world. It is true that the scholar and antiquarian Scipione Maffei had praised his work in connection with Maffei's *Verona Illustrata*, but the commission was in itself a modest one and the commissioner did not live in Venice.

Tiepolo was never to have a friendship comparable to that of Piazzetta with the gifted printer and collector Giambattista Albrizzi, devoted to Piazzetta living, and keeping alive his memory after the artist's death. Tiepolo had no dominant patron of the kind Canaletto had in Joseph Smith. Nor did any Venetian literary figure of Goldoni's stature address to him a poem of the kind Goldoni addressed to Pietro Longhi, claiming an artistic affinity prompted by his Muse and beginning 'Longhi, tu che la mia musa sorella/chiami. . .'[1]

It may be that Tiepolo's character and his circumstances—and the nature of his art —did not require, or encourage, close friendships, exclusive patronage or even literary salutes. However it had been, the arrival of Algarotti in his life was a novelty, and a welcome one. He will certainly not have met anyone quite like Algarotti before. Nor had Algarotti, for all his cosmopolitan experiences and his social mobility (worthy of any character devised by Proust), met before and become friendly with a painter of genius. To his pictorial gifts Tiepolo added those of character—amiability and extreme obligingness—which Algarotti quickly came to value almost as highly. Also, Tiepolo's relations with noble Venetian families were to prove useful to him.

In May 1743 Algarotti arrived back in Venice (where in 1712 he had been born) on an important artistic mission: to acquire paintings for the collection being built up at Dresden by Augustus III, King of Poland and Elector of Saxony. The responsibilities and the difficulties were considerable—more considerable, probably, than Algarotti at first realised—though he was quick and clever, wonderfully self-confident intellectually and genuinely interested in most manifestations of culture. He had been educated, but above all he had educated himself, not least by travel and by meeting people. And on meeting him, people were charmed.

He was the younger son of a rich Venetian merchant.[2] He had travelled widely— to Paris and London and Berlin, and also to Russia—without quite arriving or settling anywhere. He had met Voltaire. He had been found appealing by both Lady Mary Wortley Montagu and Lord Hervey. Frederick the Great, as Crown Prince of Prussia, had made a close friend of him and called him the swan of Padua, though as king he wrote complaining of Algarotti as 'cigne le plus inconstant'. Still, he had created out of the swan a count. Algarotti dabbled in all kinds of literary and scientific and artistic matters. He flitted intellectually as he flitted, and flirted, socially. He could not become attached to any one idea or person or place. Hyper-activity seems to have alternated with bursts of illness which gradually worsened. The last years of his life were spent virtually as an invalid, living retired at Pisa where he died in 1764.

From Berlin he moved to the court of Dresden. There the Elector, who had succeeded his father Augustus the Strong in 1733, was intent on assembling great art treasures, and his interests were shared by his chief minister, Count Brühl. The highly cultivated Elector had visited Venice before his succession, had an ambassador and agents in the city and commissioned work from Rosalba, for example. What he planned, and what Algarotti was intended to help form, was a collection of old-master paintings. It was Algarotti who proposed that the collection should extend to living artists, and by no means merely Venetian ones (Solimena and Panini were on his list of desirable artists, and so was Boucher). For Venice he reported that the leading representatives were Piazzetta, Pittoni and 'Tiepoletto'. After that trio came Amigoni, Fontebasso and Gaspare Diziani. He also listed the principal fresco painters of Italy, starting with Tiepolo and adding Giaquinto in Naples and 'un certo Bigaro' who worked in Bologna.

Considering how little time he had spent in Italy, Algarotti was remarkably well informed, through, no doubt, a whole series of contacts, including his brother Bonomo at Venice and probably Anton Maria Zanetti the elder ('fameux connoisseur et mon ami', he was to declare in a letter from Venice to Brühl). The visual arts were an area where Algarotti had more than a superficial interest. His own taste seems naturally to have been for Venetian art; he responded to Veronese and to Palladio, and had a fondness for picturesqueness in painting. Some aspects of contemporary Venetian painting—Tiepolo's work most obviously, when he encountered it—he responded to instinctively and enthusiastically. At the same time, he was too up-to-date to be unaware that it was open to the criticism, increasingly to be heard, that it was not sufficiently dignified or 'learned'. He was prepared to defend it, though sometimes on the dubious grounds that the addition of some erudite allusion or object had elevated its tone. Thus he was led into writing of Tiepolo's large oil painting of the *Banquet of Cleopatra* (Pl. 118) that it showed the 'learning' of Raphael and Poussin, when it palpably did not, nor was intended to. Algarotti knew how to make all the right neo-classic, scholarly noises, but seems to have been expressing what he really felt when he claimed to possess 'the most beautiful Punchinello drawings in the world', by Tiepolo.[3]

Before leaving Dresden in 1743, Algarotti had summed up the trio of history painters to be commissioned at Venice. He referred to Tiepolo without any particular emphasis, merely as 'pittore di macchia' ('painter of sketches') and as 'spiritoso'. The words mean so little that it seems probable Algarotti had only very faint ideas of what a painting by Tiepolo looked like. The pallid characterisation is in contrast to what he wrote about Piazzetta: 'a great draughtsman and a good colourist, but has little elegance of form or expression'. Indeed, he may have anticipated becoming friendly with Piazzetta and finding an ally in him. When it came to selecting a subject for Piazzetta to paint for Dresden, Algarotti typically chose an antique historical one, but an obscure one, Caesar with the pirates of Cilicia, that would permit a certain amount of uncouthness in the pirates. Rough and masculine and forceful—whether it showed Caesar fallen into the pirates' hands or his later punishment of them—the subject altogether seems to have been skilfully calculated to match Piazzetta's artistic character.

It seems likely that neither Algarotti or Tiepolo had any particular anticipation of friendship when, at last, having been held in quarantine in Verona, Algarotti reached Venice full of his mission. Yet the relationship they rapidly established remained in being, even if inevitably less close, right up to the early 1760s. As late as 1761, the year before Tiepolo left Italy for Spain, the two of them were in correspondence over a 'Gran Ritratto' on which Tiepolo was working. The lost portrait included a prominent figure of Victory and cannot have been, as sometimes supposed, a portrait of Algarotti; it is far more probable that it depicted Frederick the Great,[4] to whom Algarotti thus continued to express devotion and who was to pay for Algarotti's monument when he died three years later. Perhaps for no other patron would Tiepolo have worked on—even though possibly never completing—a large-scale, semi-allegorical portrait of a living person he had never seen.

For Tiepolo in 1743 Algarotti chose an equally ambitious but thoroughly literary subject, Timotheus, or the Effects of Music. The choice alone reveals how basically theoretical Algarotti's concepts tended to be. He had found a *recherché* subject, novel in so far as probably no painter had attempted it before and extremely demanding in its requirement of translating the effects of one art into another. Algarotti's own interest in the subject may well have been prompted by awareness of Dryden's poem 'Alexander's Feast or The Power of Musique', sharpened perhaps by awareness that Tiepolo was treating the subject of Alexander at the Villa Cordellina around this very date. Algarotti was, after all, to own Tiepolo's *modello* for that fresco. It seems natural enough that he should feel that another, far more recondite subject from the story of Alexander, the scene that follows his encounter with the family of his defeated enemy, would be highly suitable; and in this, the conqueror of Darius, celebrating success with a feast and moved by the playing of Timotheus on the lyre, would be conquered, melting into the arms of Thaïs seated beside him: 'The vanquish'd Victor sank upon her Breast'.

For the painting, Algarotti drew up an elaborate programme which seemed to offer opportunities for the greatest visual pomp: a magnificent room as the setting, Alexander, 'dressed with all the luxury of Asia', his captains around, with musicians and a variety of women and old men, and Timotheus in the centre, striking his lyre. A good deal was expected of the painter, since Algarotti envisaged Alexander shown affected by the sweetness of Timotheus' song and revealing his response in his 'trembling and lustful eyes'. A few characteristically erudite touches completed the programme, including the fact that Alexander's head would be based on medals. Yet, once again, Algarotti could not conceal his instinctive response to Tiepolo's style and to native Venetian tradition. The ornaments and the expressions, he wrote, would all be agreeably generated from the 'feconda fantasia' of Tiepolo, who had brought back to life the grace and charm 'and all the magnificence of the great Paolo Veronese'.

The tone is much more enthusiastic than that Algarotti had used when writing of Tiepolo before his return to Venice—more enthusiastic and more knowledgeable. Whatever Algarotti's defects, slowness to absorb was not among them. He came, saw and was conquered by Tiepolo's art. It could be far more suitably located in the Venetian tradition than Piazzetta's, and there was also the convenience that Algarotti was planning to acquire at least one Veronese for Dresden. Tiepolo's study of Veronese would make him the best of all experts to give an opinion, while one of his own paintings would effectively confirm how the tradition lived on in a modern exponent. And in choosing the subject he had for Tiepolo, Algarotti might pride himself that he had given the artist all he could wish for: a dramatic subject occurring at a feast, a noble hero and opportunities for the maximum 'fantasia' in terms of Asiatic luxury.

Yet the fact is that Tiepolo never painted the subject. No more is heard of it. A totally new subject was chosen, of Caesar presented with the head of Pompey, and for that composition no programme survives. While it is unclear what precisely had happened, it seems obvious that Tiepolo showed no enthusiasm to paint 'The Effects of Music' and perhaps disliked the elaborate scenario drawn up by Algarotti. Still thinking about antique rulers—the painting was destined for a ruler called Augustus—Algarotti took another episode from the life of Julius Caesar. It may not have been ideal for Tiepolo but it had a fairly exotic setting, Alexandria, and it offered an opportunity for a strong emotional effect which Algarotti was probably eager to see embodied. Possibly quite consciously, he also set up a mild form of competition between Tiepolo and Piazzetta, each to depict an incident from Caesar's life.

Both paintings were ultimately produced, but both are lost. Nothing is known of Piazzetta's composition. Of Tiepolo's a record of a kind survives in an old photograph of the *modello* he painted.[5] This does not suggest that a masterpiece was created. Algarotti had carefully indicated that the scene took place 'in una piazza di Alessandria', but apart from a slim pyramid or obelisk in the distance, Tiepolo seems to have been unconcerned with conveying Egypt. A rather stiff-looking *mannequin* Caesar stands with one hand on his hip, the other holding up his cloak presumably at the sight of Pompey's head, surrounded by Tiepolo's usual chorus of onlookers in Roman armour and oriental costume. Beside the kneeling man offering the head on a platter appears a typical Tiepolo hound—an unlearned, slightly casual note which may have been suppressed in the final painting. Various elements in the *modello* link up with work Tiepolo was doing around the same period. The figure of Caesar is similar in style to that of Alexander at the Villa Cordellina, though differently posed. The motif of a white horse, seen in profile, arching its neck, seems to be borrowed from the Verolanuova *Gathering of the Manna*; it was also to re-appear in one of Tiepolo's sketches for an Alexandrian-Roman subject he would make very much his own, the *Banquet of Cleopatra*.

Thanks to Algarotti's letters and account books, the period at which Tiepolo was engaged on the *Caesar presented with the head of Pompey* can be fixed with some exactitude. On 9 August 1743 Algarotti informed Count Brühl at Dresden that the subject had been settled on as Tiepolo's contribution, without offering any reason for the dropping of the previous subject. On 5 March 1744 Tiepolo received a first payment, possibly in connection with the *modello*. The painting itself was not finished, may even not have been started, in July, when Algarotti reported on how matters stood. Only on 26 February 1746 did Tiepolo receive a final payment, following completion of the work.

Algarotti was at least partly responsible for diverting Tiepolo's energies by giving him a more urgent and personal commission. Delighted by the accommodating attitude of the artist, whose friendship he now felt he had, he decided to have him paint a pair of smaller canvases that would be gifts from Algarotti to Brühl. Not so much learned as topical and flattering references were inserted into each composition. One of the pair was a vaguely mythological *Triumph of Flora*, a faintly Frenchified painting of the nearly naked goddess bowling through an enchanted garden in her chariot. She is distributing flowers and fertility not indiscriminately but in the direction specifically of Brühl. It was in the grounds of his country-house, Palais Marcolini, on the outskirts of Dresden, that there stood the Neptune fountain by Lorenzo Mattielli. He was a sculptor Algarotti had met in Dresden, and it was his sculpture that Tiepolo introduced into the realm of Flora.[6]

The other painting was more narrowly focused, almost 'political' in its subject and aim. It showed rather fancifully Maecenas presenting the Arts to Augustus (Pl. 117). The Palladian setting, like the Emperor's throne, is loosely derived from the Cordellina *Continence of Scipio*, and though Augustus is no portrait, the strongly individualised profile of Maecenas seems based on the outsize bust traditionally identified as of him. That suggests Algarotti's anxiety for the authentic detail, but of more concern to him was the contemporary application to be made, equating Maecenas with Brühl. Beyond blind Homer standing for Poetry (he it is who is intended by the half-oriental old man, with a stick and a boy-guide), and through the Palladian-style archway, is seen the façade of Brühl's Dresden palace, with its hanging gardens over the Elbe (the Brühlsche Terrasse of today). Presumably Algarotti had brought back to Venice, or rapidly obtained, sketches for Tiepolo to utilise; and the two insertions of modern subject-matter into such paintings are a testimony both to Tiepolo's ingenuity and to his willingness to oblige Algarotti.

The gift was not quite disinterested. What Algarotti sought, via Brühl, was the title from the Elector of 'Sur Intendant des Batiments et Cabinets du Roi'—a sort of subsidiary portfolio, as it were, in a Ministry for the Arts. His plea would surely not go unheeded, he wrote, if Maecenas intervened. He had already explained about commissioning the paintings and been thanked in rather measured tones by Brühl, stating that the paintings ought to be generally praised, if the painter was skilful enough to follow Algarotti's concepts ('Si le peintre, comme je n'en doute pas, est assez habile, pour executer Vos idées . . . ces tableaux ne manqueront pas d'etre generalement aplaudis [sic]'.)[7] Brühl duly received the paintings, though it is not established when, but he had already regretted, politely yet firmly, that no title was forthcoming for Algarotti. And after two or three years of activity and interest on behalf of Dresden, Algarotti found a convenient opportunity to resign his post with no sense of loss. He had had a *rapprochement* with Frederick the Great and was able to write to Brühl from Potsdam, expatiating on Frederick's generosity (a pension, a key as royal chamberlain and the order of merit) in a pointed though still polite manner.

In and around 1743, he still felt enthusiastic about the Dresden court. Tiepolo was to prove himself 'assez habile' in more ways than one, and his patently friendly feelings must have been very welcome as the problems of Algarotti's commission accumulated. Not everyone probably approved of the export from Venice of what would now be called 'heritage' items. With those owners who were prepared to sell there were often difficulties over price and conditions. Other representatives of the Saxon court in Venice, including the ambassador, were not very well disposed towards Algarotti, who obviously felt his own position was uncertain.

Tiepolo's expertise was a comfort and could be cited when paintings came into Algarotti's purview. Tiepolo was, Brühl was informed, particularly ecstatic about a Veronese *Rape of Europa*, which later scholarship has recognised as no more than studio work. It may well have been Tiepolo's long-standing connections with the Dolfin family which facilitated Algarotti's success in acquiring what then passed as

118. *Banquet of Cleopatra*, National Gallery of Victoria, Melbourne.

119. *Banquet of Cleopatra*, Musée Cognac-Jay, Paris.

120. Detail of Pl. 118.

Holbein's original of the Meyer Madonna, hanging in the Dolfin palace—a painting that was also to be demoted, in time, to the status of a copy. For his help in that affair Algarotti made a special present to Tiepolo.

One of his ideas was that a group of living artists should copy a group of old-master paintings, each assigned to the artist with the greatest affinity for the work and style. Tiepolo should copy Veronese's *Family of Darius*—and it might be said that he had virtually done so in the Villa Cordellina fresco. It was while working there in the autumn of 1743 that Tiepolo, on his side, expressed his feelings, writing that he would have preferred, to all the villa's considerable distractions, spending a day talking 'di pittura' with Algarotti. That may be courteous exaggeration, but nevertheless it shows that Algarotti's frank boast of having Tiepolo's friendship was no empty one. And soon this friendship resulted in Algarotti's involvement over execution of a major painting by Tiepolo, in circumstances that sound unusual and which remain partly baffling.

On 31 January 1744 Algarotti gave Brühl news of a painting by Tiepolo he had ordered for Augustus of Saxony. It represented the *Banquet of Cleopatra and Antony*. It was a painting Tiepolo had begun some time before, 'pour d'autres'. The implication is strongly that it was in Tiepolo's studio, unfinished and apparently free to be disposed of. At Algarotti's instigation, the painter was, however, prepared to finish

it, 'pour sa majesté'. Indeed, it would be finished shortly. And so it proved; in March Tiepolo received payment for it.

Algarotti's reference is the earliest known mention of Tiepolo in connection with the Cleopatra and Antony theme. However, there is a Tiepolo drawing of the subject, bearing the date 1743, and altogether it seems likely that he was giving a good deal of thought to the theme in that year. Drawings, *modelli* and large-scale oil paintings, as well as the Palazzo Labia frescoes themselves, testify to a great deal of activity—of an unparalleled kind—in illustrating the lovers' story. It is not very probable that Algarotti prompted this—or he would have said so. But he benefited from it and got involved in it. The subject extends well beyond him and requires a chapter to itself; yet it is he, after all, who first introduces it into the Tiepolo literature, as it were, starting off with the puzzling allusion to 'd'autres'.

The painting he had had finished for Dresden is the *Banquet of Cleopatra* (Pl. 118), now at Melbourne. Large, highly elaborate and obviously autograph, this is not a painting that a patron would normally leave on the artist's hands—unless, of course, he died. The style of the painting suggests that Tiepolo did not begin it much before 1743 (certainly not before 1740); it cannot have lain around unfinished for long and its handling is entirely homogeneous.

If the original commissioner was dead, Tiepolo was doubtless free to dispose of it. If, as is sometimes supposed, he finished for Algarotti a painting destined for another patron, for whom he had then to paint a substitute, he was behaving curiously: he might as well have painted the second version for Algarotti, who could have simply told Brühl that he had ordered a painting of Cleopatra and Antony from Tiepolo for the King.

Algarotti came to possess a small painting of the subject of Cleopatra's banquet by Tiepolo, which he described as intended to serve as *modello* for the large scale one and which does indeed broadly correspond (Pl. 119). Yet it is far too highly finished to be a true *modello* in the sense of a preparatory sketch of the kind Tiepolo usually produced, at least where frescoes were concerned. In finish it is closer to such a

121. F. Algarotti, *Various heads*, Staatliche Museum, Kupferstichkabinett, Berlin.

122. *Bath of Diana*, E. G. Bührle Collection, Zurich.

modello as that for the *St Clement* altarpiece (Pl. 77). But, unlike that, it is by no means faithfully followed in the large-scale composition, and Algarotti should not be taken too literally in what is anyway not a categoric statement. A carefully executed 'first idea' for the composition might be nearer the facts.

A minor mystery surrounds this small painting. It seems to have been in or by 1743 that it was engraved by Pietro Monaco as the *Banquet of Nabal* (suppressing the pearl held by Cleopatra) so that it could appear in a book he was publishing of engravings entirely of religious subjects. In its first state, before numbering of the plates, the engraving gives the owner as Joseph Smith. By the time the book was published, the ownership had changed: the painting was shown as in Algarotti's possession. He retained it for the rest of his life and bequeathed it in his will to a certain Cosimo Mari.[8] Sometimes it has been thought that Smith's earlier ownership indicates that it is he who lies behind Algarotti's reference to the big painting's being destined for 'd'autres'. On that hypothesis, Smith gives up—at Algarotti's wish—commissioning the painting, perhaps helped by receiving a sum of money instead. Yet Smith, who retained no paintings or drawings by Tiepolo in his extensive collection, is hardly likely to have ordered a large-scale *Banquet of Cleopatra* from him for himself; were he acting for others, he is even less likely to have been persuaded to surrender the painting.

The solution to the puzzling aspect of the origin of the Melbourne *Banquet of Cleopatra* remains to be found, but any fresh hypothesis takes its place best in consideration of Tiepolo's treatment of the Cleopatra and Antony theme. Algarotti, whatever he later wrote, cannot really have thought the Melbourne *Banquet* particularly learned—and it is unlikely that he intervened much to try to make it so. He seems to have accepted, for instance, the bizarre, bearded Oriental who makes a third at the table with Cleopatra and Antony, as a suitable depiction of Lucius Plancus, certainly recorded as present but someone who was as Roman in reality as Antony, in fact joint-Consul with him. Gauging the nature of his correspondent, Algarotti stressed the erudite, Egyptian elements of the painting when writing to the scholarly French connoisseur and collector Mariette, conscious also, no doubt, that Mariette's countrymen tended to feel considerable reserve about Tiepolo's work.

It may be thanks to Algarotti that in the composition for Dresden a sphinx fountain was introduced into the foreground at the left, in place of a table in the so-called *modello*. But the total effect remains resolutely un-Egyptian. And at this period Algarotti amused himself by trying his hand at etching (Pl. 121), very much under Tiepolo's influence[9] and possibly guidance; fanciful heads, half-eastern and half-Roman, profiles and mask-like decorations were his subject-matter, patently inspired by Tiepolo, almost wistfully capricious and thoroughly Venetian. Dabbling not very competently in a difficult medium, virtually doodling, and definitely having an intellectual holiday, Algarotti reveals his natural artistic preferences. Here, far from guiding Tiepolo, he gladly yields to being guided by him.

As well as the small *Banquet of Cleopatra* he owned several other paintings by Tiepolo, some of them *modelli* which were presumably in Tiepolo's studio at this period. He obtained the *modello* for the S. Alvise *Way to Calvary*, which he also bequeathed to Cosimo Mari. The paintings he owned were chiefly small, suitable for a private collection. A somewhat Boucher-style *Bath of Diana* that he owned may have been a direct commission to Tiepolo and certainly, on stylistic grounds, must have originated in the mid-1740s (Pl. 122). It is not very typical of the artist at any period, or typical of Venetian eighteenth-century painting. The very faintest echo of Titian's mythologies lies behind it, but it is Titian transmuted, turned elegant and unreal. Tiepolo had earlier treated the subject in his own highly individualistic way, with Actaeon already sprouting horns as he stumbles on the bathing goddess in a darkly mysterious, rocky landscape (a painting now in the Accademia, Venice). The Algarotti painting has as little of mystery as of conviction. The naked nymphs

are rather dutifully displayed, without much dramatic purpose, and the bounding stag in the grey-green distance is almost a flippant interpretation of the baleful metamorphosis that led to a most horrific death. Nevertheless, this treatment of a 'difficult' subject was perhaps welcome to both patron and painter.

Algarotti owned a pair of paintings of Venetian genre scenes which represent a development out of Pietro Longhi (a painter in whom Algarotti showed no interest): lively, crowded scenes of contemporary life, the *Charlatan* and the *Carnival Dance* (Pl. 123), which were to be catalogued, after his death, as by Giambattista Tiepolo. The 'feconda fantasia' of these paintings—which are far from straightforward depictions of carnival life—is indeed not unworthy of Giambattista, but they are now uncontestably recognised as being the work of Domenico, as Algarotti himself must have known. Other pairs of the two subjects exist, along with a few paintings by Domenico of comparable subjects. He was admirably equipped in every way to become *the* painter of such a charming, sub-witty genre. He had a sharp eye for contemporary foibles as well as fashion, combined with an instinctive delight in people and behaviour, costume and physiognomy, finding expression in nervous, vivid calligraphy and equally nervous, fluid, distinctly linear handling of paint.

It would be nice to think that Algarotti positively instigated the first paintings of this kind by Domenico, but that is far from clear, and the paintings themselves seem to date from a decade or so after Algarotti's return to Venice in 1743. Yet, if he did not exactly uncover this vein of talent in Domenico Tiepolo, he obviously enjoyed it, savouring perhaps its very different mood, and indeed mode, from the genre most typical of Pietro Longhi. Domenico hardly pretends to depict actual scenes of life in Venice. He is deliberately capricious, especially in the *Carnival Dance*, where the location itself is partly fantastic—almost an open-air drawing-room, which has little specifically Venetian about it. The crowd, composed of all levels of society, the semi-rustic setting, the animation and the observation are blended into an enchanted whole that is like a pictorial anticipation of Donizetti's *L'Elisir d'Amore*.

Although Algarotti may have done no more than respond to the natural wit and sophistication of Domenico's art as it developed, he is the earliest known commissioner of work, of a quite humble kind, from Domenico, and the first person to speak of him as an artist. Thus Algarotti's return to Venice coincides with the emergence of the very youthful new figure whose character—at least as much as his artistic ability—was to be so valuable to Tiepolo for the rest of his life.

Domenico was precocious, as his father had been; but with the advantage of being born into an artistic environment. The proximity of Giambattista, who obviously trained and encouraged him, could actually have proved rather too stimulating: absorbing and ultimately crushing the son's talent until he dwindled into becoming a pale imitator of his father, as often enough happened to the painter-sons of great artists. What was remarkable about Domenico Tiepolo was that he neither followed his father's style slavishly nor broke away to develop his own totally individual style and career—as, for example, did Alessandro Longhi, the talented son of Pietro Longhi. Domenico was to be in and out of the studio, increasingly assisting his father on large-scale commissions in both oil and fresco. Tiepolo had never had such a devoted and faithful collaborator; few artists have ever had such selfless support from a fellow-artist, son or not, of real creativity. For Domenico was unmistakably gifted in his own right, with artistic interests and attitudes that were only latent—if they existed at all—in Giambattista Tiepolo. Domenico's imagination, in which humour was a powerful constituent, declined to be stirred by epic history and heroic mythology and flights of lofty fancy. It was stimulated not by the past but the present, the topical and the commonplace, which yet (Tiepolo's son as he was by birth and training) he touched into a sort of poetic genre, charmed as well as charming, far removed from the prosaic. He was more ironic than bitingly satiric, perpetually diverted by life as it appeared in the shape, literally, of costume and feature, animal equally with human. Long noses and squat figures, grotesque masks, small umbrellas, tall hats, as worn by pulcinellos, fat legs, peasant head-scarves, dogs' tails —the shape of all these things, with a myriad others, it amused him to depict. He was a sort of instinctive Puck surveying the spectacle of life: 'Lord, what fools these mortals be!'

Although he mastered the art of painting, he was—even more patently than his father—a draughtsman at heart. It is in his drawings (and in one or two frescoes) that he seems most happily and utterly himself (Pl. 124).

He was not yet sixteen when Algarotti commissioned from him two drawings which were copies of two old-master paintings in Cà Renier—by Palma Vecchio and Titian—that Algarotti probably planned to offer to Dresden.[10] These drawings have not been traced but there survives a red-chalk drawing, signed by Domenico, that is a copy of a painting by Bellini[11] (and Algarotti was to own a Bellini which he definitely tried to sell into Augustus III's collection). Algarotti's patronage of the boy may seem just a graceful gesture to the father, but it was certainly more than that. Domenico must have shown himself competent, and Algarotti paid him for his pains. A few months later, writing to Count Brühl, he was explicit about Domenico's gifts: 'at a quite tender age [he] is already starting to walk in his father's steps . . . and I have no doubt at all that his progress in painting must correspond with his excellent disposition, which is infinitely encouraging for the master'.[12]

Copying had probably been part of Domenico's earliest training—copying not paintings as such but drawings, and chiefly those produced by Giambattista in the late 1730s, the years when his main tasks were the S. Alvise canvases and the Gesuati ceiling in Venice, and the ceiling of the Palazzo Clerici in Milan. The style of Giambattista that Domenico grew up to absorb represented artistic maturity. Tiepolo's studio must have been full of drawings, from scribbles to quite finished studies, perhaps cartoons as well, ranging in subject from gods and goddesses, nymphs and fauns, to the Virgin and Child, and Christ as broken, suffering man. And Domenico absorbed the vocabulary almost as effortlessly as he absorbed the style. He was equipping himself to become the perfect assistant to his father.

124. D. Tiepolo, *Walk in the rain*, The Cleveland Museum of Art; purchased from the J. H. Wade Fund (37.573).

Yet neither father nor son can have intended that this role should be the limit of his activity. He was too talented for that. Besides, for all his devotion, personal and artistic, he was of a different, younger generation. When he assumes his father's finest garments, he seems conscious that they do not quite fit him; they are a little too grand and ornate for the everyday environment where he is at home—and his tendency is to make a joke out of the discrepancy.

That he had his own approach to things—not necessarily always a flippant one— and that, originally at least, he was destined for a separate career is shown by the fact that by the time he was twenty he had received a complete commission of his own, for the series of the *Stations of the Cross* in the Oratory of the Crucifixion in S. Polo at Venice. Up to the period of leaving for Spain with his father in 1762, he continued to have separate commissions for paintings. 'I have no time to be able to engrave,' he stated irritably in 1758, 'having many things to paint, not even managing to carry out my commitments.'[13]

That his son was no mere replica or slavish adherent of his own style must have quickly become apparent to Tiepolo. Nor were qualities of irony and pointed observation, and a delight in the bizarre, absent from Giambattista's work, whether in painting, drawing or etching. But what for him was merely one ingredient of art— a dash of piquancy, flavouring on occasion some 'high', elevated subject—was for Domenico a chief preoccupation. Giambattista Tiepolo had evolved by the 1740s the richest possible fabric for creating a visionary world, the essence of which is that everything in it is distanced from prosaic, daily reality. Domenico Tiepolo had nothing to add to that fabric, though he could adroitly duplicate it when necessary. He offered instead a delightfully dyed but distinctly homespun material for clothing recognisably human human-beings, existing in the ordinary world.

In a way, the two visions complemented each other. And in one commission— one alone—father and son were given the opportunity to present their differing artistic views on a fairly extensive scale, in the frescoes they executed in the late 1750s for the Villa Valmarana (see further, chapter 9). Domenico never painted anything finer, not even in the characteristic, personal, fresco decorations he was to execute for the Tiepolo family villa.

The S. Polo paintings are inevitably immature. Even at the time there was gossip that Giambattista had 'revised' his son's work,[14] though there is little evidence for this in the paintings themselves. When they were being produced it had perhaps scarcely been settled whether Domenico was to set up independently or to remain in Tiepolo's studio, practising his own art but inevitably on call as an assistant. Other pupils had passed through the studio, but none apparently remained. Whatever was originally planned or hoped for, on Domenico's part, he was to remain by his father's side, unmarried, always available as an assistant, a collaborator, permanently in service, until Giambattista died. How much he took on in the later commissions will probably never be ascertained for sure, any more than it will ever become known what he really felt about the role of eternal subordinate that was to be his.

Where Giambattista's paintings are concerned, it is likely that his involvement became greater than is normally recognized. What is not in doubt is that Tiepolo's translation from *modello* to large-scale painting in oil began to lose its bravura vigour. The outlines hardened, and he experienced obvious difficulty at times in carrying over from still brilliant, if nervous, jagged and summary sketches the fire and vivacity of handling, the glowing colour and liquid pigment, that had been so impressive earlier in his finished paintings. And in some of the large-scale later altarpieces especially, there are whole passages where, it can reasonably be suggested, a collaborator has been at work. Judged by what is uncontestably his style, in his own documented or otherwise certain work, Domenico Tiepolo is identifiable as that collaborator.

Already in the *Stations of the Cross* his artistic character is established, even allowing for some touches here and there by Giambattista. The fairly simple compositions might be explicable through the artist's lack of experience, or because of the small scale of the paintings (each just a metre high). But composition was to remain something of a weakness of Domenico's. Here simplicity suits the subject-matter and gives a certain emotional directness to the scenes. Domenico shows his preference for humanity, for genre and at times for portraiture. His concept of Christ's Passion is, to some extent, closer to Rembrandt's than to Giambattista's. The way to Calvary is taken through crowds of ordinary people, individualised and vivid, where children are intermingled with the adult figures (Pl. 125). Simplicity achieves a poignant effect in the scene of Christ meeting his afflicted mother. The Virgin is a tragically still, dark, deeply muffled silhouette—and the device of silhouetted bodies, often seen from the back, becomes highly popular in Domenico's work.

Typical of him too is the rather heavy application of the paint. In some passages he contrives at the same time to pastiche his father's style in a remarkable manner, leaving it to be puzzled over as to whether such areas are indeed properly his or, less probably, Giambattista's. Where Domenico is very much himself is in the frequently stiff, faintly arthritic poses and gestures—an arm or leg extended with wooden, lay-figure effect—and the lack of volume altogether in the figures, so that they scarcely seem to occupy space, however crowded they may be. Both defects were to remain characteristic of his art, for all its surface vivacity. In more senses than one, depth and weight always eluded him.

Where his intervention arguably starts to be apparent in his father's work is in paintings which were, accidentally or not, destined for places outside Venice. One of the first of these is the huge *Martyrdom of St John, Bishop of Bergamo*, painted for the cathedral at Bergamo (Pl. 126). The commission was given in August 1743, not long after Algarotti had become friendly with Tiepolo and at the time Domenico was beginning 'to walk in his father's steps'. Giambattista's preliminary *modello* fortunately survives[15] and is broadly followed in the final altarpiece, which did not reach Bergamo until August 1745.

In the *modello*, the onlookers at the saint's martyrdom (including a woman at the extreme right who turns her head away, comforting her shrinking daughter) are indicated only summarily. Numerous chalk drawings were executed as more detailed studies for the altarpiece, including an additional head—of a shrieking man. This head appears in the final composition, peering round the pillars, while the mother and child are worked up into a group which in style, costume and general treatment is remarkably close to figures appearing in Domenico's *Stations of the Cross* (especially the eighth Station). The shrieking male head also has some sort of parallel in Domenico's work, being quite like that of the possessed man in his painting of a miracle of St Francis de Paul, done for S. Francesco di Paolo at Venice and dated 1748.

Of course, it may be argued that at least in the latter case Domenico is merely basing himself on his father. But the genre figures in the Bergamo altarpiece have a slightly awkward, even intrusive air. More positively, there is about the woman and child group something thin and two-dimensional, which seems to indicate the handling of Domenico. It is reasonable to emphasise the sheer size of this altarpiece and the fact that it had to be fitted into the programme of work of a very busy painter. Collaboration on it is thus not inherently improbable, especially in its subsidiary portions.

Much the same may have occurred on another altarpiece of this period, that for the convent of S. Giovanni di Verdara, at Padua, of a miracle performed by St Patrick (or St Paulinus) (Pl. 127). Although there is no surviving *modello*, the composition can be traced in a number of pen-and-ink drawings. The basis of it was apparently established quite quickly: the saint would be posed on a pedestal, with kneeling figures around him. For the saint himself in the final painting, Giambat-

125. D. Tiepolo, *Jesus comforts the weeping women*, S. Polo, Venice.

tista Tiepolo was clearly responsible. The kneeling figures, however, could plausibly be the work of Domenico, especially those shown in hard profile at the left. Much more typical of him than his father is the device whereby the woman's face is partly cut off and obscured behind the boy's. Again, there is a lack of volume and three-dimensional feel to the figures; the kneeling boy in particular seems characteristic of Domenico and might easily have strayed from the *Stations of the Cross* series.

126. *Martyrdom of St John, Bishop of Bergamo*, Cathedral, Bergamo.

127. *Miracle of St Patrick (or Paulinus)*, Museo Civico, Padua.

128. D. Tiepolo, *Miracle of St Francis de Paul*, S. Francesco di Paola, Venice.

129. D. Tiepolo, *St Oswald begging for a miracle*, parish church, Merlengo, Treviso.

Other, later altarpieces by Tiepolo suggest Domenico's intervention in comparable ways. The painting of *Sts Roch and Sebastian* for the parish church of Noventa Vicentina,[16] possibly of the 1750s, or earlier, includes the figure of an old, severely mutilated peasant woman, praying from her crude wheeled trolley to the pair of saints. In the handling of them, in St Sebastian's bare body above all, a mastery of volume and modelling is patent, indicating Giambattista. In contrast, the old woman —once again a profile figure—is seen to be more drawn than painted. The folds of her head-dress are basically linear. And her whole presence reads as something of an interpolation, if not a distraction, in a composition where the mood of piety is otherwise conveyed in terms of dignified mystery and inspiration.

Tracking Domenico stylistically is not always easy. His *St Francis de Paul* (Pl. 128) is to some extent a rather coarse performance, in which the young painter's abilities are tested and stretched too far. Hard outlines and patches of strident colour (like the vermilion coat of the possessed man)—explicable possibly through the position of the painting high up in the church—suggest someone floundering without the support and even the context provided elsewhere by his father. Yet two years later, in the altarpiece of *St Oswald* of 1750 for the church in the village of Merlengo, near Treviso, Domenico seems far more accomplished and at ease, perhaps less constrained with a less overtly dramatic subject (Pl. 129). Here possibly, as some scholars have already proposed, Giambattista has intervened to assist his son. An advance in smooth handling is anyway obvious, and the composition also is far better organised. If St Oswald's head especially might pass as by Giambattista himself, the Holy Family group is undoubtedly by Domenico, and it interestingly departs from the very types of his father in the tousle-haired Child, openly appealing and close to the sentimental. This intimate, intimist and gentle mood is as much his as is the 'genre' figure of the individualised, big-eared, sick boy.

The commission may have been judged more important than that for S. Francesco di Paolo. The Cornaro family had a villa at Merlengo, where indeed Tiepolo himself was working around 1750, and the Cornaro continued, in different ways, to be involved with the Tiepolo. A highly learned member of the family, Flaminio Cornaro, made a very early public reference to Domenico's *Stations of the Cross* in his tomes on the churches of Venice,[17] and it was to Alvise Cornaro that Domenico dedicated his own etchings of the series in 1749. The Merlengo commission to Domenico Tiepolo may well have come about as a result of Cornaro interest or direct patronage.

In growing up, in artistic terms, during the 1740s, Domenico was on hand when his father received new and important commissions for fresco schemes, for the decoration, above all, of the salone at the Palazzo Labia. There he was not involved. Nothing seems to have been delegated, and Giambattista himself undertook all the figurative work.

Less clear is the matter of precise authorship of parts of the now faded, detached and unhappily disunited fresco scheme which Tiepolo undertook before 1750 (the year he left for Würzburg) for the Villa Pisani at Mira, near Venice. For once the subject accorded with his favoured historical period and style. He was to depict the visit to the villa by Henri III of France in 1574 when the villa was owned by the Contarini. Tiepolo's patron was Vincenzo Pisani, born in 1725, who married into the Cornaro family in 1745, and the scheme was executed in collaboration with Mengozzi Colonna.[18]

One long wall was frescoed with the arrival of the King. Opposite were two narrow scenes of spectators on balconies, and above on the ceiling further spectators looked down from a balustrade framing a sky in which Fame flies trumpeting. For the ceiling design one of Mengozzi Colonna's preparatory drawings, duly annotated, has fortunately survived (Pl. 130).

In dedicating a life of Sansovino to Vincenzo Pisani in 1752, the architect Tommaso Temanza wrote a preface referring to the decorations in the villa, from the 'eccellente pennello del Sig. Tiepoletto, ed . . . del Mingozzi [sic]'. Because of their French subject-matter and the costumes, they attracted the interest of the future Marquis de Marigny, Madame de Pompadour's brother and Surintendant des Bâtiments to Louis XV, on his visit to Italy. And not only were they to be praised by Algarotti but he was proud to own the *modello* for the chief fresco.[19]

Today, the coherence of the scheme has been destroyed. The frescoes are uncomfortably installed in the Musée Jacquemart-André, the ceiling (Pl. 131) located in a room apart from the other frescoes which are found at the top of a flight of stairs. From the ceiling the spectators now look down on nothing relevant, though they include a portrait of Tiepolo himself (Pls 132 and 133) pointing at the arrival of the King and, by extension, at his own work. What obviously struck both Marigny and Algarotti was the illusionism of the effect whereby a wall appeared dissolved, opened out ('una grande apertura', Algarotti called it) in a great space, to convey a porch and a view beyond of the Brenta and other villas along its banks—Tiepolo's sole 'view-picture'. Henri III forever ascends the steps of the villa into a loggia where spectators in reality join with those in the fresco as they welcome the King (Pl. 134). And, not content with straight history, Tiepolo adds a heroine to the scene, in the stately person of a tall-proportioned blonde, turning her face from the King's gaze.

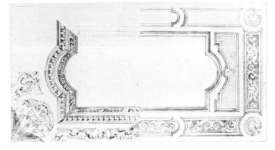

130. G. Mengozzi Colonna, drawing for ceiling of Villa Contarini-Pisani, Museo Correr, Venice.

While the ceiling, for all its faintness in places and its fairly conventional Fame, is autograph work (and is, on examination, full of vivid portraits, among them those of children and women, including Cecilia Tiepolo), there must be doubts about how far Giambattista himself was responsible for execution of the wall frescoes. The almost exaggerated proportions—as in the figures in the balconies—are only one disturbing element. There are stiffnesses and infelicities of grouping in the main fresco; and even allowing for its faded state it lacks the sense of Giambattista at his most artistically concentrated. Some collaboration seems likely, and at the period the likeliest collaborator was Domenico.

131. Ceiling of the Villa Contarini-Pisani, Musée Jacquemart-André, Paris.

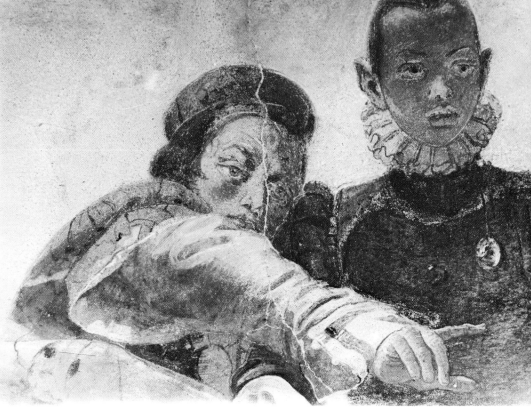

132 and 133. Details of Pl. 131.

Even harder to assess is the degree of his participation in the frescoes in the Villa Soderini at Nervesa, totally destroyed as long ago as 1917.[20] That Domenico helped on these has often been postulated, and on the evidence of the existing photographs there was clearly some studio assistance—not on the ceiling, which appears autograph and of fine quality, but on the wall frescoes. The subject of these was again a historical one, concerned with the entry or procession of Pietro Soderini as *gonfaloniere* into Florence and Niccolò Soderini sent to the Roman Senate. Tiepolo had to turn back mentally into yet earlier history here, and away from his own Venetian world. Pietro Soderini had been elected *gonfaloniere* in 1502. Tiepolo bravely suggests the typical Florentine official dress of the period and even has a good try at Florentine architecture—after which he may have been happy enough to leave other passages to Domenico, or another assistant. That he thought of himself as responsible for the final fresco seems subtly indicated by the presence of his own self-portrait, looking out from the incongruous context of very early sixteenth-century Florence, at the extreme right of Pietro Soderini's procession.

These frescoes are normally dated to around 1754, for the not very compelling reason that Tiepolo was in that year working in another palace at Nervesa. Their style, however, suggests strongly that they date from the approximate period of the Villa Pisani scheme and definitely from before the Würzburg years. Some of the same exaggeratedly tall figures of pikemen, for example, are similar to figures in the arrival of Henri III. A further slight indication of the 1740s as the most probable period of execution is in the motif of horse and rider at the right foreground of the fresco of Soderini processing through Florence, which seems patently based on the same motif, in reverse, in the *Family of Darius before Alexander* in the Villa Cordellina.

How and to what extent, and indeed whether, Domenico Tiepolo already aided his father in some of the fresco schemes of the later 1740s will probably never be settled. But he was definitely to assist his father in a further, novel way, utilising a further artistic skill. Trained perhaps in this as in most things by Giambattista, he developed an ability to etch. In time, he would produce at least one set of original etchings, but his first interest was in etching compositions that had been painted, among them some of his own. In 1749 he published his first series, etchings of his

134. *Arrival of Henri III*, Musée Jacquemart-André, Paris.

Stations of the Cross, which he dedicated fulsomely to Alvise Cornaro, referring to Cornaro's status as a Knight of Malta (and thus wearing a cross on his breast) and to the set of paintings as his first, 'immature' works.

To etch his own painted compositions had either not interested or occurred to Giambattista Tiepolo, but Domenico now started to do this for him, thus disseminating his compositions widely in a way that had not happened before. It was in part a homage from son to father. It also meant that he had to study carefully what Giambattista had painted and to translate his pictorial qualities into a very different medium. It also helped to document the father's output; and though Domenico never produced a complete catalogue, understandably enough, of all his father's work, he was sometimes able usefully to indicate by inscriptions the location or destination of some of Tiepolo's paintings (whether for Russia, Padua or merely for Venice) and to dedicate an etching on occasion. Most poignantly of all, and thanks to his practice of recording in etchings what his father had painted, he etched and inscribed as such the last painting Tiepolo completed before his death.

Like his father, he retained friendly relations with Algarotti. As late as 1761 Tiepolo was writing to Algarotti in the warmest and most appreciative way, grateful to have been mentioned in the Count's literary works and sending the thanks of 'my son Domenico', as well as politely adverting to Algarotti's one-time patronage: 'l'antica sua padronanza verso la mia persona. . .'[21]

It was on one of Domenico's etchings after a composition by Giambattista, the altarpiece in fact of *St Paulinus* (as he identified it), that the patron was to be openly commemorated along with the two artists. Domenico made the inscription on this etching unusually long and elaborate, and specific.[22] He dedicated it to 'Francesco, Count Algarotti, as highly illustrious as highly learned', who is asked to accept a composition which, when it came a while ago from Giambattista's pencil, he advised over, now etched and humbly dedicated, 'most pleasingly to my father' ('patrem libentissime'), signed: 'Jo. Dominicus Tiepolo Filius.'

The phrases seem to recall the period of greatest intimacy between the three men, when Algarotti was a friend as much as a patron of Tiepolo's, and patron as much as friend to the young beginner who was his son.

7 PALAZZO LABIA AND THE THEME OF CLEOPATRA AND ANTONY

AT SOME DATE in the 1740s—before leaving for Würzburg in November 1750—Tiepolo frescoed a complete room, in collaboration with Mengozzi Colonna, in the Palazzo Labia.[1] It was his most splendid secular commission in Venice, unique in its totality of decoration and yet undocumented, virtually unremarked on at the time by either natives or visitors to the city. Algarotti never mentions it. Domenico Tiepolo never etched any portion of it. Not until Fragonard and Bergeret de Grandcourt came to Venice, four years after Tiepolo's death, did the work receive any real tribute. Fragonard drew an airy, semi-capricious version of the *Banquet of Cleopatra* (etched by Saint-Non) and Bergeret wrote of the grandeur and richness of the frescoes in his journal: 'Tout en est grand et noble, de la plus riche composition.' He added he would do all he could to revisit the room: 'Si le tems me le permet, je ferai l'impossible pour revoir ce sallon [sic].'[2] But no second visit by him seems to have taken place; and before the end of the century Tiepolo and his work, even at its finest, were slipping into neglect. By the middle of the nineteenth century, Palazzo Labia itself was described as 'squalid and deserted'.[3]

Yet it was here that Tiepolo and Mengozzi consecrated their long partnership in a non-religious marriage, justifying all Bergeret's adjectives. Mengozzi had never provided such a sumptuous setting before, nor one more skilfully allied to the real architecture of an existing room. Carved out of the centre of the palace, and double the height of the adjoining rooms, the room itself must have been destined from the first for feasts and balls; even without Tiepolo's frescoes it would make a marvellous scenic impression of the greatest grandeur, a mixture of real and feigned decoration.

Mengozzi matched the salmon-coloured marble framing of the doors with marbling of his own, made painted balconies beneath actual windows and pierced the wall with illusionistic apertures, giving glimpses in the banquet scene of yet richer architecture, in the same idiom, opening out beyond the room. Above a cornice that Tiepolo was to animate with satyrs and other figures, Mengozzi created a ceiling of twisting, floriated, feigned, white stucco shapes, in places laid like lace against pure gold, opened in the middle with an oculus ready to suggest the sky and eternity. Indeed, everywhere the architectural screens lead the eye behind them, into apparently limitless space, which Tiepolo would enhance without cramming, just hinting at a harbour by a few flags astir, a single sail billowing whitely like a cloud, or an obelisk rising equally whitely, with blue aerial distance shimmering beyond, away into infinity.

None of the walls was unbroken by doorways or windows, all of which Mengozzi skilfully accommodated within his decorative scheme. The two main walls for frescoes lie left and right when entering the room through double doors that lead from the staircase outside; and in creating the shapes he did, allowing for two large compositions, Mengozzi must have been working closely with Tiepolo. In the two chief areas, Tiepolo painted two scenes from the love story of Cleopatra and Antony: her banquet, when she wagered Antony she would give the most costly feast ever given, and won by dissolving one of her highly valued pearl earrings in vinegar; and

135. *Banquet of Cleopatra*, Palazzo Labia, Venice.

143

the meeting of the lovers at a port (Pls 135 and 136). The first scene was a famous one, with a sporadic tradition of being painted. The second is not perhaps meant to depict a specific incident, though historically there were a number of meetings of Cleopatra and Antony at ports and harbours, and most famously she had had herself rowed in splendour down the river Cydnus to subjugate Antony—though he did not in fact meet her when she disembarked. Around this subject Tiepolo was to have more than one thought, as is shown by sketches and other paintings related approximately to the fresco. It may well be that it was never as clear in his mind—for a variety of reasons—as was Cleopatra's banquet; and it is hard not to feel that it was the banquet scene which most concerned both him and his patrons. Only, it might be suggested, when the question arose of *two* scenes being required from the lovers' story did it become necessary to evolve some sort of pendant of their meeting. It may be significant that Tiepolo painted several Banquets by themselves, but never painted the Meeting as a subject on its own.

At the Palazzo Labia, the scheme of decoration did not stop with the two scenes on earth but soared skywards, centrally with a rider who is probably Bellerophon, on Pegasus, ascending on a virtually stream-lined steed towards the gleaming, gold-draped figure of Princely Glory seated beside a pyramid symbolising Eternity (Pl. 137). And over the massive, simulated, swagged archways of Mengozzi's devising, Tiepolo set floating some of the most poetic and vivid of all his mythological imaginings, in beings who seem to inhabit their own private sphere. Above the Banquet scene a dusky god gathers a girl into his arms and his chariot. Wrongly, yet not imperceptively, this group is always identified as Time raping Beauty (though the god is patently wingless). In fact it is Pluto seizing Proserpina, one or two of whose gathered flowers are tumbling down against the dark vapour half obscuring Pluto's chariot wheel (Pl. 141). Not Time's action but the violent power of love is what the group stands for (as Ovid's account in the *Metamorphoses* emphasises); and pertinently enough it is placed above the scene where Cleopatra astounds and enchants Antony.

Yet more magically realised are the deities on the opposite wall: Aeolus, King of the Winds, naked, crowned and butterfly-winged, bestriding a cloud that drifts in front of the feigned architecture and seeming to puff into action a pair of youthful Winds, their cheeks distended as they fiercely blow (Pl. 140). Theirs is the breath that sets swelling the sail of the ship in the harbour below.

Tiepolo had never before compositionally related upper and lower zones in this way, making heaven visible to the real spectator of the whole scene but unseen by his protagonists on earth. Nor perhaps had he ever distinguished so successfully solid, earthly beings, glamorous yet human, from spirits and aerial, immortal creatures, wild and unfettered as the Winds. Here they are almost like those 'Zeffiretti lusinghieri', invoked by Ilia's aria in Mozart's *Idomeneo*, whom she begs to bear an affectionate message to her beloved. As Cleopatra advances at the harbour side she seems to increase her thrall over Antony; he can move forward only with head turned back, absorbed in gazing at her, and everything conspires to set his heart fluttering for love.

The scope and the scale of this commission were major. By any standards it must have occupied a great deal of time, quite apart from thought. Now that the documents have shown that the ceiling of the Scalzi took two years to complete, from 1743 to 1745, being worked on first by Mengozzi and then by Tiepolo, a comparable period of time seems likely enough for the Palazzo Labia decoration—arguably longer. The length of its gestation in Tiepolo's mind is impossible to fix, but he is bound to have been thinking about his contribution to the scheme well before he began the actual work. And when he began, he presumably started with the ceiling, for which there is no record or trace of a *modello*. Some slight portions of the frescoes —like a negro page and a monkey on the wall of windows opening on the palace courtyard—he could probably improvise, well enough, when it came to execution. For other portions, his preparatory work must be presumed lost. What survives in the way of drawings includes a number of chalk drawings of often small details which raise considerable problems over function, if not attribution.[4] There are also several oil *modelli* for the banquet scene and for a meeting of the two lovers, apart from large-scale paintings, of a more finished character, of the two subjects, sometimes markedly varied from the frescoes themselves.

Thus the array of work around the theme is considerable and partly somewhat confusing, especially where so little fact can be established. Even the date of pre-1750 might seem to hang on rather vague evidence, were it not that Mengozzi's part in the scheme is mentioned, favourably, in the 1753 edition of Orlandi's *Abecedario* of artists, published in Venice at a time when Tiepolo had been in Germany for some three years.[5] That reference to the Labia decorations is probably the sole one printed in Tiepolo's lifetime, and it omits to mention him in the same connection. Fortunately, there is confirmation from two non-Italian painters' sketches, made in Venice, that his frescoes had been executed before he left for Würzburg; and all the stylistic indications of Tiepolo's own Cleopatra and Antony sketches, studies and drawings point to the same approximate period.

Such preoccupation with what is virtually a single theme is untypical of him. He had never dealt with the story before and never reverted to it. While his original instigation is not established, a survey of the surviving material suggests—though it can only be a suggestion—that he received a first commission for a *Banquet of Cleopatra*, most likely a large-scale oil painting. The subject was not uncommon. It was certainly, in pictorial terms, the most familiar incident attached to Cleopatra, apart from her suicide. And as a theme for decorative painting, it could stir associations in Venice as much artistic as antique-historical, recalling the banquet and feast paintings associated particularly with Veronese and his followers.

Veronese himself had never, unfortunately perhaps, painted any scene with Cleopatra. However, her banquet for Antony was the subject of one of the sixteenth-century frescoes in a ground floor room in the Villa-Castello Da Porto Colleoni at Thiene, in the Veneto, by Fasolo and Zelotti, artists strongly under his influence. The subject appears along with scenes of Mucius Scaevola and Sophonisba. The setting is a high, open loggia where Cleopatra, classically draped but blonde and coiffeured with full, fashionable, Renaissance art, rather matter-of-factly disposes of a small pearl, almost as though disembarrassing herself of an awkward fish bone. Antony gazes across at her with a tremendously impassive, accidentally Hanoverian royal stare, recalling in his features—and even demeanour—the young George V (see Pl. 27). In that atmosphere, Cleopatra seems less a seductress than someone hovering unconsciously on the brink of an appalling solecism.

In a simple, rather deliberately non-grandiose way, this fresco happens to contain the seeds of Tiepolo's concept, though he was greatly to enhance Cleopatra when he came to the Palazzo Labia composition. He was probably not conscious of the Villa-Castello Da Porto Colleoni fresco, and not influenced by the one or two frescoes of the Banquet which occur in Venetian villas towards the turn of the seventeenth century, with no special emphasis. For much of the seventeenth century, the death of Cleopatra had been a popular subject in Italian painting. Tiepolo's master, Lazzarini, had painted a 'Cleopatra with other figures', which may well have been of that subject, and had painted the picture, as it happens, for the Labia.[6] By the eighteenth century there seems to have been little demand—least of all in Venice—for paintings of Cleopatra's death. Her banquet was occasionally painted—by Trevisani, for example, at Rome, but it enjoyed no particular popularity as a subject at Venice, leaving aside Tiepolo's treatment.

In considering the instigators of his sudden interest in the topic, there is quite a strong case for proposing members of the Labia family. Like several other families

136 (following page). *Meeting of Cleopatra and Antony*, Palazzo Labia, Venice.

for whom he was to work, the Labia ranked as very recent nobility in Venice. Of Catalan origin, possessing noble status in Spain, the family had reached Venice and settled in the area of S. Geremia by the very early sixteenth century. Trading in textiles, the Labia grew immensely rich. In 1646 there came an opportunity to buy themselves into the Venetian nobility. The Republic was desperate for money, and the golden book of the nobility was open to those who could offer a large sum of cash to the state. Giovan Francesco Labia was among the first to apply, and the first to be ennobled. He took as his arms a gold eagle on a blue ground, and giant eagles were to be carved, with ostentation unusual in Venice, along the façades of the handsome palace that was gradually built at S. Geremia. The actual entry into the ranks of the nobility was commemorated by a painting on the ceiling of the library in the palace, showing the figure of Venice enthroned, being guided by Peace as she inscribes in the golden book the name of Labia.[7]

That painting, by the fairly obscure Angelo Trevisani, may have been commissioned about 1736 or slightly later. In 1738 the head of the family, Giovan Francesco II Labia, under whom a good deal of construction and alteration of the palace had gone on, suddenly died. He left a widow, Maria, née Civran, and two young sons. Maria Labia, reputed beautiful, and the possessor of a famous collection of jewellery, which she gladly displayed to foreign visitors, was also reputed towards the mid-century to have been, in her day, 'fort galante' (as a Frenchman put it). It has been suggested that the choice of Cleopatra for the palace fresco scheme was made as a complimentary allusion to her and her jewellery.[8] At least as relevant probably, for Tiepolo, was the tradition of the lavish ways of the Labia family, summed up by the story of a banquet one of them had given, serving his guests on gold plate which he afterwards ordered to be thrown into the canal. With or without it, he punningly boasted, he would remain the same: 'le abbia o non le abbia, sarò sempre Labia'.

That occasion must have been one of the most ostentatious banquets in Venetian history—as Cleopatra's was one of the most ostentatious in ancient times. By the mid-eighteenth century the Labia, though scarcely poor, were, like Venice itself, no longer at the apogee of their prosperity, but their wealth was perhaps the most noteworthy association of the family, which had not been shy of manifesting it. That they should commission a painting alluding to their ancestor's reckless gesture seems very much in the tradition of a period in which other families celebrated achievements less personal and more patriotic, but equally from the past.

Among the Labia possessions was a collection of oil paintings, built up probably around 1700. It included no less than a dozen paintings by Giordano, of both religious and secular subjects, and work by earlier artists like Giovanni Bellini and Sebastiano del Piombo. Lazzarini was represented by some fifteen or twenty paintings, in addition to the *Cleopatra*. She was also the subject of a painting by Reni in the collection. In an inventory of 1749 covering the paintings (omitting frescoes as part of the building), three are given to Tiepolo: an overdoor of unspecified subject, an altarpiece and a portrait under glass ('con cristallo'), not otherwise identified.[9]

The altarpiece survives. It was painted for the small, family chapel in the palace and shows the Holy Family appearing to St Gaetano (patron saint of the Labia). Its style suggests a date of execution of not much later than 1740, and probably rather earlier, thus establishing contact between the Labia and Tiepolo well before he undertook the Cleopatra and Antony frescoes.

In 1743, as already mentioned, Algarotti reported that Tiepolo had in his studio a large oil painting of the *Banquet of Cleopatra* which he had begun some time before, painted for 'd'autres' but which the artist was prepared to finish so that it could be sent by Algarotti to Dresden. The oddity of this situation has often been commented on. Most intriguing of all is the identity of the 'other people' who had originally commissioned but apparently did not take possession of what was clearly an important and indeed unusual work.

A new hypothesis may be proposed: that 'd'autres' were the Labia. It would then be that they commissioned from Tiepolo—with whom they were already in touch —a large oil painting to add to their distinguished collection of paintings. The subject was settled on as the Banquet of Cleopatra, which had honourable family relevance in arguably several ways. Such a commission would have been given around 1743 and Tiepolo would have started work on it, painting first a preliminary study on a small scale, the 'modello' Algarotti was to own. At that date Tiepolo might well have found it easier to contemplate another commission for an oil painting rather than for frescoes (with the Scalzi ceiling and other ceilings in Venice, as well as the Villa Cordellina room, all in his programme). The next stage must be even more highly speculative. Possibly the Labia decided that the theme would serve better for a fresco scheme and were prepared to wait until Tiepolo was less occupied. Tiepolo himself might have suggested that the subject would lend itself to more grandiose treatment, discovering and developing further fresh ideas as he pondered the subject.

In some such manner, it could be, the painter was left with an unfinished oil painting on his hands without feeling aggrieved, while its original commissioners could look forward—once Tiepolo's commitments permitted—to his providing them with something of greater quality and greater grandeur, a permanent monument on their palace walls. Anyone might own oil paintings of the subject. Only the Labia would have Tiepolo's frescoes of the theme, set in a mythological and decorative framework that was unique.

Certainly, to return from conjecture to fact, it seems that awareness of the commission for the frescoes was what stimulated Tiepolo's continued thinking around the Cleopatra and Antony story. And although he had dealt with so many subjects— battles, visions, allegories—he had never depicted a feast, in either a religious or a profane context. A sense of richness and exoticness, with an array of spectators, was virtually the given element, which Tiepolo would naturally tend to invest with a festive air. Somehow, a banquet of his devising might be predicated as unlikely to have the baleful, disturbing menace of those given by Phineus or Belshazzar.

The concept of Cleopatra's banquet provided opportunities even richer than normal. It arose from an encounter between East and West, symbolised by two great personages, a queen and a Roman ruler. He had come to conquer her and her kingdom, but was in fact conquered by her. Different though the actual incident depicted was, the *Family of Darius*, as painted by Veronese, might continue to reverberate in Tiepolo's mind. There East and West met as opposites, each with its train of pageantry, on a high, public, Palladian stage. It was a drama, yet played out with a minimum of dramatic action or gesture. Calmness, dignity and splendour were conveyed, reinforced by the frieze of foreground figures and by the long horizontal of the architectural screen extending behind them. Tiepolo had studied the composition for the Villa Cordellina frescoes, if not before; he did not forget it when he came to concentrate on the *Banquet of Cleopatra*.

Part of the attraction and novelty of the theme for him must have lain in the fact that he had a heroine to depict as his central personage. He who had turned the captured Carthaginian woman in the *Continence of Scipio* into a queenly figure could have no problem in re-creating a real and famously beautiful queen. No supposed 'likeness' inhibited him. No traditional type of figure was associated with her. Each age and each artist had interpreted Cleopatra for themselves. The scene of her banquet was Alexandria—which was to say, from Tiepolo's point of view, Ruritania. Cleopatra's court, her retinue, even her plate and tableware, could be summoned up from pure fantasy. And Tiepolo seized every freedom he was offered.

The story of the banquet was told in Pliny's *Natural History* (Book IX), in connection with the properties of pearls. At the actual feast, the lovers were accompanied by Lucius Plancus, who was joint-consul with Antony and who agreed to adjudicate

over Cleopatra's wager. To Tiepolo it may be that another Roman figure at table would have distracted from or diminished Antony—or perhaps he never quite realised who Lucius Plancus was. Whatever the explanation, he made him, from the first *modello* through every variation to the Labia fresco, an eastern potentate, a combination of Pharaoh and Herod. As a result, Antony's isolation, his incongruousness, within an oriental environment was emphasised. Arriving from a world outside, he is—for all his renown and his Roman origins—bewildered as well as bewitched.

In broad compositional terms, Tiepolo established his characters and setting, and the approach he would adopt, in what seems to be the earliest treatment of all, the small-scale *modello* that Algarotti acquired soon after his return to Venice in 1743. Everywhere, beginning with the setting, Tiepolo paid subtle homage to the influence of Veronese, but at this stage he saw the scene as comparatively intimate. Cleopatra is dressed much as any fashionable sixteenth-century Venetian lady, and quite unostentatiously clasps her pearl, seated at the left of a modest table, laid in a tiled, open-air loggia. Antony, placed nearer the front of the picture-plane, is shown in profile, wearing a plumed helmet. A dwarf, a negro page, two dogs—a minute, pet one peeping out from under the fringe of the tablecloth—and some bizarrely clad attendants complete the composition.

In concept, as in execution, the effect is a little tame. It needed to blossom more boldly, especially where Cleopatra was concerned. For the big picture which Algarotti had Tiepolo finish for Dresden, there is an emotional enrichment, as well as literal expansion and development. Almost everything has been subtly rethought. The setting is now far more elaborate, and enclosed by a heavy architectural screen borrowed directly from the *Family of Darius*. From that composition too comes the suggestion, at the left, that the scene is taking place on a platform raised above the level of the ground behind. But the most noticeable change is in the figure of Cleopatra (Pl. 139), more opulently dressed and more arresting in pose, as she holds up in her left hand, extended in a commanding way, the pearl suspended over a slim, fluted glass, in place of the silver tankard she had previously been shown grasping in somewhat taproom manner. At a glance, the composition makes the central point of the story visible and comprehensible.

Whatever Algarotti's learned condiments, the banquet is very much improved by a more glamorous Cleopatra, with a piquantly pretty face (possibly that, as has

138. Detail of Pl. 136.

139. Detail of Pl. 118.

140 (following page). *The Winds*, Palazzo Labia, Venice.

before now been proposed, of one of Tiepolo's own daughters) and a toy-like lap-dog. She is beautifully clad in a jewelled dress of apricot-buff—last seen worn by Pharaoh's daughter in the *Finding of Moses*, but now enhanced by a stand-up, frilled ruff of icing whiteness and crispness, and by a sash that might be that of some self-awarded order. She has become recognisably a typical Tiepolo heroine.

That was as well, since the artist and his patrons were far from finished with the theme. Despatch of the large-scale *Banquet* to Dresden in 1744 left some commission unfulfilled on almost any interpretation of the scanty evidence. There are drawings of Cleopatra and her attendants, of Antony seated at table, bareheaded, and, most absorbing of all, pen-and-ink studies on a double-sided sheet (Pl. 142), reversing the position of the two lovers in a series of rapidly flowing thoughts, doodles almost, though doodles of an inspired kind.

This sheet bears on it the numbers '1743', and it would seem perverse not to accept this—odd though putting a date on such a sheet may be—as the year of execution, given that in 1743 Tiepolo was definitely working on the subject. Some of the studies are of single figures, others of the pair of lovers. But one suggests a composition on a colossal scale—far bigger, it may be thought, than was feasible for an oil painting and done perhaps with some idea of a fresco in mind. In a vast arched space, not unsuggestive of the setting of Raphael's *School of Athens*, the banquet is served at the top of a huge flight of steps and witnessed by a concourse of people. All this is conveyed in a tiny scribble which might be read as an excited after-thought or a radical re-thinking of the concept, to express the maximum grandeur. Looking at this, one can see how Tiepolo might have managed the composition that never was —*Timotheus, or the Effects of Music*—with its Asiatic pomp, its crowded palatial setting and at its centre, of course, a feast.

In another sheet with a pen-and-ink drawing, more meditated, a complete compositional study in itself, Tiepolo retained the motif of a raised platform, though with steps at the right, and reduced the architectural grandeur to a simple 'quote' from, once again, Veronese's *Family of Darius* (Pl. 143). In this scene, Plancus is omitted entirely. Most of the gesticulating is done by Antony, and Cleopatra's significance is slightly muted.

These drawings all indicate that Tiepolo had settled on a revision which he would eventually adopt in the Palazzo Labia fresco, that Cleopatra should be at the right of the composition. Instead of starting with her, the eye would follow Antony's gaze and read across, from left to right, to stop at her figure.

At some point, however, he executed one large-scale Banquet picture, echoing the Dresden painting in several ways (though showing Antony bareheaded), apparently weaker in execution and with extremely commonplace features for both Cleopatra and Antony.[10] This, it has sometimes been supposed, is the 'replacement' canvas, done for the patron or patrons who were previously to have received the Dresden picture—in which case, he or they definitely had the worst of what would appear an extraordinary proceeding by Tiepolo, quite close to bad faith. But it seems most unlikely that any such switch or substitution took place.

It was, as far as can be deduced, the germ of the tiny scribble which proved most fruitful in Tiepolo's continued thinking around the Banquet subject. The scene called for scenic grandeur. Preserving the concept of a raised platform with a central staircase leading up to it, he expanded the composition in an oil sketch of horizontal format, a true *modello* in its liveliness and vigour (Pl. 144). Inevitably, the figures of Antony and Cleopatra are small in relation to the architecture, and set back in the middle distance, verging on insignificance against the long, unbroken outline of the pillared screen that extends rather monotonously across the composition. For some reason Plancus is absent from the composition, probably because Tiepolo wanted the lovers' gaze along and across the table to be uninterrupted. Even though the story required him, Plancus was something of an artistic intrusion. It proved not

141 (preceding page). *Pluto and Proserpina*, Palazzo Labia, Venice.

154

142. *Banquet of Cleopatra*, Nationalmuseum, Stockholm.

143. *Banquet of Cleopatra*, Victoria & Albert Museum, London (D.1825.32–1885).

possible to dispense with him entirely, but eventually Tiepolo solved the problem of accommodating him without letting him interfere in the eye-locking exchange of the two lovers. At the same time, in this *modello* there are new or newly developed motifs: a fine, pawing white horse (amost a brother to the Horses of the Sun at the Palazzo Archinto); a dwarf on the steps, watching Cleopatra; and buffets of piled plate flanking the central episode on either side.

The format of this sketch may at first seem to disqualify it for any relationship to the Labia fresco, but that is not necessarily so. It could have been executed before the precise nature of Mengozzi's decorative framework was fixed; and even as it is, there is a strong horizontal emphasis to the concept of the wall area, which requires

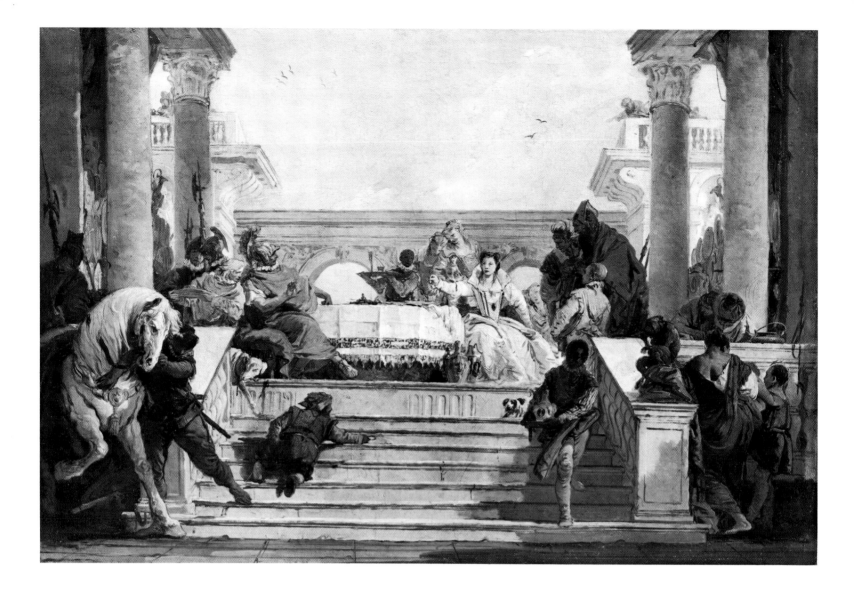

144. *Banquet of Cleopatra*, National Gallery, London.

lateral spaces to be frescoed. Tiepolo filled them with one or two attendants but chiefly with buffets piled with plate (surely a reference to the rich tableware associated with the Labia family's lavishness).

That this sketch is somehow connected with the frescoes is further suggested by the fact that it has a pendant, conceivably a little later in date, but basically of the same period, and very similar in handling (Pl. 145). This shows a seashore meeting between Antony and Cleopatra—and introduces therefore the idea of two scenes, in effect for the first time. At this stage the main motif was of Antony bending in homage to kiss Cleopatra's hand, having landed in what is clearly meant to be Egypt and bringing in his train booty and captives.

The central motif was isolated and studied in a wonderfully luminous pen-and-wash drawing, where Antony grabs at Cleopatra's fingers with an almost greedy gesture, while she looks down pensively, if not quizzically, at this treatment of her hand (Pl. 146). In the oil sketch—with its brilliant yellows and reds, and its characteristic, nervously rapid pencilling in paint—the incident passes off with greater dignity on both sides. Instead of letting Antony's left arm hang limply down, as in the drawing, Tiepolo puts it gracefully across his breast, increasing the earnestness and courtesy of the lover's homage. Egypt is summarily conveyed by a pyramid and a palm tree, and Cleopatra stands beside them expressive of being on her own territory, very much in command of the proceedings. The windy coastal setting is

145. *Meeting of Cleopatra and Antony.* Wrightsman Collection, New York.

evoked by a flag or two flying in the breeze, and the bustle of landing, like the booty and the captives and the surrounding soldiery, is all evoked with economic yet totally convincing touches. Even more than the *Banquet*, this is a public, nearly a political, scene, another testimony to the sway exercised over Antony by Cleopatra.

Another pair of *modelli*, slightly discrepant in handling as in size, yet clearly related, were made by Tiepolo in upright format, concentrating in each case on the central areas of the Labia fresco scheme. There can be no doubt that these are directly related to the frescoes themselves, as they reveal yet further thoughts and improvements, though even these ideas were to undergo some drastic revision when Tiepolo set to work on the actual fresco compositions.

It was the scene of the Meeting that kept being revised. In the upright *modello*, the format dictated greater concentration, suppression of the pyramid and so on, and a shift from seashore to harbour (Pl. 147). The composition changed totally. Although Antony still kisses Cleopatra's hand, there is no sense of encounter. Gone is the booty being brought from the ships. In very stately fashion, Cleopatra advances from the left, barely glancing at her lover, whose ardour seems hardly to interrupt her progress, for all its public manifestation. Whether Antony has just landed, or whether the lovers are about to embark, is unclear. But Cleopatra herself has certainly not arrived by ship, judging by the general direction of her entourage, which includes the head of a horse (last seen in the horizontal *Banquet* sketch).

To search in historical accounts for this exact scene is probably a waste of time. Tiepolo is likely to have been thinking of it as a prelude, in a general way, to the *Banquet*, and in artistic terms he was seeking perhaps for something less static than that composition was bound to be. In the *modello* of the *Meeting* there is already a hint, to be developed finally in the fresco, of movement out of the composition, as a page-boy tugs aside a hound, as though making room for the lovers to advance.

The upright *modello* for the *Banquet* (Pl. 148) has not got the sparkle—the suitably marine sparkle—and the inspired agitation which make its pair one of the most brilliant in Tiepolo's *œuvre*. It is more hasty, less glowing in colour and mildly disappointing as the penultimate stage for the fresco of the same subject. Yet it is obviously autograph work, and its thinking—as opposed to its execution—is pro-

146. *Meeting of Cleopatra and Antony*, Metropolitan Museum of Art, New York, Rogers Fund (37.165.10).

found. The upright format again compels rigid concentration on essentials. The architectural setting grows proportionately tall, opening up a vista not merely of sky but of vertical motifs: trees and a thin obelisk or pyramid. Some of the attendants are reduced or suppressed, while the dwarf on the steps is moved closer to Cleopatra. In profile now, she raises her head and the pearl in a patently challenging manner. At her right, in a silhouette which helps to give emphasis to her pose, a negro servant bends, holding a salver with a glass of vinegar.

It is, however, the placing of Antony which has been most extensively re-considered. Instead of being on the near-side of the table, where his legs always gave a certain amount of compositional trouble, he has been put on the far side, looking outwards and towards Cleopatra, and shown bareheaded. Where he sat, Plancus is now shown in discreet, undistracting profile, emotionally excluded from the significance of the event to Cleopatra and to Antony. Perhaps the very simplicity of this sketch's final solution to all the problems raised by the *Banquet* composition accounts

147. *Meeting of Cleopatra and Antony*, National Gallery of Scotland, Edinburgh.

148. *Banquet of Cleopatra*, Stockholm University Art Collection.

149. Studies of jewellery, Meyer-Ilschen Collection, Stuttgart.

151 (facing page). Detail of Pl. 135.

150. F. M. Kuen after Tiepolo, *Pluto and Proserpina*, Library, Weissenhorn.

for its tame effect, and yet is a tribute to Tiepolo's determined pursuit of the essence of the subject. He was now ready to execute this fresco and its pendant.

For the two frescoes there exists a mass of drawings, chiefly chalk drawings on blue paper, studying often details of jewellery, position of a hand and folds of drapery, as well as heads, and so on. The precise status of these drawings is vexed, and so in part is the matter of their attribution. If it is too sweeping to assign them to Domenico Tiepolo, or to studio assistance, it is nevertheless very far from established that they are all Giambattista's autograph working drawings corresponding to the actual areas of fresco worked on a time. The frescoes themselves reveal clear traces of incising, suggesting that cartoons were used in preparing the plaster surface—cartoons probably destroyed in the process. Several of the chalk drawings are oddly weak to be from Tiepolo's own hand, with wavering outlines that are quite untypical of his normally firm draughtsmanship. Nor are the often fussy details with which they deal the sort of details Tiepolo might be expected to need to study before executing a fresco. His imagination and his improvisation—not to mention his great experience by the mid-1740s—were such that it is hard to think he now felt he must draw a brooch (Pl. 149) or a sash before incorporating such objects in, of all things, a fresco. And it seems an oddity that for the ceiling no drawings exist.

The stylistic evidence of the large oil paintings, and especially of the *modelli*, would point to the period around 1743–4 as that when Tiepolo's thoughts were most actively engaged with the Cleopatra and Antony theme. But execution of the Labia frescoes is quite likely to have been delayed, perhaps edged out by the pressure of other commissions which were running behind schedule. By about 1746 the pressure had probably slackened. Around then Tiepolo may have started the frescoes, but it is by no means impossible that they took more than one season to complete.

That they were completed, however, before he left for Würzburg would anyway be a reasonable supposition, and it finds confirmation of a kind in a rough drawing of the *Meeting* fresco done in Venice in 1752 (when Tiepolo was still absent in Germany) by the future Sir Joshua Reynolds. There is another piece of comparable evidence in a drawing of the Pluto and Proserpina group (Pl. 150), copied by a German artist, Franz Martin Kuen, who was in Venice for a longish period apparently in 1746–7. Kuen must have had good access to the palace, for he also copied Tiepolo's altarpiece in the family chapel. It is slightly surprising that he should have singled out from the whole salone scheme only the admittedly beautiful, but subsidiary and loftily positioned, mythological composition and not bothered to record the chief frescoes below. Tiepolo's task will have begun, of course, with the ceiling, and it is tempting to wonder if at the time of Kuen's visit he had not yet reached the Cleopatra and Antony frescoes themselves.

If the frescoes were not begun until, say, later in 1747, when Tiepolo had, by his standards, something resembling leisure, the silence of Algarotti would also become explicable. By then he had flitted away from Venice, from Italy altogether, and did not return to the country until 1753, the year Tiepolo returned from Würzburg. By then, both he and Tiepolo had other concerns; extraordinary as it might now seem, the episode of the Palazzo Labia frescoes was only an episode in the artist's busy life, eclipsed perhaps for him by the even greater, grander achievements at Würzburg.

Yet it was in the Palazzo Labia that Tiepolo gave fullest expression to his dream of classical antiquity, focused on a woman who was no conventional heroine, no chaste warrior-maid, no humane ruler or faithful wife. Cleopatra was simply a queen, beautiful and opulent. Whether or not he was aware of Plutarch's words, Tiepolo celebrated the person he had memorably described: 'But yet she carried nothing with her wherein she trusted more than in herself, and in the charms and enchantment of her passing beauty and grace.' That is very different from the stern

152. *Negro page and monkey*, Palazzo Labia, Venice.

Roman ethos of the Palazzo Dolfin canvases of some twenty years earlier, and far from the heroic acts of an Alexander or a Scipio, controlling their emotions; whereas Antony, under Cleopatra's spell, surrenders his will and yields frankly to pleasure.

In a room decorated to make a sumptuous ambient for feasting and presumably dancing—for people to enjoy themselves in—that 'lesson' might seem enough. Yet it may be doubted if such pure hedonism, more characteristic of the court of Louis XV than of Tiepolo's Venice, was the motive behind the frescoes, in the eyes of either the artist or his patrons. Not Antony but Cleopatra is the subject. And there is a sense in which she can be seen as admirable, skilful, even heroic in her Scarlett O'Hara fashion, as she sets out to defend what she possesses in the only ways open to her—the only ways, it could be claimed, open to most women. To some extent, the frescoes arguably do not tell a love story, as Shakespeare or Dryden understood it. Tiepolo's Cleopatra gives no hint of the world being well lost for love. She enchants, astounds and dominates, acting more like Armida in seducing Rinaldo than a mere mortal woman swept by passion; but unlike Armida (who admittedly falls in love) her motives are 'good': she disarms a potential enemy, to keep her kingdom.

The fact that the whole room was to be decorated, giving Tiepolo opportunities to enhance the illusionism already apparent in Mengozzi's contribution, made for both coherence and impact of a strongly theatrical kind. The actual disposition of space meant, however, that the main entrance wall and that opposite, largely occupied by windows, could receive only a light garnish of frescoes by Tiepolo, though even there he deliberately contrasted mood and mode. Over the entrance doorway he painted a sober statue of Minerva (scarcely a goddess associated with love), giving classical dignity to the room, and placed directly above a sculpted, gilded Labia eagle. On the facing wall Mengozzi had conjured up a solid-seeming marble balustrade. This Tiepolo enlivened with a negro page holding a plate of food and apparently trying to tempt a mischievous chained monkey, scrabbling along the interstices of the balustrade (Pl. 152). The concept of these figures derives from one version of Cleopatra's banquet, positively that of the horizontal *modello*, where a negro page descended the steps and on the adjoining balustrade was perched a pet monkey.

Between Minerva and the monkey-business, each effective in its way, two facets of Tiepolo's art are aptly symbolised. Grave and lively constantly mingle, and the presence of both in the Palazzo Labia scheme is only one indication of its richness and complexity. All the aspects of Tiepolo's imagination met here. Within one room are united allegory, mythology and history. The ceiling is pure vision, remote and timeless, with its own idiom of eternal triumph. Closer to the spectator, though still removed, floating into the room frequently in front of the architecture, come the figures of mythology. Finally there are the two scenes of mortals on earth—though earth is scarcely the word for the magic soil where pageant figures, blended of East and West, hybrids redolent of Veronese but grown taller, wilder and more fantastic, flowers of glass-like irridescence, take final shape. Such a scheme, on so many levels, is too rich, too intoxicating—too perfect—to bear repetition. And Tiepolo was never again to repeat it.

On the left-hand wall he frescoed Antony meeting and greeting Cleopatra; on the right-hand wall her banquet. For the banquet setting Mengozzi had contrived a loggia of vast dimensions, with giant Ionic pilasters at the uppermost level, echoing those he feigned as within the salone itself, and a balconied gallery supported by Corinthian pillars. Glimpses of this colossal loggia are given through the screen of architecture he devised to cover the complete wall. In the gallery Tiepolo put, in place of onlookers as earlier, an orchestra (again an echo of the never-executed *Timotheus* is detectable), with a bespectacled conductor. On either side of the main area he piled up silver dishes and gold flagons, with a massy splendour suitable at once for Cleopatra and for the Labia.

162

In the upright *modello* he had shown his awareness of the architectural setting Mengozzi would execute, or had already executed. He had decided the placing of the three figures seated at table. Not much more remained, it might be thought, but to transfer the concept to the large-scale fresco. At this point Tiepolo reverted to one earlier idea, and gave Antony again a helmet, perhaps to increase his military, Roman appearance. Around Cleopatra, however, his thoughts continued to accumulate. Instead of appearing in profile, she appears in the fresco three-quarter face. Instead of her left hand lying idly in her lap, it is raised to take the glass of vinegar. The result is that less abruptly, though with far greater ease and assurance, she becomes the composition's cynosure, almost seeming to call for silence, and definitely for attention, as she balances pearl in one hand and glass in the other, fixing her gaze upon Antony like a conjuror mesmerising an audience.

Closely examined, the appurtenances of the banquet are quite simple, as are the attendants grouped around. Plain costumes and a plain, white tablecloth act as visual forms of discreet throat-clearing, ensuring that nothing distracts from Cleopatra (Pl. 151). And now Tiepolo exerts all his dress-making arts to clothe her with unparalleled magnificence. Her dress is no longer buff-yellow or white but a pale, mauvish pink, and wonderfully patterned. Her breasts are bared, the dress itself supported on the shoulders only by two strands of pearls. Pearls are around her throat and looped across the stomacher of her dress, where they meet a grass-green sash. The high, white, upstanding collar of a pale-blue cloak, swirling about her raised arms, sets off the blondeness of her skin and hair; and in her hair, itself twisted into diadem-like curls, are pearls, a cameo, the peaks of a golden crown, and a jagged fall of scarf or ribbon of an intense, brilliant blue.

Among those gazing with Antony at this apparition, a full-blown pink peony that far exceeds nature, are two bizarrely clad men at the extreme left, one bony-faced, the other with rounder, fatter features (Pl. 153). Tiepolo is easily identifiable as the first. That Mengozzi is the other can be only conjecture, but it is a very attractive one. Side by side, witnesses of their own creation which extends around and beyond Cleopatra—which is everywhere in the room—they deserve their place at the feast of astonishment they have together, so memorably, created. No signature or date is on the frescoes, but Mengozzi and Tiepolo are declared to have been here—and here, it may be more than sentimentality to feel, was where the whole scheme finished, with the subject with which Tiepolo's thinking had most certainly begun.

Yet he did not fail to respond to creating the fresco opposite. A new idea occurred to him, and in place of the motif of all his previous proposals, of Antony kissing Cleopatra's hand, he made Antony advance, leading her forward, as though to descend the painted steps (matching those in the *Banquet*) and enter the actual salone. Only marginally less splendidly dressed, incredibly tall and stately, Cleopatra is colder in costume and manner, wearing what in reproduction appears a white dress but is actually white suffused with a mauve tint: she is a magnolia in place of a peony, and a little more fragile-seeming.

Pomp and animation, the press of people in a breezy place as a royal progress gets under way: such seem deliberate contrasts with the more static scene of the *Banquet*. There is immediacy in the action of the negro page, worked up from the upright *modello*, tugging out of the lovers' path a pale-brown hound, as refined and delicately proportioned as Cleopatra (Pl. 138). A beautiful piece of *recherché* colour complements the boy's dark skin with a tunic of crushed blackberry—itself an unusually dark tone to find in a fresco painter's palette. Above all, Mengozzi had allowed for space. He had left quite blank the background perceived through the vast architectural screen—in contrast to the setting of the *Banquet*. Tiepolo too was to leave the background largely blank, though he turned it into sky and gave it aerial depth and scale by a pennant or two, rigging, tackle and masts, all as foreshadowed in his *modello*.

In that sketch a sail is discernible behind the thickest of the masts, up which a

153 (following page). Detail of Pl. 135.

163

seaman clambers. For the fresco, in a moment of sheer inspiration, whether pondered or improvised, he brought the sail forward, hiding the mast, and made the great arc formed by its yard and yard-arms curve beyond the main scene into the subsidiary portions of fresco at the right, almost touching the standing man in profile who closes the whole composition. White as any cloud, the sail falls like a backcloth, and the seaman is retained, leaning over it at what appears a dizzy height, engaged perhaps in furling it now the voyage is done (Pl. 154). Already in the *modello* Tiepolo had conceived another, more marvellous barque, with a prow carved into a torso of Neptune. In the fresco he modelled this with such proud virility that the figurehead takes on the character of an additional, living personage. In the *modello* too he had sketched the blonde page-boy standing halfway up the gangplank. For the fresco he changed the colour of his costume from lemon-yellow to lime-green, and instead of holding a salver, the page now holds a cushion, on which rests the stake for which Cleopatra is playing, more precious to her than any pearl: her crown.

If this fresco is slightly the less famous of the two, it still has its own poetry, poetry of motion seen at its most enchanted in the Winds who puff and blow high up in the heavens, who have, it seems, blown Antony hither. Turbaned and helmeted figures —eastern and western—watch the pair of lovers, while other more menial figures toil. Recalling a motif from his horizontal *modello*, Tiepolo retained the men unloading huge urns of precious metal, though they are glimpsed only briefly through an aperture flanking the main fresco area. Their presence tends to confirm that the action is of Antony's disembarkation.

He himself is the most lost, the most absorbed of all the figures, locked in a personal dream; apparently leading Cleopatra but led by her; apparently so splendidly armoured but patently vulnerable; heroic-seeming, martial and magnificent, 'the greatest soldier in the world', but weak and hopelessly in thrall. He cannot advance without turning back. Tiepolo probably echoed his own concept of the affianced Carthaginian couple in the Villa Cordellina *Continence of Scipio*, but here it has almost tragic significance, symbolising the dominance exercised by Cleopatra.

One or two other isolated frescoes were painted by Tiepolo in the Palazzo Labia, but the results are hardly memorable after the impact of the Cleopatra and Antony scenes. He also executed a large pair of horizontal oil paintings of the two subjects, in or around 1747 (the date that has been deciphered, rightly or wrongly, on one of them). In reproduction, at least, these look disappointing and unsatisfactory, an odd mixture of motif (though there is one new one in Antony's confronting Cleopatra, in a rather ungainly way, at their seashore meeting) and undistinguished in execution. Studio assistance seems the most likely explanation for paintings which, though they may well be based on the horizontal *modelli*, come as a somewhat laboured and fatigued postscript to Tiepolo's epic handling of an epic story.

The room at the Palazzo Labia was organised into being a complete theatre, the theatre to which Tiepolo had always been aspiring, where for his *dramatis personae* Mengozzi created the most splendidly effective of prosceniums. All is illusion in the room, or so it seems, making the visitor lose—like Antony—any awareness of reality beyond. Art occupies every centimetre of space, and indeed defines what is space. There is no sense, as at the Villa Cordellina, of the frescoes as merely pictures on the wall. To the concept of total decoration that recalls the patriarchal gallery at Udine is joined a thematic linking of ceiling to wall that has something in common with the Villa Pisani and which Tiepolo would make most dramatic of all in the hall of the Villa Valmarana.

But nowhere else was to have the almost overpowering profusion of the Palazzo Labia salone, an effect that must have been only the greater when the frescoes were in pristine state. Today, after nineteenth-century neglect and twentieth-century damage, caused in the Second World War, they have lost the startling freshness of, for example, the Palazzo Sandi ceiling. Gone also from Tiepolo's style is something

154 (preceding page). Detail of Pl. 136.

of earlier piquancy. In its place is superb assurance, a quality the theme imperatively called for. It shows in Tiepolo's depiction of Antony, especially in the harbour scene: he is made far more convincingly a noble hero of antiquity than had been Tiepolo's Alexander or Scipio.

Altogether, the style of the Labia frescoes is less 'mannered', as well as more matured, confident and balanced. The strongly centralised compositions are part of that balance, but it is also present in less analysable ways, partly perhaps arising from the very fact that the incidents chosen concern not solely Cleopatra but also Antony. There is an element, rare in Tiepolo, of two protagonists, male and female. Cleopatra's may be the more dominant role (though in the harbour scene, as finally evolved for the fresco, Tiepolo gave Antony visual precedence), but that does not detract from the close involvement of two great personages—in, operatically speaking, a duet. No fading here and there can damage the frescoes' almost autumnal ripeness, suitable again for the theme of lovers no longer young, doomed, it is true, but wonderfully well matched, equal and united in death:

> No grave upon the earth shall clip in it
> A pair so famous.

And no pictorial representation of them, it may be claimed, approaches closer to the Renaissance splendour with which Shakespeare had invested them than does Tiepolo's.

8 THE YEARS AT WÜRZBURG

WHENEVER EXACTLY the Palazzo Labia frescoes were completed, they cannot have been worked on during the winter months. In the later portion of the decade of 1740 Tiepolo had commissions for other palaces in Venice, chiefly—it is worth noticing—for oil paintings. He also had one or two major religious compositions to paint in oil. At the Palazzo Barbaro he painted a ceiling on canvas, showing the apotheosis of the sixteenth-century family hero Francesco Barbaro, and four oval overdoors of somewhat recondite, still partly baffling subject-matter, focusing on virtuous heroines of antiquity.[1] Lucretia is easily identified; and a scene ironically often supposed to depict Cleopatra is actually of Roman women offering their jewellery to Juno (not, presumably, a subject likely to have appealed to Maria Labia).[2] Another, perhaps slightly earlier canvas for a Venetian palace was the brilliantly coloured, highly Veronesian *Marriage Allegory*, which commemorated a marriage in the Cornaro family, faithful patrons of Tiepolo.[3]

In the summer of 1749 Tiepolo received a commission for an altarpiece with the unexpected destination of London (Pl. 155). Unfortunately, although executed and still surviving (today located, even less expectedly, in Budapest), the altarpiece gave rise to difficulties from its arrival in London onwards and was apparently never installed. Not the least strange aspect of a fascinating story, with international ramifications, is that this, the first major Spanish commission to Tiepolo, resulted in his painting being effectively rejected—a rare occurrence in his career, but one that was to be repeated in Spain at the end of his life, over his altarpieces for the church of S. Pascual Baylon.

It was in August 1749 that the Spanish ambassador in London, Ricardo (or Richard) Wall, by birth an Irishman, gave Tiepolo a commission for a painting of the Apostle closely associated with Spain and Spanish history, St James the Greater, intended for the altar in the embassy chapel.[4] The reasons for the choice of artist are not known. Wall did not claim to be knowledgeable about painting and may have been guided by the Spanish ambassador in Venice, the Duke of Montealegre. Even after the commission was given, Wall was hesitating, assuring his ministerial master in Spain that, if he could get work on the painting suspended, he would send the necessary measurements to Madrid, clearly with a view to the altarpiece being executed there.

Tiepolo, however, went ahead with the commission. The painting reached London just about twelve months later, by which time Tiepolo's thoughts must have been very much concerned with his impending journey to Würzburg. Before the *St James* altarpiece left Venice, it had been warmly approved. The Doge, Pietro Grimani, had seen it (perhaps more as a diplomatic courtesy to Spain than as an expression of artistic interest), and in London it was to be inspected by a number of connoisseurs, among them Frederick, Prince of Wales, and to receive varied assessment. When Wall reported these facts back to Madrid, on 3 December 1750, he was frankly seeking a different subject for the embassy altarpiece, preferring a Christ

155. *St James of Compostella*, Szépművészeti Müzeum, Budapest.

crucified and, by implication, a different painter to execute it. That was just as well, since Tiepolo, having set off for Würzburg, was no longer available.

In giving Tiepolo the subject of St James, Wall or his intermediary is likely to have had in mind a famous incident connected with the saint: his miraculous appearance, on a white horse and carrying a banner, at the battle of Clavijo between the Moors and the Spaniards. Thanks to the saint's intervention, the Moors were defeated. The subject was naturally popular in Spanish art, though occurring elsewhere in churches dedicated to St James.

The painting was an altarpiece, not therefore to be composed as a pure narrative. Tiepolo made the statuesque saint on horseback central, prominent and dignified, detaching him from the melée of battle glimpsed in the middle distance at the right. For St James there is no struggle. One touch of the saint's sword vanquishes the foreground Moor, whose scimitar and turban have fallen to the ground like symbols of his total submission.

Not since the Palazzo Dolfin series had Tiepolo dealt with a battle theme, but a figure on a white or piebald horse, facing frontally, with similarly arched neck, is included in the *Family of Darius before Alexander* fresco in the Villa Cordellina and again in the *Entry of Pietro Soderini into Florence*. This motif of horse and rider may owe something in pose, and also in use of it at the edge of a composition, to the armoured equestrian figure at the extreme left in Tintoretto's vast *Crucifixion* in the Scuola di S. Rocco. More frontal and dynamic in pose is St Martin's horse in Pordenone's *Sts Martin and Christopher* in the church of S. Rocco. There the angle of the horse's head, and even the saint's gesture towards a figure at the left, could have had some influence on Tiepolo's motif of an equestrian figure but seems particularly close to the treatment in the composition showing St James.

It is not surprising that Tiepolo should quote himself, with subtle variations, for the pose of St James's horse, though he has made the saint's animal more nervously thoroughbred, pure white and almost soulful in expression. The lightly idealised saint's head is soulful also, in its heaven-seeking gaze and pious air, and though the upturned face is hardly new as a pose in itself, it conveys a mood of devotion and ardour which becomes a tendency in Tiepolo's later work.

Against an unbroken blue sky, enhanced by recent cleaning, the saint and his horse appear very much visionary forms. St James, dressed in cream garments, on his milky steed, has a supernatural radiance and pallor. Apart from the scarlet of the horse's trappings, the sole strong colour comes from the red area of the saint's triumphant, parti-coloured, Christian banner. It is with a gesture slowed down—as ceremonial as a dubbing—and outside the tempo of ordinary fighting that he subdues the youthful, unresisting Moor, sinking in recognition of a superior force. Perhaps there is some suggestion—since he is not slain—of the Moor's conversion at the point of the sword.

On the feigned balcony of the ceiling of the Villa Pisani Tiepolo had placed beside him a figure who must be his own Moorish or negro servant, whose existence is traditional and also, to some extent, documented. A chalk study for the Moor's head in the *St James* may be based on that of his own servant's, while the theme of conversion, rather than killing, might well appear to Tiepolo a sympathetic—not to say more Christian—approach to infidels.

The very presentation of the saint is simpler, more 'human' and less dramatic than had been Tiepolo's earlier tendency. The intervention of heaven is restricted to a pair of cherubs' heads, something which can be compared with the Noventa Vicentina altarpiece of *Sts Roch and Sebastian*. There is also a striking similarity between the upturned face of St Roch and that of St James, and now that the painting for the Spanish embassy in London is known to have been executed by 1750, it is tempting to consider if the Noventa Vicentina painting is not equally pre-Würzburg in date.

That the *St James* at least looks forward to later developments in Tiepolo's style, though its actual handling has none of the hard outlines that then occur, is indicated by the general acceptance of it as a painting of the late 1750s, or later still, until the documents about its commissioning were discovered. Not every painting of the last period, even among those with religious subject-matter, is simple in composition and treatment, blending realism and piety in a way less ostensibly stylish than was earlier typical of the artist, but that becomes a marked tendency, well before Tiepolo went to Spain.

It is not credible that such a shift of mood, gradual rather than violent, can be attributed solely to the influence of Domenico Tiepolo, though it results in the father coming closer to the ethos of his son. Nor can it be attributed, as it used to be, to some influence arising from the years in Spain, since it obviously preceded that period. Tiepolo was not retreating from the world nor, as far as can be deduced, from his art, undergoing some spiritual crisis. But he may have felt that his art needed to evolve, to become less consciously aristocratic and aloof, less visually splendid, particularly where religious subjects were concerned. Whether he was aware of it or not, the style he was most widely associated with was dropping from favour with 'advanced' opinion in Europe. Not gods and goddesses but ordinary people were to appear on the stage, in the plays of Goldoni, to take a Venetian example. The imaginative scenes of Tiepolo were to be compared, by the Venetian *littérateur* Gasparo Gozzi, with the realistic ones of Pietro Longhi; and Gozzi pointedly stated that the latter were by no means inferior.

Tiepolo conceivably chose to emphasise the 'human' and the un-grandiose in the *St James* altarpiece because of its destination. For a German rococo church, say, he might have felt a more sumptuous and astonishing effect was required. He must anyway have been only too conscious that the English did not patronise him.

When the painting reached London, Wall found first that its measurements were wrong: either the embassy altar needed to be dismantled or the canvas would have to be cut. Worse than this was the subject of the painting. Although he recognized it had been done by the 'famoso pintor . . . de venecia', he—or at least his chaplains at the embassy—feared that the figure of the horse would cause a scandal, given English attitudes to the cult of images. When people came to see the painting a few months later, they were divided in their judgment of it, he was to report; though the feared-for scandal seems not to have arisen—perhaps because the painting was not placed on the altar. Nobody seems to have known what to do with the painting, but probably it was despatched to Spain. Wall himself was recalled to Madrid in 1752 and was still in royal service when Tiepolo arrived there ten years afterwards.

Almost a lull can be detected in Tiepolo's career, if not in his output, as the mid-point of the eighteenth century approached. With the Palazzo Labia frescoes finished, he had, it seems, no major commission, no further fresco scheme to undertake. Around 1749–50 he may have painted his sole official decoration for the Doge's Palace, the *Neptune bringing Venice the treasures of the sea*, though the exact dating of that painting is hard to settle.[5]

Europe was drawing its breath, following the Peace of Aix-la-Chapelle in 1748. 'The year which we are now closing', pronounced *The Gentleman's Magazine* in 1749, 'has not been made memorable by any great events. The European nations are engaged in repairing the ruins of the late war.' Among the less remarked-on events of 1749 was the succession of a new Prince-Bishop, Carl Philipp von Greiffenklau, in the Franconian city of Würzburg. It may have had little political resonance but it was to prove of the greatest significance for Tiepolo.[6] By March 1750 a complex series of incidents had left the enlightened Prince-Bishop with an urgent wish to see suitably painted the main room of his imposing palace, the Residenz, built by the brilliant architect Balthasar Neumann, but with no painter for the task. Thoughts turned to Italy, and specifically to Venice, which had some useful commercial links with Würzburg. Approached about the commission, Tiepolo was interested, and soon terms were agreed. The Prince-Bishop was delighted by the news. The programme devised for the fresco scheme was sent to Venice, but so eager was the Prince-Bishop to obtain the painter that he would not insist on proposals in the programme if Tiepolo had better ones to make.

The culmination of all arrangements, negotiations and travel came on 12 December 1750 when Tiepolo, accompanied not only by Domenico but also by his younger son Lorenzo, aged fourteen, and by a servant, arrived in Würzburg, to be lodged in the Residenz. For the first time in his life, Tiepolo had left Italy, going north as Titian had once done, and partly over the same route. Just as with Titian, Tiepolo's paintings went travelling out of Italy before he did. As well as the *St Clement* altarpiece for the Elector of Cologne, he had painted the *Martyrdom of St Sebastian* for the new church of the Augustinian canons at Diessen, designed by the Bavarian rococo architect, Johann Michael Fischer.

In 1750 another distinguished foreigner was drawn to a German court: at last Voltaire had yielded to Frederick the Great's entreaties and arrived in Berlin. The mid-point of the century was the year that the prospectus for the *Encyclopédie* appeared, a quintessence of all that the Enlightenment stood for. Yet 1750 was also the year of Rousseau's *Discours sur les Sciences et les Arts*, attacking luxury and the corruption that art brings—and an example of such corruption might well have seemed to Rousseau the refined court environment of the Prince-Bishop for whom Tiepolo was to work.

Commercial and artistic links between Würzburg and Venice were partly represented by a native of Würzburg, the merchant and banker Lorenz Mehling, living in Venice, who seems to have opened negotiations on the court's behalf with Tiepolo.[7] Mehling had earlier signalled devotion to his native city by sending home from Venice the gift of a reliquary-monstrance. Before Tiepolo was prepared to go in the same direction, a number of matters had to be settled (not least that of money), but Mehling must have been able to report favourably at quite an early stage. A letter of 24 May 1750, from the Prince-Bishop's treasury to Mehling, told of Greiffenklau's pleasure that 'the famous fresco painter Signor Tiepolo has decided to come. . .' Longingly and eagerly was he awaited, and it was then that the Prince-Bishop gave emphasis to his eagerness by dispensing Tiepolo from being bound by the subjects outlined in the 'programme'. It was not the 'programme' but his fees over which Tiepolo bargained, in addition to the cost of the journey and the number of people who would accompany him. No doubt the commission and the flattering reception he was promised were tempting factors, but the final one must have been the high sum of money it was agreed he should receive: 10,000 Rhenish florins, apart from subsidiary payments for travel and board and lodging.

Commissions needing to be completed could have been responsible for some delay in his setting out for Würzburg, but he was also ill, twice, during 1750, as the court authorities learnt in August. These illnesses may have been early attacks of the 'gout' of which he was later to complain but which seems never to have incapacitated him in any serious way. In itself, the journey to Würzburg was not daunting. Sebastiano Ricci, Pellegrini and Amigoni had travelled and worked not only in Germany but as far as England (as had Canaletto, of course). Amigoni had eventually gone south as well, to Madrid. Rosalba Carriera had visited Paris and Vienna, and Fontebasso was to go off to work in St Petersburg.

Whatever Tiepolo and his party expected, their first sight of the Residenz at Würzburg can hardly have failed to impress them. The colossal scale of the building, situated on the edge of the city, itself attractively set along the Main and surrounded by vine-clad hills, was almost unparalleled in Germany, princely in a way that recalled the magnificence of Versailles, though with far greater elegance of effect (Pl. 156). Its huge entrance courtyard was then enclosed by elaborate ironwork gates, minor masterpieces of baroque style. At the centre of the building, behind the vast,

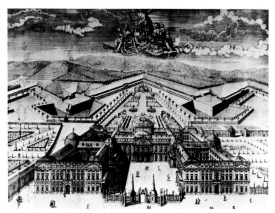

156. Eighteenth-century engraving showing a view of the Residenz, Würzburg.

carved coat-of-arms, and looking on to the formal gardens at the back was the Hauptsaal—the Kaisersaal, as it was soon to become known—where Tiepolo would work.

The undamaged Würzburg of the eighteenth century, with its cathedral and other fine churches, must have been a pleasant enough city. It was to strike Mozart sufficiently for him to note it as 'eine schöne prächtige Stadt', though he stopped there only briefly, for coffee, on his way to Frankfurt in 1790. Italians had contributed to the handsome architecture of Würzburg, under the patronage of successive Prince-Bishops, since Antonio Petrini (from Trento) had settled and built there in the mid-seventeenth century. Tiepolo was to find a talented fellow-Italian artist, Antonio Bossi, a stucco-worker, active in the Prince-Bishop's service.

The traditions of Würzburg went back a very long way and were proudly upheld. Greiffenklau was the seventy-fifth bishop in the seat of St Burkhard, the first bishop who had been consecrated by the great saint of Germany, St Boniface, in the tenth century. A strong sense of history, combined with consciousness of the city as the site of great events, was to play its part in shaping the 'message' behind Tiepolo's frescoes, though the final expression of these in terms of personalities, rather than a theme, was possibly the painter's own contribution.

It was not only great architectural achievements that Tiepolo encountered at Würzburg but also a great architect, in the person of Balthasar Neumann. Franconia was Neumann's artistic kingdom, with Würzburg its capital. Eleven years older than Tiepolo, he possessed a genius that was admirably complementary, and in an ideal world architect and painter would have worked together in Franconian churches and in other palaces as well as in the Residenz.

Neumann had trained in military engineering, served as a lieutenant of artillery and in 1720 became surveyor of the episcopal palace being planned at Würzburg on a gigantic scale by the then Prince-Bishop, Philipp Franz von Schönborn, the second outstanding member of a famous family to reign there.

At the Prince-Bishop's instigation, Neumann made plans for the city in addition to the Residenz, and his responsibilities increased with the succession in 1729 of a third Schönborn as ruler. Like Tiepolo, he was to be much in demand and highly influential, as far away as, for example, Vienna.

The genesis of the Residenz at Würzburg is complicated. By an odd coincidence, the concept may go back to a Venetian source: the germ of the design has been traced to the project for a palace near Heidelberg, envisaged by an architectural superintendent who was Venetian. A multi-national flavour was introduced when French architects were brought in to give advice, and Neumann himself travelled not only to Paris but to Vienna to consult a distinguished contemporary, Hildebrandt, creator of the Upper and Lower Belvedere there. All the various contributions contradicted the proverbial saying of 'too many cooks'. The final building was a splendid achievement: it incorporated a richly decorated chapel, and, above all, a vast and magnificent staircase, with a huge vault, bare when Tiepolo arrived.

It was under the third Schönborn Prince-Bishop, Friedrich Carl, that the Residenz had been completed in 1744. He died two years later, and after the brief reign of his successor Carl Philipp von Greiffenklau, himself a Schönborn on his mother's side, became Prince-Bishop and possessor of the palatial Residenz.

Its interior was no less splendid than the exterior, though bombing in the Second World War destroyed many of the exquisitely decorated rooms, with their stucco, lacquer and mirrors. Behind the strong, baroque façade the idiom was more rococo, with much elegant stucco decoration by Bossi (a native of Lugano), who occasionally worked also as a painter. Fortunately, there survives his 'white salon', acting as an ante-room to the Kaisersaal, and almost a grotto of stucco decoration, twisting and branching out in forms where mingle associations of white coral and frosted foliage, with an effect at once ornamentally rich and tonally austere.

There was one area of artistic activity where Franconia notably failed to generate or attract great talent, and that was painting. No native painter approached Neumann's stature. In their various palaces, as for churches, even the Schönborn family had not always succeeded in obtaining first-rate painters, though on occasion looking abroad, to Italy. Early in the eighteenth century Andrea Pozzo had declined to execute frescoes for the Residenz at Bamberg, where the walls had been kept simple and flat to form a convenient surface for paintings. There the proposed theme had been 'Roman history or something connected with it with moral implications' ('so in das Moralische einläufet').[8] What was finally produced, by a painter from the Tyrol, was less moral than historical and imperial in its connotations: the Roman emperors were depicted with their German successors. In a very faint way there gleams there some hint of the 'idea' or programme, and certainly the train of thought, that was to be expressed by Tiepolo in the Kaisersaal at Würzburg.

The greatest patron of the Schönborn family, Lothar Franz, had had built early in the century the grandiose and monumentally baroque Schloss Pommersfelden, where again architectural achievement was not matched by the decorative painting of the interior. The subject of the vast staircase-ceiling fresco (Pl. 157) (executed by a much-travelled Swiss artist, Johann Rudolf Byss)—Apollo as the Sun adorning the World as Virtue adorns mankind—has a moral, enlightenment 'message' which may also have had its relevance for Tiepolo's second commission at Würzburg—in terms of subject rather than composition or, still less, technique. Imperial German history was to be disposed of in the Kaisersaal, and was so successfully conjured up in such a superb decorative way by Tiepolo that he became the obvious artist to undertake decoration of the staircase ceiling, where the theme eventually selected would be entirely allegorical, of Apollo illumining the world.

Carl Philipp von Greiffenklau had inherited two major problems of decoration in the Residenz, of which the staircase one was easily the more daunting by its sheer scale and the demands it made on those who drew up its programme, as well as on the executant of any scheme.

The Hauptsaal, which became the Kaisersaal, was a challenge of a different kind, where the scale was still big but where the chosen painter had to match the sumptuous décor and add the final adornment to a room intended as a state dining-room. It seemed sensible to give priority to the painted decorations of this room and reserve the question of the staircase for later.

In 1749 the Swabian painter Johann Zick, six years younger than Tiepolo, had been invited to Würzburg to fresco the ceiling of the ground-floor Garden Hall. It was on Neumann's advice that this commission was looked on as in the nature of a trial, to see if Zick had 'all the necessary ability' to be entrusted with the frescoes of the Hauptsaal overhead. The Garden Hall was an ungrateful space—low because of the high room above—and Zick must have been judged—quite rightly—to lack sufficient skill and lightness of touch for the greater task.

Before that conclusion was quite clear, the Prince-Bishop had allowed himself to be persuaded by a plausible rogue, a certain Joseph [sic] Visconti from Milan, otherwise unknown as a painter, that he, Visconti, and his son could successfully fresco the Hauptsaal. The episode is most curious, but Visconti impressed both Greiffenklau and Neumann by a sketch he showed them for one of the frescoes, of an 'Imperial marriage'. During the winter of 1749–50, while Zick retired to his own studio, Visconti was installed in the Hauptsaal, where stoves were introduced, and began, or failed to begin, to fresco. Perhaps he had no experience or adequate technique. Court officials soon realised that no progress was being made with the work, and on 2 March 1750 Visconti was ignominiously dismissed.

From patronising the totally obscure, the Prince-Bishop turned, perhaps with relief and possibly prompted by Neumann, to the most famous of fresco painters. Tiepolo accepted the Hauptsaal commission. He arrived in Würzburg with his two sons. Quarters were assigned to the family in the Residenz, and they were to be seated for meals at the table reserved for persons of knightly rank, though Tiepolo seems to have preferred to sit at the court servants' table, where the court artists sat. Eventually he ate in his own quarters, where his suite of rooms included a studio.

No frescoing was proposed for him during the winter months, which were occupied presumably in finalising ideas for the frescoes now he could inspect the actual room and see on the spot what was involved. Before he left Venice, Tiepolo had received the 'programme' for the Hauptsaal, a document that had gone through several stages over a considerable period of years, and one that the Prince-Bishop might well fear was calculated to deter any artist of genius, especially a foreign one.

Proposals for the theme of decoration went back to 1735, to the reign of Friedrich Carl von Schönborn. Originally the intention was that the decorative scheme should be spread over a whole series of rooms, to include the staircase area. Although illustrated by various examples and incidents, the central concept was plain and coherent. It revolved around the bishopric of Würzburg and the duchy of Franconia, from their origins to late medieval times, in a positively historical pageant of a kind now more often associated with the decoration of nineteenth-century town halls. The Empire and Germany were stressed throughout in a document of impressive learning, if of doubtful inspiration for an artist. But the imperial, dynastic overtones and the deep seriousness of what was proposed made it likely to appeal to a ruler who combined in himself the spiritual and temporal.

Some rooms were intended to be frescoed, while others would be decorated by oil paintings. The Hauptsaal was among those destined for frescoes, as was the staircase ceiling which, partly perhaps because of its size, would be divided into five scenes. One of these had as its subject: 'How the Emperor Frederick Barbarossa was married to the Burgundian Princess Beatrice and not only confirmed Herold, Bishop of Würzburg, in the duchy of Franconia but also invested him at the same time, which could be shown by presentation of the ducal banner. . .' In the Hauptsaal, sacred and secular strains were to be united, with a distinct emphasis on the subordination of the latter, however great in worldly terms. Thus the Emperor Otto IV would be shown at his marriage—at the Imperial Diet held in Würzburg—

to the daughter of another Emperor; and St Boniface would be depicted crowning Pippin as King of the Franks.

Frescoes for some rooms, as they were completed, were put in hand in the 1730s, though the Prince-Bishop expressed doubts about the proposal for as many as five scenes on the ceiling of the staircase. In a revised programme of a few years later, new proposals were made, omitting the marriage of Frederick Barbarossa and his investiture of Bishop Herold. One or both of these important subjects were probably then assigned to the Hauptsaal. There, in the winter of 1749–50, Visconti attempted to execute his fresco whose subject was a 'Marriage'.

By the time Tiepolo received the programme in Venice, it was in its fourth and final state.[9] It set out clearly the two historical scenes to be frescoed in the Hauptsaal: Frederick Barbarossa's marriage and the Imperial Diet, held by the same Emperor, with the consecration, investiture and homage of the Bishop of Würzburg. These scenes would be painted 'right and left above the cornice'. The ceiling was to be in more allusive, poetical vein. The Genius of *Imperium* would be seated on a throne, being brought the bride by Apollo, 'Phoebus orientalis', in the chariot of the Sun.

That is very much a précis of a lengthy document. The smaller areas of the room also required to be filled, with portraits and semi-political allegories, all specified in erudite and minute precision. The programme had retained all its learned, literary, chronicler-like origins. It quoted in Latin from the patent Frederick Barbarossa had conferred on the Bishop; it cited Claudian in connection with the ceiling and Hosea, chapter two, for the allegories.

Tiepolo neither neglected it nor was overawed by it. He may have encountered pedantry before (there are no surviving programmes for the frescoes in the Palazzo Archinto or the Palazzo Clerici), though not always in quite such proliferating, excruciating detail. There should be, the programme specified, for example, an oratory in which the Bishop of Würzburg blessed the bridal pair, with Rainier, Count of Burgundy, standing at the left, and depiction of the devices on the imperial banners and on the Burgundian shield (made up, it was to be noted, of eight portions, parti-coloured blue and yellow).

Tactfully and confidently, Tiepolo took no initiative over the Prince-Bishop's anxious assurance that any of this could be changed. He cheerfully undertook to work, 'with all possible attention, art and industry'—as the contract he signed phrased it—having had the programme translated into Italian. Further translation, into his own pictorial idiom, would follow once he got down to conceiving the frescoes. A significant twelfth-century event in a country he had never seen was—regardless of the stipulated form of the Burgundian shield—likely to emerge as set firmly in Tiepolo's entirely homogeneous concept of the historical past in sixteenth-century Venice. For the rest, princely couples and imperial events, bishops and banners (supplemented by dwarves and dogs, unspecified but to be volunteered) were the very stuff to excite his imagination, as they had always done.

Of more concern probably to him at this earliest stage, before he left Venice, was the plan that accompanied the programme, giving a description of the Hauptsaal. Luminous and beautiful though the room was, it by no means offered easy areas for fresco decoration. Unlike, say, the ballroom of the Palazzo Labia, where large walls were available for *quadratura* painting, supplementing the real architecture, the Hauptsaal was so rich in coloured marble and stucco that only above the cornice was there any space for frescoes—and then the two main spaces, north and south, were restricted and somewhat awkward, roughly triangular, with a floridly curved oval space forming the ceiling.

The challenge, as Tiepolo must have realised when he saw the room itself, was a double one: not merely had his compositions to fit harmoniously within the given areas, but they must match in quality the exuberantly sumptuous room, airy yet of great grandeur and of the finest workmanship. From its exquisitely patterned

158. View of the interior of the Kaisersaal, Residenz, Würzburg.

159. *The River Main*, Residenz, Würzburg.

stone floor to the gilded stucco surround of the ceiling, it was a masterpiece of interior decoration. Already *in situ*, presumably, and increasing the sense of drama, heightening anticipation of what the frescoes would show, were huge curtains on either side of the spaces, moulded out of plaster and painted blue and gold, heavily fringed, sparkling from inset portions of mirror and raised by winged putti to reveal the stage, as it were, on which the historical scenes would be acted out (Pl. 158).

In sending details of the room and its programme to Venice, the Prince-Bishop's officials had thought it unavoidable that execution of any preparatory sketches by the artist would have to wait until he actually saw it. Tiepolo probably agreed, though that is not to say that he did not turn over the subjects in his mind, especially in their essential components of a marriage, homage to a ruler and—most familiar of all to him—a 'heaven' of various deities.

Not until the winter was well over, by which time he must have been settled in at Würzburg, did Tiepolo begin work positively on the frescoes. Before that, on 17 April 1751, the Prince-Bishop came to visit him in his apartments in the Residenz. The court was about to move to Veitshöchheim, not returning until July, and a convenient period thus occurred for the frescoes to be started. On this visit, the Prince-Bishop apparently saw some sketches or drawings Tiepolo had prepared, conceivably for all three frescoes. The most likely thing is that, much as usual, oil *modelli* had been executed for approval by the patron. Whatever Tiepolo showed him on 17 April clearly gained the Prince-Bishop's approval. Ten days later he began work on the ceiling fresco. A court official (perhaps recalling the fiasco of Visconti's frescoes) looked into the room and noted that Tiepolo had started to paint and to 'durchpauschen': pricking the design, possibly with the aid of cartoons, on to the surface of, in this case, the ceiling. On 8 May, the same official noted, doubtless with relief, that the ceiling fresco had 'come along well'.[10] On 8 July, the feast of St Kilian, the Prince-Bishop returned for celebrations to Würzburg. The Hauptsaal could not be used, but he gave a dinner in the Garden Hall below, and after dinner took his guests to inspect the ceiling, now complete and unveiled for the first time.

Tiepolo had been faithful to the programme. Across a sky of bright blue, Apollo guides a quadriga of laurel-wreathed cream and white horses, rearing and snorting as they bear the chariot in which the bride sits, speeding on with thrilling velocity (Pl. 161). Before and around them stream and cluster cupids and personifications; Ceres and Bacchus hail them in their celestial progress; and leading the way is Hesper as Hymen, with a flaming torch ('mit einer brennenden fackel', as had been stipulated in the description). Awaiting the arrival of this bridal train, seated on a throne seen at a precipitously steep angle, surrounded by banners and emblems, is the figure of *Genius imperii* (frequently mistaken for the Emperor himself). 'Ein prächtiger thron' was the programme's requirement—one hardly necessary to urge on Tiepolo, who devised an eminence of satisfying, architectural solidity, compounded of curving white steps, jutting cornices, and a sheer plinth from which hangs a great bolt of peach-coloured fabric. At its foot he placed the river Main, referred to in the programme as desirable to include somewhere on the edge of the composition (Pl. 159). Just as the bride, Beatrice of Burgundy, is Tiepolo's usual blonde heroine, with high, pearl necklace and Veronese-style dress of gleaming white topped by a sweep of white ruff, so the Main is his familiar river-god, aged and naked except for a few sedges, clasping a nubile nymph.

Yet here the group is given its own additional, sensuous, watery allure. The stream tipped from the terracotta pot held by the river-god is thin and grey beside the cascade of shimmering blue silk that sets off his and his companion's flesh and spills out of the fresco frame altogether, rippling away in fluid fold after fold, as though tugged by gravity, like an element that refuses to be contained on the ceiling. Nearby, clouds mass and bulge beyond the gilt edge of the composition, suggesting that the sky is drifting down into the room. Flowers, scattered by cupids, are falling too, forever about to drop on the spectators below. And in this euphoric bursting of the bonds, the fresco seems to symbolise Tiepolo's refusal to be constricted, to feel inhibited—rather, the contrary—in the wonderful cage of pink, white and gold created by Neumann. Within it, his art would sing only the more loudly. If anything was needed to complete the room and complement the décor, it was use of the

160. *Apollo bringing the bride*, Staatsgalerie, Stutt-gart.

colour blue and a sense of space beyond the spaciousness already conveyed archi-tecturally. Both were provided by Tiepolo's skies, and by his consistent use of a brilliant blue for key areas of costume and drapery.

For the ceiling fresco two related oil sketches exist, one a rather slight, almost scratchy, affair,[11] the other more fully developed and acceptable as a true *modello* by Tiepolo himself (Pl. 160). Between them, they show that the main disposition of the

161. *Apollo bringing the bride*, Residenz, Würzburg.

162. *Homage to the Emperor*, Residenz, Würzburg.

163. Detail of Pl. 162.

groups as seen in the fresco was fixed from the start, with movement across the composition from right to left, the central motif being necessarily Apollo and the bride's chariot. Typically, the painter disposed the groups more spaciously when it came to the actual fresco, tidying up the group around *Genius imperii*, which had tended to seem confused at the sketch stage, and giving even greater *élan* to the real protagonists of the composition, the dark-eyed, pink-muzzled horses, creatures of barrel-bellied solidity, seen from below, but also poetically wild and rampant, careering through the sky like scudding clouds.

The working practice for translating the Residenz frescoes from *modelli* to final scenes is even more obscure than at the Palazzo Labia. Related chalk drawings that survive are not pricked and can scarcely be cartoons in the proper sense. The role of Domenico Tiepolo is no less obscure.[12] He was to be allotted some minor parts of the decoration in the Hauptsaal (oil paintings for three overdoors, one of which he signed) but must have been employed by his father in other ways. Lorenzo too, though very young and inexperienced, cannot have been taken to Würzburg solely for the pleasure of his company; to learn, he had to be active in the studio, even if in the humblest capacity. It seems obvious that Tiepolo, travelling abroad to a major task, in a building he had never seen, thought in terms of a team. He was perhaps conscious also that another, even more major task in the same building might be offered to him if the first was completed successfully.

foreground hound, introduced into the fresco of course but lacking in the preliminary sketch.

With touches like that, and the addition of the pair of Orientals (Pl. 165), the eventual fresco lightens solemnity, while actually reinforcing seriousness by portraying Greiffenklau, seventy-fifth bishop in the succession from St Burkhard, as his twelfth-century predecessor. The assurance of 'in perpetuum', provided by the imperial patent, is given pictorial resonance. And although Tiepolo filled Barbarossa's Diet with figures from his own, deeply Venetian imagination, he also introduced one or two heads, wearing ermine-bordered caps, who have an authentic northern flavour.

After the Hauptsaal ceiling, he turned to the two side frescoes, tackling first the *Marriage of the Emperor*, and only in July 1752 completing the *Homage* fresco opposite. He managed to finish it shortly before the feast day of St Kilian, and it was then, with the whole scheme concluded, that the room became known as the Kaisersaal.

The Marriage subject was to be treated purely historically. At Würzburg in 1156 the Emperor Frederick Barbarossa had married as his second wife Beatrice of Burgundy in, as the programme put it, 'the presence of many princely persons'. The moment to be depicted was the solemn benediction by the Bishop of Würzburg (Gebhard von Henneberg, though he was not identified in the text). The bride was a great heiress, bringing Burgundy to add to the Empire, while Würzburg gained— the compiler of the programme emphasises—from the imperial good will.

Such were the dynastic and local associations of a subject not immediately promising or inspiring. Tiepolo took it, lifted it outside time into his own private kingdom of the imagination and created what is possibly his most perfect non-allegorical fresco. It is certainly his most sumptuous.

Not even Tiepolo could match it or quite find sufficient inspiration in the companion scene, with its entirely masculine cast of characters and narrower local significance (Pl. 162). Bishop Herold kneels to the Emperor as a vassal to his feudal lord, while the Emperor confirms the Bishop and his successors ('Suisque successoribus in perpetuum...',[13] quoted the industrious compiler of the programme, citing the very words of the patent issued on the occasion), as holding full authority throughout the bishopric and duchy of Würzburg. Thus the scene was central to the existence of the Residenz—itself no mere *Lustschloss*, but the outward, visible and imposing sign of the Prince-Bishop as a ruler.

Tiepolo made all he could of the somewhat bare bones, clothing them with ermine and armour, rich robes and an imperial eagle, as well as adding pretty pageboys, a Palladian archway, two unexpected Orientals and a large, seated, Saint-Bernard-style dog. The effect is splendid in detail, but slightly inert. The kneeling Bishop and the enthroned Emperor do not hold much interest, even though Tiepolo gave the features of his own patron, Greiffenklau, to the twelfth-century prelate and dressed Barbarossa with a regal opulence even Louis XIV might have thought excessive. The surrounding court is, though distracting, more striking: from a dignified, aged noble holding a sword of state or justice, to the blondest of the pageboys winsomely turning to gaze out of the composition, as conscious as a choirboy of the effect of youthful looks allied to a fanciful costume, here of pale blue and white (Pl. 163).

For the composition there exists an oil sketch upright in format and somewhat puzzling as the original *modello*, yet clearly from the hand of Giambattista Tiepolo himself (Pl. 164). At this stage the central incident was located in a powerful architectural framework, with the Emperor seated within a deep porch or archway that rises to the top of the canvas. Tiepolo seems to be recalling partly the *Continence of Scipio* at the Villa Cordellina, and its preparatory sketch, and also aiming at an effect of much greater depth than he sought in the final fresco. Since the format of that had a more horizontal emphasis, he had to abandon the central arch, transferring the architectural element to the left and making it a screen running parallel, rather too patly, with the line of the Emperor's throne. As a result, the composition lost something in concentration but it gained in literal airiness and spaciousness, being now set in an open, sunny atmosphere. The original programme had stipulated an interior. In changing that, Tiepolo also managed to hint at the physical setting of Würzburg; a castle-crowned slope rising at the right of the fresco serves to convey the fortified castle of the Marienberg on its hill, as it is seen from the windows of the Residenz. Single figures are worked up and elaborated in chalk drawings, if those existing are truly preparatory; a typical sheet shows studies of the chief page-boy and the halberdier at the left, the head of the nobleman who holds the sword and the

Court life in eighteenth-century Germany is no more portrayed than is life there in the earlier period, but there is more than one reflection of it, and not least in the very choice of subject. Five centuries had elapsed since the original scene, but in 1752 it was still thought worth recapturing. With just fifty years more to survive, the small, unimportant yet civilised and essentially *ancien-régime* kingdom, centred on Würzburg, saw itself thus. In the palace of its ruler it had no thought of depicting those who are ruled or even the benefits of good government. Church and Empire were its twin concerns, highly individualised and localised, with a sort of sunny optimism felt in the very weather Tiepolo created. Here the Church kneels, pleasantly and courteously, yet definitely, to acknowledge the secular power. In the opposite fresco, the situation is reversed: Emperor and Empress kneel before the Church, personified in the blessing Bishop who is again given the features of Greiffenklau.

The *Marriage* fresco has priority of execution, but that offers no explanation of its flawless quality and perfect fusion of all Tiepolo's gifts. The subject seems ideal in retrospect, largely because of the freedom with which he interpreted it, frankly subordinating the imperial groom to his ice-princess bride whose long, apparently unending sweep of blue robe is in itself expressive of triumph and dominance.

The genesis of this fresco composition is unfortunately difficult to establish, not through any lack but rather through the existence of two oil sketches, often treated as preliminary *modelli* and as by Giambattista Tiepolo, when on both counts their claims are at least dubious (Pls 166 and 167). Not only in their handling, which can be compared with numerous undoubted autograph *modelli* by the artist himself, but in what they depict, these two sketches fail to impress and, ultimately, to convince.

The upright oil sketch at Boston is often described as Tiepolo's preliminary thought for the fresco. If that were so, he was wise to think again. The basic elements of the eventual composition are present, it is true; but by separating the bride and bridegroom, and placing the officiating Bishop between them, the author of the painting has contrived an awkward, confused knot at the very centre of the scene (and compounded confusion by the page-boy placed in front of the bridegroom). Another aspect of feeble designing is the plethora of mitred heads depicted behind the chief bishop's own—thus dissipating the impact of his presence, just as the Emperor's profile obscures the action of the blessing.

To suppose that Tiepolo, at the height of his artistic powers and for one of his most important commissions, conceived this 'first idea' is a good deal more difficult than relegating it to the category of the Tiepolesque following, while admitting that an exact author is not easily proposed and its original purpose unclear. A lack of vigour in the handling is only the clinching aspect in excluding the sketch from consideration.

The upright sketch, if sketch it be, in London is hardly more satisfactory as the creation of Tiepolo himself. At first glance it improves greatly on the Boston composition by grouping the bride and bridegroom together under the gaze and upraised hand of the Bishop, himself now given adequate presence and visual emphasis. At the same time, the Emperor is placed nearer than his bride to the foreground picture-plane. That in itself would be no oddity, but what is distinctly peculiar is that next to him is seen a page-boy in a pose explicable only (from the completed fresco) as adopted to hold up the bride's train. Thus the painter of the London picture has either introduced a figure meaningless in the context or perpetuated the clumsy, virtually impossible device of the bride's train held up behind the bridegroom. Far more likely is it that the painter had seen the completed fresco, borrowed largely from it and in introducing his own variations failed to spot the inconsistency.

The London painting is highly and heavily finished for a true *modello*, and has a heavy, more than faintly prosaic, touch. Its very colours—far from those of the

166. Studio (?) of Tiepolo. *Marriage of the Emperor*, Isabella Stewart Gardner Museum, Boston.

165 (facing page). Detail of Pl. 162.

167. Studio (?) of Tiepolo. *Marriage of the Emperor*, National Gallery, London.

168. Giambattista Tiepolo (?). *Apollo, page boy and other studies*, Staatsgalerie, Stuttgart (No. 1474).

169. Rubens. *Marriage of Marie des Médicis*, Louvre, Paris.

fresco—are hot and garish. Whether Domenico was its author is not entirely clear, though that is certainly more credible than assuming that it is the work of his father.

What must ultimately tell most strongly against both the Boston and the London paintings as true *modelli* are their radical compositional differences from the fresco. Tiepolo's *modelli* are often enough summary, and there are frequent departures from them, as charted by some of the commissions already discussed, in execution of the final work, but these tend to be minor and easily explicable. The point is well illustrated by the relationship between sketch and fresco of the Homage subject. It would be most unlike Tiepolo to sketch in oil paint proposals as far from his eventual solution as are the Boston and London compositions, leaving aside the other grounds for questioning them as autograph.

Removal of these unsatisfactory, though undoubtedly related, paintings from evolution of the eventual composition, leaves only some chalk drawings, chiefly studies of heads and arms in the fresco. There exists additionally a sheet of studies which includes the page-boy train-bearer of the fresco (Pl. 168). The same sheet has a study also for the figure of Apollo, clearly connected with the staircase-ceiling fresco Tiepolo was to go on to execute—but which at this date had not been begun or even commissioned. That is a further puzzling point in connection with these sheets of drawings.

In conceiving the *Marriage* fresco, to be set in the 'oratory' required by the programme, Tiepolo may have had in his mind two compositions by great artists of the preceding century. One of these is admittedly a distant echo—assuming it is an echo at all—but possibly in Rembrandt's grandly conceived etching of the *Marriage of Jason and Creusa*[14] lay some germ which could have proved fruitful for Tiepolo's thinking. Far more striking is the compositional parallel provided by Rubens's *Coronation of Marie des Médicis*, engraved earlier in the eighteenth century (Pl. 169). It cannot be established that Tiepolo was aware of this wonderful, characteristic blend of allegory with history where, at the Queen's coronation, Plenty and Hymen are as solidly present as Henry IV and the royal retinue. Tiepolo is required to be more strictly literal and historical, though in his own richly charged terms. Allegory has been accommodated in the zone of the ceiling overhead. Where the Rubens composition has its analogies is in the kneeling figure of the Queen and her train, seen in profile and disposed to make maximum effective use of the horizontal shape, leading up to the altar at the extreme edge. The general spread of figures across the composition, forming a comparatively shallow screen, also anticipates, whether accidentally or not, Tiepolo's way of arranging his figures in the Würzburg fresco (Pl. 170).

Most difficult to prove, and yet possibly the most significant of all influences, would be the guiding of Tiepolo, via the Rubens, towards the concept of placing so much pictorial emphasis on a woman. It was to make her his protagonist in a way that the programme and the ethos behind it had never envisaged.

Out of the briefest references to Beatrice of Burgundy, a person he could make vivid only by transmuting, Tiepolo conjured up a blonde figure of icy demeanour, aloof, virginal and intensely regal, a princess of pearls and cool silks, who eclipses in her splendour even his Cleopatra (Pl. 171). In her stiff, white dress and fan of stiffer, white ruff, set off by the long, trailing, white-lined, blue robe that is gathered up into a great sequence of folds by a white-clad page, she could stand for the heroine of some northern folk or fairy tale, compacted of sky and snow, forever frozen and liable to dissolve if touched by the rude hand of reality. She is more patently idealised, colder and prouder than any of Tiepolo's previous heroines: the incarnation of no mere woman but an Empress.

While the Emperor—carefully shown red-haired and red-bearded—raises his eyes devoutly, hers are half-closed. Beside her swelling presence, he is subordinated to a consort's role. And everything else seems to have swelled, just as the 'oratory' has, to become a vast basilica, in Palladian style, with only marginal suggestions of religious usage. This edifice of grey stone and giant, mauvish marble pillars needs its scale to accommodate the mingled concourse of onlookers, drawn from Church and state (Pl. 175). There are cardinals and a standard-bearer in gold armour, a choir and counsellors, a bridal attendant clutching a miniature dog, a page holding the imperial crown—and a dwarf, borrowed from Cleopatra's banquet.

Only the legs of Christ on the largely obscured crucifix at the left are a reminder of anything specifically religious in the pageant splendour of the scene. The eye, directed by a diagonal shadow, runs down from that almost incongruous, veiled hint to the imposing, portly figure of the Bishop in embroidered cope, at the top of the apricot-velvet steps, and follows the line of the Empress's curving robe, a wave that breaks on the barrier formed by the packed bodies of the spectators. To suggest the excitement and the difficulty of seeing the ceremony, Tiepolo has one man clambering up, clasping a pillar—a device he borrowed from Veronese, who often uses it in scenes of the Adoration of the Magi.

Everywhere he suggests that individuals were present, and behaved as individually as people do at such ceremonies. He characterised each head, in age and type and even in deportment. While one prelate turns away, as though meaning to chat to his neighbour, an official stands rigidly to attention but cannot stop his glance wandering outside the scene altogether, seeking the real spectator in the room below. The preoccupation of the pages is with the Empress's train and with keeping the crown anchored to its cushion. Aloft, the choir of singers and musicians concentrates intensely on its music. In a touch bold, even by Tiepolo's standards, the foreground dwarf is engaged—at the very moment of the benediction—in pushing forward another cushion for the Empress to kneel on.

It was by a myriad of such devices that Tiepolo 'realised' and, as it were, humanised the impact of the scene. People, not stuffed dummies, were gathered there; and under the splendid costumes beat very human hearts. To justify such treatment, were justification necessary, he could have pointed to the tradition of Venetian painting. Veronese especially, but Titian too on occasion, had introduced comparable notes of simple humanity which have almost poignant effect when found amid grand and elevated subjects. In Veronese's *Family of Darius* a Persian dwarf shielding his dog and frightened by a monkey expresses humanly, and possibly humorously, to a sixteenth-century eye, a sense of being defeated. It was daring of Titian to introduce into the solemn theme of the *Vendramin Family worshipping* (in the National Gallery, London) the little boy, with his pet dog, who sits unconcerned on the steps of the altar on which a fragment of the True Cross is displayed.

Yet, when he had individualised so much, Tiepolo did not falter in his instinctive aristocratic preference—in art—for great personages, whose glamour partly derives from position and from being quite unlike ordinary people. And again and again, for him, the personages were female. It is as if he could not fasten imaginatively, in the same way, upon a man. Sometimes, the subjects he was allotted—Rachel, Cleopatra, Armida—fully justified the emphasis he gave to the charm and power of the eternally feminine. But the *Marriage of the Emperor Frederick Barbarossa*, as intended for the Prince-Bishop's Residenz at Würzburg, was certainly not one of them. He was working not for Louis XV but for the celibate ruler of a portion of the Holy Roman Empire. Of course, the result was perfectly decorous and dignified. It showed the bishop of the day (at once the twelfth-century day and the modern one) with an Emperor at his feet. It celebrated Würzburg at an apogee of enjoying imperial favour. Nevertheless, what Tiepolo made the fresco celebrate, most memorably of all, was his own homage to the whole idea of woman.

★　　　★　　　★

170. *Marriage of the Emperor*, Residenz, Würzburg.

171 (facing page). Detail of Pl. 170.

172. *Assumption of the Virgin*, Chapel, Residenz, Würzburg.

The Kaisersaal occupied Tiepolo for a considerable time—longer, it would appear, than he normally took for a fresco scheme. The working season may have been shorter in northern Europe, or there was simply less pressure on him, away from home, to cram every minute with activity. The winter of 1751 must have interrupted his progress on the two facing frescoes, but he is unlikely to have remained idle. He was probably quite eager to demonstrate his abilities in oil as well as fresco—as he would certainly urge at the Spanish court late in life, when his fresco commissions were completed. During the winter of 1751–2, with the Kaisersaal unfinished, he undertook two altarpieces for the Hofkapelle, the chapel of the Residenz: the *Assumption of the Virgin* and the *Fall of the Rebel Angels* (Pls 172 and 173).

The chapel was as elegant and as splendid an interior as the Kaisersaal. Neumann had designed a glittering, gilt shrine, oval in plan, with a screen of marble pillars supporting a gallery. The ceiling of the chapel had been frescoed in 1735 by the painter Byss, who had worked at Pommersfelden. Some of Bossi's liveliest sculptures animated the various levels of the chapel, on the high altar of which is no painting but a sculpted Crucifixion with Christ on a tall cross, to which Tiepolo perhaps alluded in introducing a crucifix into the oratory where Frederick Barbarossa's marriage is blessed. At the entrance to the chapel were two large-scale altars, framed by massive, twisted columns, for which Tiepolo's canvases were destined. When the Prince-Bishop visited Tiepolo in his own quarters in February and March 1752, work on them was apparently in progress and presumably approaching completion.

Both paintings are signed by Tiepolo and must be accepted as largely his own work. No convincing *modelli* survive, though numerous chalk studies of heads and arms and other details once again exist and can only have been done in preparation for the altarpieces.

Yet the overall effect of the two paintings is—for some reason—disappointing. Neither composition possesses Giambattista Tiepolo's natural felicity, and in passages the handling of paint, like the draughtsmanship, is mechanical. Here and there, a struggle to appear forceful makes for uneasy, exaggerated rhetoric—especially in the *Fall of the Rebel Angels*. Perhaps Tiepolo was suffering, understandably enough, from diminished energy. The paintings are of a standard that in another artist's output would be labelled 'studio', though at Würzburg this can only mean the intervention of Domenico—and it seems unfair that someone so gifted in his own right should be held responsible for the unsatisfactory parts of his father's paintings. Nevertheless, the canvases are very big—not as tall as those for Verolanuova but far taller than the central painting in the Scuola del Carmine—and Tiepolo may have been indisposed as well as tired. The final result probably satisfied the Prince-Bishop, and seems to have satisfied such modern critics as have commented on them, but examination of especially the lower portion of the *Assumption* points definitely to some assistance in the execution.

The subject of the rebel angels had never been handled totally successfully by Tiepolo. At Würzburg there is a stridency and a banality about the St Michael, clothed in a slack expanse of meaninglessly agitated, bright-vermilion drapery, which is painful to think of as Tiepolo's achievement. An overgrown, ungainly street urchin the archangel appears, yelling at a rabble of fellow-urchins more naked than he. At least the *Assumption* offered a more grateful opportunity, though here too there is exaggerated gesturing and a rather tepid, almost sentimental air to a scene that had, after all, inspired the tremendous, engaged drama of Piazzetta's superb altarpiece of the subject, now in the Louvre. That was installed not far away, at Sachsenhausen, near Frankfurt, and recollection of it might well inhibit Tiepolo when he came to paint the subject on an even bigger scale.

Because of the sheer height of the Würzburg *Assumption*, it is difficult to judge the quality of the area occupied by the Virgin, but much of it looks characteristic of

Giambattista—and notably fine is the modelling and feathery, swan-like conviction of the angel's wings at the left. On earth there seems greater unevenness of handling among the Apostles. The bald Apostle, seated at the left and seen from the back, is extremely tame in concept as in execution. The *Assumption* calls for something rather more dramatic as a reaction than just sitting it out and vaguely gesticulating with one hand—as though disturbed at a picnic by a persistent fly (not even a wasp). A very similar type of figure, used in the same way, to close off the composition at one side, had been introduced by Domenico into his *Stations of the Cross* (in the second painting of the series); and his intervention at this point in the *Assumption*, if not elsewhere in the lower half, seems probable enough.

Nor need it be an objection to his assistance that Giambattista signed the painting as his own work, since his was indeed the responsibility. The Prince-Bishop is unlikely to have felt cheated, had he been made aware of any collaboration, as the father and son worked so closely together—and anyway he seems to have admired and encouraged Domenico's artistic activity.

If in the spring of 1752 Giambattista did not give his entire attention to the chapel altarpieces, this would not be entirely surprising and could be quite unrelated to any temporary loss of energy. A new and most ambitious project was close to becoming a reality. At some so far unascertained date the Prince-Bishop and his entourage must have opened positive discussions with Tiepolo about frescoing the vast vault of the staircase ceiling in the Residenz. All along, perhaps, this prospect had been in the minds of the patron, his architect and the painter. Something about it may have been adumbrated before Tiepolo left Venice, with the implication that this commission would follow if the Kaisersaal frescoes proved a success.

On 20 April 1752 the Prince-Bishop made a further visit to Tiepolo's apartments, a court official noted, and it was then that he was shown 'das Project von der Hauptstiege, so der Maler Tiepolo entworfen'.[15]

Rarely in Tiepolo's career is the precise moment documented when he presented a project in sketch form to his patron—and this one was to be the culmination of all his artistry, as well as the culmination of so many hopes and plans for dealing with the decoration of the staircase.

Tiepolo had been living in Würzburg, in the Residenz, for well over a year when he received the Prince-Bishop on that April day. He had come to know the building and its chief occupant, as well as Neumann, the architect of the staircase that, from almost modest beginnings, artfully unfolds, bifurcates and doubles back on itself under the huge expanse of high, unbroken vault. A master of ingeniously devised staircases, as at Schloss Brühl, Neumann had conceived at the Residenz a gradual, thrilling spatial experience on the grandest scale. It asked to be complemented by frescoes or a fresco of equal spatial grandeur.

Earlier projects for the ceiling had never supposed that such an area could be covered by any single composition. It was to be divided up into historical scenes of import for the bishopric of Würzburg and for Franconia, very similar in kind to those Tiepolo had frescoed in the Kaisersaal. Indeed, the two subjects there had at one period been included in the programme for the staircase.

History had been splendidly dealt with by him in the Kaisersaal, leaving the way clear for a much more exciting yet traditional treatment of the staircase ceiling: as a heaven. To some extent that was the obvious solution, though how it was reached is not known. Perhaps the existence of Byss's ceiling for the staircase at Pommersfelden prompted the thought of something comparable being executed for the Residenz. A single, coherent subject is likely to have appealed to Neumann; and, far from daunting Tiepolo, it can only have excited him by its possibilities, vaster than any he had previously enjoyed.

By the time he showed the Prince-Bishop a sketch, possibly the sketch that survives (Pl. 176), the theme must have been settled. It was suitably cosmic for the

173. *Fall of the Rebel Angels*, Chapel, Residenz, Würzburg.

174 (following page). Detail of Pl. 186 showing the portrait of the Prince-Bishop.

colossal space. At its thematic centre Apollo as sun-god, bringing light and enlightment, rises over the world, encircled in the sky by Olympian deities, the Hours and the Horses of the Sun; and at the edges of the composition are disposed the Four Continents.

Once conceived, this huge yet luminous and entirely coherent design could easily be seen to solve all the problems. As the visitor ascended the first flights of steps he would encounter the Continent of Europe and then, in pausing at the landing where the staircase divided, see the figure of Apollo rising high in the heavens above; only as he turned and took the second flight would the other Continents take shape along the sides of the ceiling: Asia and Africa left and right, with America over the entrance to the state-rooms (including the Kaisersaal).

The sketch that exists is unusually though not inappropriately large. In it Tiepolo devised pairs of stucco figures for the four corners of the ceiling and sufficiently realised the various groupings in the fresco for the patron to grasp not only the illusionism of the radiant central space but the character assigned to each Continent. Europe alone would be shown enthroned, surrounded by various arts and civilized activities. Figures in feathered head-dresses, the chief one seated on an alligator, symbolise America. Asia would be seated on an elephant, Africa on a camel. Already Tiepolo provided sufficient indication of the Moors and page-boys, traders and Orientals, as well as the exotic birds and beasts, that would enliven each group.

All that remained was to turn the bravura concept into the fresco itself. Preparations for that work perhaps took some time. Not until 29 July did Tiepolo sign the contract for the ceiling.

In evolving the concept that won the Prince-Bishop's approval, Tiepolo must have been aided by recollections of what he had achieved on the ceiling of the Palazzo Clerici at Milan. It was there that he had first depicted Apollo rising to illuminate the Continents of the world in an Olympian heaven. The Würzburg court might be more conscious of Byss's fresco at Pommersfelden, but Tiepolo would be able to think additionally of his Apollo ceiling in the Palazzo Archinto and, closer at hand, the 'Phoebus orientalis' he had frescoed on the Kaisersaal ceiling. All his life he had been practising, in effect, for the commission he had now received; and a line can be traced back from the staircase fresco that is rightly his most famous masterpiece, executed for a masterpiece of a building, to the ceiling, so comparatively little known, in the modest Palazzo Sandi at Venice. There it was that he had early disposed four incidents along the edges of the composition, leaving the central zone free and as airy as possible—to be the domain of gods and goddesses floating in an enchanted, light-filled space that conveys optimism and exhilaration.

How Tiepolo went about tackling the gigantic task at Würzburg is unclear. There are a mass of related chalk drawings, of variable quality, but including some that are presumably autograph (Pl. 177). A number of them may be working drawings of some sort, arguably connected with the amount of painting to be carried out on the plaster on a given day. Whatever their purpose, they do not help document the changes and additions that were at some point decided on.

The first perhaps, and the most fundamental, was an exchange of location between the Continents of Europe and America. The result of this is that the 'discovery' of Europe is made only after the turn of axis at the landing, and Europe is now placed within the Residenz, above the wall leading to the state-rooms. No longer, it is true, does Apollo rise over Europe, but Europe is given dominance by occupying greater space, while some equation of it with Würzburg was also to be introduced.

At some stage, when the scheme was presumably not settled in every detail, there was a project for treating the south wall, below the European portion of Tiepolo's fresco, with some playful painted illusionism, alternating with the stucco decoration, to be carried out possibly by a native court painter. A drawing, now destroyed, showed that between the two main doorways, and under his family coat-of-arms, the Prince-Bishop would be depicted, with some of his retinue, gazing up from a balcony at the fresco overhead.[16]

Although that concept was not pursued, it lingered on and seems to have emerged finally in the form incorporated by Tiepolo into the fresco itself. What the composition had lacked at the sketch stage was any reference to its instigator, Carl Philipp von Greiffenklau. His rightful place was to be found on the ceiling, and he was to be portrayed, still in profile but in his own semblance, in a medallion-type image hovering low over Europe (Pl. 174).

The device was one never previously or subsequently used by Tiepolo, and is more often associated with the images on baroque funerary monuments. No less baroque, splendidly so, is the way Tiepolo supports the suspended portrait with winged and laurel-crowned Glory at its top and trumpeting Fame at its side; it nestles on a mantle of ermine-lined, crimson velvet, while a griffon from the Greiffenklau arms punningly claws at the portrait's frame.

177. *Study for 'Africa'*, Staatsgalerie, Stuttgart (No. 1477).

178 (following pages). Detail of Pl. 186 showing 'Europe'.

To have such an enlightened ruler, lightly apotheosised in his lifetime, is Europe's distinction. Europe itself charmingly dwindles into being mid-eighteenth-century Würzburg, with hints of the bishopric, a concert in progress and the presence of local figures (Pl. 178). There the arts flourish, including the art of Painting, and also Architecture. It is all more than empty flattery, for the Prince-Bishops had proved good patrons, and Tiepolo had cause to pay specific tribute to the one who was reigning. These are the activities fostered by the enlightenment, symbolised by Apollo, god of the arts and patron of music; as he almost dances in his effortless ascent through the sky, a butterfly-winged figure at his feet accompanies him, holding his lyre.

The message of the ceiling becomes metaphorically as well as literally one of enlightenment. Adumbrated at the Palazzo Clerici, it is here restated and expanded on a majestic scale. Apollo's radiance is no blinding, destructive force. Nothing baleful interrupts the universal beaming of the sun-god, worshipped throughout the world, who scarcely needs to summon his chariot or the immortal Horses, so inevitable and air-borne is his course.

After the clarity of this solution to the problem of composing a theme to cover the whole ceiling comes the clarity of execution. Tiepolo did not present new images as such of Apollo or the other gods, or the Continents. He relied chiefly on traditional iconography, interpreting it with his own and his century's elegance and wit. The crisp stylishness of his Continents in particular—developed beyond the figures that fringe the Clerici ceiling—has some analogy with northern, particularly German, porcelain of the period, where groups of Continents are often modelled. It is not the concept of a Nubian woman on a camel symbolising Africa, or that of a turbaned figure on an elephant for Africa, that constitutes in itself anything novel or interesting, but what Tiepolo can make of such personifications. Setting off Africa's blue-black skin with a pure white head-dress and billows of cream drapery, hanging in her ear a solid gold earring the size of a saucer, Tiepolo creates a major symbol, exotically sensuous, dignified and compact, as it were an essence of Africa in his eyes (Pl. 179). This figure, gazing up fearlessly, half in worship of the sun which pigmented the bloom of her dark skin and which gives nourishment, ripening the sheaf of grain she holds, sums up the theme. When Tiepolo exchanged the places of America and Europe on the ceiling, and put over the latter the Prince-Bishop's portrait as a sort of minor sun, certainly a celestial phenomenon, he preserved the upward gaze of Africa, directed now towards that portrait, possibly in intentional adoration of it. The theme 'Africa' stated by this figure is echoed and expanded down the long side of the ceiling with a skilfully orchestrated series of variations. Trade is expressed by merchants western as well as African; bales and barrels, in addition to a casket of pearls, are prominent, and the whole pageant—for such it is—is far more developed than at the Palazzo Clerici.

One convention unites fantasy and nature, the allegorical and the actual, the playful and the serious: the convention established by the force of Tiepolo's imagination. He fuses everything to make a world which is wonderfully well ordered and unfailingly delightful: the Nile is a typical, naked, white-haired old man, accompanied by a sharply observed pelican; a lively monkey seems to tweak an ostrich's tail, and a dromedary's rear obtrudes towards the spectator, the front half of it bizarrely blanketed by a rich carpet. Ivory tusks and a bulging blue-glazed jar lie, with a quiver of arrows, at the feet of Africa, herself reclining on a camel beside a low-slung tent broadly striped in grey and white. In homage to her a Moor kneels, dressed in Veronese-style costume, holding in one hand a smoking incense-burner, while protecting himself against the sun's rays, that she unblinkingly enjoys, by a parasol.

For all its sense of heterogeneous, tumbled variety and exotic richness, with little tricks of illusionism (so that the monkey and ostrich, for example, appear standing on the cornice, outside the main scene), the composition has been most cunningly devised, each incident linked to the next and kept literally in perspective. This is as it were only the fringe of Africa—its coast rather than its heart—for ultimately the subject is subordinated to the central theme, and the eye is directed up to the heavens and to Apollo, divine animator of the marvellous segments of the globe that frame this vision.

By contrast with *Europe*, the other Continents are natural, cruder but none the less absorbing to Tiepolo. They have their marvellous artefacts, like pearls and ivory, and also the beauty of their magnificent bodies, set off by turbans and brilliant, feathered head-dresses. Life is shown as wilder, with the hunting of a female tiger in *Asia*, and preparations for roasting a dead crocodile in *America*. Yet Asia is shown as also the site of Calvary. Those Continents have their arts too, and music-making of a kind is going on in *America*, with the beating of tambourines by figures in feathered capes (Pl. 182).

Compared with the exoticism and excitement of these scenes, *Europe* seems rather staid, and the figure of the Continent herself somewhat smug in her proprietory gesture of resting a hand, with its sceptre, on the head of the Jovian bull. The horse and hound which have to serve as Europe's fauna cannot compete with the elephants, tigers, camels and macaws of other places, and the temperature of Tiepolo's imagination distinctly drops (even the composition lacks ebullience). After the fruits of the earth, the fruits of the mind, admirable as they are, seem less appetising.

Yet Tiepolo tinged the scene with local allusions and, probably, local portraits which must have given it particular meaning at the time. The foreground figure in military uniform, reclining on a cannon, may well be, as traditionally supposed, Balthasar Neumann (enlisted among the palace guards at Würzburg as a lieutenant of artillery at the age of twenty-seven). He died in 1753, aged sixty-five—much older than this figure's apparent age—but his presence in Tiepolo's fresco would be a deserved compliment and would also complement the portrait not far away of the other begetter of the total *mise-en-scène*.

Neumann became a colonel and perhaps retained a pride in his military rank which this man, though so negligently posed, may be felt to express as he lounges, handsomely periwigged, in a bravura uniform of silver and violet. If this is Neumann's portrait, it could hardly be in greater contrast to the discreet bust-length of Tiepolo himself, tucked modestly away, in *Europe*, at the corner of the ceiling, between two large figures modelled in stucco (Pl. 180).

All fancy and exuberance are quenched by this intensely sober portrayal. Tiepolo had so often been present as a personality in his own work, always fancifully dressed and very much a part of the scene. He had studied his features over the years, without any self-flattery. There was one guise he had not attempted: a direct image as he appeared when at work, at work especially perhaps, as in the Residenz, on a fresco scheme. Images of him, drawn or painted, were to be produced by other artists, showing him in gentlemanly costume, very much the prosperous artist. Only he, and only on this occasion, depicted the worker, with what seems almost pride, paradoxically, in the plainness of his cap and the negligence of the untied cravat or scarf, hanging loosely like a sweat rag round his neck. Admittedly, there is a glint of gold, either embroidery or, more likely, a chain, decorating his drab-coloured coat, but it is discreet to the point of near-invisibility; it does nothing to take away from the sobriety of the depiction, enhanced by the worried, slightly worn features, familiar from many earlier paintings, but now grown gaunt with age.

The painter does not stare out, as self-portraits traditionally tend to do and as Tiepolo had frequently amused himself by doing from his own compositions. His earnest glance is downwards and across to Würzburg-Europe where Neumann sits at ease, as if seeking his place there. And this is how he chose to leave his image, outside—to some extent—the cosmos he had conceived for the ceiling.

179 (following pages). Detail of Pl. 186 showing 'Africa'.

199

The plain garb and the workaday appearance would be less striking if Tiepolo's head were not so closely juxtaposed to the smart and *soigné* head of a much younger man, Domenico, in powdered wig and bright blue costume, calmly regarding the spectator with a bland air. At first sight, he might be mistaken for some youthful patron, from a social level above the artist's, so piquantly different is the appearance of son and father. Yet his presence here is probably Tiepolo's tribute to him as his assistant on the vast scheme, assuming that this portion of the fresco is Tiepolo's work. Alternatively, it might be worth considering whether it was Domenico who caught so vividly his father's features and then added his own portrait, in a subsidiary position but in a typical self-portrait pose, in this spare corner of the ceiling. Were that actually so—though the handling of this area seems to have all Giambattista's vivacious, confident touch—Domenico might be paying oblique tribute, in his characterisation of his father, to the true begetter of the ceiling. If, more likely, the father executed these two portraits, there is perhaps some paternal pleasure, not unmixed with humour, at showing himself the artisan with such a fine young gentleman as his son. And, beyond doubt, the juxtaposition of the two generations, however different in outlook, speaks of collaboration as much as affection. At Würzburg Domenico had, as it were, won his spurs.

A third head, very much subordinated, obtrudes at the far left of the figure of Tiepolo himself, with boyish features and a homely air. Various identifications for this face have been suggested; the most likely one must be that it is Lorenzo Tiepolo, shown as at once loosely associated with Giambattista and Domenico, yet not on their level and not sharing in their intimate relationship. Nevertheless, Lorenzo had been brought to Würzburg, and it would be natural enough that he too should be included in a record of the family's presence and activity there.

If he took any part in actual execution of the frescoes, it will not now be identifiable. Yet, wonderfully homogeneous as is the ceiling fresco in overall effect, there are places where the hand of his elder, much more gifted brother, seems to be present, especially in depiction of some of the subsidiary fauna enlivening the cornice. Assessments of any such intervention are bound to be subjective, but one area which seems to suggest Domenico's hand is the group in *Asia* capturing a female tiger. This is in itself (though envisaged already in the *modello*) a minor portion of the whole composition of the Continent. Not only does the handling there lack the spirited quality of Giambattista but the draughtsmanship, and even the physiognomy and the poses, point to Domenico. Elsewhere, in the occasional gaudy macaw, and more definitely in the ostrich and mischievous monkey, Dom-

180. Detail of Pl. 186 showing Tiepolo's self-portrait with Domenico.

181. Detail of Pl. 186.

182 (following pages). Detail of Pl. 186 showing 'America'.

enico may well be detected, in his own typical idiom, more at home among the *exotica* of the natural world than with allegory or gods (Pl. 181). Domenico certainly made an amusing pen-and-ink study of an ostrich striding along with a ludicrously lofty air (and two black-chalk drawings, apparently signed by him, are recorded, with motifs including that of an ostrich). So vivid is Domenico's study that it comes as a surprise to realise he has copied it from Stefano della Bella's etching, *The Ostrich Hunt*.[17] In another pen drawing, he introduced the monkey from the Würzburg ceiling, so, whether or not he is credited with that portion of the fresco, it proved exactly the kind of motif that appealed to him.

No doubt there are plenty of minute areas not assigned to him to fresco but where he completed a jewel, added a plume, touched up a turban or a striped drapery, copying as faithfully as he could his father's manner. Both father and son enjoyed contriving visual witticisms and the freedom to improvise given by fresco. Either of them might have thought up the light-hearted piece of illusionism whereby, just below Asia seated on her elephant, a parrot perches on a *trompe l'œil* garland adorning the feigned cornice; and nearby there appears to have rolled, as it were out of the fresco, and come to rest, a turban-cum-pointed fez, forever propped a few inches above the real cornice.

But the supreme triumph of the staircase fresco is not in details, nor in anything concerning Domenico. For all the charm and imagination lavished on the Continents, it is the centre of the ceiling that best conveys Tiepolo's unrivalled ability to create air and illumination, and to fill his own radiant heaven with beings solid yet aerial, only extending by their presence the atmosphere of liquid, streaming light (Pl. 186). To cover the vast surface of the Residenz staircase ceiling with that unified vision, a very heaven of heavens, and retain its visionary quality, was the essence of Tiepolo's achievement. The gods recline majestically on a bank of purplish cloud. Amid rifts of paler cloud there float and soar butterfly-winged figures of the Hours and flocks of sporting putti, bringing the Sun's chariot and the immortal Horses, forming concentric waves of movement around the shimmering fan-like focal point—the heart of the radiance, where Apollo rises calmly and inevitably, to dominate the earth Tiepolo has created to match this heaven (Pl. 187).

Although there seems something a little grandiloquent in a cosmic view which gives such prominence to Carl Philipp von Greiffenklau, ornament of the western world, what his patronage helped bring into being justifies his claim on the world's attention. There is, thanks to Tiepolo, more than rhetoric to the idea of his fame and glory. An artistic Joshua, Tiepolo has stopped the sun. He has reversed the decline of the *ancien régime* and offered on the Residenz ceiling the most optimistic of all philosophies, a complete harmony of mankind and nature and art, on a stupendous scale and with a confidence and exhilaration that he never surpassed.

★   ★   ★

Not until November 1753 did Tiepolo and his sons leave Würzburg to journey back to Venice. Although some friendly contacts were to be kept up after their return, chiefly, it seems, through Domenico, the Prince-Bishop died in 1754, not having lived long to enjoy the fruits of his enthusiastic, enlightened patronage.

During the years at Würzburg Tiepolo executed no frescoes elsewhere in Germany. But he executed some major oil paintings for other places and patrons. It was probably while in Würzburg that he accepted a commission for a large-scale painting of mythological subject-matter, showing Apollo mourning for his beloved Hyacinth, whom he has accidentally killed (Pl. 183). For Tiepolo the subject is an unusual one. The sun-god is no longer radiant but distraught, more man than god, and crouched over the dying youth from whose blood there blossom the first

183. *Death of Hyacinth*, Baron Thyssen Collection, Madrid.

185. Veronese, *Adoration of the Magi*, National Gallery, London.

184. *Adoration of the Magi*, Alte Pinakothek, Munich.

flowers of the hyacinth. In Tiepolo's strange concept, the scene is set in a courtyard or semi-formal garden and is witnessed by a group of male figures, old and young, who might have strayed from the *Capricci* etchings and will reappear in the *Scherzi*.

It is as if Tiepolo felt the need to frame the foreground incident, even possibly mitigate it, by this device of a chorus, which lessens the emotional impact but increases the hallucinatory aspect of the scene.

While virtually nothing is known as to the circumstances of this commission, those for a religious commission of about the same period, also for a large-scale work, are firmly established. It was for the Benedictine abbey church at Münsterschwarzach, a building of Neumann's unfortunately destroyed early in the nineteenth century, that Tiepolo painted the *Adoration of the Magi* (Pl. 184), a splendid altarpiece, dated 1753, which quite eclipses the altarpieces for the Hofkapelle in the Würzburg Residenz.

Some drawings exist related to the altarpiece, the subject of which is also that of Tiepolo's largest etching, of apparently later date and of only very loosely similar composition.[18] Behind his painting lies awareness of Veronese's sumptuous treatments of the theme, notably the big canvas then hanging in the church of S. Silvestro at Venice (Pl. 185). From that is derived the kneeling elderly king closest to the Child though Tiepolo creates his own, far cooler colour scheme for the costume, a harmony of gold and pale fawn and white, complementing the sky-blue cloak of the Virgin. Veronese's painting had earlier inspired Sebastiano Ricci's large *Adoration of the Magi* (now in the British Royal Collection) which in Tiepolo's day belonged to Consul Joseph Smith. Ricci, however, had evolved his own pose for the standing Moorish king, and Tiepolo perhaps recalled it in the almost swaggering, showy figure which is his version of the same king, a tall silhouette topped by a great gourd of scarlet turban, with matching tunic and hose, and a sleeve of dazzling stripes. Such a person might have stepped from the ceiling of the Residenz, and Tiepolo permits himself a frank quotation, not from the ceiling but from the *Marriage* fresco of the Kaisersaal, in the page-boy seen from the back in the foreground. Dressed in white, he had there been the Empress's train-bearer, while in the *Adoration of the Magi* he is in chestnut-brown and has become a bearer of gifts for the Infant Christ.

The *Adoration of the Magi* is in one sense a highly traditional, emphatically Venetian piece of painting, planned to hold its own in a northern architectural setting. At the same time, in Tiepolo's development, it looks forward—both in handling of paint and in concept—to trends of his work during the late 1750s and onwards. Although richly applied, the pigment is worked in a new and almost agitated manner, in places a sort of sketching on a large scale. Details of beards, eyebrows and eyelids are rapidly established, and then the brush passes on, not lingering to define the contours more exactly. The result is a vibrancy of surface, combined with what seems new emotionalism, felt, for example, in the intense exchange of gazes between the ardent, aged king and the candid, new-born Christ Child he so yearningly adores. Rubens has sometimes been quoted in connection with the painting, but in terms of sentiment and humanity Murillo would be nearer the mark. The kings may make up an opulent trio, symbolic of the world's riches and pomp, but the mother and child they have come to worship are thoroughly intimate (even simple, in comparison with some of Tiepolo's earlier, near-disdainful Madonnas) and tender. Unobtrusively, the Child curls his right hand around his mother's fingers, as though humanly seeking some slight reassurance on this tremendous first public occasion of the recognition of his Godhead.

Compared with Veronese's usual treatments of the subject, and with Ricci's altarpiece, Tiepolo's concept is remarkably simple and direct. No glories of angels stream down from heaven—just two cherub heads, themselves not immediately obvious. In the Magi's train are no noble horses or hounds—nothing, in fact, that can distract from the central significance, conveyed with the economy of the words

186. *Apollo and the Continents*, Residenz, Würzburg.

187 (following pages). Detail of Pl. 186, showing Apollo.

209

of St Matthew's gospel: '. . . they saw the young child with Mary his mother, and fell down, and worshipped him'.

Most remarkable of all here is Tiepolo's interpretation of St Joseph (assuming that it is he who is shown behind the Madonna, and the figure certainly has a halo). Instead of the conventional old man depicted by Veronese and Ricci, and by Tiepolo himself in his etching, St Joseph is shown as barely middle-aged, a handsomely vigorous, if slightly unkempt figure, standing prominently over the maternal group, and gesturing in a way at once respectful and protective. Even if it were to be thought that this figure was intended for a shepherd, and that the halo is a later addition, there would still be something remarkable about this *Adoration*, for St Joseph would then be lacking from it.

While at this period Giambattista Tiepolo evolved new approaches, and in part a new style, moving away from the colossal, profane grandeur of the Residenz frescoes, Domenico too revealed a new aspect of his ability, also with a religious theme. In 1753 he completed and published his set of twenty-four etchings on the subject of the Flight into Egypt. It was dedicated to 'Sua Altezza Reverendissima Monsignor Carlo Filippo, Prencipe del Sacro Romano Impero Vescovo d'Herbipoli e Duca di Franconia Orientale, Ec. Ec.', and declared to be invented and executed by the artist, 'in Corte di detta Sua Altezza Reverendissima. . .'

It was a typically eighteenth-century undertaking: a virtuoso display of the variations possible on a given theme. And Domenico proudly proves his virtuosity, as he takes the Holy Family, seen from the back as they descend a slope, seen from the front as angels come to escort them, on foot and on a donkey, in a boat, embarking and disembarking, through the country and eventually, safe at last, into the town. In one scene it is St Joseph who carries the Child. Once, angels support the walking, footsore Virgin, and St Joseph humps the pannier, giving some relief to the donkey. The series opens in a homely interior, as St Joseph announces the need to flee. It closes with the Virgin, now seated backwards on the donkey, poised to enter a town gateway that smacks more of the Veneto than of Egypt. The gateway is thronged with types of character favoured especially by Domenico, part-peasant, part-oriental, and including a page-boy, a bald-headed man and an inquisitive woman turning to scrutinise the arrival of the Holy Family.

188. D. Tiepolo, *Arms of the Prince-Bishop of Würzburg* (frontispiece to the *Flight into Egypt* series), National Gallery of Art, Washington, Rosenwald Collection (B-19, 935).

Nothing could seem further removed from the world of Giambattista's highest imaginings and most glorious visions. Yet this series of 'Idee pittoresche' clearly pleased the Prince-Bishop, and it was Domenico who created a vivid souvenir-cum-farewell of the Würzburg experience in his etched frontispiece to the volume. There, Fame flies through the air, accompanied by angelic figures bearing up the arms and appurtenances of the Prince-Bishop, blowing a trumpet blast over a view of the Marienberg castle, picturesquely located up on the hill overlooking Würzburg. Not Neumann's modern Residenz but this early seventeenth-century Gothic-revival building, with its four bulbous-roofed towers, was the image of the city Domenico chose, perhaps for its association with Mary but also perhaps as the 'sight' which best summed up for southerners like himself and his father the impact of Würzburg (Pl. 188).

Giambattista Tiepolo had left a more subtle memorial to his stay. In placing himself within, yet apart from, the context of his own creation spanning the ceiling of the staircase of the Residenz, it was as though he felt his art had reached its zenith. No longer playfully disguised but with total, sober straightforwardness he portrayed himself there exactly as he was, as its creator. He needed no label to identify him, no flourish of signature to declare his presence, but the message is as strong as any Renaissance one in its pride: 'iste perfecit opus'. And his image is there quite solemnly, to remain long after he has gone from Würzburg, and by implication from life, reinforcing the fact within his own painting that Giambattista Tiepolo 'fuit hic'.

9 THE LAST YEARS IN ITALY

BY THE TIME Tiepolo and his sons reached Venice from Würzburg, the year 1753 was closing. They returned to a city and society little changed during their absence. A novel animal, a rhinoceros, had been exhibited in Venice in 1751. A new Doge, Francesco Loredan, had been elected in 1752. The two events were of about equal significance.

It is true that for the fostering of the visual arts, especially in the way of teaching, a new institution, the Venetian Academy, had been approved by the Senate, in September 1750, and given premises in the Fonteghetto della Farina, on the quay facing S. Maria della Salute. The first Director appointed was Piazzetta, not merely distinguished and respected as an artist, and now the oldest among his peers, but recognized as a gifted teacher. Around him, in contradistinction to Tiepolo, had formed a group of talented painters who remained in effect his pupils.

Nevertheless, there was little sign at Venice of new styles, still less new categories of painting, being introduced by a new generation of artists. Piazzetta's pupils worked very much in his manner. To contemporaries, Francesco Guardi, then emerging as a view painter, seemed a 'buon scolaro' of Canaletto. Alessandro Longhi, one of the youngest and most individual of talents, was to be complimented on his 'nuova maniera' of painting, but he was something of a solitary example.

The decades from 1750 onwards are marked by the deaths of the great elderly Venetian figures and by an absence of worthy or even interesting successors. Much of Domenico Tiepolo's originality was obscured by his filial piety, and compliments paid to him usually emphasised his role as faithful follower of his father. Broadly, it was tradition, not innovation, that society welcomed. If, here and there, advanced literary opinion might praise the 'reality' of Pietro Longhi's modern genre paintings and display distinct reserve at the continued spectacle of Tiepolo's fabulous and imaginary ethos, it did not affect patronage of Tiepolo by the Church and nobility. Indeed, his most grandiose expression of the Venetian aristocratic principle, the ceiling of the Villa Pisani at Strà, was finished as late as 1762, on the eve of his departure for Spain. Had he remained in Venice, there is no reason to think he would have lacked further commissions of the same kind, if not always on the same scale. A society less determinedly conservative would have suited him and his art less well.

While Tiepolo had been away in Würzburg, he had perhaps been out of the collective Venetian mind. No contemporary appears to show awareness of his absence—never mind his achievements—in Germany. He was probably quite prosperous before he went there. He returned wealthy. It was after his return that he purchased a country property, the villa at Zianigo, in the Veneto, which the family were to occupy and Domenico to decorate. His financial position was such that in the 1750s he could lend money to the governors of the church of the Pietà, where he was also to be involved artistically, frescoing the ceiling. As no workmanlike figure but in thoroughly gentlemanly guise (a worthy parent of Domenico as depicted at Würzburg), he was portrayed by Alessandro Longhi in his *Compendio* of famous modern history painters—Venetian, understood—which was first published in

189. *Virgin appearing to St John Nepomuk*, S. Polo, Venice.

1760.[1] In the second edition, published two years later, the portraits were accompanied by brief biographies; that for Tiepolo spoke of his fame and also of his living 'signorilmente'. And in 1756 his status in the artistic hierarchy was acknowledged by his being appointed the first President of the Venetian Academy.[2] By then, fame and success must have made him recognized almost universally as one of the leading painters of Italy—perhaps the leading painter, whose fame within the century would be rivalled eventually only by Batoni at Rome.

Tiepolo's prosperity, consolidated by the years in Würzburg, is only the more vividly underlined by Piazzetta's poverty. Tiepolo had not been back in Venice long when, on 29 April 1754, Piazzetta died. Like Tiepolo he had a wife and numerous family. Unlike him, however, he left them in extreme indigence and deep distress. Quite without facility, limited in his range, never able or perhaps eager to achieve total popular success, Piazzetta may, to some extent, stand as Thackeray to Tiepolo's Dickens. With his dogged integrity and stubborn devotion to his art had gone instinctive artistry, though his life might seem to end in failure and misery.

After his death, a moving document was drawn up on behalf of his widow and children, desperately appealing to the Doge for some financial help. The 'Inquisitor sopra l'arte', a member of the Dolfin family who had patronised Tiepolo, also submitted to the Doge a long and eloquent memorandum, strongly supporting the case and incorporating the testimony of Piazzetta's parish priest.[3]

From these statements the different circumstances of Piazzetta and Tiepolo are made clear—almost, at times, painfully pointed. That Piazzetta's devotion to Venice should be emphasised was natural in the circumstances, but the stress on his refusal ever to go abroad or accept advantageous offers from foreign princes seems to carry a faintly personal allusion. As a result of his determined patriotism, Piazzetta died poor. He laboured for the future of Venetian art by the training of pupils. It was dissatisfaction with his own art that made him destroy a number of his works which could otherwise have fetched money. Fame rather than prosperity was always his goal.

Finally, inevitably, the Inquisitor's memorandum invokes tradition—the tradition of renumeration from public funds of great Venetian painters, drawing on Ridolfi's *Lives*, and citing Bellini, Titian, Veronese and Tintoretto as all beneficiaries. To them, tacitly, Piazzetta is added in terms of artistic stature; and perhaps the combined eloquence and the stark facts won some small pension for the painter's widow. She lived on somehow for another eighteen years, by which time Cecilia Tiepolo was herself a widow, one whose husband had left her very comfortably provided for.

Tiepolo's sheer industry was always remarkable. Rarely did he ever decline a commission, and he cannot have been back many months from Würzburg before he was working on an altarpiece of *St John Nepomuk* for the church of S. Polo in Venice (Pl. 189). The painting was unveiled on 8 May 1754, shortly before the saint's feast day and barely a week after Piazzetta's death.

The interior of S. Polo is notably dark, and Tiepolo may have taken this into account in giving a livid brilliance to St John's agitated white surplice and to his intense, illuminated head. As a young man, Tiepolo is recorded to have painted a *St Paul before the Tyrant* for the church.[4] That painting has disappeared but might have made a constructive comparison with the *St John Nepomuk*—not necessarily to the latter's advantage. The saint himself, a comparatively new figure for pictures, having been canonised only in 1729, is realised with much of Tiepolo's new, emotional-seeming fervour, anticipating the late Spanish altarpieces. The prominent palm of martyrdom at his feet is no lightly sketched symbol but a solid, vegetable branch, almost roughly uprooted, it seems, and thrown down to join the book fallen half-open on the steps. A gigantic crucifix held by the saint has its own harsh vigour, and the effect exuded by him is of quivering, burning, fierce piety.

Only the vision to the saint, of the Madonna and Child, seems unworthy of his ardour. It fits rather awkwardly into the composition, almost as an afterthought. The Child, markedly, and the Madonna, both fail to relate to the kneeling St John, in style as much as in other ways. Not merely is haste suggested but some inner uncertainty, or possibly a forced coming together of new and old concepts in one composition. The very human baby and the rather haughty, heavily lidded Madonna are not themselves ideally matched. In comparison with St John they seem mundane and commonplace; their thin haloes lack the fiery radiance flaring around his head and investing him with the visionary quality in which they are defective.

For all Tiepolo's industry and energy, he was probably liable more often to flag on work in progress as he grew older, and to require assistance. Nor could even he always summon up a fresh solution to the theme of saints, single or grouped together, for an altarpiece. During the 1750s there began to be distinct unevenness in his large-scale oil paintings. The splendour and confidence of the Schwarzach *Adoration of the Magi* was not to be repeated on every occasion. Yet, although the *St John Nepomuk* seems a somewhat disappointing celebration of Tiepolo's return to his native city, he was able to rally and rouse himself for other altarpieces, outside Venice, in both design and execution.

Physical weakness and illness had scarcely affected him, it would seem, before the age of sixty or so. By his mid-sixties he refers to what was certainly not his first attack of 'la Gotta insolentissima', and one serious enough to keep him in bed for a month.[5] It may be that this 'gout' was some form of arthritis. If it affected his hands in any way, as is conceivable, it never proved as crippling for him as it had been for Rubens and was to be for Renoir.

If at times a big canvas was a daunting prospect to cover, especially to fill out from his own *modello*, Tiepolo seems to have lost nothing of his verve and invention and accomplishment in any work on the scale of drawings, *modelli* or etchings. As for fresco, it remained the medium where all sense of effort was banished. The challenge of fresh decorative schemes stimulated him to fresh solutions; and at the Villa Valmarana particularly, he was to handle fresco with a new directness and facility, dispensing with the elaboration of the scenes at Würzburg but with a summary confidence that is equally masterful.

Nothing better testifies perhaps to the continued, sustained power of his imagination in the immediately post-Würzburg period than his second series of etchings, the *Scherzi di Fantasia*, which became available in the 1750s and which the balance of probability would place as executed in these years.[6] The date of their origin has been a matter of hot debate among recent scholars and cannot be taken as settled. What does seem apparent is the advance, in both invention and technique, on the *Capricci*. The *Scherzi* are as poetic but more bizarre, wilder in their fantasy and yet more private and idiosyncratic in subject-matter. Even after so many years of giving expression to his imagination in painting, Tiepolo had something personal to say and relished the freedom of creating in etchings a highly personal dream-world of fancy and musings, filled with favourite motifs of his, without the need to illustrate known scenes and incidents. These are his 'idee pittoresche' variations, however, on a theme of his own devising, with hints of the magical and the occult, though lacking any linking 'story'.

Magic and strangeness are enhanced by the delicacy of handling—which it is hard not to see as evidence of increased mastery of the medium. The touch is light and flickering, giving an almost shimmering effect to the compositions, and there seems greater economy in the spaces of sky and foreground where the needle has barely pricked the plate.

Nothing seems to have substance in this mysterious countryside—and again it is a country world, a distinctly pagan one that is delineated (Pl. 190). Tree-trunks rise and curve in ghostly silhouettes, their boughs stripped mostly of leaves but frequently forming the perch for a staring owl. The ground is littered with strange

190. *Seated woman with a child and ox, (Scherzi),* National Gallery of Art, Washington, Rosenwald Collection (B-19, 908).

191. *A magus and other figures with Punchinello, (Scherzi),* National Gallery of Art, Washington, Rosenwald Collection (B-19, 899).

shapes that are not always easily read: a broken branch or stick may be entwined with or become a snake; or a snake may wreath itself around the scabbard of a fallen sword. The skulls of animals long dead are propped beside a half-buried shaft of masonry or bas-relief. Relics of an older age linger, without disturbing the reverie of brooding, bearded magus-like figures, often accompanied by a youth or child. Through a heat-haze screen of dots and flicks and nervous scribbles, like cabbalistic signs or an infant's attempts at writing, is glimpsed a world of uncertainty, in eternal flux, with shapes on the point of changing into something else: skull into vase or owl into skull. Abruptly, Punchinello pops up to confront a magus in one of the most haunting of all the compositions (Pl. 191). At the magus's shoulder is an untidy, gipsy-like figure, while behind there lounges in negligent nudity a young man quite indifferent to the confrontation. An antique altar, a slab of bas-relief, an owl perched on a sword provide additional touches of disassociation. Elsewhere, a child seated near to a woman is seen to have the legs of a satyr. In a scene that might look at first like a Repose of the Holy Family on the Flight into Egypt, the whole family are shaggy satyrs.

Although all the scenes are open-air ones, the mood induced is, intentionally or not, claustrophobic. Intimations of mortality may not be as obvious as in the *Capricci*, but they pervade most of the compositions, and become quite explicit in the etching of a group of ill-assorted figures scrutinising the effigy of Punchinello on his tombstone. Yet death, it seems, is itself something piquant and peculiar, not so much painful as a natural process, a dissolution or transmutation into other things. This is perhaps the secret of life that the magi pore on and ponder over in other etchings: the ultimate knowledge. Everything passes and changes; even for Punchinello there is death, but in death he is still an object of curiosity and wonder.

There is a sense in which the *Scherzi di Fantasia* could be claimed as the most perfect productions of all Tiepolo's art. In their ruminativeness, as in their bizarreness and their humour, they are wonderfully mellow. They exude a wisdom which has nothing to do with their philosopher-style magi or the paraphernalia of globes and books, but has to do with artistic accomplishment. Nothing is forced—least of all the vein of serious fantasy, of preoccupied, concentrated apartness, which runs through figures and landscape, making for intense strangeness but no feeling of fear or distaste. They seem to represent Tiepolo's innermost imaginings—his thoughts at their freest and most personal—and it need therefore not be surprising that they remain forever elusive and tantalising, for all the spell they cast.

'Tout s'anéantit, tout périt, tout passe', Diderot was to write of a painting of ruins by Hubert Robert. 'Il n'y a que le temps qui dure'.[7] But he recognized the pleasure of the sensation aroused by such reflections. Something rather similar can be sensed in two vignettes of pastoral scenes with ruins drawn by Piazzetta and issued as engravings, with verses beneath referring to Time's ruinous process which affects not only rustic habitations but pyramids, columns and busts; a monument was once erected to flatter a conqueror and now gives shade to peasant lovers. Tiepolo's intentions in his etchings are more complex. Incongruities and fancies are there because they amused him. What it all *means* he himself might have failed to be able to explain; even mortality is not preached about, and no moral can be drawn. These 'jokes' start from the basis of diverting their creator. Not merely are they peopled by children of his brain—sometimes conceived and fostered through preliminary or related drawings—but they are, as it were, favourite children; in type, face, costume, gesture and accessory, offspring he had always loved and whom now, exercising a parent's prerogative, he brings together to play for his own delectation.

The very freedom of the *Scherzi* from ulterior significance is probably at least half their point. And there certainly lies much of their fascination, in the career of a busy artist who was to spend the greater portion of his life in the service of others, illustrating specific subjects and investing them with strong doses of application for patrons and subsequent audience.

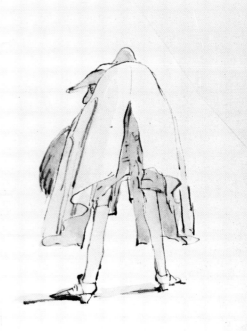

192. *Caricature of a man*, Museo Civico, Trieste.

As an etcher, Tiepolo seems closer, perhaps not unexpectedly, to Canaletto than to Goya. His 'sleep of reason' produces marvels, not monsters. He attacks nothing, possibly because in the end everything diverts and delights him. After all, he found in the exterior world plenty to smile at, and, when he wished, was as sharply observant of 'real' people as was his son. In probably the decade of the 1750s he showed himself a shrewd, even harsh caricaturist in drawings (Pl. 192), and was certainly an illustrator, before Domenico, of Punchinello's antics.

In the *Scherzi* there appears to be a mood of transience, indulged pleasantly. The spectator can savour the slow process of time in a world that is remote from the everyday and so old that it is positively reassuring. The strange figures that sit beside masonry fragments, stare at skulls or globes, seek to instruct or understand, are like embodied associations conjured up by the mouldering obelisk and the overgrown altar or urn. Very different though Tiepolo's compositions are, they seem foreshadowed in some of Canaletto's etchings, like the so-called *Landscape with two ruined pillars*, with its poetic, half-desolate flavour of nature regaining the world from man. And at a step beyond Tiepolo's etchings lie the late caprice landscapes and watery ruin-pieces of his brother-in-law, Francesco Guardi, escaping perhaps from the conventional requirements of commissions.

Tiepolo cannot have wished seriously to escape at all. He had energy enough—and fecundity enough—to be at once a private and a public artist. Major fresco commissions took him travelling through North Italy in these years, from 1754 to his departure for Spain in 1762, just as they had been doing since his earliest activity.

Indeed, he would return to work at Udine. And where he did not go, fresh oil paintings of his would carry his art.

In Venice too he continued to be active. Before the *St John Nepomuk* altarpiece was unveiled in 1754, he had entered into a contract with the governors of a new, unfinished church, S. Maria della Visitazione, or the Pietà, to fresco the main vault and two subsidiary spaces. This must have been his chief task during the summer. The work was completed by 8 October of that year, when he received the last instalment of the total sum due to him.[8]

The church was an old foundation, on one of the most splendid of sites, down the Riva degli Schiavoni, facing towards Palladio's S. Giorgio Maggiore. Originally an orphanage (of compassion, 'pietà'), the institution became famous for the music-making activity of its female orphans, given additional impetus by the long association of Vivaldi with it. For the foundlings he composed oratorios, masses and concertos, and partly as a result the Pietà gained the reputation of being the first of the four Ospedali with orchestras of girl inmates. The Président de Brosses (in his *Lettres familières sur l'Italie*) singled it out in 1739 for its disciplined musicality, while also noting appreciatively a pretty young girl, dressed in white and with flowers in her hair, who led the orchestra. Some of these associations, if not precisely all, were to be caught by Tiepolo in his main fresco.

The new church had been designed by Giorgio Massari, the architect of the Gesuati, and building of it started officially in 1745, when the first stone was solemnly blessed in the presence of the Doge, Pietro Grimani. Completion of the church's roof was celebrated in 1750, and in 1751 the governors expressed their intention of selecting an artist for the ceiling frescoes. Work was delayed, however, because of financial costs—the hospital had to be reconstructed more urgently. As a result, nothing was done to the church for two years. By the time work went forward, Tiepolo was back in Venice and available. Once again, for the last time, he and Piazzetta were to be linked in the decoration of a church, for the high altarpiece, to depict the Visitation, had been commissioned from the older painter, who died before he could complete it. It was to be finished by one of his devoted pupils, Giuseppe Angeli.

Massari's original plan was for the façade of the church to form the centrepiece of a single edifice, large in scale and severely regular in style, with the two wings of the hospital flanking the Palladian, pedimented church. The building would have occupied the complete site between two small canals. Although this plan was never carried out, and the façade of the church itself completed only in 1906, and then not accurately, Massari was able to design the interior and its furnishings in some detail. Inside, the church is a remarkably consistent, unspoilt example of Venetian taste and patronage—and varied artistic skills—in the latter years of the Republic.

The plan is a gentle oval, with four altars at the curved corners; the high altar is recessed, forming in effect a separate chapel. Less imposing than the Gesuati and more of a single spacious room or hall—almost a concert-hall—the Pietà interior is coolly pale and highly restrained, setting off the more elegantly the wrought-iron screens, with their exuberantly sprouting flowers, and the exquisite, fragile-seeming gilded shell of the fully rococo pulpit. For the altars various individuals took responsibility. The Doge Francesco Loredan donated that with Angeli's painting of a sainted Doge, Pietro Orseolo, and the will of a Greek doctor provided for the opposite altar, the altarpiece of which showed a miracle performed by St Spiridon, a Greek (or, more properly, Cypriot) saint of the fourth century, painted by another of Piazzetta's pupils, Domenico Maggiotto.

Tiepolo's two smaller frescoes are in the wall and ceiling immediately above the high altar. On the wall a roundel in *grisaille* shows an angel appearing to King David. On the ceiling are frescoed Faith, Hope and Charity in a composition that inevitably recalls the painting of the subject in the Scuola del Carmine and which yet is marked-

193. *Coronation of the Virgin*, Pietà, Venice.

ly different. Faith now floats on the clouds (not standing) and the child held by Charity is not nursed on her lap but appears precociously upright, individual in physiognomy, looking down inquisitively with much of the air and assurance of a third generation of the Tiepolo family.

For the centre of the very high ceiling of the church proper, the subject chosen was the Triumph of Faith, represented by the *Coronation of the Virgin* (Pl. 193). At first sight the overall effect is somewhat disappointing. Very much constrained, as

194. *Vision of St Anne*, Gemäldegalerie, Dresden.

well as contained, within its oval framework, the fresco is a single painting placed on the otherwise unadorned ceiling. There is no attempt at the elaborate patterning and subsidiary scenes that cover the Gesuati vault or the fusion of the whole area into one tremendous piece of illusionism as was achieved at the Scalzi. And in the fresco the feigned architectural elements are of the slightest. Two curved balconies, more baroque than rococo in style, provide at top and bottom choir-lofts for some of the massed angelic performers singing and playing the organ, strings and brass, all in celebration of the central event.

Yet, as it is conceived, that event becomes a triumph of illusionism more extreme in its way than any Tiepolo had created before. The steeply foreshortened Virgin is poised dizzily, tilted inwards as she retains her balance on the spinning globe of the earth. Far above her, the equally foreshortened figure of God the Father gestures down welcomingly, with arms raised in a vast, majestic, arching shape that culminates in a smaller arched shape, the crown of her glory. They are the two figures attracted—as it were—towards each other. Even Christ and the Dove, making up the Trinity, are visually subordinated to this magnetic pull which sets the heavens quivering. The beat of angels' strong wings and the music of instruments and voices combined add their stir of excitement to a scene where all is pure triumph and joy. Nothing is overthrown. No forces of evil need to be depicted crushed. There are no bodies hurtling downwards, and indeed the whole movement is of thrust upwards, *into* the ceiling, with a centripetal urge which might perhaps have been encouraged by northern examples of ceiling painting seen by Tiepolo in Germany.

Related to the fresco is an oil sketch, where the paint is handled with a furious, hectic energy, and the pencilling is rapid with a rapidity that becomes a mark of Tiepolo's late style.[9] The evidence of this sketch, were it not connected to a documented fresco, would suggest a date after, rather than in, 1754. The *modelli* that follow share much of its gifted impatience and almost savage speed. As shorthand to record his own ideas, Tiepolo's *modelli* become more terse with time.

The Pietà fresco was not, apparently, unveiled until 1755, when Tiepolo is recorded as having gone back 'to retouch the painting of the ceiling. . .'.[10] It was the last of his religious frescoes in Venice, as it proved, and the penultimate religious fresco of his career. It associated him with a thoroughly 'modern' yet characteristically Venetian project, and his own friendly attitude to the Pietà is suggested, along with his prosperity, by the loan two years later by him of a substantial sum of money to the governors.

The commissions which came to him for altarpieces were also from outside Venice. The resulting paintings are somewhat uneven in quality, at times rather laboured after the inspired handling of their *modelli*. Tiepolo showed no sign, though, of refusing work. The locations in convents or parish churches might not be very significant, nor the patrons of much importance. Yet between 1755 and 1760 he produced a number of altarpieces—for Parma, Rampazzo (near Vicenza), Folzano (near Brescia), Cividale and, largest and most memorable, for the Duomo at Este.

In most of these paintings a saint is the subject, and the treatment varies from pious meditation via narrative to visionary drama. At Rampazzo, where a Count Thiene and his wife were the commissioners, S. Gaetano da Thiene is shown floating on a cloud, eyes raised to heaven, one hand pointing down to his small church being built.[11] At Folzano, the site of a new church with an elaborate high altar, the subject was Pope St Sylvester baptising the Emperor Constantine—a subject to arouse Würzburg associations—and Tiepolo made an impressive scene out of the hunched figure of the Pope, splendidly clad, absorbed in his task of pouring water over the bare-shouldered, sick Emperor, his arms crossed in humility.[12] While a *modello* exists for the Rampazzo altarpiece, for that at Folzano there is none, though an impressive chalk study was made for the Pope's head—summary but very sure.[13]

220

It was presumably in these years (if not earlier) that the altarpiece of *Sts Roch and Sebastian* was painted for the church at Noventa Vicentina. Here the commissioner may have been of considerable importance, in himself and to Tiepolo. Cardinal Carlo Rezzonico acquired a palace at Noventa in the late 1750s. Tiepolo was certainly working for the Rezzonico family at Venice in or around 1758, and in that year the Cardinal became Pope, as Clement XIII. The Rezzonico retained an interest in the Tiepolo, and the Procurator Lodovico Rezzonico was to be a witness at Domenico's marriage in 1776.

No *modello* exists for the Noventa altarpiece, and in the absence of documentation it can be only a surmise that the future Pope commissioned the painting. The head of St Roch is, as has often been pointed out, remarkably close to that of St James in the altarpiece destined for London. It may be that eventually it will emerge that the Noventa painting dates from pre-Würzburg. Whether or not it does, it seems to contain passages of collaboration, most obviously in the figure of the mutilated beggar-woman at the left (as already referred to in chapter 6), whereas the two saints must have been conceived and modelled by Giambattista alone.

The altarpiece at Cividale is a far more clear-cut case, where Domenico's hand is patent (Pl. 194). There the commission came from a convent of Benedictine nuns, who chose an unusual, though not inappropriate, subject. The Virgin Mary as a child is shown not—as sometimes supposed—presented to God the Father by her parents (which would indeed be an odd theme), but being presented *to* them—borne by cherubs, as it were from heaven, to them on earth. That St Anne is kneeling to receive the divine gift of her daughter is obvious.

For this composition, signed and dated 1759, Tiepolo executed a *modello* with all the spontaneity and hasty confidence of a drawing, the sketchiest of sketches that, however, not merely settled the placing of the figure-groups but, by rapid, minute touches, conveyed the ecstasy in the faces of the protagonists and the very creases of their drapery (Pl. 195). Although the impression is of great summariness, along with speed, a remarkable amount of information is provided in economical form. With scaffolding like this, a complete edifice could be constructed; and it was.

Hardly any alterations in design were made in painting the large-scale picture, though where Tiepolo had suggested a rather generalised patch of landscape at the left a view of the convent at Cividale was inserted. But what has altered is the artistic temperature. Cold in tone and heavy, rather pasty, in application of paint, the final altarpiece has lost inspiration, even as what set out to be airy, visionary and mystic has grown inert, prosaic and far too solid. Space and interval have been disturbed. God the Father is bigger, and so is the child Mary, and the clouds which promised to drift vaporously under and around them are pudgy affairs that might be modelled out of pastry.

Some of the facial mannerisms, the chalkiness and the doughy texture of the paint are found, more glaringly, in work documented as Domenico's from the mid-1750s onwards and exemplified by the *Four Camaldolese Saints*, now in Verona but done for S. Michele di Murano. Compared with that work, the Cividale altarpiece is a superior piece of painting, and the hand of Giambattista Tiepolo must be on a good deal of it, though it is a hand that, temporarily, has lost its highest cunning.

Ironically, perhaps, the years after the return from Würzburg saw the career of Domenico Tiepolo starting to develop in its own right. He received a commission from Münster Schwarzach, to paint a *Stoning of St Stephen* altarpiece as a pendant to his father's *Adoration of the Magi*.[14] At Brescia he executed frescoes in the church of SS Faustino e Giovita. At Venice he signed a separate contract with the Scuola di S. Giovanni Evangelista as 'Signor Domenico Tiepoletto figlio del celebre professore . . .' Yet the compliments paid to him always came back to the one Algarotti had paid him as a boy: 'most diligent imitator of such a father', as Longhi's *Compendio* put it. 'Closely following, faithful disciple', was a poetical variant, celebrating the

195. *Vision of St Anne*, Rijksmuseum, Amsterdam.

Palazzo Rezzonico fresco of 1758 and the marriage that had instigated it.[15] Meaning it kindly, the Prince-Bishop of Würzburg had written to him after the return to Venice, expressing belief that one day his talent would come to be 'a true copy of the original—that is, of the virtuoso, your father'.[16] And, in religious commissions especially, Domenico could not contrive an alternative idiom; he was doomed to mouth, usually leadenly, the language learnt in his father's studio and practised as his father's collaborator. Fortunately, before they left Italy, Domenico was to receive a reward and be permitted, encouraged possibly, to be entirely himself, playing his individual part in the fresco scheme at the Villa Valmarana.

With Giambattista's last great altarpiece in Italy, the greatest of this period, the *St Tecla interceding for plague-stricken Este*, Domenico had probably little or nothing to do. The painting was put in place on the high altar of the Duomo, the abbaziale di S. Tecla, at Este on Christmas Eve, 1759. The Cividale altarpiece, which was mildly overdue, had reached its destination only in September of the same year, and perhaps it suffered from Tiepolo's lack of attention to it (not that it lacks anything in 'finish' of a dutiful kind) while he devoted himself to the bigger, more ambitious task.

The scale of the *St Tecla* was its own challenge, being nearly 7 metres high. The subject recalled the outbreak of plague in the city in 1638, and the painting is likely to have been commissioned not long after the approval given by the Commune of Este on 29 June 1758 to a proposal for such a picture to be done, by 'un valente pittore' yet to be selected.[17]

The *modello* Tiepolo produced has a certain compositional assonance with that for the altarpiece for the Benedictine nuns of Cividale (Pl. 196). In both designs a shallow platform occupies the foreground where the chief figure, a female, kneels to receive a vision (which happens in both cases to include prominently God the Father). But while these similarities indicate that Tiepolo was thinking of the two subjects at around the same period, the mood and approach of each are radically different. For Cividale he conceived what is essentially a pious meditation, illustrating if not precisely a mystery, at least a holy event that could be conveyed only symbolically. It is in effect set outside time, and its visual tempo is slow and dignified. Even the view of the convent building does not localise the vision, but it does help to suggest the continuity of it: God's gift of the Virgin to Anna and Joachim (and hence to all mandkind) is for ever valid and to be celebrated.

What Tiepolo conceived for Este was a drama, an appeal out of depths of shocking human affliction for the intervention of the Almighty. It was a subject for Tintoretto, whereas the Cividale painting might have been assigned to Veronese or Bassano. The presence of Este itself in the background was already there in the *modello*, for the location was very much part of the story. The kneeling saint was not thought of as detached from the actuality of the scene, not locked away in some sumptuous chapel or church, but almost touching with her trailing robes the group of living child and plague-stricken, dead mother sprawled out alongside her. And in place of the reclining God the Father of the Cividale painting, manifested as blessing calmly from on high, the figure in the Este altarpiece comes with Michelangelesque dynamism, full-length and imperious, with tremendous state and angelic attendants, in a pictorial thunderclap. Echoing his gesture, obeying his charge, angels cleanse the sky of Plague, a crushed and shrinking body, falling away defeated behind St Tecla's head.

For the *modello*, Tiepolo gave the saint a sole companion, a woman too overawed, tearful and distressed to be other than huddled before the splendid vision which fills so much of the upper part of the composition. The city of Este, deserted and sickly even in tone, was sketched in starkly. No human presence animates it. The effect of the plague is conveyed by the single foreground incident of the child desperately clambering on the livid corpse of its mother, while a man holding his nose against the stench attempts to tug the child away.

196. *St Tecla interceding for plague-stricken Este*, Metropolitan Museum of Art, New York.

The tonality of the *modello* has its own restraint and delicacy. There are touches of vivid scarlet and blue for the man's tunic and the dead mother's cloak. For the rest, the tones are chiefly golden buff, greyish white and blue. God the Father's flying cloak is suitably sky-blue, and the saint is dressed in white and pale biscuit-yellow. For the theme, the tonality is possibly too delicate and harmonious, but it is wonderfully subtle. Its airy blondeness adds its visionary quality to one of Tiepolo's most majestic and affecting visions.

The subject seems to have encouraged him to new powers of thought, and to combine, in a dramatic way he had not done before, pathos and grandeur. The motif of the dead mother and living child was one he had used for a comparatively minor part of a canvas of the *Brazen Serpent*, for the Venetian church of SS Cosma e Damiano, some twenty-five years earlier.[18] There, amid other incidents of the dead and dying, it took its place, with the child a baby, seen trying to suck at the dead mother's breast. In the *modello* for the *St Tecla* altarpiece, the motif is isolated and developed into a complete, not so miniature drama. The child is more than an infant, and its distress is part of the emotional impact, further heightened by the desperate man, its father possibly, trying to tear it away from the contagion to which it clings.

There is a new mood of 'realism' too, it might be said, in the very gesture of his holding his nose. Certainly there is an absence of rhetoric of the kind that had made the S. Alvise *Way to Calvary* something of a pageant, for all its feeling. Sketching economically, yet very fully realising his scene, Tiepolo gives concentrated intensity to the open-mouthed, imploring St Tecla, a lonely figure who seems nearly convulsed under the burden of her interceding role and the spectacle of tragic death so close beside her. The vision of God the Father is shown as a further drama, a drama of the heavens, with its own grandeur yet also intensity.

Visions had been one of Tiepolo's most consistent, favoured themes, going back at least to the appearance of the three angels to Abraham in the Patriarch's palace at Udine. There, as often later, the vision was a half-lulling day-dream, enchanting but undramatic in impact, coming in no thunderclap but like slow, summer lightning. On the ceiling of the Scuola del Carmine he had achieved a much more thrilling effect, truly hallucinatory, in which the vision virtually *is* the subject, and earth, along with the saint crouching on it, becomes ignored, if not obliterated.

In the *St Tecla* composition Tiepolo made almost a clash out of the interaction of the two zones of earth and heaven—one emotionally dark, confused and prayerful, the other supernaturally bright, comforting and supremely dominant. God the Father does not merely appear; he acts. With a gesture of tremendous authority, which might elsewhere serve to divide day and night, he banishes the plague. Tiepolo gets part of the exciting, commanding effect of this figure from its full-length, extended pose, from upraised hand to flying foot, unobscured by any cloud. He may have glanced at the memorable, running silhouette of Jehovah in Tintoretto's *Creation of the Animals*, but for greater awe and majesty he set his deity high in the heavens, attended and borne up by angels, bringing with him weightlessly the globe of the world. And he may have recollected also some of Castiglione's vigorous and dynamic drawings that include Jehovah. A striking example is the brush drawing of *Moses receiving the Tablets of the Law* (Pl. 196a), where Moses kneels humbly before the magnificent, Michelangelesque group of Jehovah amid angels. That drawing is one of many by Castiglione in eighteenth-century Venice, entering eventually the collection of Consul Smith.

In Tiepolo's concept, the saint looks up from earth, fixed in an agony of prayer for aid, and is answered from heaven, even as she turns her eyes upwards. The Almighty is at hand—as intensely immediate in his response as St Tecla in her appeal. About this vision there is no languor, no graceful decent of shimmering distance. Instantly,

196a. G. B. Castiglione, *Moses receiving the Tablets of the Law*, Royal Collection © 1994 Her Majesty the Queen.

it seems, God the Father is manifested, filling the sky with his glory and mercy and omnipotence.

Extreme though the emotional gamut of the scene is—from human affliction, through faith, to divine assurance—the painter is in complete control of his effects. The paint is not wild, though it may be agitated; and despite its inevitable sketchiness, the *modello* is very full of detail, very cogent in its planned impact. The location of the scene is strongly emphasised. The composition reads very rapidly, and that the subsequent altarpiece will be large is already indicated.

Whereas the Cividale altarpiece fails to live up to its *modello* in execution, the Este altarpiece (Pl. 197) retains, in places even deepens, the grandeur, intensity and stark pathos that characterise the preliminary sketch. Its impact in the church, seen as it is, central and dominant, at the end of the nave, is tremendous. Much, if not all of its powerful handling must be Tiepolo's own. He enhanced the authority and the physical presence of his God the Father. New incidents enrich the background. As well as larger, distraught and pointing figures, there is a group resembling a secular Bearing of Christ's Body to the Tomb: mourning, muffled people stagger with a shrouded corpse through the countryside, watched by another, static group, under the shadow of the haunted-seeming city and the mountains beyond (Pl. 198).

Tiepolo had never before pushed his imagination so far into such a bleak region. For the altarpiece he re-thought the foreground group, suppressing entirely the man who tugged at the child's arm, and leaving the horror of the entwined bodies of dead mother and frantic, living child to make its own assault on the emotions. For that incident he was probably inspired by a similar group in the foreground of Poussin's *Plague at Ashdod* (Louvre), early copied and also engraved. From Poussin too may have come the device of combining a formal pavement foreground with a specific distant landscape, used here and in the Cividale altarpiece (compare Poussin's *Ecstasy of St Paul* (Louvre)). It was most likely from the *Plague at Ashdod* that Tiepolo took the idea of having the poignant incident of mother and child witnessed by onlookers, and typical of Poussin in its psychological subtlety is Tiepolo's invention of two men affected by the sight, one tearing his hair as he gazes at it despairingly, the other unable to contemplate it further, bowed down, with his face buried in his hand.

The motif of a man holding his nose against the stench of plague was retained. Tiepolo transferred it to the centre of the composition, giving this figure fresh intensity and significance by setting it in profile and having it point to a plague-horror outside the canvas, forever unseen but imagined. Again, the device is novel for the artist and seems to anticipate something of the *frisson* of David's *Brutus*.

Yet not every addition and alteration in the altarpiece is an improvement. Tension is not heightened but lowered by the introduction of an upraised bearded oriental head between St Tecla and her bent, grieving female companion—and the frank curiosity, bordering on the quizzical, of this face is an odd lapse of judgment. A drastic change in the colour of St Tecla's robes, to a strident red, could be explained as effected for greater visual emphasis in the church, but it is unexpected and somewhat crude. Even the handling of this expanse of paint lacks subtlety.

The cumulative impression of the altarpiece is, nevertheless, profoundly moving and grand. It is Tiepolo's last major religious statement in oil paint in his native land, and it remains one of his finest and most original works. The splendour of its vision might have been anticipated, though even that has a directness, urgency and un-rhetorical tautness which suggest new thinking about a familiar theme. Also novel is the influence of Poussin. What could not have been anticipated was Tiepolo's determined realisation, with equal directness, of the earthly and earthy elements of the subject; it is as though he welcomed the departure from the world of glamorous heroes and heroines, Palladian architecture and well-bred suppression of emotion.

225

197. *St Tecla interceding for plague-stricken Este*, Duomo, Este.

198. Detail from Pl. 197.

Humanity and faith in God are now asserted, with almost desperate seriousness. The Este altarpiece takes on additional resonance as it points the way towards Tiepolo's final activity, and indeed his final painting—of a supernatural vision to one of the humblest of saints, in the simple setting of a Spanish monastery garden (see Pls 231 and 238).

★   ★   ★

Apart from the *St Tecla* altarpiece, Tiepolo's triumphs in the last years of his career in Italy were to be in frescoes. At Venice, however, no very demanding fresco commission came his way after the Pietà ceiling. For the Rezzonico family he frescoed the ceilings of two rooms in what had become their palace on the Grand Canal, built by Longhena but completed by Massari only in 1756. One of the rooms has a subject often identified as an *Allegory of Merit between Nobility and Virtù* and which probably had specific connotations for the family. Certainly the other room, with a marriage allegory, commemorated the marriage in 1758 of Ludovico Rezzonico and Faustina Savorgnan.[19] For that fresco Tiepolo borrowed the motif of Apollo's chariot and horses from the ceiling of the Kaisersaal, but the original poetry and *élan* are missing.

It was outside Venice that he was more fully employed and more artistically creative. He worked at Treviso and returned to Udine; he was active at Verona, and in and around Vicenza. These tasks occupied the years up to 1761, by which time he was engaged on the task of tasks, described by himself as 'grandissimo sopratutti', which was frescoing the ceiling of the ballroom of the Villa Pisani at Strà.[20]

Time and war have made sad victims of Tiepolo's work for palaces in Vicenza and Verona. Little is known of the frescoes he is recorded as early as 1779 as having painted, with Mengozzi Colonna's assistance, in the Palazzo Marchesini at Vicenza. His frescoes in the Palazzo Trento there were largely destroyed by bombing in 1945; the decorative scheme he executed for the Palazzo Porto has been partly repainted and dismantled. At Verona his ceiling of the *Apotheosis of Hercules* (Pl. 199) for the Palazzo Canossa was gravely damaged, also in 1945.

That fresco is important as indicating that in decorative subjects too Tiepolo was re-thinking his approach and evolving new ways to treat old or familiar themes. The Canossa ceiling, 'la superba volta', was to attract the attention of local poets when there were celebrations in Verona for the marriage of Matilde, daughter of its commissioner, Carlo di Canossa, to Count Giovanni Battista d'Arco;[21] but the poets' praise is more interesting as a testimony to Tiepolo's stature than for anything perceptive or particularly detailed.

The ceiling was painted in the summer and autumn of 1761, shortly before Matilde di Canossa's marriage, which (following the poetical references at the time) it was apparently commissioned to commemorate. In itself, the fresco suggests a triumph of heroism, with Hercules carried in a chariot through the skies to the temple of Glory. If there is a distinct echo of Würzburg in the motif of horse-drawn chariot, it is virtually misleading in any consideration of the style. For one thing, Hercules crosses the ceiling on its shorter axis, leaving even more spaciously empty than on earlier Tiepolo ceilings great expanses of sky.

All the figures seem on a smaller scale than at Würzburg and distributed around the composition more centrifugally than centripetally. Nor is there any sense of penetration up and into the ceiling, as at the Pietà. Apart from the figure of Fame and a few, scattered putti, there is little real sense of movement; and despite the pawing horses, Hercules and his chariot are more fixed than hastening in their progress towards Glory. A leisurely, placid mood seems to affect Time, with beside him Cerberus (perhaps as an allegory of Prudence), and the reclining gods and goddesses, loosely dispersed throughout the composition, giving at first sight a somewhat

199. *Apotheosis of Hercules*, Palazzo Canossa, Verona.

fractured air to the composition. Under what appears a vast canopy of sky, striped by a band of the zodiac, is taking place a gentle Olympian masquerade, more stately than dynamic. And that leisureliness, combined with a spaciousness that seems more than merely compositional, characterises Tiepolo's two last great ceiling frescoes, at the Villa Pisani and in the throne-room of the Royal Palace at Madrid. He had always been concerned with achieving a luminosity and an aerial distance in which his figures could breathe and move. More liquid than ever, more all-embracing, these late skies seem to reduce people to particles floating in an ether which has become, if not the chief subject, then at least the chief interest from the painter's point of view.

Quite different aims and ideas were needed for the most absorbing task Tiepolo enjoyed in this period, shifting from large-scale palace decoration, with themes of cosmic grandeur, to new, intimate effects, to pure poetry in place of allegory and only modest, moderate illusionism. Between work at Vicenza itself and work at Verona, Tiepolo frescoed the Villa Valmarana, not far outside Vicenza, with a considerable contribution from Domenico. The two schemes—which is what they became—were completed in 1757, the year in which their commissioner died. Giambattista, with only slight assistance, frescoed in the villa the hall and four rooms on the ground floor, frescoing walls as well as ceilings. In the adjoining foresteria, a guest house, the chief frescoist was Domenico, and there were seven rooms to decorate.

Although the task as such was extensive, the rooms are all small in scale. None was designated for banqueting or dancing. No dynastic statements were to be called for,

229

200. *Sacrifice of Iphigenia*, Villa Valmarana, Vicenza.

201. Detail of Pl. 200.

or moralising themes; but neither was the decoration to lack substance, to be just 'decoration' in a pejorative sense. Tiepolo was being employed in a house—a home, it might be claimed—where highly civilised values were celebrated and presumably esteemed. He would make the villa a positive library, in pictorial terms, or a private theatre, with scenes from some of the world's greatest poems being acted out for a family audience. But the villa was also a country property, and in the foresteria the literary tone was allowed to drop and be replaced by scenes of contemporary peasant life. In Shakespearean terms, Bottom and the rude mechanicals took over from fairies and noble lovers.

The commissioner of the two series of frescoes, both marvellous and each with its own magic, was Count Giustino Valmarana.[22] He had acquired the property, previously belonging to the Bertoli family, and situated on the Monte di San Sebastiano, on the outskirts of the city, in 1720, when he was aged thirty-eight. It was there, in the 'palazzina', rather than in the family palace at Vicenza, that he seems increasingly to have spent his time. Around this modest house his thoughts clearly revolved as he grew older. In 1752 he made a careful will, ensuring that at his death it would descend through his eldest son to that son's eldest son, if he had one, and so on in perpetuity.

Yet when it came to decoration of it, he was singularly free from dynastic concerns. He did not look to see a glorification in paint of the Valmarana family. Unlike Count Niccolò Loschi, he did not stress morality; unlike Carlo Cordellina, he did not choose subjects from history. The very scale of the villa, with a ground-floor

plan of four small rooms leading off an entrance hall, larger than them but still of modest dimensions, would not have encouraged grandiose themes and offered little scope for grandiose treatment.

How he chose Tiepolo is unclear, though the painter's presence on occasion in Vicenza or even his work at the Villa Loschi (Count Giustino's sister had married a Loschi) may have played some part, leaving aside his wide repute as a great fresco painter. Unfortunately, Count Giustino left the commission until very late in his own life. One of the frescoes in the foresteria bears the date 1757, and on 20 June that year he died at the villa. A contemporary, noting his death, mentioned that he was very rich and that he was currently having his villa painted 'by the famous Tiepoletto'.

Nothing is known as to how the programme of decoration was drawn up, and whether from the first—as seems quite probable—the palazzina was seen as having its own distinct ethos, patently literary and more elevated than the rooms of the foresteria, where freedom and fantasy would reign. The existence of the two levels of the decorative schemes virtually called for two artists, or at least for two styles. However it came about, it gave Domenico Tiepolo an opportunity he was never to have again. Not even on the walls of the Tiepolo's own villa did he fresco with such fertile, delightful invention and so perfectly exploit in paint his keen, amused observation of country life and manners. He found—sadly, it was to be briefly—his own artistic voice and vocabulary, utterly distinct from those of his father.

For Giambattista Tiepolo the commission was to be hardly less stimulating. With him it would not provoke a new style or new subject-matter as such, but it produced a new approach, fostered no doubt by the intimate setting and by the poignant mingled theme of love and duty which underlay most of the incidents depicted by him.

The four symmetrical rooms called for some broadly unifying concept, and it was found by matching scenes from the poems of the two greatest epic poets of antiquity, Homer and Virgil, with scenes from those of the two greatest epic poets of 'modern' Italy, Tasso and Ariosto. The *Iliad* and the *Aeneid* were thus matched with the *Gerusalemme Liberata* and the *Orlando Furioso*. From each poem three or four scenes were selected to decorate the walls in each room; on the modest-sized ceilings was feigned sky animated by a relevant deity or allegory. The total effect is of a balanced but highly novel pictorial *paragone* between ancient and modern—almost, between classical and romantic—and a resolution, peacefully, of all quarrels and rival claims about the superiority of the geniuses of one age over those of another. All four are treated as in effect love poets, and in that Homer is perhaps the poet most ruthlessly adapted to a strand of eighteenth-century taste. Yet, paradoxically, Tiepolo showed himself at his most imaginative and original in dealing with the scenes from the *Iliad*.

The hall of the villa was also associated with the overall theme, announcing it on a scale and with a dramatic *coup de théâtre* that could not be attempted in the adjoining rooms. The subject chosen for this was the Sacrifice of Iphigenia (Pl. 200), a familiar subject, excluded from the *Iliad* but treated by both classical antique writers and painters (most famously by Timanthes, whose masterpiece of the scene survived through literary allusions).

It was not a new subject for Italian painting and still less for Tiepolo and his contemporaries. It had, for example, served for one of Piazzetta's rare 'history' paintings,[23] while Tiepolo had dealt with it previously in oil and fresco (the extremely damaged painting in the Villa Corner at Merlengo).[24] The subject was virtually a pagan variation of the Sacrifice of Isaac. It set up oscillations of violent emotional conflict—a father compelled by divine injunction to sacrifice his beloved child—without actually depicting bloodshed, since at the last moment the sacrifice is arrested.

231

In his earlier compositions of the subject, Tiepolo had combined in the one scene the moment of imminent sacrifice and the dramatic arrival of the goddess Diana, halting it and substituting a hind as the victim. Even at Merlengo, where he had other walls and the ceiling to utilise, he preserved this unity. On a short side wall he showed Iphigenia carried away by the goddess to Tauris, and on the ceiling an apparently vague triumph of Diana in the clouds.

For the Villa Valmarana, something much more ambitious was realised. The hall is treated as a complete, three-dimensional stage, on to which the visitor steps unprepared, directly on entering the house. The long right-hand wall depicts, on a raised platform, framed by pillars, Iphigenia at the altar about to be sacrificed, amid a throng of spectators. On the opposite, shorter walls are other spectators and a glimpse of the becalmed Greek fleet. From both walls the spectators' eyes are raised to the ceiling, following the grave and despairing gaze of Calchas and of Iphigenia respectively, and the visitor's gaze is equally guided upwards. There, on the ceiling, Diana appears—a true *dea ex machina*—commanding the priest to drop the knife from Iphigenia's bared breast; and, floating in on a cloud illusionistically painted hovering in the air in front of the pillars, the hind is brought by a winged boy.

Only gradually does the full import break. The first visual sensation is of the half-naked, fainting blonde girl, the knife blade, the additional sacrificial instrument of an axe and the dish held by an attendant for the blood. At the furthest end of the ceiling Diana appears. The hind floats down from the far left. At the far right, closest at hand to anyone stepping into the hall from the outside world, is an armoured figure, isolated and not gazing at all but with head buried in his cloak: Agamemnon, the father, unable to witness what he has been compelled to order, and unaware of the dénouement (Pl. 201). It was precisely the solution of Agamemnon's grief chosen by Timanthes and the subject of traditional literary praise.

A series of emotions are meant to succeed each other, all triggered off by the first, not quite disagreeable shock. Tiepolo's Aulis, partly created by the Ionic pillars and severely elegant architectural framework devised, once again, by Mengozzi Colonna, is so clean, pure and restrained, raised emotionally as well as literally out of anything merely natural or ordinary. There is nothing here of the 'realism' of the Este altarpiece. A quite different convention is operating. Tiepolo always remembers—and at the Villa Valmarana Mengozzi Colonna is at hand should he have a lapse of memory—that fresco decoration, however serious its subject, ought ultimately to please.

Yet Iphigenia's situation is tragic, though it is staged so formally. She is a heroine at the centre of the scene, but also a victim, as innocent as the wretched hind that will be sacrificed in her place. Human-beings can do nothing for her—and Tiepolo surrounds her by mutes, looking up pale or amazed at the intervention overhead of a divinity. Of a contemporaneous painting of the *Sacrifice of Iphigenia* by Carle van Loo, the French theorist the Comte de Caylus pronounced approvingly that the spectator was struck only after shedding tears ('le spectateur n'en est frappé qu'après avoir versé des pleurs. . .').[25] Tiepolo's Iphigenia also is a touching and appealing spectacle; after that sensation comes surprise at the goddess's arrival—and pleasure in the illusionism by which it is contrived. A whole gamut of sensations is experienced by the beholder, who gradually realises that the outcome of what at first seemed a scene of human sacrifice is—if not exactly happy—at least calming. Duty has been done, and the goddess is appeased. As well as Diana, the Winds appear on the ceiling; flags are already stirring, and soon the Greek fleet will be on its way to Troy.

Although grander and more formal than the scenes that follow in the rooms around, the *Sacrifice of Iphigenia* serves as introduction to them. It has grandeur and formality as befits what is a sort of frontispiece to their stories, where duty triumphs over love and where—pagan or Christian—a warrior learns to suppress his passion. Achilles must give up Briseis; Rinaldo leaves Armida, as Aeneas is bid to leave Dido.

Only the rustic idyll of Angelica and Medoro is undisturbed and happy, though that love is what drove Orlando mad.

Yet the effect of the four stories is far from being unmitigatedly stern. Just as in the *Sacrifice of Iphigenia* there is frank delight in Iphigenia's semi-nudity, so in the other frescoes there is a strong vein of sensuousness in depiction of the female body. Tiepolo's is no boudoir art, but at the Villa Valmarana, more than elsewhere, it comes closest to the style of *dix-huitième* eroticism associated with Boucher.

From the hall, the first room at the right is that of the *Iliad* and it would seem intended to be entered first. Here Mengozzi Colonna made even more pronounced the classical architectural framework for each subject, creating a proscenium arch and platform for the chief action, with wing-like porches at the sides. The sense of witnessing scenes on the stage—scenes from opera—is strong, enhanced by the noticeably few protagonists, painted in powerful, silhouetted shapes, and by the unusual device, akin to a backdrop, whereby a more naturalistic setting is placed behind and below the foreground platform.

Homer was a rare source for painters when Tiepolo was working at the Villa Valmarana (though in that year Caylus published his *Tableaux tirés de l'Iliade, de l'Odyssée d'Homère et de l'Enéide de Virgile*, and at least one copy reached Venice because Consul Joseph Smith owned one). Unknown to Tiepolo, and probably to his patron, new ideas about attitudes to the antique past were being expressed in aesthetics. Neo-classicism was to become a trend, a European vogue and then in turn die away long after Tiepolo's death. It stood for a more sober, learned, correct approach, not only to the past of Greece and Rome but to painting subjects derived from those sources. Tiepolo was not, by his own standards, unlearned, and certainly not careless in dealing with any subject-matter. What concerned him was the significance of the story to be illustrated, not historical accuracy of costume or setting—as he had already patently shown in dealing with the story of Cleopatra and Antony under the promptings of Algarotti.

Judged by the general idiom of neo-classicism and by what most learned people would expect by the end of the eighteenth century to be the proper approach to classical themes, both Tiepolo's *Iliad* and *Aeneid* rooms, and his *Sacrifice of Iphigenia*, would seem flippant in their indifference to accuracy and frivolous in their lack of dignity. While he and Mengozzi might feel they had striven for a particular chastity of effect and achieved a dignity of framework that is indeed chaste and dignified in comparison with the near-reckless exuberance of the decoration of the patriarchal gallery at Udine, advanced aesthetic taste could well question the presence at Aulis of Orientals mixing with the Greeks, and look askance at the introduction of a large, seated dog, taken from the *Homage* fresco at Würzburg. Tiepolo's Minerva is not particularly noble. His Dido is wearing a sixteenth-century ruff, and hints of the sixteenth century and Veronese haunt most of the costumes of his classical antique people.

Tiepolo's interpretations would never have won the approval of Winckelmann any more than of Caylus. Goethe's judgment (recorded in the *Italienische Reise*) was to be that Tiepolo (he did not distinguish between father and son) succeeded far better in the 'natural' foresteria frescoes than in the 'elevated' ones of the palazzina.

Yet for the palazzina frescoes, and especially for those with antique subject-matter, Tiepolo seems to have reflected deeply, curbing his normal love of enrichment and worldly glamour, his irony and high spirits and being determinedly serious, simple even, and emotionally direct. If classicism means clarity and control, Tiepolo was there at his most classical. What is beyond argument is that he sought new effects and created them in ways new and unforeseen.

The *Iliad* room tells in three scenes of Achilles' love for Briseis and hers for him. Angry with Agamemnon's demand for her surrender, Achilles is shown restrained from killing the Greek commander only by Minerva's sudden appearance to him

202. *Briseis led to Agamemnon*, Villa Valmarana, Vicenza.

203. Detail of Pl. 202.

alone, tugging at his hair. The action and incident were awkward for any painter to depict; Tiepolo tried valiantly, but could not disguise the awkwardness or illustrate other than rather too literally Homer's drama. He was far more at ease in the subject of the largest fresco, *Briseis led to Agamemnon* (Pl. 202), for which the poem gave merely the briefest sanction—'the woman went with them unwillingly'. He made a martial, somewhat baleful silhouette of Agamemnon standing on the foreground platform, waiting while the two aged heralds bring away from the tents of Achilles the reluctant, seductive bundle of white draperies and blonde hair and skin that is Briseis (Pl. 203). Homer saw her as a captive, a female chattel, handed over, albeit reluctantly, from one chieftain to another; but for Tiepolo she becomes a heroine. Her unwillingness to leave Achilles in wonderfully conveyed in her drooping pose, as is her distaste for what lies ahead in the form of Agamemnon, to whom one of the heralds points, as she is virtually harried on, stirring the spectator's pity as another victim.

234

Tiepolo's ability to find inspiration in his text was demonstrated most poignantly in the third scene, *Achilles mourning on the seashore* (Pl. 205). This is the most original of all the compositions in the palazzina. Less classical than romantic was his response to Homer's lines about the grieving Achilles, weeping, away from his comrades, 'on the beach of the grey sea. . .' Damaged though this fresco is, it retains its haunting mood. The hero is placed outside the proscenium arch, in a piece of *trompe l'œil* that intensifies his lonely, brooding misery. Under the beetling cliffs and out of the 'grey sea', Thetis rises to comfort her son, accompanied by a sea-nymph, their heads only barely breaking the line of the horizon where the sea and sky meet. Here there is no more sense of jarring anachronism than in a Renaissance painting of comparable subject-matter. The freedom from any established iconography (for the subject is very rare indeed in painting) has helped Tiepolo to seize the essence of the incident in a free and truly affecting poetic way. Though the ostensible grief is Achilles' for the loss of Briseis, the inner sadness is that of Thetis, mourning for her son whose lot on earth she knows is doomed to be brief.

The *Iliad* room leads into that of the *Orlando Furioso*, perhaps pairing Ariosto with Homer as certainly Tasso was with Virgil. For these scenes Mengozzi dispensed with platforms and architecture, framing them in a thoroughly Venetian rococo *quadratura* of scrollwork and flowers, recalling the decoration of painted Venetian furniture of the period. Within this more relaxed framework the elements of setting are of the simplest: a tree-trunk, a thatched roof, a rock. One scene shows Angelica romantically rescued from the orc by Ruggiero on the hippogriff, but the romance of the other three scenes is more gentle and non-heroic, concerned with Angelica in a less passive role: taking care of the wounded Moorish knight Medoro, fondly carving his name on a tree (Pl. 204), and seated beside him in a peasant hut. The mood of these scenes is poetically tender, almost surprisingly so. The language of the heart, expressed through the eyes, had been no theme of Tiepolo's, even though it was a commonplace of his century. He had painted so many subjects, but scarcely the subject of two people in love. Yet the Angelica who bends to nurse the fainting body of Medoro is meltingly affectionate, and her feeling is reciprocated in the scene where, gazing at him as she carves his name, she is confronted—as is the spectator—by Medoro's upturned face suffused with passionate ardour.

Paired on the other side of the hall of the villa are the rooms of the *Aeneid* and the *Gerusalemme Liberata*. There lay the literary origin of the whole programme, it may be, for in the scenes chosen both poets dealt with the theme of the warrior-hero who must abandon the spell of a woman. Duty conquers love. On the ceiling of the *Aeneid* room Venus triumphs not as the personification of love but as the mother of the hero and founder of Italy. The ceiling of the *Gerusalemme Liberata* room is usually interpreted as showing Light dispelling Darkness, and though the triumphing winged figure is probably Nobility or Merit, rather than Light, the triumph implies a conquest of mind over body, of intellect over emotion.

Granted the fame and popularity of the story of Dido and Aeneas, the frescoes in the *Aeneid* room are somewhat tame and disappointing. The room is the least successful in terms of theme, decoration and execution. Mengozzi's Chippendale-style twisting fronds, medallions and birds provide a slightly disconcerting framework for illustrations that themselves seem rather uncertainly pitched in tone. Dido appears only in the scene where Aeneas arrives at her court with his son Ascanius (Cupid, in fact, disguised). Tiepolo's new simplicity and directness make him avoid, almost too brusquely, opportunities for lavish treatment. The queen of an exotic empire is firmly dressed in sixteenth-century costume and might be an allegory of good government by a follower of Veronese. Neither Dido nor Aeneas is accompanied by much in the way of retinue, though Virgil wrote of 'quinquaginta . . . famulae' present in the Carthaginian court. More successful are the visionary scenes of Venus appearing to Aeneas on his landing in Africa and Mercury appearing to the

204. *Angelica carving Medoro's name*, Villa Valmarana, Vicenza.

236

sleeping hero, warning him to depart. A distinct oddity is the fourth fresco, taken from a later book of the *Aeneid*, a scene of Venus at the forge of Vulcan, executed in *grisaille* and patently attributable to Domenico Tiepolo. This is only the most obvious example of his intervention in the villa frescoes. It helps to underline the homogeneity of the room adjoining, the Tasso room—the most successfully integrated and decorated of the four rooms.

The theme of Rinaldo, the young Christian knight, a paragon of beauty and chivalry, ensnared by the enchantress Armida, herself beautiful, brave, intelligent, but evil, had seduced plenty of Italian painters before Tiepolo, among them Guercino, Pietro da Cortona and Giordano. It had attracted composers too, from Lully's *Armide* of 1686 onwards, including Handel and Jommelli, and later Gluck and Rossini.

Tiepolo had previously depicted in oil paint incidents in the story of Rinaldo and Armida, on both a small and large scale, and doubtless knew it well.[26] The task of the Christian knights is to free Jerusalem, and that of Armida is to prevent them. In his poem Tasso asks how the crusaders could be expected to withstand love, considering that such heroes as Achilles, Theseus and Hercules were conquered by it. And—in this like Dido—Armida falls genuinely in love. When she pleads with Rinaldo not to leave her, she pleads sincerely, not out of guile; and at the moment of parting Rinaldo pities her. She attempts suicide but eventually is reconciled to the now purified Rinaldo, still admiring of her as he virtually converts her to Christianity. At one point in the poem she is called 'a second Cleopatra', and by the end she has not lost her exotic glamour, though she has, or will, become good.

At the Villa Valmarana Tiepolo made the chief scene the episode of the painful parting of the lovers (Pl. 206). The other three frescoes show Armida falling in love with the sleeping Rinaldo; the lovers on her magic island, discovered by the warriors Carlo and Ubaldo, sent to seek out Rinaldo; and Rinaldo's shame when he realises the spell he has been under. In Armida's garden the lovers are seated side by side, exchanging glances, merging into a single figure, so closely and intimately are they juxtaposed. Tiepolo seems to have sketched, some years earlier, ideas for a sculpted group of Rinaldo and Armida, and now achieved even greater cohesion. No less intensely conveyed is the sense of Rinaldo's shame: he turns from the shield that reflects his subjugated image and tears at the flower-garland symbolising it, while on his beautiful, asexual face, with its huge eyes, is an expression of profound, bitter chagrin, Tiepolo makes him seem almost to taste self-disgust, with lips puckered by a rapid flick of paint applied like a squirt of lemon-juice on the mouth.

Probably more than once had Tiepolo dealt with the most poignant scene of all— the actual parting of the lovers—before he dealt with it in fresco. In all the compositions, Armida is seated on the ground, in varying poses of despairing expostulation. The chief changes affect the pose of Rinaldo, always standing and naturally in the hands, sometimes literally, of Carlo and Ubaldo. In a small and brilliantly handled *modello* he is sinking physically under the stress of emotion. In another larger composition he stands inert, eyes downcast; in yet another he makes a gesture half of apology and half of farewell.

Only in the fresco is Rinaldo placed close to Armida—so close that her outstretched, imploring hand crosses in front of his bare leg. The policeman-like warriors no longer grasp his arm or gesticulate; though one of them has his fingers at Rinaldo's shoulder, they seem tacitly to have recognised that the struggle is his: he must conquer himself. Not fainting and far from inert, Rinaldo gazes down at Armida, lovely, dishevelled and beyond dignity in her despair. A stoic grief seems to invest his whole figure. His body is turned in the direction of departure, but his head inclines towards her. Affection, reluctance and pity can all be read in his pose and in the complex expression on his face. His very cloak, billowing like a sail, seems stirred by conflict and bearing him away against his instinct. Most expressive of all

206. *Rinaldo leaving Armida*, Villa Valmarana, Vicenza.

are his arms. Tiepolo has crossed them over his body, with left hand tightly clasping right arm, as though Rinaldo is arresting himself, suppressing his impulses, taking himself in hand and tearing himself away under pressure from his own physical grip, even while he longs to yield and stay.

Great poems were the subject of the whole fresco scheme in the villa, and two of them were available to Tiepolo in his and their native language. Yet in itself that is not sufficient to explain the intensity of his response, with its emphasis on the tender, passionate and strongly human elements of the incidents depicted. Iphigenia's distress, Angelica's care and cure of Medoro, Achilles' lonely brooding on the seashore, possess an emotional plangency which in the Tasso room reaches its bitter-sweet climax. Framed in a fourth variation of decorative painted mouldings, with flattened rococo shell and leaf motifs, these scenes are a climax also in terms of Tiepolo's art. Here, and here alone in the villa, every part of every fresco speaks—and the verb is in the circumstances no rhetorical one—of his hand as much as of his mind.

So integrated is the scheme of this room, and so high the quality of execution, that it is tempting to suggest that Tiepolo started the whole series here, and possibly in 1756. It can be only a hypothesis, but it seems possible that Count Giustino's death interrupted work in the villa or caused it to be hastened on, with more speed than might have been desirable. In 1757 work can hardly have started on the frescoes much before March, and within three months or so the patron was dead. Only the Tasso room and the hall have total consistency of execution. Elsewhere, lapses of thought occur, whatever the reasons to be assigned, as well as lapses, or departures, from Giambattista's own standards of fresco painting.

Neither in the *Iliad* nor *Aeneid* rooms are the ceilings very successful, in concept or execution. In the *Orlando Furioso* room it is usually agreed that Domenico Tiepolo intervened by painting the pair of peasants and the rustic hut in the scene of Angelica and Medoro seated there. Domenico's presence in the *Aeneid* room is demonstrated by the *Forge of Vulcan* fresco, unique in the series in being done in *grisaille*. Oddest of all is the fact that in the *Iliad* room a complete classical-style framework was painted by Mengozzi for the fourth fresco but filled by nothing more than a cupid flying through a huge expanse of sky and a slight, sketchy, North-Italian landscape, complete with peasants, that is as patently by Domenico as it is unrelated to Homer. It is difficult to explain this other than as an impromptu, last-minute substitution, in haste, of what had been intended to be a further 'history' scene.

What that might have been can only be conjectured. Two horizontal oil sketches, not necessarily *modelli*, exist from about this period, showing the Madness of Ulysses and, more pertinently, the Rape of Helen.[27] The latter subject was also painted by Tiepolo in an upright sketch, at around the same period or arguably later, and it is conceivable that some such incident was to be illustrated in the Villa Valmarana. That Helen is the subject of these existing *Rape* compositions is most probable, but just worth considering, if the villa was in mind, is whether either of the paintings is meant to show the capture, rather, of Briseis.

An oil sketch of the *Death of Dido*, also datable to the later 1750s, has been linked to the scheme for the *Aeneid* room, with the proposal that this subject was intended originally for the fourth wall.[28] Attractive though this suggestion is, it takes no account of the most unusual aspect of the Valmarana frescoes, the fact that no oil *modelli* for them exist. All the preliminary work seems to have been done in pen-and-wash studies.[29] These drawings are among the most fluent and accomplished in all Tiepolo's œuvre, uninhibited in their economy and often leaving unresolved— almost deliberately, it might be supposed—detailed problems that could be resolved on the frescoes themselves. In fact, there must have been more to it than that, but the directness and freshness of the frescoes by Giambattista would encourage the idea that he gave himself licence to improvise. In some cases it can anyway be demonstrated that he changed his mind between the execution of the pen-and-wash drawings and the fresco. In the drawing of Angelica tending the wounded Medoro is included a cupid flying in with more herbs, and a parrot perched on some sort of pediment or column (Pl. 207). These decorative and somewhat 'rococo' touches are omitted from the fresco composition. Instead, more suitably and more soberly, appears a peasant holding a horse beside a tree.

The extent of the collaboration between Giambattista Tiepolo and Domenico in the palazzina may never be precisely settled, nor may the reason for it. Yet it is obvious that the commission was undertaken largely by Giambattista. Down in the foresteria, the situation is the reverse. Only one room out of seven, the so-called 'Sala dell'Olimpo', was frescoed by the father. In the remaining rooms Domenico was free to let his imagination soar, for once unfettered. And it soared not in any Olympian direction but into a world no less wonderful, made up partly from observation and delight in human antics and fashions, chiefly country ones, and partly from fantasy.

The word 'genre' is too weak and prosaic to cover scenes that are often bizarre as well as witty, frankly enchanted and wonderfully carefree. Peasant life is no more laborious, it would appear, than patrician life. Smartly dressed ladies out walking in winter and rustic women out walking in the summer are equally presumed to be enjoying themselves. Peasants repose and eat contentedly enough under heavy-

207. *Angelica curing Medoro*, Victoria & Albert Museum, London (D.1825.23–1885).

foliaged trees (Pl. 208). A complete room of Chinese scenes is more overtly exotic but hardly less 'realistic' than Domenico's pair of well-washed, charmingly clad country lovers (Pl. 209); and the playful, Gothic-style setting Mengozzi devised for this couple, as well as for other comparable figures, emphasises the extent to which this is an enchanted, semi-artificial world—distinct no doubt from that of the palazzina, with its epic heroes and passions of love, but equally divorced from plain, everyday concerns. Despite the wit and irony, there is something reassuring in Domenico's vision. No hint of harsh weather spoils his winter scene. He never depicts people working—just diverting themselves, in country or town.

It would be wrong to make too sharp a contrast between palazzina and foresteria, between Giambattista's elevated ethos and Domenico's more lowly one. The foresteria is the location, after all, of Giambattista's Olympian gods and goddesses, reclining on clouds in a thoroughly relaxed siesta mood. And in the palazzina rustic touches have, for one reason or another, crept in. Working together, if not exactly side by side, father and son have managed to devise what amounts to a single idiom, accommodating Achilles and Angelica, Columbine and Pantaloon, the love story of Rinaldo and Armida, and the love-making of two peasants. Past and present eventually come together, magically synthesised, leaving the spectator to conclude that 'All the world's a stage...'

208. D. Tiepolo, *Peasants eating out of doors*, Foresteria, Villa Valmarana, Vicenza.

209. D. Tiepolo, *The declaration of love*, Foresteria, Villa Valmarana, Vicenza.

A sense of theatre and theatrical presentation was detected in the frescoes well before it was known that the patron had been involved a good deal in theatrical matters in Vicenza. He had a share in a theatre there, where *Demetrio*, an opera by the Venetian but Viennese-based composer, Antonio Caldara, was performed with notable success in 1734. 'Good alike at grave and gay', Caldara could range from serious operas and religious music to drinking songs and musical *jeux d'esprit* based on a card game or even a visit to the dentist. If Count Valmarana savoured his work, he might well enjoy the comparable pictorial range provided by the Tiepolo, father and son, for his own private delectation in his own small, much-loved property.

A private air still hangs around the villa, strikingly unostentatious compared with the Palazzo Labia or the Villa Pisani at Strà. More poignant than exuberant, Giambattista's palazzina frescoes have a touch of autumnal tone about their flavour and their colouring. Parting and farewell form a distinct thread in leading from the hall to the rooms, and from one room to another. Already in the *Sacrifice of Iphigenia* there is parting adumbrated: though she survives, she is lost and, as it were, dead to her father.

Maturely beautiful, deeply expressive and yet devoid of rhetoric, the frescoes are

210. *Assumption of the Virgin*, Oratorio della Purità,
Udine.

suffused with soft tones of russet and pale gold and pinkish fawn. Apart from the skies, blue is used rarely. The colour harmonies are not new ones for Tiepolo but they are developed here in subtle ways that seem to complement the quiet novelty of concept and approach in the frescoes themselves. Tiepolo had not achieved precisely these effects before, and he was not to do so again. Although Count Valmarana died before he could thoroughly appreciate all that had been executed for him, he deserves a high place among Tiepolo's patrons. What he gave the artist was by no means the most splendid of his fresco commissions, but in a certain sense it was the most subtle, and unforeseen, of all.

In the late summer of 1759, Tiepolo travelled out of Venice for another fresco scheme, again taking Domenico with him. This time he was returning to a city, Udine, that was associated with some of his earliest and most brilliant frescoes. Again he was to be working for a Dolfin patron, Cardinal Daniele Dolfin, nephew of the old Patriarch and himself obviously eager to employ Tiepolo to decorate a modest building, though one with which he was closely involved.

Two years before, the Cardinal had acquired a site close to the Duomo for the institution of a school of Christian doctrine for children, the Oratorio della Purità. A simple yet elegant building was designed, with a pedimented façade, its doorway gracefully carved with the three dolfins of the patron's arms. On the first floor, in the usual way of Scuole, is the chapel, a fairly low-ceilinged room, where the Tiepolo were to work. For the pretty stucco and marble altar Giambattista painted an altarpiece in oil of the Virgin Immaculate, standing on a pedestal carefully designed to match the colours and style of the architectural surround. The main ceiling fresco continued the theme of the Virgin, depicting the Assumption, and was also executed by Giambattista (Pl. 210). Around the walls eight scenes from the Old and New Testaments were selected, apparently by the Cardinal, involving children and relating to the purpose of the foundation. These are in *grisaille* on a gold ground and were Domenico's contribution to the scheme.[30]

Domenico's task was nicely gauged to suit him, especially in scenes allowing him to be at his most natural and touching, as in depicting a delightful family of Maccabeus children or the sons of Jacob clustering about his deathbed. He even made an effort to take seriously the more monitory subject of Elisha cursing the children who mocked his bald head and were thereupon eaten by bears—though the distinctly sheep-like bears remain more playful than carnivorous.

On the ceiling, Giambattista Tiepolo had an opportunity to return to the subject he had painted for the chapel of the Residenz at Würzburg, but it was with fresh, invigorated and now inspired power that he depicted it. The heavenly portion of the Oratorio fresco has all the radiant spaciousness and almost literal buoyancy so lacking in the Würzburg altarpiece, and even more drastically improved is treatment of the group on earth. Tiepolo foreshortened the tomb and the figures of the Apostles around it, while reducing them in number and prominence; one alone, standing with hand raised aloft in a dramatic gesture of amazement, is dominant against the expanse of cloudy sky. In his effective pose and domination over the rest of the group, this figure seems to echo the gesticulating Apostle of Piazzetta's great altarpiece of the *Assumption*.

The Virgin owes nothing to Piazzetta's treatment. A decorously clad sister, artistically speaking, to the Iphigenia of the Villa Valmarana, or even Armida, she has the same expressive features as they, with open mouth and large, soulful, upturned eyes. She is ascending to heaven, not as Piazzetta had conceived the event, in a stormy blaze of white light, but in a tranquil, cool, semi-afternoon glow that gives translucence to her sky-blue and white robes and to the pale gold and olive-green draperies of two angels who aid her effortlessly in her ascent.

The effect is very different, again, from the great cosmic drama of the Pietà ceiling. At Udine the Virgin, exemplifying total purity, is the central focus of the composi-

tion. Purity extends to the soft clouds and the atmosphere of the heavens themselves, emotionally dominated and occupied by the Virgin. At once elegant and eloquent, her gestures are those of a heroine, and she is an active not passive participant in her assumption. The motif of her coronation is removed to a subsidiary compartment where angels bring a light wreath of lilies—a further symbol of purity. Simple piety, not majesty, is the emphasis of the composition, and charm, expressed at its sweetest in the roses that fall miraculously around the empty tomb as the Virgin is borne steadily towards paradise.

The work of frescoing in the Oratorio seems to have taken Tiepolo a bare month —from the middle of August to the middle of September. It was during that period, presumably, at the height of the summer, that he looked again at the countryside around Udine and made a number of pen-and-wash studies evocative of strong sunlight and luminously dark shadow. One study is of the crossing of the Duomo at Udine, and the others are economical sketches of rustic roofs, gateways, a well-head in a farm courtyard (Pl. 211), always devoid of any human presence. Each shape is firmly reduced to essentials, moulded by the light and baked by the heat, so that from them there seems to exude a smell of dry straw and tile and earth, like the perennial scent of the Italian countryside in summer.

Tiepolo made no use of these drawings. They simply record his visual sensations when outside his native city, and some of them seem to have been done when working earlier at the Villa Valmarana. He may even have based some of them on farm buildings around his own villa at Zianigo, when he retreated there for a rare break from work.

His appetite for work was undiminished, though, writing to Algarotti from Venice in March 1761, he referred to his 'molti impegni'.[31] What they consisted of, he vividly conveys. He must shortly proceed to Milan, but also manage to complete two paintings for a church in Rome, while labouring on at a ceiling canvas for 'the court of Moscow' and facing the task of frescoing the ceiling of the main salone of the Villa Pisani at Strà. Less than a month later, his commissions included the prospect of travelling to Verona 'to paint a room', and he was finding some time, so he said, to work on a 'Gran Ritratto', commissioned by Algarotti. This large-scale,

212. *Girl with a parrot*, Ashmolean Museum, Oxford.

now lost portrait was almost certainly not, as sometimes supposed, of Algarotti himself, but an equestrian portrait of Frederick the Great. The commissioner of the paintings for Rome was Cardinal Dolfin. The 'court of Moscow' seems to refer to the Empress Elizabeth Petrovna, Frederick the Great's enemy, for whom Tiepolo is recorded also as painting some half figures 'di donne a capriccio' in December 1760.[32] These 'fancy' paintings are as unexpected an aspect of Tiepolo's activity as is a portrait of the King of Prussia, but, unlike that, examples of them survive (Pl. 212). They develop out of Rosalba's pastels, and the models may very well be, as has been suggested, Tiepolo's own daughters.

With such tasks of all kinds, Tiepolo was perhaps ill-advised to agree in September 1760 to paint a ceiling in the Scuola di S. Giovanni Evangelista at Venice, and it is scarcely surprising that he never managed to undertake it. By May of that year he had accepted the Villa Pisani commission—which he was himself to describe as the greatest, 'largest of all' his tasks. As soon as he recovered from an attack of gout, he turned to executing the *modello* for the ceiling, work on which he estimated—with perhaps deliberate exaggeration—as likely to take three or four years.

Events were to cause that leisurely estimate to be sharply revised. The Pisani, famous as a Venetian family and descended from a recent Doge, came close to being out-bid by a royal trump: Charles III of Spain had decided that the huge throne-room of the new royal palace in Madrid should be frescoed by Tiepolo. To the pressure of 'molti impegni' was soon added this one, which became a diplomatic issue, raised by the Spanish ambassador to the Republic. Eventually, Tiepolo found time to complete the Villa Pisani ceiling, as he had wished, before accepting the high honour—as he termed it—of the Spanish king's summons, which grew more peremptory even as Tiepolo sought to delay the start of his journey. What he wished was to be, in his own words, 'quiettissimo e tranquillo' in mind, before leaving. Whether he really was, cannot now be known. But at least he left Venice with the knowledge and satisfaction of having finished the ceiling of the Villa Pisani (Pls 213 and 214).

By a happy accident, the ceiling became his final work in his native country. It was in the medium of fresco, where he was always at his best. It was a thoroughly Venetian commission, involving an ancient and distinguished patrician family, in a modern building on an impressive scale—the largest fresco he ever executed in a private dwelling. And, somewhat ironically as things proved, it stressed a glorious future for the Pisani, and by implication for Venice. It was the least backward-looking of all Tiepolo's subjects, for it combined allegory and personification with the living members of the family, portraying them positively up in the clouds, serene and assured, almost gods themselves, in a very heaven of optimism.

History compounded the irony when the Villa Pisani was chosen as the official country residence for Napoleon's viceroy in Italy, Eugène de Beauharnais, after the overthrow of the Venetian Republic. Decorations in a very different style from Tiepolo's, lightly Pompeian in manner, were to be frescoed in adjoining rooms. A bedroom was prepared for the Emperor not far from the salone where Tiepolo had splendidly summed up the *ancien-régime* ethos of privilege, benevolence and peace in the best of all possible worlds. And eventually it was to be recorded that Napoleon slept there.

The sumptuous villa on the Brenta had been built, to the designs of Francesco Maria Preti, to express the fresh distinction of the Pisani family with the election of Alvise Pisani as Doge in 1735. Most of the extensive painted decoration of the interior was executed after the Doge's death in 1741, much of it during the 1760s.[33] Before that, however, it seems, a Tiepolesque painter, possibly Crosato, had frescoed a *Triumph of the Arts* in one of the rooms, mingling conventional allegory and personal allusion by introducing into it the Pisani coat-of-arms and a putto holding the Doge's cap. In that ceiling there seems to lie a hint of the far more developed and

ambitious ceiling, in theme and execution, that Tiepolo himself would create. Among the painters eventually working in the villa may well have been a young amateur of the family, Almorò Pisani, a dilettante artist who died in 1766 at the age of twenty-six.

The commissioner of Tiepolo's fresco was one of the Procurators of St Mark's, another Alvise Pisani, who chose for the largest and most important room in his palatial villa the leading and most important painter in Venice. As usual with such private work, documentation of the commission is non-existent, but the theme of the ceiling decoration must have been settled between patron and artist by the time Tiepolo turned to work on the *modello*.

Past no less than present was to be conveyed in the painted decoration of the villa. In the two courtyards that flank the grand salone were painted contemporaneously the Twelve Caesars and the Kings of Rome, along with other figures of antiquity.

Thus grandiose echoes of the classical past in the architecture combined with the grandeur of the patron's family to make a thoroughly imperial and consciously Roman effect. Like several noble Venetian families, the Pisani claimed descent, by quite fanciful genealogy, from Roman ancestors. Theirs were identified as the Calpurnii Pisoni. In a more allusive way the Caesars and the Kings were fitting figures to adorn a villa built originally in honour of a doge.

The central salone, nowadays often called the ballroom, is vast and very high, divided by a gallery running the whole way round it at first-floor level. A comparatively restrained, classicising *quadratura* framework was devised by Pietro Visconti, a Milanese expert in this type of décor; he had previously collaborated with Tiepolo at the Palazzo Canossa in Verona. The figurative portions of the scheme included quite large scenes to be frescoed on the walls at the upper level (and perhaps the intention had once been to fresco also the lower areas, which remain blank). Whether Giambattista himself planned to paint the wall frescoes that do exist is unclear, but in the event they were carried out by Domenico.

A few decorative figures over doorways and a parrot perched on the feigned capital of a pillar were painted by Giambattista immediately below the ceiling proper. The huge area of that was marginally sub-divided and framed by Visconti's somewhat flat and only mildly illusionistic decorations, leaving the big central area for Tiepolo to fill. Although Tiepolo could not resist making a leg or two project out of his fresco and over the framing, there was to be no excited breaking of the

214. Detail of Pl. 213.

visual barrier Visconti established—no bulging clouds or falling figures, and altogether an absence of strong *sotto in sù* effects. Accepting or sharing the implications of Visconti's idiom (far less exuberant than Mengozzi's typical one), Tiepolo was also to be comparatively restrained. The subject conveniently assembled a number of his favourite motifs but offered the novelty of their being blended with positive portraiture in the living members of the Pisani family who would share the space with Fame, the Virtues and the Continents and other personifications. The Prince-Bishop of Würzburg had appeared on his ceiling only in effigy, and elsewhere in Tiepolo's work the direct allusions to patrons had been restricted to figures fancifully dressed—not, at least, in contemporary costume—and to their coat-of-arms. Essential to the concept at Strà is that the inhabitants of the villa are depicted under the eye of eternity, as it were, forever fixed outside time but very much a part of the universe.

The *modello* conveyed, even more faithfully perhaps than usual, how Tiepolo would deal with the ceiling (Pl. 215). The composition was conceived in two distinct, not precisely equal portions, of which the larger and lower one was the more significant. There, a calm vision of the Arts and the Virtues includes chiefly male members of the Pisani family seated amid the clouds, with Fame at the zenith of the heavens blowing a trumpet. No single dramatic vision was suggested but rather one of generalised, easy assurance, with figures lightly and confidently disposed in groups throughout an airy sky. The eldest Pisani boy is placed on the lap of Venice, her nursling as it were, whose future seems so calmly, unassertively, assured. The central presiding figure in this cosmos is a female figure who symbolises perhaps Divine Wisdom, and the tenor of the scene is strongly Christian as well as pacific. Only on the outskirts are there repercussions from the calm, central statement. To the left Evil, or Heresy, is put to flight, in company with a scaly dragon. At the upper end of the composition, below the Continents grouped on clouds, there are men fighting—Christian conquerors probably, rather than symbolic of warfare as such.

In the *modello* some passages were possibly too striking and obtrusive—as, for example, the scarlet-draped America and the writhing figures of Evil—and on the ceiling they have been modified, either in tone or prominence, surrounded by areas of greater space, in a sky more blonde and golden, evocative of a perpetual noon. In the fresco another Pisani has been added, an adult, bewigged male who must be Alvise Pisani, its commissioner. Tiepolo has developed the sketch of the eldest boy into a complete portrait of tender actuality. In blue suit and cloak, with smart boots and miniature sword, this youthful cavalier looks down solemnly yet not unapprehensively, as though sitting for his likeness in an artist's studio and conscious of the family hopes for the future placed on him.

Tiepolo blended, with no incongruity or awkwardness, such touches of acute observation with his more familiar idiom of graceful, bare-breasted Allegories, as lightly tinted as they are lightly clad. The overall effect is of harmony—a vast, heavenly harmony. In Tiepolo's grandest universe and among noblest abstractions there is always room for the play of life, often at its liveliest. Although the ceiling is a great pageant of heaven, earth is present, and in an unusual way. At the lower left, and conceived already as a feature in the *modello*, is a screen of trees and an unallegorised couple, with flask, goblet and stringed instrument, who seem to symbolise pleasure of the senses, wine and music, with no doubt the promise of love. In quite undignified fashion beside them is shown a table, covered by a table-cloth, from which a booted leg somewhat surrealistically protrudes. However to be explained, it is bound to raise a smile—not least because of its proximity to the serious group of the Arts nearby. Even there, as with other subjects he was repeating (like the Continents), Tiepolo contrived to give new life by means of new poses and new devices, still apparently as inventive as ever.

215. *Apotheosis of the Pisani family*, Musée des
Beaux-Arts, Angers.

From among plenty of examples, the figure of Charity, not the most obvious in the composition, may be singled out. For Charity, placed high in the ceiling, Tiepolo foreshortened the figure severely and gave her to hold a naked, mischievous-looking infant who treads on nothing more solid than her draperies and cloud-vapour: an infant whose vivid physiognomy suggests that he too is of the Pisani family. And in his vitality he might symbolically stand as the very daemon of Tiepolo's art.

★　　★　　★

If the Villa Pisani ceiling proclaims Tiepolo as undiminished in vigour, and capable of reaching a fresh eminence, even under pressure, it reflects the position he had consolidated since his return from Würzburg. By 1760 further tokens of recognition had been given to him. The newly formed Academy of Fine Arts in Parma had elected him as Honorary Academician (he had Anton Maria Zanetti to thank that he was elected with that rank and not as a mere 'amatore', as first proposed at Parma). It was apparently in 1760, according to a now lost but presumably genuine letter, that he received some splendid recognition from Louis XV for a painting that he had presented to the King. In 1761 he was gratified by what he modestly termed the indulgence of Batoni, who had seen some of his *modelli* in Rome and praised them. Tiepolo, the Venetian diarist Gradenigo noted in 1760, is the most acclaimed artist for figure painting 'of halls, rooms and churches, in fresco and oil'.[34]

To his great fame Tiepolo owed the fact that Charles III of Spain had invited him —summoned him, rather—to Madrid. Delay as he might, anxious to remain in Venice for the marriage of a daughter, if not for other reasons, and fearful as he probably was of the journey, Tiepolo was bound to accept; and he set off bravely, stating in a letter to a friend that he expected to be in Spain for only two years.

The summer of 1761 was his last in Italy. Soon after, he probably began to make domestic and legal arrangements for his family during his absence, perhaps with the possibility in mind of his death. There was the property of Zianigo, in which, it seems, each child had some share. Of Tiepolo's sons, Domenico and Lorenzo were to accompany their father to Spain. Left in Venice was Giuseppe, who had become a priest in the order of the Somaschi, founded by Blessed Girolamo Miani. The chapel at Zianigo was dedicated to him and to the Purity of the Virgin, and Domenico had frescoed in it scenes from the Blessed Girolamo's life.

The immediate family Tiepolo was leaving is portrayed in an unfinished painting variously attributed to Domenico or Lorenzo (Pl. 216), in which an artist is taking a likeness in pastel in a room where Cecilia Tiepolo is seated along with three of her daughters, while behind her chair stands Giuseppe in priestly black. The fourth daughter, Elena, was already married. The pastellist at work seems to be Lorenzo. Of the three girls depicted, the central one, holding a dog (on whose collar are the initials 'B.T.', for Battista Tiepolo), is likely to be Angela; she and her elder sister Anna, seen probably at the right, never married. The third girl, Orsetta, eventually married Giovanni Giacomo Poli.

It is not hard to recognize in the girls, in Angela perhaps especially, the models, or at least the types, which had served for several of Tiepolo's women, and not solely for the 'fancy pictures' destined for Russia. If not a positive model, the whippet-like dog is certainly of a kind that also occurs in his work.

The most vivid portrayal, however, is that of Cecilia Guardi, no longer the piquant, youthful blonde of *Apelles painting Campaspe* or *Rachel hiding the idols*, but a handsomely upholstered, middle-aged woman, with fan and fur, wearing, it might almost be, one of the flowered dresses she fondly itemised among the bequests in her will: 'my dark dress with yellow flowers, the Lyons [silk] dress with green flowers. . .' The detail does not extend to showing her gold watch, with its gilt chain, or the

216. D. Tiepolo, *The Tiepolo Family*, British Rail Pension Fund, on loan to Doncaster Museum and Art Gallery.

rose-diamond brooch, also mentioned in her will, but from her cap to her high-heeled shoe she is recognizably the person to whom Tiepolo would send presents from Spain of pearl jewellery and garments garnished with lace. And, as she gazes across at her son, she seems also the affectionate, maternal person she describes herself as in her will: 'una Madre . . . sempre amorosa et affetuosa'. Her worldly goods she would dispose of prudently and thoughtfully, chiefly within her family, and for the salvation of her soul she begged her son Giuseppe to remember her when he said mass.[35]

Tiepolo was leaving Venice at the height of his prosperity and fame, and leaving it in highly flattering circumstances far more publicly disseminated than when he had left for Würzburg twelve years earlier.

Nothing suggests that commissions in Italy, least of all in Venice, were coming his way less frequently. In going to Spain he was in no sense retreating from the artistic scene. Yet by 1762 taste generally in Europe was turning more and more against the style of decoration and the 'grand machine' that he represented. Nature and the natural were standards by which the century would, outside Venice, judge that his work failed. Soon it would come to be stigmatised as 'false', where he himself would probably have claimed that it was imaginative—deliberately and supremely so. Just as Picasso could draw well, conventionally, so Tiepolo could, when he wished to, record 'nature' and the natural as well as Canaletto or Pietro Longhi.

Even in Venice, by 1762, voices were heard which championed truth and naturalism in painting. Gasparo Gozzi had published in the *Gazzetta Veneta* of August 1760 a comparison of Longhi and Tiepolo which concluded that Longhi's imitations of life around him, what he saw with his own eyes, were 'no less perfect' than Tiepolo's great imaginative scenes. For all his polite way of putting it, Gozzi probably felt far more interest in Longhi's art than Tiepolo's. In the world of Goldoni's plays, the conventions of Metastasio might well seem faintly absurd. Tiepolo never encountered a critic as openly hostile to him as in France Diderot proved towards Boucher; yet Diderot's biting comment on Boucher's lack of truth amid his talents—'Cet homme a tout, excepté la vérité'—might have been muttered in Venice about Tiepolo by the more advanced literary figures, and possibly by some connoisseurs, before he left the city. The point had been put by at least one foreign visitor, Charles-Nicolas Cochin, with a sly wit as sharp in its way as any invective, when he regretted that nature 'which is so beautiful', was not nearly as beautiful as the paintings of Tiepolo and Piazzetta.[36]

The voice of Tiepolo himself was to be heard, shortly before his departure for Spain, quoted at second hand but convincingly enough reported in the *Nuova Veneta Gazzetta* in March 1762.[37] Large-scale commissions could hardly fail to be in his mind. He had just completed the ceiling at Strà and had recently prepared the *modello* for the throne-room of the Royal Palace at Madrid—'fatica grande', as he described it in a letter, adding that for such a work one must have courage.

As quoted by the *Nuova Veneta Gazzetta*, Tiepolo seems defiant, virtually re-actionary, in asserting his belief that painters must try to succeed in 'opere grandi', that is, in work capable of pleasing 'the nobility and the rich'; it is they who make artists' fortunes and not the other sort of people, 'who cannot buy paintings of much value'. His whole career had borne out the truth of that. He might have summed up his art in the same words Rubens had used of his: 'I am, by natural instinct, better fitted to execute very large works than small curiosities.'

What he did apparently go on to say was that hence it followed that the painter's mind must always aim 'for the sublime, for the heroic, for perfection'. It was with this determination that he may be thought of as setting out for Madrid, a few weeks after his sixty-sixth birthday.

217. *Triumph of Spain*, National Gallery of Art, Washington, Samuel H. Kress Collection.

10 SPAIN: FROM 'GRANDIOSAS IDEAS' TO DEATH

IT WAS a real chapter in Tiepolo's life, the final one as it happened, that opened with his long and exhausting journey to Madrid. Summoned at last, it might be said, to a European court, and on loan, as it were, from the Serene Republic of Venice to his Hispanic Majesty, he was not exactly Apelles going to Alexander but he was travelling as a famous artist to undertake a major commission in a foreign capital at the pressing request of a monarch—one who, as Tiepolo himself put it, 'can command'.

Artistically, at least, he must have travelled hopefully, his passport the *modello* he had already executed (Pl. 217). The plans of what was required from him in the throne-room had been provided by September 1761, by which time also Tiepolo had recognised that he must accept the commission and go to Madrid, though he then hoped to delay the date of his departure. He went believing he had 'only one room to do' ('non haverò [sic] a fare che una salla [sic]') and flattered himself that he would be home again at the end of two years.[1]

To propel him to Spain a considerable amount of heavy machinery had been brought into play, all set in motion by the wishes of Charles III. The King's minister in Madrid, the Marqués de Esquilache, the Spanish ambassador in Venice, the Duque de Montealegre, the Supreme Inquisitor Foscarini and the Procurator Pisani, were all involved in the high-level diplomacy needed.

A first approach to Tiepolo seems to have come from Charles III's 'intendente general' in Venice, Count Felice Gazzola, an artillery expert and amateur archeologist with an interest in Paestum who later moved to Spain. He was to commission from Tiepolo the design of the dedicatory page,[2] to the King, of his book on Paestum, published posthumously in 1784, and he was conveniently in Venice in 1771, when he witnessed a document Tiepolo's widow had drawn up, itemising the gifts her husband had sent her from Spain.[3]

The Inquisitor Foscarini took a hand, on behalf of the Republic, by approaching Pisani to see if he would release Tiepolo from his work at Strà—and thus, perhaps, the lower part of the salone of the villa remained undecorated. Another member of the Foscarini family, Sebastiano, was the Venetian ambassador in Madrid, and he too was doubtless made aware of the situation.

Tiepolo could probably count on a good deal of sympathy and admiration from the Spanish ambassador in Venice, who had been ambassador at the time of the commission of the *St James* for London and who now stressed in letters back to Madrid his respect for the painter's 'generous way of thinking' ('su generoso modo de pensar') and his justified confidence. The ambassador had offered Tiepolo money —which was refused—in a gesture of open, express friendliness ('como de Amigo à Amigo') that was not to be typical of Tiepolo's treatment by the Spanish court after he reached Spain. As for any delay in setting out, the ambassador soothingly spoke of this as being in fact no loss of time, for Tiepolo had assured him that he would be occupied in finalising 'las grandiosas ideas' that he was preparing for the throne-room.[4]

This was no form of words, for Tiepolo was working on the *modello* as late as mid-March. It was his hope, he told an unidentified correspondent, possibly Algarotti, that the finished design would be well suited and appropriate for the 'Great Monarchy' concerned. That phrase provides the nub of the theme: the Glory of the Spanish Monarchy. At the thematic centre of the sketch that survives, Spain is depicted enthroned between statues of Hercules and Apollo, while Fame flies overhead. Paying homage, actually or implicitly, are the Virtues and the relevant Continents, the Oceans and the Spanish Provinces, with Columbus and his ships, the Pillars of Hercules and the inevitable overthrow of Ignorance or Envy. At the bottom of the highly finished composition, with sketches at each corner for the stucco statues decorating the corners of the throne-room, a slim, brick pyramid rises, symbol of the glory of princes, and adorned by a blank cartouche.

Nothing could be more appropriate, or on a more suitably cosmic scale. The *modello* itself is nearly two metres long, in anticipation of the vast length of the actual room, and is the most extensive and perhaps the airiest of all Tiepolo's many heavens. He was more than ever determined to keep many of the attendant figures and attributes to the sides of the composition; and, as in the Villa Pisani, the most significant groupings in the sky are placed in the lower half, with the result that at the centre there is simply infinite space.

Almost roughly handled in terms of paint, with nervous, fretted, half-impatient outlines, despite its high degree of finish, the *modello* is remarkably elaborate—as, for example, in realising the detail of the stucco shell and statue décor—and impressively apt in its Spanish allusions. For those Gazzola had probably provided the necessary references, and Spain shown majestically enthroned in the throne-room of the capital of the Spanish empire must have been chosen well before, as the obvious theme of the ceiling. Yet the *modello* should not be regarded as necessarily Tiepolo's first thought. It may have been preceded by studies or sketches in pen and wash, of the kind of which one survives for the design of an overdoor in the throne-room. It probably is, nevertheless, the *modello* which served as guide to execution of the ceiling, and which Tiepolo carried to Madrid; its unusual elaboration could be explained by that fact. The more detailed the 'programme' proposed, the more it might be expected that the King would wish to see it had been followed by the painter. The theme of the throne-room decoration was to be positively located in his reign; and on the cartouche on the pyramid in the final fresco it is specifically he who is praised and commemorated.

For all the vigour and invention, however, of the *modello*, the 'grandiosas ideas' of which were obviously approved of in Madrid, it cannot count as exactly novel in Tiepolo's *œuvre*. Not even he could think up an entirely original composition for a subject which was bound to stir associations from so many of his previous commissions for ceiling paintings. And when he began to put ideas down on canvas, it seems as though there flocked around him recollections of Würzburg which then blended with the layout of the ceiling at Strà and the almost equally recent ceiling of the Palazzo Canossa at Verona. A ceiling for Russia had depicted Princely Glory, with a pyramid, and he conveniently adapted it, though for Madrid as a subsidiary, if important, motif. Among the allegorical personifications Faith was to appear, and for that figure he went all the way back to the Scuola del Carmine ceiling.

Indeed, the *modello* is a near-perfect anthology of all Tiepolo's favourite devices and groupings, assembled without any overt drama, and sedate compared with the Apollonian vision of the staircase of the Residenz, yet spacious with the spaciousness that had always been in his art but which the late ceilings tend to emphasise. And in some ways it is less the Residenz ceiling that the composition recalls than that of the Villa Pisani—understandably enough, given the close relationship in date of the two commissions. The Madrid composition positively develops out of that for Strà, but there it had not been necessary to provide a fringe of figures all the way round the central, heavenly scene. At Madrid, the imperial, historical theme, more far-ranging in its references, required a global framework: Spain rules the world (or much of it). And so Tiepolo went back and borrowed from his own device at Würzburg, itself developed out of the Palazzo Clerici ceiling, to set the visionary portion of the composition within a busily peopled border. Fusing his two most ambitious earlier schemes, separated in execution by about a decade, Tiepolo created an offspring which recalled each of them, though in that blend lay its individuality.

With the *modello* accomplished, and in the knowledge that he would have Domenico and Lorenzo as companions in execution of the fresco, Tiepolo had every reason to travel hopefully. An earlier proposal to go partly by ship was put aside. In the event, he travelled by land, via Barcelona, accompanied by his sons and also by a certain Don Joseph Casina, oddly described by the Spanish ambassador as a Paduan nobleman and a merchant in mirrors. All April and May were occupied by the journey. On 4 June 1762 Tiepolo at last reached Madrid, so exhausted that he retired to bed, being put up temporarily at the Venetian ambassador's residence.[5]

Although he had arrived, he seems to have been hardly expected. No accommodation for him had been settled. The court was at Aranjuez, but Tiepolo was not sufficiently well to go out to present himself, as the Italian architect and local artistic factotum Francesco Sabatini explained apologetically to the Marqués de Esquilache when he announced Tiepolo's arrival.

Esquilache's response was cool, if courteous. The King did not agree with Sabatini's suggestion that Tiepolo should be lodged in the house previously occupied by the Neapolitan painter Giaquinto, and he left it to Sabatini to decide if it was worth Tiepolo's going out to Aranjuez when meanwhile he could prepare for the work in 'la Sala Grande'. As for housing him, something should be found by Sabatini in the neighbourhood of the royal palace. A house was rented in the small Plaza de San Martìn, and he occupied it until his death. A few days after Tiepolo's arrival his annual salary was fixed at 2,000 doubloons, the same sum as Giaquinto and Mengs, also employed in the palace, received; like them, he was given an additional sum for a coach.

In coming to Spain Tiepolo might seem to have been following a traditional Italian path, metaphorically in the steps of Titian, whose work had increasingly been despatched to Philip II, and more literally in the wake of Giordano in the late seventeenth century, followed by Amigoni. When Amigoni died, Ferdinand VI, Charles III's predecessor, had replaced him by Giaquinto who had frescoed several ceilings in the royal palace.

The situation that Tiepolo entered was a complex one, and much about it is still obscure. No letters of his exist that would throw full light on how he was received or how he felt at the Spanish court. On the one hand, he was to choose to remain in Spain and in the King's service when the royal palace frescoes were completed— from which it might be argued that he was content enough. On the other hand, it is possible to detect some unease about how both he and his art were being regarded, from a late letter of his to a court official; and events subsequently proved his unease to have been justified.

Part of the complexity, and for Tiepolo perhaps the novelty also, lay in the fact that he was now in the service of a real monarch, one who was himself no simple personality, the governor of a kingdom that he sought very consciously to change and reform. The King who was to expel the Jesuits from Spain in Tiepolo's lifetime was deeply devout, almost superstitiously so. He was no idle ruler, no mere figurehead, but someone to whom quite minor decisions had to be referred. He lives most vividly in Goya's portrayal of him in hunting costume, holding his gun; and hunting was a passion with him. His life-style, as it might be called, is equally vividly conveyed in a small painting by Paret of his dining in semi-state, occupied, characteristically, in feeding his dogs at table. In art he had tastes which seem to have been

218, 219, and 220 (following pages). *Triumph of Spain*, throne-room, Royal Palace, Madrid.

257

strong, if not entirely coherent, and which were probably coloured more than he realised by his own piety. An English visitor summed up the matter a few years after Tiepolo's death by commenting that the King 'has naturally no great relish for the arts', but thought it a sovreign's duty to encourage them.[6] He deeply admired the work of Mengs, and that admiration appears to have been shared by his Franciscan confessor, Joaquín de Eleta, an unlearned, not totally amiable, though not necessarily sinister, figure of considerable influence at court.[7]

What is clear is that Tiepolo's earlier, other direct experience of a foreign court—that of the Prince-Bishop at Würzburg—was a poor preparation for his experiences in Madrid. There was far greater formality and much stiffer protocol at the Spanish court, where the business of ruling was a serious matter and where the personality of ministers and officials had to be considered, in addition to the King's. Too much cannot be deduced from silence, but there seems to have been a notable lack of cordiality at court with regard to Tiepolo and certainly little recognition of his artistic stature. No particular sign of pleasure was manifested on his arrival, and protocol alone can hardly account for the frigid brevity with which the eventual news of his death was received by the King.

Charles III had come to the Spanish throne in 1759, having earlier ruled, almost as a boy, in Parma, before inheriting the kingdom of Naples and the Two Sicilies. In Madrid he inherited a new royal palace, for which Juvarra had prepared designs before his sudden death in 1736, and which was built in modified form by Juvarra's pupil Sacchetti. The result is big and imposing, without being distinguished or attractive. Its palatial interior, in particular, despite the fresco decorations of numerous artists, has the air of a large, impersonal, not quite first-class hotel. At the centre of the building is the throne-room, the biggest room in the palace, looking out on the wide space of the Plaza de Oriente.

Decoration of the palace interior began under Ferdinand VI. During his reign artistic projects of all kinds had been fostered and artists of all kinds, especially Italian, invited to Spain. He had retained the famous castrato Farinelli, whose singing had charmed the melancholy Philip V, and created him a Knight of Calatrava. On the accession of Charles III, Farinelli was required to leave Spain. Giaquinto continued to be employed, however, and his silvery, fluent, ever-efficient if ultimately monotonous frescoes decorate several rooms of the palace, including the chapel.

It seems to have been the arrival in Spain of Mengs, far younger and already patronised by Charles III in Italy, that precipitated Giaquinto's withdrawal. He left the country in or shortly after 1761, the year Mengs arrived in answer to the King's summons. Had he stayed, he might possibly have received the commission for painting the throne-room. Alternatively, it may have been intimated that this task would be assigned to someone else. And although Mengs was capable of painting ceilings, in a style very different from that of Giaquinto or Tiepolo, he may well have drawn back from the physically, not to say artistically, arduous task of frescoing the ceiling of the throne-room. For that, the obvious European candidate was Tiepolo.

In a letter apparently dated 23 December 1761, and written from Madrid, Mengs speaks of having 'per competitori' both Giaquinto and Tiepolo,[8] but he cannot have meant it literally, since Giaquinto was soon to depart and Tiepolo had definitely not yet arrived. That he and Tiepolo were or would become rivals, in some sense, is undeniably true, though no personal animosity need have arisen. Nor is there any evidence to suggest that Mengs intrigued against Tiepolo; any legends to that effect might aptly be compared, not least in terms of their respective talents, to the story of Salieri poisoning Mozart. Where their two styles may have been contrasted most sharply, to the apparent detriment of Tiepolo, was over the commission for altarpieces for the royal convent church of S. Pascual Baylon; but whatever the precise facts, Mengs himself was not involved.

Nevertheless, the difference in the style and the approach of the two artists was as great as the gap in their ages. Mengs, born in Bohemia in 1728, was precocious, but his career was to be plagued by ill-health, and he died only nine years after Tiepolo. His glossily finished, somewhat waxen paintings pay at least as much homage to Raphael as Tiepolo's do to Veronese—and the orientation is significant, quite apart from the predestined influence intended by Mengs's father in having him christened Anton (after Correggio) Raphael. A certain dignified naturalism and mildly classical simplicity are characteristic of Mengs's style. He had probably been influenced by seventeenth-century Bolognese painting, especially the work of Reni, almost as much as he had been directly by Raphael. A careful draughtsman, he made a good representative of Rome as opposed to the Venice represented by Tiepolo. In contrast to Tiepolo, he was an active portraitist, always competent and on occasion sensitive. And he stood also for the rising trend that would become neoclassicism: serious and slow in comparison with the apparent frivolity and the speed of Tiepolo; a thinker, whereas the Venetian was, by implication, merely a decorator. Hence the characteristically biased judgment of Winckelmann (in the *Abhandlung von der Fahigkeit der Empfindung des Schönen in der Kunst*, 1763), uninhibited by the likelihood he had never actually looked at any of Tiepolo's frescoes, that while Tiepolo's work, once seen, is forgotten that of Mengs remains for ever ('bleibt ewig').

The royal palace in Madrid allows that judgment to be tested practically, and where Mengs is not present himself, it is often the work of his Spanish pupils Maella and Francisco Bayeu (the brother-in-law of Goya), the latter an odd stylistic waverer, now quite vigorous under the influence of Giaquinto and now timid and nerveless in pale imitation of Mengs. Only Charles III, in all Europe perhaps, would have proposed patronising both Mengs and Tiepolo, and bringing their work together in a single building. In the palace chapel is an altarpiece by Mengs, representing the private, devotional aspect of the King's character (he is said to have carried on his travels Mengs's *St Anthony of Padua with the Infant Christ*). In the throne-room Tiepolo's fresco celebrates the public monarch, apostrophised on the ceiling as 'Carole Magnanimum', who raises lofty monuments that time cannot affect (Pls 218, 219 and 220).

Unfortunately, it is now difficult for the ordinary visitor to assess Tiepolo's achievement fully and fairly. The throne-room is very long, high, rather narrow, not brilliantly lit, and cordoned off, so that much of the area of the ceiling has to be peered at down a diminishing perspective. The area furthest from the spectator is precisely that where Tiepolo concentrated significance, with Spain herself enthroned. That is some indication that the present disposition of the room (which goes back to at least early in this century), with the throne placed halfway down the longest wall, facing the windows, contradicts Tiepolo's intentions and, possibly, the original layout. The ceiling seems to have been composed on the assumption that the throne would be at the end of the room, under the eyes of the figure of enthroned Spain and of Princely Glory with the pyramid extolling Charles III. The living monarch would have taken his place at the key point in the pageantry extending overhead and visually resounding up the room. To eighteenth-century minds, and doubtless first to the King's, there would surely have been something incongruous, if not improper, in the present arrangement whereby the canopy of the throne appears about to receive out of the ceiling the falling body of vanquished Evil.[9]

Yet even in the best conditions, the ceiling would perhaps not rank with those at Würzburg and Strà. The scale is, as Tiepolo rightly emphasised, 'vasta', and the proportions of the room would always make it difficult to take in the overall effect from any single viewpoint. At Madrid there could be none of the unfolding drama of the staircase in the Residenz, and there is certainly none of the subtle use of natural light. At Würzburg, as at Strà, the architectural setting, in its broadest sense, must have been an inspiration to the painter. In the royal palace, the huge, unfurnished empty room in which Tiepolo had to work must have looked more daunting than inspiring.

To execute such a fresco at all was a *tour de force*; and objectively it is hard to detect much diminution in the artist's powers or think him inhibited by the thoroughly foreign environment in which he was working, for the first time, in his mid-sixties. His Spanish patrons were unlikely to trouble themselves over comparisons with his earlier achievements, or indeed over the degree of assistance he obtained from his sons. His task was to cover the ceiling with a vision of the Glory and Grandeur of the Spanish Monarchy. Certain details not in the *modello* were added in the fresco itself —notably putti prominently carrying the Golden Fleece. Other changes, as in the masts of Columbus's ships, seem to have been dictated by aesthetic considerations. Finally, and largely as envisaged in the *modello*, the ceiling was completed. It took about the two years Tiepolo had estimated. He signed and dated it in 1764, and in that year Charles III, a widower, and his family moved into the palace.

Nevertheless, though the finished decoration appears to have gained royal approval, and is largely a success, it remains perhaps more a matter of effective detail than a totally coherent, impressive whole. Even where it cannot be precisely demonstrated, there is a sense that Tiepolo is repeating himself. His feathered Americans, exotic creatures—dead or alive—turbaned or helmeted figures, sea-gods and striped draperies, and all the familiar apparatus of his richly layered imagination, are dutifully brought out and disposed across the ceiling. The images are as splendid as ever, as solid and voluptuous, if not quite as exuberant as before. Perhaps only in the main, aerial portion of the ceiling, around the throne of Spain and the pyramid of Princely Glory, is Tiepolo at his happiest. Several of the figures along the cornice are, by contrast, more dutifully than vivaciously executed, pleasingly decorative yet rather crowded and lacking the bubbling invention of the great earlier frescoes.

The packed figures tend to become genre—enchanted genre, admittedly—of the type associated with Domenico, but a little earth-bound and obvious. Some of this genre element has, significantly perhaps, crept into the fresco without any origin in the *modello*. Tiepolo planned there for one corner to show the Pillars of Hercules, but in that place the ceiling somewhat unexpectedly shows an ostrich or two, with some other birds. And perhaps it is not unfair to think of Domenico as responsible.

At the other end of the ceiling are changes which are distinctly not improvements on the *modello*. One corner of that has the foreshortened silhouette of a man restraining a rearing horse, with a woman seated nearby, reclining along the cornice in a typically complex, twisted pose, looking up in profile at the man to her right, while flexing her left leg to accommodate herself more easily. Giambattista Tiepolo could —would, perhaps it should be said—have had no difficulty in translating these crisply sketched forms of energy and grace respectively into full-scale figures in the fresco. Instead, the silhouette of the man is lost amid a jumble of doubtfully relevant eastern heads and shoulders, and flapping flags; and he is, in the fresco, far less vigorously conceived and, as far as can be judged, far less vigorously executed. Yet more inert is the fresco's interpretation of the seated woman, where all attempt at her complex pose and foreshortening has been abandoned. The artist of this figure on the ceiling clearly found the master's concept beyond his skill to realise. He produced the barest approximation to the *modello* at this point, just a stolid woman, seated slackly in amorphous drapery on the cornice, her head in a three-quarter position, scarcely turned, scarcely indeed animated. By itself the figure would pass as no more than vaguely Tiepolesque, so far is it from the idiom of either Giambattista or Domenico at his most sedulous in pastiche of his father. It is clearly the work of a not very gifted assistant—ungifted, at least, in following Tiepolo's style—and may reasonably be assigned to Lorenzo. The head in particular, unidealised to the point of prosaicism, relates quite well to his undoubted work.

Lorenzo was twenty-six in the year the three Tiepolo arrived in Spain. He seems to have developed only slowly as an artist, one whose preferred medium was pastel and whose speciality was portraiture. Yet he certainly studied his father's compositions, especially those done in the late Italian years, and etched both the *Vision of St Anne* and the *St Tecla*, as well as recording in etchings three of Tiepolo's ceilings for Russia. In Madrid, his career became a reality. He was appointed a 'pintor de cámara' to the King, married a Spanish wife and executed a number of pastel paintings of Madrid street-scenes, with faint echoes of Piazzetta in their head-and-shoulder genre format and a strong dose of Mengs in their competent 'realism'.[10] After his father's death, Lorenzo preferred to live on in Madrid, in the King's service until his own death in 1776, often urging fruitlessly an increase in his annual stipend.

However work on the ceiling is to be apportioned, it is patent that Tiepolo was assisted on it, and must have expected, in taking Domenico and Lorenzo with him to Spain, that he would be so assisted. The likelihood is that both sons were involved more directly than in any previous scheme.

With the throne-room ceiling completed, Tiepolo may well have thought of returning home. But whereas at Würzburg the largest task had been reserved for last, at Madrid completion of the throne-room led to further employment on ceilings in smaller, as it were easier, rooms of the palace. Giambattista was responsible for two of these; a third room, the Antecámara de la Reyna, was frescoed by Domenico in closest possible imitation of his father. It was his most sustained secular tribute to Giambattista's influence and the last fresco he executed during his father's lifetime. It too was a glorification of Spain, seen with Hercules, who holds the Golden Fleece, and Neptune and Mars; and several of the figures are direct quotations from Giambattista's ceiling of the *Apotheosis of the Spanish Monarchy* in the saleta (Pl. 221), the room adjoining the throne-room.

Here Tiepolo rallied his forces for one last or penultimate expression of Olympus. A presiding Jupiter high in the heavens witnesses Mercury bearing down with a crown on the seated Spain, who is accompanied by a lion, while Apollo, nearly nude and full length, benevolently and radiantly hovers over Spain's head. Neptune is among the other gods in attendance, and Hercules heaves at a pillar.

For this fresco, at least planned by Giambattista, two oil sketches exist, one very slightly larger than the other and both now conveniently in the same place, the Metropolitan Museum.[11] Their similar theme and oval format, and roughly similar compositions, relate them convincingly to the final ceiling, though not quite straightforwardly.

Neither can claim to be in itself the *modello*. For the composition of the ceiling, Tiepolo perhaps eventually utilized them both, and both may have been submitted to the King as preliminary ideas. Both show the crowning of Spain by Mercury, with Jupiter in the upper part of the scene and Hercules, plus pillar, in the lower portion. In the smaller canvas Mercury flies down in a pose and position very similar to those in the fresco, though shown approaching Spain from the right. Other motifs, including Neptune, Hercules, Mars and Venus—and the chariot of Venus—are also sufficiently similar in depiction to suggest that Tiepolo made considerable use of this sketch. Where, however, it fails to offer a basis for the fresco is in the figure of Apollo, merely glimpsed in the background lying on and behind a cloud.

The larger canvas, otherwise less close in every way to the fresco, is remarkable for its inclusion of the god, posed exactly as on the ceiling. He is as radiant and vital, as dominant almost, in the sketch as in the final work. The creation of that figure was the inspired contribution of the larger sketch. By bringing Apollo into prominence at the right, Tiepolo had inevitably to shift Mercury to the left; and in the fresco the balance between the two flying male bodies, each present to honour the demure, blonde and ermine-clad Spain, has been achieved with maximum effectiveness.

One oddity in the larger sketch is also worth remarking: a minor quotation from

221. *Apotheosis of the Spanish monarchy*, Saleta, Royal Palace, Madrid.

a detail in the throne-room fresco (not found in its *modello*). In the American portion of that fresco a puma appears, staring out over a bale. The animal appears again, in precisely the same pose, at the bottom of the sketch but not in the saleta fresco.

Little can be deduced from this, and the sequence of the two sketches seems impossible to fix. What is clear, however, is that the prominence given to Apollo in the larger sketch was approved—by the patron, presumably, as much as by the painter. In the throne-room, Apollo had been shown in the form of a statue flanking Spain, but in the saleta he comes totally to life, shining out—for the last time—in Tiepolo's work. Perhaps he is present in flattering yet not false allusion to the enlightenment Charles III was trying to bring to his country, but he can be seen in the context too of Tiepolo's work and career.

At the Palazzo Sandi, some forty years earlier, Tiepolo had depicted Apollo as god of music cruelly punishing the presumption of Marsyas, and even earlier he had shown the contest of the god and satyr, judged by Midas, in a companion painting to the *Rape of Europa*.[12] On the Palazzo Archinto ceiling he had frescoed Apollo for the first time, showing him in all his brilliant splendour, the focus of a cosmic court and inhabitant of an Olympian dwelling. At the Palazzo Clerici Tiepolo had again frescoed Apollo, rising now in his chariot to illuminate the world. At Würzburg Apollo had driven his steeds in thrilling course across the sky, bringing Beatrice of Burgundy to her marriage. Most triumphantly of all, he had been set as the prime illumination, the generative principle of all things, in the great hymn to light—mental and physical—that was the staircase ceiling of the Residenz.

In the saleta of the Royal Palace at Madrid, his is inevitably a lesser triumph, on a smaller scale, in a composition of which he is not the ostensible centre. Yet he shines forth, haloed and solidly modelled (conceivably, not uninfluenced by Mengs), still the god of Tiepolo's idolatry. And it is he, a risen, Christlike figure to the Jehovah of Jupiter aloft, rather than Spain, whose greatness and power the ceiling comes to symbolise and celebrate. Indeed, an oval sketch exists,[13] unrelated to any known project, late in style and conceivably executed in Spain, in which Apollo is the chief emphasis—and also impetus, as he and his train rush almost riotously to their work of illumining the world. In a pose somewhat similar to that in the saleta fresco, but more urgent, and lit by a bigger nimbus, Apollo there blazes forth as undisputed lord of creation. Had that composition ever been realised in fresco, it would have been among the most stirring, and perhaps the most intense, of all Tiepolo's paeans to the Sun.

Compositionally, and in terms of execution also, the saleta fresco is probably the most satisfactory of Tiepolo's frescoes in the palace. A third one was required, for the ceiling of the guard-room, reached at the top of the staircase which Giaquinto had frescoed. A large, upright painting by Giaquinto, of Venus giving arms to Aeneas,[14] may conceivably have been planned to be utilised, with decoration of the guard-room in mind. Its date is not certain but the subject is obviously appropriate, and was only marginally changed into an *Apotheosis of Aeneas*—with a good deal of emphasis on arms and armour—for the fresco that Tiepolo undertook. In his composition Venus awaits the arrival of Aeneas in Olympus, holding a splendidly plumed helmet, the product doubtless of the forge of Vulcan, seen in action at the base of the composition.

The fresco itself was probably very much a collaborative effort (Pl. 222). Yet its design, zig-zagging up from Vulcan, through a wonderfully posed, majestic Time, to the mid-point of Aeneas' ascent and then to the cloud where Venus proudly waits, is certainly Giambattista's own, and two sketches by him relate to it, one indeed with good claims to be the *modello*. What both suggest is that Tiepolo conceived a stronger *sotto in sù* effect than is conveyed by the fresco as executed. A slight tameness in presentation there may be partly explicable not through any failing powers, nor through any involvement of the Tiepolo sons, but through some adaptation to a Mengs-like idiom, whereby a ceiling painting does not aim at virtuoso foreshortening and perspective. Instead, for all it is on a ceiling, it is composed much as an easel painting. That style may have suited the King's taste better, where it could be practicably used (as it patently could not in the vast tunnel of the throne-room). It is hinted at in the way the saleta fresco is composed. And certainly, by Tiepolo's standards, the fresco of the *Apotheosis of Aeneas* is very much a picture hung on the ceiling rather than illusionistic in the manner of his great ceilings.

The sketch with every claim to be Tiepolo's *modello* has a harsh and vibrant touch, very typical of Giambattista's late, last manner in sketches and small paintings (Pl. 223). Handling in these Spanish works has increased in 'nervousness', of a masterly kind, for it has become even more expressive and personal. In the *modello* for the *Apotheosis of Aeneas* the pigment on the wings of Time and on other figures, as on some passages of the drapery, is jaggedly applied, fretted and worked, as though angrily directed by a convulsive, feverish impulse, whereby the hand is compelled to obey the dictates of the mind.

222. *Apotheosis of Aeneas*, Guard-room, Royal Palace, Madrid.

The effect is of determined seriousness. The style would prove well suited to depiction of religious, semi-mystical subject-matter but, as the *Apotheosis* sketch shows, it could be used no less impressively for allegory and mythology. Only the pose of Aeneas himself is rather awkwardly devised, unusually mannered, with a somewhat flabbily extended left arm and with the air generally not so much of

223. *Apotheosis of Aeneas*, Museum of Fine Arts, Boston.

224. *Apotheosis of Aeneas*, Fogg Art Museum, Cambridge, Mass.

rising confidently to immortality as of going up unsteadily in a dubiously powered lift. Otherwise, there is a faintly baleful force and intensity about the foreground male figures, summed up in hunched and, as it might be, half-envious Time, propped on a rock, while Venus and her attendants, beings of no ordinary sort, watch the hero's ascent with grave aloofness. From the serene sky to the depths of the smoky earth, lit by flickering flame from Vulcan's smithy, the composition is profoundly resolute, as earnest in its imagined Olympus as any Christian heaven.

A smaller sketch of approximately the same composition lacks the compressed power and painterly fury of the *modello* and could well be rather earlier in date, executed conceivably even before Tiepolo left Italy (Pl. 224). In it, Aeneas (presuming the hero here is he—and Vulcan's forge is again a feature) is more gracefully posed. He kneels to greet his mother as she somewhat casually welcomes him among the immortals, gesturing in a way so flippant that it leaps the centuries and seems to call out for cocktails and a long cigarette-holder. Although Tiepolo was sensible to suppress that concept of Venus for the guard-room fresco, he might have considered adopting the kneeling pose, which also gave a better sense of being air-borne, for her son.

But motifs in this sketch, and also partly in the *modello*, relate back rather than forward. The figure of Mercury falling from the top of the composition is common to both and followed in the fresco; and that figure derives directly from a ceiling of Tiepolo's of the *Chariot of Venus*, etched by Lorenzo Tiepolo and recorded in

Domenico's catalogue of his father's work as 'In Petroburgh'.[15] Lorenzo etched the ceiling in reverse (as can be established by a surviving preparatory sketch), and in that reversed pose Mercury occurs in the two *Aeneas* sketches and the finished fresco. The ceiling for St Petersburg must certainly have been painted before Tiepolo left Italy, as must also a ceiling of *The Graces with Mars*, again etched by Lorenzo. Presumably because of its Russian destination, Tiepolo had included here a wolf (seated at the left in the etching); similarly placed, in the left-hand corner of the smaller *Aeneas* sketch, the wolf re-appears. It might be thought highly appropriate for a Roman theme as well, but the fact is that neither in the *modello* nor the guard-room fresco did Tiepolo incorporate the animal.

It is not surprising if, especially after completion of the throne-room ceiling in 1764, Tiepolo's mind turned back to earlier motifs and concepts, rummaging in the storehouse he had built up, when called on for further work in the same vein. That his originality was not exhausted he would prove conclusively in the paintings for the church of S. Pascual Baylon, but his energies were perhaps beginning to diminish. In fact, his activity as a painter of mythologies and allegories, and ceiling paintings altogether, was coming to an end, though less through any failure on his part than from lack of patronage once he finished working in the royal palace.

In 1764 the future was far from clear, and in the absence of documents it can only be presumed that Tiepolo then received commissions for the saleta and guard-room ceilings. He seems to have felt himself under distinct pressure. In a letter—the more valuable as being the sole one known to have been written by him from Spain to anyone outside the country—sent from Madrid on 7 August 1764, he tells his un-identified but almost certainly Venetian patrician correspondent that he has numer-ous ceilings ('molti soffitti'), to execute.[16] He begs the favour of borrowing a car-toon, the 'cartone della gloria di Anfitrite' [sic] that he himself had executed, many years before, for his correspondent's father, among the designs for paintings on the staircases of his palace. This remarkable request shows Tiepolo frankly calling on past achievements to help him out, and perhaps save time, as he faces the demand for further decorative frescoes.

His plea was obviously no idle one, since he goes on to specify that his son Giu-seppe would take charge of the 'cartone' (for which he would provide a receipt) and have it sent to Spain by the first ship. The implications of the letter are many, and not the least fascinating aspect of it is the revelation of a 'cartone' by Tiepolo being kept in a Venetian palace where he may or may not have carried out actual painting. The letter stresses that he *designed* compositions for his correspondent's father; and it may be the fact that these, or some of them, remained otherwise unexecuted which prompted the thought of borrowing one for execution in Madrid. Whatever response his letter received, Tiepolo painted no 'Glory of Amphitrite' for the royal palace.

The 'molti soffitti' became two, assuming that Domenico was separately com-missioned for the antecámara, and work on them perhaps occupied the Tiepolo, on and off, until 1766. Tiepolo was in the King's service and may well not have been free to execute work for other patrons. He received in these years no other royal commissions, as far as is known. Perhaps unfortunately, he had no opportunity to work in the more attractive and relaxed environment of the palace at Aranjuez. And although the charming, intimate Casa del Labrador there was not to be begun until the end of the century, in the reign of Charles IV, it would have offered scope for Domenico Tiepolo to show off his true talent as a decorator, just as would a com-mission for cartoons of genre subjects from the Royal Tapestry Manufactory.

Nevertheless, it must have been in Spain that Tiepolo was impelled, and surely not just at his own instigation, to return to one more earlier secular theme and re-inter-pret it, on a reduced scale. For one of the Contarini palaces in Venice, he had painted during the 1750s a canvas ceiling composition of Venus entrusting an infant boy to

Time (the painting now in the National Gallery, London). That the boy is Venus' child seems clear—the composition was etched by Domenico Tiepolo and given the title *The Childbed of Venus*—and he may be identified as Aeneas, destined for immortality. Such a subject might refer generally to the Contarini's allegedly Roman descent or, more specifically, to the birth of an heir.

The ceiling is one of Tiepolo's most alluring late paintings, tender in its delicate, dawn-like colouring and in its sentiment: a masque of beauty in which Venus quietly triumphs as a mother, a goddess and a half-sleepy, sultry beauty.

It was this subject that in Spain Tiepolo took up again, producing a very different composition, though preserving the chief actors (Pl. 225). Time now kneels in a mysterious landscape, before what is virtually a vision of the goddess who seems about to hand over some chain or locket for the infant that Time holds out in obedient pose. At the right are suggestions of a temple, with an altar on which perches Jupiter's eagle. Though no more than a small, sketchily handled painting, the picture may have been intended to be complete in itself, rather than a preparatory *modello*. In it, grace and bewitching charm have been replaced by an urgency and earnestness that are characteristic of Tiepolo's last paintings. There is a new solemnity about the scene. The child no longer sits looking out of the composition, as in the ceiling picture, but is cradled, dormant, in Time's huge, rude arms, and Time himself is a wilder, untidier figure than before, more gaunt and more visionary, with a pair of ragged yet powerful pinions, like those of some giant bird of prey.

The precise dating of this painting within the Spanish years is not easy, but if it could be as late as 1768—as is conceivable—a birth in Charles III's family might have occasioned it. In February that year Charles's daughter María Luisa, married to Leopold, Grand-Duke of Tuscany, gave birth to a son, the future Francis II. He was to become Emperor of Austria and the last Holy Roman Emperor. The boy's place in the scheme of things was important from the first, since his father was heir to his childless brother, Joseph of Austria, ruling since 1765 with his mother Maria Theresa.

Sufficient interest in the boy is shown by the fact that in the summer of 1770 Mengs painted his portrait in Florence; it was sent to Spain, and before the end of the century is recorded as at Aranjuez (today in the Prado).[17]

Apart from this small painting, *Venus and Time*, the work of Tiepolo's last years in Spain seems to have been entirely religious in subject-matter. Apart from one major royal commission, that for the church of S. Pascual Baylon, he seems to have worked most of the time on a small scale, creating a few sketch-like pictures which are, as is *Venus and Time*, complete works of art in their own right. It is not possible to say for whom such paintings were done, but presumably they were private commissions, not interfering with the painter's availability as a royal artist. These paintings, which it is tempting to see as the latest, as they are certainly among the most personal, of all Tiepolo's huge output, are simple and devotional in theme, dealing chiefly with Christ as a baby and as a corpse: the Flight of the Holy Family into Egypt and the aftermath of the Passion.

In style they form a homogeneous group, but in concept they seem to evolve—even within the handful that they are—to a point of daring, intense originality, the more moving for the undoubted fact that their creator was old, he was a long way from his homeland and had perhaps begun to guess that he would never return to it.

A depiction of the Deposition is at once stark and mystical. Christ's body is stretched out in *rigor mortis*, his head arched agonisingly back and propped on the lap of the wildly grieving Virgin at the foot of the Cross, and all around kneel bowed and equally grieving angels, in a flurry of wings. This scene of sorrow is set in no fanciful or oriental Holy Land but in Spain, on the outskirts, as it were, of Madrid, a view of which is glimpsed in the background.[18] Yet starker and more original in concept is the *Entombment*, where again the agony Christ endured is suggested by the broken, collapsed corpse being laid in the tomb (Pl. 226). There is no rhetoric here, and no conventional nobility. The difficulty of getting the dead body into the box-like sepulchre is graphically conveyed. The Virgin, seated stoically, and now grown rigid in grief, turns away from the sight. A rocky cavern is the burial-place, and it fills the whole area of the canvas, shutting out any hint of sky or even air. Almost intolerable desolation is the mood. And though angels hover above, they too are mourning; and their presence does not mitigate the sense of loneliness and loss.

The subject of the Flight into Egypt, so delightfully treated in Domenico's series of etchings of over a decade earlier, now attracted his father, who set it in much harsher and more mountainous landscape, a Pyrenees of the imagination, though perhaps partly inspired by the countryside traversed on the journey from Venice to Madrid. Adored by an angel or rowed by an angelic boatman in a boat accompanied by two swans, the Holy Family is shown, in two compositions, as being looked after on its journey; in a third the Family is alone, but has paused for rest and is within sight of a familiar city—that of Madrid.

A fourth treatment of the theme is the most radical of all (Pl. 227), hardly foreseen in Tiepolo's œuvre, unexpected in his century and almost disturbing in its originality. Landscape as a subject had often appealed to him, but it had remained a subsidiary aspect of his paintings. His response to it, however, can be seen in the early *Rape of Europa* and in the more mature *Finding of Moses*, as well of course as in the purely landscape drawings of the 1750s. Now, in treating the Flight into Egypt, he conceived it as a landscape in which the figures would become subsidiary; they are the more haunting for the sense they convey of being lost in the wilderness of a magnificent but alien nature and dwarfed by its forms. The effect strangely recalls the artists of the sixteenth-century Danubian School, though even they did not depict as inhospitable a terrain as that Tiepolo paints with a sort of savage, agitated handling which increases the feeling of nature's power.

In cold, mountainous country, where crags rise steeply, bare of all vegetation, there is only a solitary, towering pine tree, its giant trunk sloping upwards the

226. *The Entombment*, Pinto-Basto Collection, Lisbon.

227. *The Rest on the Flight into Egypt*, Staatsgalerie, Stuttgart.

whole height of the composition, to provide inadequate shelter for the minute figures huddled at its base: the Virgin and Child, St Joseph and their mule. Over a dark expanse of sombre water, a white bird glides, complemented overhead by the silhouette of a dark bird against cloud—floating there like a detached frond of pine foliage. Their wheeling freedom in the air only heightens the impression of remoteness and isolation. Poor and exhausted, the family at the base of the tree is stripped of sanctity; a man and a woman, nursing a baby—vagrants, it might be, or gipsies—have stopped for rest in a natural setting hostile to all human presence and on a journey that shows no sign of ending.

Although the painting fits in well enough with other late paintings done by Tiepolo in Spain, its composition remains unusual and so patently Northern as to suggest it was inspired by some sixteenth-century print, Netherlandish if not German. And the extreme subordination of the figures to the landscape recalls certain pictures by the elder Pieter Bruegel (e.g., *Landscape with the Flight into Egypt*, Princes Gate Collection, Courtauld Institute, London).

Tiepolo had always painted to affect the spectator—and not solely with astonishment and delight. Christ's Passion, for example, had been conjured up with maximum drama in the S. Alvise *Way to Calvary*, at approximately the mid-point in his career. What is remarkable in the late, Spanish-period, religious paintings is not their strong emotionalism as such, but their absence of bravura, their steady concentration on the chosen theme, with the fewest possible compositional elements. Speaking more rapidly than ever, Tiepolo is less exuberant in figures of speech, less free in fantasy, grown artistically parsimonious but only the more measured and

228. Detail of Pl. 231.

270

telling as a result. Just as his early works seem full of youthful *joie de vivre*, reflecting his own enjoyment of his powers (and doubtless of his life), so the late works seem to reflect a meditative, sober mood, ultimately more serene than sad. To claim it as wise would be too much, where so little is clear, but it may reasonably be described as experienced. The last paintings testify to Tiepolo's power to keep changing and evolving. Impressive though they are in themselves, they gain by coming, after the sustained drums and tuckets of his grand, public manner, like insistent *pianissimi*. And in that final shift into a semi-private, movingly human view of religious subjects, as in the curve of his career, he really seems to echo Titian.

By January 1767 he had completed his fresco commissions for the King. The question must have been whether he would now return to Venice. He decided not to. He wrote a suitably flowery letter to the King's secretary, Miguel de Muzquiz, showing he had mastered, or been guided towards, the elaborate forms of Spanish court language. He saw himself assured of the possession of the great honour of serving for always ('siempre') such a great sovereign; he remained always ('siempre') at the command of his royal will. A little more pointedly, he indicated as a way he might serve, 'even painting in oil' ('aun pintado á Olio'), adding, not without due pride, that he had happily occupied himself thus, 'in other Courts'. With a few more flourishes and expressions of obedience, he closed with an assurance of awaiting orders.[19]

Tiepolo's decision seems, on the face of it, somewhat surprising. His output in Spain must so far have been restricted largely, if not entirely, to the royal palace frescoes; and he had been in Spain for four and a half years. It was double the length of time he had originally calculated being away from Venice. Yet however wearisome the return journey might appear, he would presumably have undertaken it if he was seriously dissatisfied at the Spanish court and felt poorly paid or unappreciated.

The reason why he wrote as he did, introducing the matter of his ability in oil paint, to be read as meaning he was more than a decorator, is very likely because he was aware there was a major royal commission in the wind which would be for oil paintings.

In 1765, if not earlier, Charles III had decided to build on what were then the outskirts of Aranjuez, some distance from the palace, a fine church and convent, dedicated to S. Pascual Baylon, for the mendicant order of Alcantarine Franciscans (whose founder was the Spaniard, St Peter of Alcántara). Although Marcel Fonton, a Neapolitan who had already worked for the King in Italy, was the architect, there was much involvement by Francesco Sabatini as overseer, at least on the financial side. From Sabatini, if not from others, Tiepolo would easily have learnt that plans for the interior of the church included no less than seven altarpieces.[20] Why Mengs was not commissioned is unclear, but his health was not good and in fact he was not particularly happy in Spain (he was later to seek and obtain permission to return to Italy). Unlike Tiepolo, he was probably uneager to take on such a large task.

The King took a close personal interest in what was always referred to as a royal foundation. Fonton's rather light-hearted baroque façade incorporates the royal arms and the Golden Fleece in a cartouche above the central window of the façade, and reference to the King's name, and probably to the dead Queen's too, was made in the choice of saints for the altarpieces. It was the King, after all, who was paying, a fact of which the King's confessor had occasion to remind Sabatini.

It was not probable that an Alcantarine Franciscan friar so close to the King would not play some part in the building and the way it was decorated, and Padre Eleta soon became the chief instrument in completion of the project. It was the King's orders that he conveyed, or said he conveyed, but he was clearly in a position of considerable authority. He seems to have preferred to communicate with the architect through Sabatini, thus distancing himself from too overt an involvement.

On a document of 16 January 1767 informing him that Tiepolo had decided to remain in Spain, Charles III noted: 'Esta bien' and added that he would give the painter works ('obras') to occupy him.[21] A second note by the King mentions a commission for works which will be indicated by 'el P.[adr]e Confessor'. By the end of March Tiepolo had received the news that he was to paint the seven altarpieces for the new church, which was still in the process of being built.

The subject, sizes and disposition of these had been carefully settled. For the high altar, St Pascual Baylon, the humble sixteenth-century Spanish mystic, a lay-brother of the Alcantarine rule, was the inevitable choice. In the right and left transepts would be respectively the Stigmatisation of St Francis and the Immaculate Conception. The latter subject was already very popular in Spain, and a cult fostered by the Franciscans, as well as being a personal one of the King's. In the chapels, right and left, halfway down the church would be St Charles Borromeo and St Joseph with the Christ Child. St Charles had been a cardinal protector of the Franciscan order and was the King's namesake. St Joseph was also a popular subject in Spanish art, and Charles III's wife had been called María Amalia Josefa. Two oval paintings in the chapels immediately right and left on entering the church would show St Anthony of Padua, a famous Franciscan saint, and St Peter of Alcántara.

The commission brought together church and state, with a strongly Franciscan emphasis in terms of piety, though scarcely in terms of holy poverty. The altarpieces were destined for a handsome church, itself part of a sumptuous, royal foundation, to be inhabited, somewhat ironically, by friars of a rule noted for its extreme austerity. The requirements for accommodating the friars in their own gallery inside the church sadly affected the interior, robbing the nave of height and light and cutting off virtually all source of illumination for the chapels halfway down the side aisles.

However, for Tiepolo the commission was the thing. Not only did it come most opportunely, giving him every chance to display his talents in oil painting and in religious themes, but it was the most extensive single commission of its kind he had ever received. Indeed, few painters anywhere, at any period, have been called on to supply all the altarpieces for one church. Tiepolo was in effect being offered a temple to his own art, comparable to Tintoretto's Scuola di S. Rocco or Veronese's S. Sebastiano, though that is not how Charles III or Padre Eleta would have cared to think of their patronage. Almost certainly, Tiepolo benefited from some lack of eagerness or willingness shown by Mengs, quite possibly connected with his health; and it may well be that neither for the King nor his confessor would Tiepolo's have been the chief part, let alone the sole one, in the commission, had Mengs urged his own claim. That factor possibly lay in the background from the first, influencing what was eventually decided.

On Tiepolo any such consciousness would seem to have acted only as a positive stimulus. Between receipt of the commission and the beginning of August, he executed the *modelli* for presumably all seven altarpieces. Sabatini was able to send news of their completion to Padre Eleta, who was with the King at Ildefonso (La Granja), north of Madrid, perhaps proposing that Tiepolo should go out to the palace with his paintings. On 5 August Eleta replied dryly that the King had decided that the painter should send the *modelli* without troubling to come himself. A month elapsed before approval was given for Tiepolo to paint the altarpieces.

Five of the *modelli* fortunately survive, and now, no less fortunately, are permanently in one place, the Princes Gate Collection[22] (Pls 229, 230, 231 and 232). Missing are those for the two oval paintings which happen to be the less important, artistically at least. No trace seems to exist of the *modello* which was presumably executed for the *St Peter of Alcantara*, but the remaining six paintings were in the collection of Francisco Bayeu at his death in 1795.

The surviving *modelli* are broadly very similar in handling, and, though there

may be some slight variations of quality between them, the total effect is profoundly impressive. Restrained and yet rich in colour, animated in surface and intense in their grasp on the essence of each subject, they match thought with execution in a way that shows how determined Tiepolo was to bring his art to its highest pitch for this important, testing commission.

As *modello*, each painting is wrought to be much more than a mere sketch. The agitated outlines, which actually aid expressiveness, are no sign of haste. Nothing is left unresolved; the format of each altarpiece is carefully conveyed, whether its top will be curved or rectangular. Although the scale is small, the different settings, the attributes, the pale-blue and white flowers in the garden where St Pascual kneels (Pl. 228) the inside of the mouth of the serpent on whom the immaculate Virgin treads, the dotted lines of the rays that stream from the seraph to imprint the stigmata on St Francis—all are conveyed with a felicity of touch that is like a release of energy.

The subjects nicely blended the familiar and the new. All were conceived, no doubt as instructed, in meditative not dramatic terms, emphasising the sanctity of the saints and their privileged apartness, exemplified by the Virgin. Where a vision was involved, as most notably with St Pascual, Tiepolo eschewed the stirring excite-

229. *The Immaculate Conception*, Courtauld Institute Galleries, London (Prince's Gate Collection).

230. *St Joseph*, Courtauld Institute Galleries, London (Prince's Gate Collection).

231. *St Pascual Baylon*, Courtauld Institute Galleries, London (Prince's Gate Collection).

232. *St Francis receiving the stigmata*, Courtauld Institute Galleries, London (Prince's Gate Collection).

ment of, for example, the *St Tecla* composition. No less fervently does the youthful Spanish saint kneel in prayer, but he kneels not to invoke heaven, but as the result of the heavenly vision he has been vouchsafed. His personal piety is what is depicted: piety for its own sake, it might be said, as here and in the other subjects no miracles are shown, no healing or helping of others, no charity in a social context. Each saint is very much alone, humanly speaking, cloistered in the cell of his own virtue.

The subject of the Immaculate Conception was by no means new for Tiepolo. Quite apart from the painting on the altar of the Purità chapel at Udine, he had earlier painted it for a church at Vicenza,[23] and had established his own treatment of a theme which allowed for little variation. At Vicenza, the Virgin was dressed in a clinging garment of shimmering white silk, painted with sensuous response to

274

233. Two surviving fragments of *St Pascual Baylon*, Prado, Madrid.

material shaped by the limbs beneath it, that might well not suit in Spain—and which Tiepolo himself may no longer have thought appropriate. With decorously covered head and bulky draperies, the Virgin of the Aranjuez *modello* seems a true 'vessel of honour', filled with mystic grace, a dignified image of womanhood free of sexual overtones, elevated above the globe, unheeding of the angels and cherubs at her side and all around her.

No more novel for Tiepolo was the scene of the stigmatisation of St Francis. In addition to a now lost painting, he had prepared a drawing of the subject for engraving by Pietro Monaco pre-1739 (Pl. 53). In that the drama of the moment had been very much his concern. Stormy, elemental atmospherics had accompanied the ecstasy with which the saint received the mystic imprint.

For Aranjuez Tiepolo re-thought the scene, investing it with that mood of quietism and poignant humanity which seems characteristic of his last years. Without drama in the heavens or on earth, the saint submits, almost in weary resignation, to the ordeal of great sanctity, his eyes fixed on the frail, wooden cross before him. In a tranquil sky the seraph appears, and an angel, half-embracing the saint, seems to comfort him as he gently creates the rent in his habit for reception of the sacred wound. The saint's companion-friar—a necessary part of the incident—abases himself in utter humility, and is visually abased, excluded from the awe-inspiring loneliness of being singled out by God.

After the impact of this *modello*, those for the *St Charles Borromeo* and the *St Joseph* are somewhat more conventional. A drop in emotional temperature is marked. The *St Joseph* indeed raises several problems, both in concept and handling, whereas the *St Charles* is uncontestably autograph, even if not entirely satisfactory. The grandiose Palladian setting Tiepolo chose for the saint was certainly sumptuous enough, vaguely recalling the setting of such earlier paintings as the *Vision of St Clement*. He had not depicted the saint before but followed the traditional iconography of his features, took pleasure in his cardinal's robes and made a giant crucifix out of the normal attribute of the cross he is shown adoring. At first Tiepolo seems to have painted St Charles in three-quarter face, his hands—his left hand at least—raised in a gesture of wonder over the cross.[24] For the mood of these paintings, he probably felt that that was too rhetorical. He suppressed it, preferring the simpler motif of the saint's hands folded on his breast. For that he executed a chalk drawing.[25] He moved the saint's head and put it in profile, nearer the cross, deepening the sense of fixed adoration. A *pentimento* of that kind by Tiepolo on a *modello* is rare, and it indicates how carefully he approached this major commission. Nevertheless, the angel and the curtain in the top right corner of the composition are rather perfunctory adjuncts, hardly more than frank space-fillers.

Much odder is the composition of the *St Joseph*. In an attractive if somewhat irrelevant landscape, a cloud has risen to form a convenient seat for the saint, who sits upright with the Christ Child, holding a book beside him. Overhead, a pair of angels fly in with a lily-wreath, echoing in motif, though not precisely in pose, the upper compartment of the Purità ceiling at Udine. The fact that only in this composition, of those preserved by the *modelli*, were the main figures to be totally altered for the altarpiece may be explicable in several ways. If Tiepolo was meant to illustrate St Joseph's adoration of the Child, he has not done so very satisfactorily. And then the seating of the saint on a cloud—as though he were himself a vision—sharing it with the Child, on equal if not superior terms, might meet with disapproval.

Aesthetically, also, the design is disappointing. The creation of the cloud is a banal, nearly ludicrous device, not enhanced by being painted in a pudgy, lumpy way devoid of any vaporous suggestion. St Joseph's stiff and upright pose is notably lacking in fervour—conveying, rather, a sense of uneasy responsibility for the Child juxtaposed to him. Oddest of all is the draughtsmanship of St Joseph's figure, for his left leg has been omitted entirely and must be presumed muffled somewhere in the cloud. Yet while that is skimped, the foreground is busy with the littered tools of the saint's trade: his hat, a basket, a saw and even a plank of wood.

All this should point to intervention, at least, by Domenico, but it is difficult to believe he could pastiche his father's style in an oil *modello* as skilfully as here, where the actual painting of the angels in the sky, and the handling of the angel heads at the left, seem characteristic of Giambattista. Collaboration on such a small scale seems improbable. It may therefore simply be that Giambattista's inspiration faltered, for some reason, on this *modello*. The interesting point is that its design was rejected.

The *modello* for the high altarpiece was obviously going to come under a scrutiny both aesthetic and doctrinal. Tiepolo was depicting a saint little known outside Spain, canonised less than a century earlier. Charles III had given the name Pascual to one of his own sons. He was a humble, youthful saint, the Alcantarine Franciscan lay-brother gardener who had enjoyed a vision of the Holy Eucharist in a monstrance held by angels. What details Tiepolo had been given are, as usual, unclear, yet he instinctively understood and responded to the subject. In essence it was already very much his, though the accidents of it were new. Realisation of them is part of the sober, impressive effect of the resulting composition. Where the vision takes place is powerfully conveyed—avoiding the generalised countryside of the *St Joseph*, as much as the Palladian grandeur of the *St Charles*, but combining the open-air and the architectural.

A monastic garden, stony yet not infertile, is the setting, with a slightly battered wooden fence, beyond which is visible a portion of monastery building and the severe, Doric portico of its church. Tiepolo gave particular firmness and prominence to these structures that fill much of the background, as though evoking something of the concept of the actual church and monastery that was being built at Aranjuez. So lively and crisp is Tiepolo's handling that the foreground, even where bare, is as animated as the rest of the composition, made tactile and interesting by countless little hooks and flecks of paint suggesting the bumpy soil on which lie the saint's hoe and a thoroughly Spanish-looking, striped bag. In this austere and artistically uncompromising setting, the saint's vision comes as miraculously soft and vaporous and glowing. A gently rising spiral of cloud partly blots out the verticals and horizontals of the church portico, drifting up and away skywards, while the eye follows the direction of the saint's upturned head towards the monstrance held by an angel wrapped in a golden-yellow humeral veil that prevents contact with the sacred vessel itself.

In this *modello* was summed up all the sense of visionary mysticism which the other subjects alluded to, without depicting exactly this meeting of the earthly and the divine: a meeting made harmonious and tranquil, as though inevitable. The angel's appearance, borne on strong wings and holding aloft the gleaming Sacrament, is as natural, it seems, as the prosaic garden and the plainly clad saint, whose simple occupation has been put aside as the vision is manifested to him.

This was, as it were, Tiepolo's last word on the theme of divine intervention. He had begun as early as the Ospedaletto *Sacrifice of Abraham* some fifty years before, delighting in his own virtuosity and savouring the drama of the scene. His virtuosity was as present as ever in the S. Pascual *modello*, but it had matured and become absorbed in a profounder artistry where all effort seems concentrated on expressing the essence of the subject and its inner significance.

It was apparently on 5 September 1767 that Tiepolo learnt that formal approval had been given by the King to his proceeding to execute the seven altarpieces. Sabatini thereupon renewed the painter's request for a larger studio, 'of the same kind as the Pintor de Cámara Don Antonio Rafael Mengs has in his house', now that Tiepolo was to work on the 'quadros grandes al olio'; and in October this was granted.

By August 1769 Tiepolo had completed the altarpieces. They were ready to be shown to the King or to Padre Eleta, and Tiepolo was only too willing to alter anything in them, as he assured the King's secretary, if they did not meet with 'complete Royal approval'.[26] In fact, the church was not finished. In March 1770 it was decided that the paintings should remain with the painter, and they were moved to Aranjuez only in May of that year, after Tiepolo's death.

Tiepolo had written of his willingness to change anything in the altarpieces, but already a certain number of changes must have been made between the *modelli* and the altarpieces as executed. The most drastic was the change of composition of the *St Joseph*. The saint was now depicted kneeling and clasping the Child, a baby cradled half in his arms and half supported on a cloud. The result was a more obviously devotional image. St Joseph is humbled and privileged at the same time; his human nature is contrasted now with the divine nature of the Child, whose divinity is emphasised by the added motif of adoring angels close by, one holding a basket of flowers. For the new pose of the Child and the new motif, chalk drawings were made.[27]

On the other altarpieces the alterations were comparatively minor, and it is not possible to say whether Tiepolo was asked to make them or whether they arose from his own second, not always better, thoughts. They tend to simplification. Thus the large angel accompanying the Virgin in the *modello* of the *Immaculate Conception* was removed. More surprisingly, Brother Leo, St Francis's companion, was removed from the *St Francis* altarpiece, as well as the wooden cross at which the saint was shown gazing. On the high altarpiece, the humeral veil previously worn by the angel was converted into a similar-coloured drapery held by, but not wrapped around, that figure, whose right arm is now bared and whose hand touches the monstrance; and a stole was added to the angel's costume. Again, Tiepolo executed a drawing in chalk for the new detail (Pl. 235), which may well have been proposed on the grounds that a supernatural being, an angel, should not wear the humeral veil which is worn by the priest when, for example, elevating the monstrance at Benediction. The drawing must be among the last executed by Tiepolo, and its quality is markedly above many of the chalk drawings now accepted as by him. In the angel's heavy-lidded gaze, as in the summary grasp on his wing, Giambattista asserts an unfailing, personal authority.

Since no *modelli* survive for the *St Anthony of Padua* and the *St Peter of Alcántara*,[28] it remains uncertain whether changes were introduced there, but it may be significant that a chalk drawing exists of the *St Anthony* composition very close indeed to the altarpiece.[29]

The altarpieces themselves had, from the first, a sad and chequered history. Today they are dispersed throughout the world, partly mutilated and divided into fragments, offering a vivid testimony of how little they were—from the first, it seems—either understood or cared for. Yet, taken together, they are a slightly disconcerting phenomenon, recalling in their execution less the *St Tecla* than the laboured *Vision of St Anne*. The high quality of the *modelli* was only fitfully carried over on to the large canvases, though *in situ* in the church that would not have been easily apparent, and the effectiveness of the images remained.

Nevertheless, whether explained as partly collaborative work or as the efforts of a single hand now grown tired, the intact altarpieces—four out of the seven—are at their best dutiful, heavy in paint texture and reliant for what vitality they possess on rather obtrusive outlines and drawing. The *Immaculate Conception* is perhaps the most impressive, though even there some of the angels' heads are slack and weakly sentimental. But it has an autograph air to it, which is more than can be said of the *St Anthony of Padua*, with its poorly executed perspective of wall and window, and its general perfunctoriness; here it is not a matter of some rather slack details but of a pervasive weakness and painful commonplaceness (Pl. 236). Indeed, it seems the

234. *Allegory of the Immaculate Conception*, National Gallery of Ireland, Dublin.

weakest of the seven paintings, inferior to its companion oval, the *St Peter Alcantara*, a work for which only a single chalk drawing appears to exist.

By comparison with the *St Anthony*, the altarpiece of the *Stigmatisation of St Francis* looks impressive, at first glance (Pl. 237). But the poignancy and fervour which characterised concept and handling in the *modello* have gone, quite apart from the compositional changes that leave such a void at the left. St Francis's head seems rather too patently based on that of St Pascual in the high altarpiece. More clumsy is the angel—a commonplace interpretation of the tender figure of the *modello*— whose wings have been, if not exactly clipped, certainly made thin and conventional. They are flatly drawn rather than painted, lacking modelling and density. And it happens that a good comparison can be made on this very point, since the two fragments, all that remain, of the *St Pascual Baylon*, are of the key areas, of the saint himself and the angel with the monstrance.

Sadly reduced though the *St Pascual Baylon* thus is, enough survives to suggest that on this major item of the series Tiepolo toiled virtually unaided (Pl. 233). The heavy outlines and the solid impasto give it a quality more dogged, perhaps, than inspired. He has worked at the saint's head until it has taken on something of the character of Spanish wood sculpture; inserted in this carved mask, the upturned eyes might be of glass, while the nostrils and the open lips, parted to show a glimpse of teeth, have all the slightly uncanny detail that makes such sculpture disturbing in its piously obsessive realism. The angel, however, is modelled with a lighter touch, suitably spirited and quite masterly when it comes to creating the curve and weight and downy shadow of the angel's wing. In reproduction it may look very similar to the angel's wing in the *St Francis*, but in reality it has all the conviction and implicit power under the plumage—a true swan's wing—that the other merely echoes. Here Tiepolo stamps his full authority on the canvas, with a piece of pure painting that might have made his 'competitor', Mengs, weep for envy.

It is not subjective to see Tiepolo as deeply engaged in getting this painting right, for himself as much as for his patron. Although he declared in August 1769 that the altarpieces were completed, he probably found—when they remained on his hands throughout the following winter—that on the *St Pascual Baylon* at least there were touches he could yet add.

236. *St Anthony of Padua*, Prado, Madrid.

237. *St Francis receiving the stigmata*, Prado, Madrid.

Of the remaining two altarpieces only fragments remain: the head and shoulders of St Charles Borromeo with the upper portion of the crucifix he contemplates; and St Joseph holding the Child and two smaller canvases of angels.[30] The composition of the *St Charles Borromeo* altarpiece is recorded by an etching, showing it to have been not significantly different from its *modello*. More complicated is the evidence for establishing the eventual composition of the *St Joseph*. A squared-up pen drawing exists,[31] attributed to Domenico Tiepolo, which presumably records the composition at some late stage, and the surviving three fragments of the altarpiece accord with that. One minor feature of it is unexpected. In the foreground lies, half-buried, a bas-relief with helmeted heads—a motif borrowed from Giambattista's *Scherzi* etchings and somewhat incongruous in a religious painting. Whether that was eventually incorporated in the altarpiece cannot now be known.

Tiepolo's state of mind at the end of August 1769, when the altarpieces were ready to be seen, is documented by a letter he was impelled to write to the King's secretary, Muzquiz, frankly appealing for guidance and assistance. He was less concerned perhaps about the altarpieces than about some future commission, and he referred to the difficulty he and his sons had experienced in trying to discover if Padre Eleta had any further work for him, now the St Pascual series was done. He had not managed to speak to Eleta and so had written to him, without success. Now he feared he may have failed to execute the altarpieces to Eleta's complete satisfaction which would be a grave mortification for him ('que seria para mi la mayor mortificacion. . .'). He appeals to the King, via Muzquiz, asking Muzquiz to tell the King not only that the altarpieces are done—though he is very ready to alter them if they do not meet with royal approval—but that he seeks other tasks, showing his wish to be constantly employed ('de ser continuadamente empleado') in the glorious royal service.[32]

The fate of the Aranjuez altarpieces was, happily, not to be known to Tiepolo, and it may too easily colour interpretation of a situation which in the summer of 1769 was by no means clear-cut. Eleta's silence may have signified not merely his disapproval at being approached directly by the painter, and his sons, but also his comparative powerlessness to give commissions unless instigated by the King. He was closely involved in the building and decoration of the monastery and church of S. Pascual, but elsewhere Charles III might himself openly take the initiative; and it seems that he now did so, without Eleta's involvement.

Tiepolo's appeal to Muzquiz was something of a bold move, for it criticised by implication the King's confessor. And just as in 1767 Tiepolo had expressed a pointed willingness to receive a commission for oil paintings, doubtless aware that such a commission was under consideration, so his eagerness for fresh employment in 1769 suggests that he had heard of a new project which might involve him. Once again, it was a matter being handled in Madrid by Sabatini, whose good offices and friendliness towards Tiepolo continued to be valuable.

It had already been decided that the dome of the collegiate church of S. Ildefonso at La Granja should be decorated, with stucco and with frescoes. The 'grange' which was the basis of the site, was and is most famous for its gardens and fountains, laid out by Philip V but finished only in the reign of Charles III. The lighter side of royal life in the summer palace—'the antithesis', wrote Richard Ford, 'of the proud, gloomy Escorial'—is commemorated in the Casa del Gòndola, housing one of Charles III's pleasure-boats. A more solemn aspect was in the chapel or Colegiata, dedicated to St Ildefonso, seventh-century Archbishop of Toledo, a musician and a writer whose best known extant work is a treatise on the Virgin. In the chapel are buried Philip V and his wife, who did not die until 1766.

The result of Tiepolo's appeal to Muzquiz could hardly have been speedier or more gratifying. On 2 September Tiepolo was awarded the commission for the S. Ildefonso frescoes by the King, and he was asked to press Sabatini to produce the designs for the stucco decoration for the King's approval. Muzquiz had clearly written back to Tiepolo, for on 13 September Sabatini wrote to Muzquiz himself, referring to a meeting that day with Tiepolo who had shown him the secretary's letter. They had settled that Sabatini would send two different ideas for the stucco decoration, to allow the King to choose between them. Once that was settled, Sabatini would have the duty of giving the painter 'the subjects to be painted', as he and Tiepolo had agreed.

Tiepolo followed up Sabatini's letter with one of his own, written two days later, very different in tone from his earlier appeal. Full of 'joy and elation' he was delighted that the King was (as it seemed) satisfied with the Aranjuez altarpieces and had charged him with the task of painting the dome of the Colegiata, to which he would give 'all my attention and care' ('toda la atencion y cuidado').[33]

This is the last known letter from Tiepolo, and it closes his long career proudly and victoriously. He had won a third major commission from the King and justified his continued stay in Spain. He had begun there with the secular task of the royal-palace frescoes. He had gone on to paint in oil the seven altarpieces for the church of S. Pascual Baylon. Now he had received a commission for religious subjects in fresco, the medium in which he never failed.

He began to put down his thoughts for the S. Ildefonso decoration.[34] Pen-and-ink drawings of the four Evangelists, composed to be seen from below, and suitable to fill pendentives, were almost certainly done for the scheme, as was probably the oil sketch of the *Allegory of the Immaculate Conception*, of a quality to be ranked with the *modelli* for the Aranjuez altarpieces—accomplished in execution and as personal in its handwriting, as also in its fervid mysticism (Pl. 234).[35]

The Colegiata was dedicated to the Trinity, and the triangular halo of God the Father (not used in the Este altarpiece, for example) emphasises the solemn, triune aspect of this prophet-like deity who raises both arms majestically in benediction of the Virgin, kneeling before him, created immaculate from eternity: 'I was set up from everlasting, from the beginning. . .' Charles III's personal devotion to the Immaculate Conception, St Ildefonso's treatise on the Virgin and the Colegiata's dedication seem brought together in a special way, for a special destination. Around the totally visionary central scene, with the Virgin kneeling on the globe of the world on which lies the Serpent, cluster angels in adoration and the attributes of her purity and uniqueness: the tower, palm tree, the crescent moon and the spotless mirror. And although God the Father occurs in other depictions of the subject, he is seldom as prominent, or as memorable, as Tiepolo makes him here. This is no benign old man with picturesque wrinkles and swirling drapery, but a fierce figure, heavily bearded and grim-visaged, plainly dressed in a timeless, semi-monkish tunic, whose very gesture of holding his arms aloft seems achieved only by trembling effort. It is he who dominates the painting; and eternity is symbolised as the will at work in a physically frail and aged body. Instead of those Shakespearean associations which Tiepolo's earlier work often prompts, he seems here to suggest the ethos of Milton.

If this is not Tiepolo's last painting, it must certainly be among his latest, and along with the other late surviving works it evokes a mood of exalted and intense feeling, not explicable merely through the subject-matter. A small, late sketch of *Angels appearing to Abraham*, the subject of the early, enchanted, insolently beautiful fresco in the patriarchal palace at Udine, reworks the theme with extremes of austerity and emotionalism: the angels are now of elemental dignity, not impudence, and Abraham is bowed utterly to the ground before them, reduced to a quivering bundle of piety.[36] Yet, fascinatingly, all the elements of this fervent composition, which seems profoundly mystical, remote and poignant, almost painful, in its expressiveness, can be found already in the Udine fresco.

Tiepolo's energies may have been waning, but his appetite for work was un-

238. D. Tiepolo after G. B. Tiepolo, *St Pascual Baylon*, Museo Correr, Venice.

diminished, and so, it seems, was his creative urge. Perhaps he saw the La Granja commission as truly his final one in Spain, after which he would return to Venice; or perhaps, more realistically, he guessed he would never make that journey. Though no letters exist, there is touching evidence that he did not forget his family. By various methods he sent home presents from Spain. When a Venetian patrician lady, Chiara Zen Mocenigo, came back from Madrid to Venice she brought pearl bracelets and a pearl necklace that Tiepolo had entrusted her with for his wife and daughters. In May 1769 he bought a number of lace and lace-embroidered items of lingerie specifically for Cecilia; they were never despatched but eventually reached her the following year, brought by Domenico,[37] and they constitute Tiepolo's last gift to the wife he had married half a century before.

On 5 March 1770, Tiepolo became seventy-four. During the winter months his work seems to have included putting a few finishing touches to the high altarpiece of S. Pascual Baylon, which was still in his studio, along with the other six paintings for Aranjuez, awaiting orders for their removal to the new church.

Without any warning, without any preliminary illness, Tiepolo died suddenly, on 27 March, dying so rapidly that there was no time for him to receive the sacraments.[38] He was buried in his local parish church of S. Martín, where Juvarra had been buried. No interest or importance was attached to preserving his tomb, such as it was, and—like his birthplace—it long ago disappeared.

Charles III was staying at the Pardo palace, outside Madrid, where he often spent the winter hunting. Sabatini promptly informed the King's secretary, Muzquiz, of Tiepolo's death, and on 28 March Muzquiz replied tersely that the King had learnt of the painter's death. Sabatini was commanded to assemble the paintings he had finished for Aranjuez so that the King could see them on his return to the capital.

Tiepolo had not had time to get far enough with the La Granja commission, and probably Domenico took back to Venice, later in 1770, the oil sketch of the *Allegory of the Immaculate Conception*. Eventually, two years afterwards, the Colegiata frescoes he had hoped to execute were painted by Francisco Bayeu.

In May of 1770 Tiepolo's altarpieces for Aranjuez were moved to the church, where the first mass was celebrated on St Pascual's feast day, 17 May.[39] The altar dedicated to St Charles Borromeo had been given a different association, with the crucified Christ, so that altarpiece was not put up. The remainder were, but they failed to please, for reasons not entirely clear. By November 1770, it was settled that they should be replaced, and Padre Eleta was able to inform Sabatini that the King had decided that Maella and Bayeu should paint the five altarpieces required, leaving aside the high altarpiece; that was reserved for Mengs, on his return to Spain. So ended the 'competition' between Tiepolo and Mengs. In 1775, after Mengs's return, Tiepolo's paintings started on their travels, moved first to the convent building, then partly moved to the Prado museum on its foundation and partly cut up and dispersed. Although the altarpieces by Maella and Bayeu were to be destroyed in the Spanish Civil War, Mengs's much darkened altarpiece remains—seeming almost to vindicate Winckelmann—on the high altar of the church.

For Domenico Tiepolo, his father's own painting for the high altar took on particular significance, not for what it represented but for when it had been done. He etched the composition and printed under it the legend that it had been painted by Giambattista Tiepolo, Venetian painter in the service of the King of Spain, in 1770, 'before his death' (Pl. 238). Faithful to the end, he thus made of this, the largest and the most important of the Aranjuez series, and probably the finest in quality, Tiepolo's last piece of completed work.

It was a fitting choice, as well as moving homage. Domenico's brief yet explicit wording suggests a career that continued until the end—to be interrupted only by death. In that way it was to be paralleled in France, only a few months later in 1770, when Boucher died suddenly, in his studio and at his easel.

The calibre of the painting Domenico etched showed that with Tiepolo there had been no artistic decline, no weakening of his creative powers, even if his brush now moved more slowly and handled paint more heavily. And his death was merciful in its swiftness and even in its timing. Tiepolo did not live to experience a humiliation as public as it would have been, for him, unprecedented: for his work to fail, and to be removed, and for the commission to be given to other painters. Only in the Spanish embassy in London had something similar happened, but in a much less important way, without his being on the spot or indeed in the service of those involved. He died believing presumably that he had, once again, succeeded in a major task, pleased his patron and produced art of which he himself could be justly proud. Domenico, unwittingly, vindicated his father. Without his etching, the composition of the *St Pascual Baylon* in its final state would not now be known.

For Tiepolo, the Aranjuez paintings, done in his old age, in a foreign country and for a foreign monarch, must have seemed proof that he could still sustain the creativity which had astonished Venice when, at around the age of twenty, he first incited applause and showed the *Crossing of the Red Sea* at the Scuola di S. Rocco. Down the years he had gone on to greater and greater success, louder applause and more profound achievements. One commission led to another, as he always hoped it would; for him the Aranjuez paintings became in turn stepping-stones towards the task at La Granja, and that doubtless he envisaged leading to something new, a further challenge, a fresh opportunity to display his ability.

Although he had expressed few opinions about art in general, he had certainly been wonderfully confident about his own. Never slow or hesitant, and rarely declining a commission, he had gone on constantly creating, testifying—by example after example—to a fiery imagination that only death could extinguish. In writing to Muzquiz on 13 September 1769, in the belief that his Aranjuez paintings were approved and in anticipation of working at La Granja, he declared that he had 'always held with fulfilling my obligation' ('siempre he tenido de cumplir con mi obligacion').

Those words, of quiet yet firm assurance, take on additional resonance, not merely because they are the last expression of Tiepolo's personality but because they seem to sum up his attitude to his art and to his own powers. Actively and always he had sought obligations—opportunities to demonstrate how extensively he could create—travelling far to fulfill them, encouraging himself when even he half-faltered at the magnitude of the task (as in Venice, contemplating the scheme for the throne-room ceiling in Madrid).

He had always put total trust in his own artistry, understanding somehow that it performed the more magnificently the greater the pressure. And always he had been justified. He had not merely fulfilled his obligations, he had surpassed them. In the long unfolding pageant of his work lie the justification, the fulfilment and something more: the bright, vital flame of art that, when the artist is dead, burns on, 'As long as men can read and eyes can see...'

EPILOGUE

FORTUNATE IN LIFE, Tiepolo was perhaps equally fortunate in the moment of his death. It came before he could be aware of a rejection more fundamental and wide-sweeping than Charles III's rejection of the Aranjuez altarpieces.

The style Tiepolo supremely stood for, whether represented in the Residenz at Würzburg or on the ceiling of the Scuola del Carmine at Venice, in the Duomo at Este or in the Villa Valmarana at Vicenza, was coming under increasingly unsympathetic scrutiny, passing into scorn and near-neglect. For over a century after his death, Tiepolo's work was broadly to be dismissed from serious aesthetic consideration. Even now, two centuries later, it is by no means certain that his reputation has been fully restored.

The process of dethroning him began in his own century. The veiled hints of Gasparo Gozzi and the more open objections of Cochin indicated the basis of critical reserve and eventual denigration. In Tiepolo's art there seemed to be a flagrant absence of 'truth to nature'; and that absence was equated with a lack of discipline, encouraging artistic licence, undignified or shocking treatment of subjects and a general superficiality. Such apparently unserious art could not hope to be taken seriously, least of all in circles where the need both to define and to follow nature was an urgent major concern. To an age much obsessed with pursuit of naked fact, Tiepolo might appear to be providing merely a heavily costumed fiction. And politics mingled with aesthetics, to Tiepolo's eventual detriment, for his patrons had tended to be aristocratic and privileged figures, authoritarian even when 'enlightened', themselves addicted to living in a world of myth and allegory, sacred as well as profane, which was increasingly to be scrutinised, doubted and rejected.

After the upheaval of the French Revolution, whatever monarchies survived, that old world became the *ancien-régime*, a world of such anachronisms as periwigs and Prince-Bishops. Within thirty years of Tiepolo's death, the Serene Republic of Venice, declining rapidly in the last decades of the eighteenth century, had ceased to exist. It was almost as if, as it sank, it took Tiepolo's reputation with it.

The coming of the nineteenth century could offer little likelihood of salvaging his reputation. Art had also undergone revolution, less in terms of neo-classicism, or any other single movement or style, than through the powerful individual figures of David and Goya. No doubt, as is frequently said, Goya was influenced by some of the work of Tiepolo he was able to see, but among Italian artists he was influenced also by Luca Giordano and even more by Giaquinto. The colour and style and handling of paint of all three painters appealed to him. In no sense was he an inheritor, still less a cultivator, of Tiepolo's art. He was too individual, and also too revolutionary. He might begin with charming, decorative genre paintings, more akin anyway to Domenico than to Giambattista Tiepolo, but he would end by creating scenes of appalling violence, beyond 'realism' and psychologically far more deeply disturbing, illustrating truths of the human heart and the human condition that the eighteenth century had scarcely dreamed of.

Painting in Venice was by 1800 a spent force. Domenico Tiepolo lived on, having become President of the Venetian Academy in 1783, still capable of delightful genre frescoes—for what was now his villa at Zianigo—and of wonderfully spirited, mildly fantastic and partly satiric drawings, exemplified by the Punchinello series, 'Divertimenti per li regazzi' (the work of someone with no surviving children of his own). He continued faithfully to keep his father's name alive, etched and listed Giambattista's compositions, and published an edition of the family's etchings dedicated to the reigning Pope, Pius VI.

Painting in Europe by 1800 was not just a matter of Goya and David but of Turner and Constable, and Caspar David Friedrich—to take only a few outstanding names representative of new aims, new energies and a new age.

The nineteenth century saw sporadic, limited and largely amateur interest in Tiepolo's art, perhaps as much in France, ironically, as in Italy. In England he was, in the main, ignored or abused. One or two collectors acquired his paintings, but his reputation in Europe remained low. He was the subject of an 'elogio' at the Venetian Academy in 1856, but no book on him was published in any language until the 1880s. Only in 1883 was a bust of Tiepolo put up, in the arcades of the Doges' Palace, near to one of Canova. Even then, in an anxiety to bind him to the Venetian tradition, the inscription on it robbed him of individual genius, echoing the poetic compliments of his own century though now with a touch of the elegiac: 'In the sunset of the Republic, he renewed the glories of Titian and Paolo [Veronese].'

Some modern historians and art historians have implied that Tiepolo's art, however brilliant, is symptomatic of decline, either of an artistic tradition or of a society —or both. That implication separates him from the general re-appraisal of Baroque art in recent years; it would take considerable courage, or sheer foolhardiness, to make Rubens and Bernini, for example, symptoms of a 'decline', and it is difficult not to think that Tiepolo and his age, when so judged, are being assessed rather too simplistically in the light of subsequent historical events. In any case, it is extremely doubtful if the artistic tradition of Venice was in decline during the eighteenth century, given the quantity and quality of artistic activity there. Compared with, say, Florence or Bologna, Venice appears bursting with talents, not only in painting but in sculpture and architecture. Not fettered by tradition, far less overshadowed by the past than had been the seventeenth century, the eighteenth century extended the achievements of the Venetian school in ways quite unforeseen. In Canaletto alone stands a genius unparalleled as a view painter anywhere at any period; yet he is profoundly of his city.

Tiepolo was a more traditional figure in terms of training and patronage, in the type of art he produced and, above all, in provoking associations with the art of Veronese. So much has been made of his 'debt' to Veronese that it is often forgotten how little Veronese had to teach him in the area of fresco painting. The frescoes by Veronese in the Villa Barbaro are not an essential step for Tiepolo's evolution in the medium. Tiepolo did not need and scarcely heeded, any earlier examples of fresco painting. It was, from the first, his natural medium. He understood instinctively how to make it serve decorative ends but be serious and imaginatively powerful, vivid and convincing. He remains unchallenged as a painter of frescoes, and there he positively enriches the Venetian tradition. Whatever he had borrowed from Veronese, he was to repay it a thousandfold, with fresh, new-minted currency.

But as regards his reputation with posterity, Tiepolo chose a dangerous road in becoming a decorative painter, whether in oil or fresco. Veronese himself, though conveniently cited to imply his superiority to Tiepolo, has been little understood, rarely discussed in depth until very recently and certainly under-appreciated generally in what passes for the history of art. The amount of visual pleasure both artists set out to give—cannot help enjoying giving—is a positive disadvantage when it comes to being assessed. That colour and invention and wit and fantasy can co-exist with a serious view of art, can fuse into a vision just as profoundly imaginative as any pursuit of significant form, is still only grudgingly recognised, if recognised at all.

And in Tiepolo's case, the disadvantages to any just appreciation are legion. His century, his city, his style—each represents a handicap; but perhaps the greatest of all is his style. It is indeed the essence of his art, his natural speaking voice—not adopted—and it cannot be detached from what he has to say.

That he was not blind or indifferent to nature and natural appearances is obvious throughout his art, and in his drawings lies the final evidence. Yet he was not content with transcribing 'nature' and the natural; he could not be, because of the fermenting force of his imagination, whereby the ordinary environment and the everyday were transfigured into something more exciting, more highly coloured, far richer and more strange, though seldom disturbing.

He was born to create an alternative universe, solid-seeming, well built, which should be as beautiful as possible. There is the frank goal of his art, and that is its sole 'message', to be accepted, derided or ignored. Perhaps, for the sake of his reputation, he should have been a composer, not a visual artist. Between an actual scream of rage and Mozart's second aria for the Queen of the Night in *Die Zauberflöte*, there has intervened, quite acceptably, art—artistry of the most supremely stylish kind ever known. In Tiepolo's painted equivalents of opera the stylish beauty of the images, so crystalline and so finely wrought, and so effortlessly succeeding each other, may disconcert the earnest seeker of plain realism, of unadorned nature, and also the ruralist, the purist and the puritan. That Tiepolo's vision is of a world not previously experienced, and one which is indeed strictly impossible, unrealistic, though not unreal, is exactly what gives it point.

Ultimately, it is his confidence in his own creativity, combined with the scale of his vision, that makes his images impressive as well as beautiful. About his art he was intensely serious—which does not mean he excluded humour. He worked hard for his effects: for that illusionism which could convert a room into a personal realm of sheer magic, inhabited by opulently dressed people, moving in settings of marvellous splendour, amid all the trappings of magnificence, from noble dogs to benevolent deities—and often enough including himself, an actor too, if he saw cause, in a play of his own devising.

If his faith was first and foremost in his own art, he certainly knew how to express convincingly acts of faith in the Christian story, which fortunately for him frequently involved the supernatural. About his own private faith, it is impossible to state anything, but everything would suggest a devout believer (like his wife and eldest son) who would have welcomed Domenico's solemn stipulation in his will that masses should be said in the villa chapel at Zianigo, 'per li Deffonti di mia Famiglia' and who would have approved Domenico's practical charity in bequeathing a sum of money for distribution to the 'poveri della Villa. . .' In every way, it was easy for Tiepolo to put his faith in a god, whether Christian or pagan, who descended from heaven and was manifested as the light of light, 'lumen de lumine'. It is not the least of the claims to be made for Tiepolo that he is the last great religious painter of Europe.

For Tiepolo light was divine, and he worshipped it. It gave clarity, colour, sparkle, vivacity and vitality to his images. Darkness for him is associated with evil and ignorance, in a thoroughly eighteenth-century-enlightenment way. His perpetual subject is of day dawning, literally or metaphorically, and illumination coming in some form to assist, instruct or delight humanity.

The whole school of painting to which he belonged had over the centuries continued to give primacy to light and colour. Sensuous effects in painting were fostered in a city that was itself a triumph of light and colour, the most sensuous of all cities, the one that had made of itself a wonderfully picturesque work of art.

No richer or more sympathetic inheritance and environment could have been provided for Tiepolo. He absorbed it all and then set out to create his own pictorial kingdom, a Venice of the imagination, more highly coloured, more suffused with light, more graceful, more sheerly enchanted. Yet it is intensely real and profoundly convincing. His contemporaries and fellow-citizens responded, from the first, to what he drew and painted and etched. The palaces and churches of Venice received additional ornament and enhanced splendour at his hands. However far he travelled, he remained the typical and inevitable product of his birthplace, deep-dyed in its traditions, the greatest exponent in his century of all that it stood for artistically. And when all the other adjectives have been exhausted, he is perhaps most succinctly summed up by concluding, as one began, that he was in every sense Venetian.

NOTES

1. BACKGROUND, BIRTH AND EARLY YEARS

1. The diarist was Pietro Gradenigo; see the extracts printed as his *Notizie d'Arte*, ed. L. Livan, 1942, pp. 191–2.

2. The document of Tiepolo's baptism published first, fairly accurately, by G. M. Urbani de Gheltof, *Tiepolo e la sua Famiglia*, 1879, pp. 2–3. The precise text, provided by Dr F. Pedrocco, reads: 16 aprile 1696/Gio. Batta figlio del sig. Domenico q. Zuanne Tiepolo, mercante, e della Signora Orsetta, giogali; nacque li 5 del pass.o: sta in C.S. Dom.co C. il N.H. Gio. Donà fu di C. Nicolò B.P. Gasparo Solta canonico nostro (Libro 18 dei Battezzati, p. 6).

3. Baptismal entries for the other children are printed by Urbani, *op. cit.*, pp. 3–4.

4. For the full text of this dedication, see the catalogue, edited by D. Succi, of the exhibition, *Da Carlevarijs ai Tiepolo, Incisiori Veneti e Friulani del Settecento*, Gorizia and Venice, 1983, no. 518.

5. It was omitted by Urbani (see note 2) and thus several of the older monographs assume the date as not known.

6. Urbani, *op. cit.*, p. 6, n. 1 for the death entry in the register of S. Pietro di Castello.

7. Eugenia Tiepolo's will published in part by Urbani, *op. cit.*, pp. 17–18, misreading the words of the bequest as 'li quadri de Rame . . .' I owe to Dr F. Pedrocco the correct reading and a transcript of the full text of the will (which includes bequests to other members of the Tiepolo family).

8. The painting appears as a small reproduction in A. Pallucchini, *L'opera completa di Giambattista Tiepolo*, 1968, no. 1a; see also the same author in *Studi di storia dell'arte in onore di Antonio Morassi*, 1971, pp. 303–7.

9. Portraits of the Cornaro, including one of the Doge Giovanni II, published by E. Martini as by Tiepolo in *Notizie di Palazzo Albani*, 1974, no. 1, pp. 30–5; see also E. Martini, *La Pittura del Settecento Veneto*, 1982, p. 509, n. 190; his plate XIII reproduces the Doge Giovanni II portrait in colour.

10. A. M. Zanetti, *Descrizione di tutte le pubbliche pitture . . . di Venezia*, 1733, p. 255. That a number of the paintings are by Tiepolo has been more than once suggested by modern scholars. The arguments are set out and discussed at length in an important article on the whole problem by B. Aikema in *Mitteilungen des Kunsthistorischen Institutes in Florenz*, 1982, pp. 339–82.

11. The precise circumstances of this commission were published by L. Moretti in *Arte Veneta*, 1973, pp. 318ff; see also the entry for Piazzetta's *St James* in the exhibition catalogue, *Giambattista Piazzetta, il suo tempo, la sua scuola*, Venice, 1983, n. 15.

12. Further for this painting, see the entry in the exhibition catalogue cited in note 11 above, no. 5.

13. Pallucchini, *op. cit.*, 1968, nos 6 and 28. References henceforward to Pallucchini, *tout court*, are to this.

14. It is reproduced by Aikema, *loc. cit.*, p. 367, as of a mythological subject.

15. For the four paintings, see Pallucchini, nos 19, A, B, C, D. The date of commissioning of the S. Aponal painting, referred to in the text above, has now been established as 1 December 1721 (cf. L. Moretti in *Atti dell'Istituto Veneto . . .*, vol. CXLIII, 1984–5, p. 379), though the painting had not been delivered in April 1727.

16. For this previously unknown letter, see G. Bortolan in *Notizie di Palazzo Albani*, 1973, no. 3, pp. 51–3.

17. I am indebted to Dr F. Pedrocco for these new documents, drawn from the Libro dei Morti of Santa Ternita, 1700–1730 (S. Francesco della Vigna). The entries for Tiepolo's children are: Adì 18 dito (October 1723)/Gio. Dom.ico figlio del sig.r Gio. Batta Tiepolo di mesi tre incirca da vaiollo in giorni 12 incirca; si sepelisse con P.Z./ Sepelito in S.ta Justina. Adì 30 ditto (October 1723)/ Elena figlia del sig. Gio: Batta Tiepolo d'anni tre da vaiole in mesi due incirca. Si seppelise con P.Z./Sepolta in S. Justina.

18. Cecilia Tiepolo's will published by Urbani, *op. cit.*, pp. 62–9, whence are drawn the facts about her children other than those referred to in the previous note.

2. THE FIRST FRESCOES

1. Da Canal's *Vita di Gregorio Lazzarini* was published by G. A. Moschini in Venice, 1809; for his 'life' of Tiepolo, see pp. xxxi–xxxv. As an art critic Da Canal is discussed briefly by N. Ivanoff in *Arte Veneta*, 1953, pp. 117–18.

2. This presumption went unchecked until the discovery published by A. Mariuz and G. Pavanello of an Assumption fresco in the abandoned church, attributed by them to Tiepolo (see *Il Giornale dell'Arte*, October 1985, p. 3).

3. *E.g.* A. Alciatus, *Emblematum Libellus*, Paris, 1542, pp. 226–7.

4. Pallucchini, nos 33 A and C.

5. See the document quoted in part in A. Morassi, *A complete catalogue of the paintings of G. B. Tiepolo*, 1962, p. 230. Its existence was first noted by V. Joppi and G. Bampo, *Contributo quarto ed ultimo alla Storia dell'Arte nel Friuli . . .*, 1894, p. 43.

6. An extract from this letter, by a certain 'Pre Gioseffi', written from Udine, was first published by A. Morassi in *Le Arti*, 1942, p. 97. For considerable discussion of the dating and the partly political significance of Tiepolo's work for the patriarchal palace, see M. Muraro, 'Ricerche su Tiepolo giovane', extract from the *Atti dell'Accademia di Udine*, 1970–72, to which the present text is indebted. Specifically for the galleria frescoes see also W. L. Barcham, 'Patriarchy and Politics: Tiepolo's *Galleria Patriarcale* in Udine revisited', in *Interpretazioni Veneziane* (Studies in honour of Michelangelo Muraro), 1984, pp. 427–38.

7. For Ricci's Sacrament chapel, see J. Daniels, *L'opera completa di Sebastiano Ricci*, 1976, nos 93–5.

8. Da Canal, *op. cit.*, p. xxxv.

3. 'THE CELEBRATED VENETIAN':
AT HOME AND AWAY

1. For some of the background see the chronology compiled by R. Morozzo della Rocca and M. F. Tiepolo in *La Civiltà Veneziana del Settecento*, 1960, pp. 231ff.

2. For discussion in detail of the investment in buildings and a table of the buildings put up at various dates during the century, see the relevant chapter in J. Georgelin, *Venise au siècle des lumières*, 1978, pp. 441ff.

3. Cited in W. G. Constable, *Canaletto*, 1976 ed., revised J. G. Links, vol. I, p. 14.

4. S. Maffei, *Verona Illustrata*, 1732, pt III, p. 215.

5. On Tiepolo's relations with Monaco, see further the fundamental article by G. Knox, 'A group of Tiepolo drawings owned and engraved by Pietro Monaco', *Master Drawings*, 1965, pp. 389ff.

6. Pallucchini, no. 64; see additionally G. Knox, 'Giambattista Tiepolo: Queen Zenobia and Ca' Zenobio . . .', *Burlington Magazine*, 1979, pp. 409ff.

7. See F. Haskell, *Patrons and Painters*, 1980 ed., p. 252 and also G. Tassini, *Curiosità Veneziane*, 1933 ed., p. 218 (under *Delfina*).

8. The letter itself appears lost or untraced since the nineteenth century, but there is no reason to doubt its authenticity; for quotation from it, see Morassi, *op. cit.*, 1962, pp. 230–1.

9. Fresh facts, utilised here, about the Archinto commission published by P. L. Sohm in *Arte Lombarda*, 1984, pp. 70–8; Sohm, *loc. cit.*, p. 74, for the subsequent mention in the text of the letter of August 1730 referring to Tiepolo. For the guide-book reference, see S. Lattuada, *Descrizione di Milano*, 1737, vol. III, p. 152.

10. Printed in S. Townley Worsthorne, *Venetian Opera in the Seventeenth Century*, 1954, pp. 25–7.

11. The relation to each other of the various existing oil sketches, apart from drawings, is by no means clear. A third oil sketch in a private collection is published by Martini, *op. cit.*, 1982, pl. XXX and p. 510, n. 194. A fourth sketch, of almost the same size, sold at Sotheby's, London, 11 December 1985 (lot 19).

12. See Morassi, *op. cit.*, 1962, p. 231.

13. The letter, of 17 November 1734, written from Venice, published by G. Fogolari posthumously in *Nuova Antologia*, 1942, pp. 33–4.

14. See note 13.

15. Morassi, *op. cit.*, 1962, p. 232 implies that a plaque in the villa records the commissioning by Loschi of Tiepolo's frescoes in 1734. In fact, the plaque speaks only in general terms of Loschi's rebuilding and decoration in that year: 'a fundamentis/erexit ornavitque/Anno MDCCXXXIV'. The text given, with other references, in *Gli Affreschi nelle Ville Venete dal seicento all'ottocento*, ed. R. Pallucchini, 1978, vol. I, p. 133 (cat. no. 17).

16. A group of the relevant drawings is in the Victoria & Albert Museum; see G. Knox, *Catalogue of the Tiepolo Drawings in the Victoria & Albert Museum*, 1975 ed., pp. 40–1; his no. 12 is a drawing based, as he points out, on Ripa's illustration. A larger group is at Trieste, for which see G. Vigni, *Disegni del Tiepolo*, 1972 ed., nos 7–22.

17. For Tiepolo's activity in Sant' Ambrogio, Pallucchini, no. 115.

18. This important letter published by O. Sirèn, *Dessins et Tableaux de la Renaissance Italienne dans les collections de Suède*, 1902, pp. 107–8.

19. For this engraving, see the catalogue of the exhibition, *Immagini da Tiziano*, Rome, Dec. 1976–Jan. 1977, no. 36.

4. FULL MATURITY:
THE YEARS 1736–40

1. See note 18 of chapter 3.

2. Morassi, *op. cit.*, 1962, p. 232 for these and other payments by the Cardinal to Tiepolo for paintings.

3. Daniels, *op. cit.*, no. 281; Ricci's composition is in reverse. For the Veronese, see T. Pignatti, *Veronese*, 1976, no. 242.

4. For the history of the church and documents concerning Tiepolo's activity there, see A. Niero, *Tre Artisti per un tempio, S. Maria del Rosario-Gesuati*, 1979.

5. Daniels, *op. cit.*, no. 517.

6. See further the exhibition catalogue of the exhibition, *Giambattista Piazzetta, il suo tempo, la sua scuola*, under no. 32.

7. Pallucchini, nos 122A and C.

8. Reproduced by Martini, *op. cit.*, 1982, fig. 927.

9. Pallucchini, no. 122B.

10. Niero, *op. cit.*, p. 22.

11. Niero, *op. cit.*, pp. 44–5.

12. *E.g.* by G. Knox, already in the first edition of his *Catalogue of the Tiepolo Drawings in the Victoria & Albert Museum*, 1960, p. 18; see also A. Rizzi's catalogue of the exhibition, *Disegni del Tiepolo*, Udine, 1965, under no. 86, with further references.

13. Pallucchini, nos 129 and 125.

14. Probably that engraved by Monaco; see F. Vivian, *Il Console Smith mercante e collezionista*, 1971, pp. 223–4.

15. Pallucchini, under no. 128.

16. The documents published first by Urbani, *op. cit.*, pp. 100 ff; transcribed not entirely accurately but with no significant error.

17. See Sohm, *loc. cit.*, p. 77, n. 2. Disappointing as a text is P. d'Ancona, *Tiepolo in Milan, The Palazzo Clerici Frescoes*, 1956, as documentation and interpretation.

18. A fine group of these is divided between the Metropolitan Museum of Art and the Pierpont Morgan Library, New York; see the catalogue by J. Bean and F. Stampfle, of the exhibition, *Drawings from New York Collections*, III: *The Eighteenth Century in Italy*, New York, 1971, nos 74–93.

5. 'MOST EXCELLENT PAINTER OF OUR DAY . . .'

1. Zanetti's comment published by Urbani, *op. cit.*, pp. 103–4.
2. For some of these influences see the excellent discussion by H. Diane Russell in the catalogue of the exhibition, *Rare Etchings by Giovanni Battista and Demenico Tiepolo*, Washington, 1972. For more recent bibliography and further discussion of Tiepolo's etchings see the exhibition catalogue, *Da Carlevarijs ai Tiepolo . . .* pp. 354 ff. For Domenico's collection of prints and drawings (sold in Paris in 1845), see J. Byam Shaw, *The Drawings of Domenico Tiepolo*, 1962, p. 18, n. 8.
3. For Ricci's activity as an etcher see the catalogue cited in the note above, pp. 328–43.
4. For this latter point, see Knox, *op. cit.*, 1975, p. 61 (no. 111); see also M. Santifaller in *Pantheon*, 1975, pp. 331 ff.
5. See A. Mariuz, *L'opera completa del Piazzetta*, 1982, no. 97.
6. In a dedicatory letter, dated 24 January 1751, to the Prince of Liechtenstein, conveniently quoted in the exhibition catalogue, *Da Carlevarijs ai Tiepolo . . .*, p. 357, n. 6.
7. For these, see the exhibition catalogue cited in the note above, pp. 166–9. Left unidentified there as merely 'Dama con cortigiane, paggi e guardie' (no. 189) is a scene of ancient history, showing either Sophonisba or Artemisia.
8. For the documentation so far published, see the references in the catalogue edited by A. Rizzi, of the exhibition, *Mostra del Tiepolo: Dipinti; Disegni e Acqueforti*, Passariano, 1971, under no. 33.
9. Pallucchini, nos 126–7. Those sketches are in the museum at Buenos Aires and have probably not been examined by many scholars.
10. See Urbani, *op. cit.*, p. 106, and *ibid.* for subsequent quotations.
11. W. E. Addis and T. Arnold, *A Catholic Dictionary*, 1952 ed., under 'Scapula'.
12. For very full discussion of the ceiling, its significance and the circumstances of its commissioning, see W. L. Barcham in *The Art Bulletin*, Sept., 1979, pp. 430–47, utilised for what follows in the text.
13. *Ibid.*, p. 440.
14. Reproduced in *Gli Affreschi nelle Ville Venete . . .*, plates volume, fig. 274.
15. Pallucchini, no. 143; the modello, after cleaning, in the exhibition at Agnew's, London, *Venetian Eighteenth-Century Painting*, 1985, no. 25.
16. Pallucchini, *op. cit.*, no. 160 O.
16a. See L. Münz, *Rembrandt's Etchings*, 1952, vol. I, pls. 55–57.
17. See the discussion in *Gli Affreschi nelle Ville Venete . . .*, no. 118, pp. 197–8.
18. The letter published posthumously by G. Fogolari, *Nuova Antologia*, Sept., 1942, pp. 34–5.
19. Daniels, *op. cit.*, nos 267 and 268.
20. See G. B. Rodella, *Le Pitture . . . di Brescia*, 1760, p. 149.

6. THE FRIEND AND THE SON

1. Quoted in T. Pignatti, *Pietro Longhi*, 1968, p. 70.
2. On Algarotti's artistic activities and career, see particularly Haskell, *op. cit.*, pp. 347 ff and pp. 409–10, with earlier references. The fundamental article on Algarotti's relations with the court at Dresden remains H. Posse in *Prussian Jahrbuch*, 1931, *Beiheft*, pp. 1–73, publishing Algarotti's correspondence, and his accounts, from which quotation is made here.
3. Letter of 13 February 1751, to Mariette; see Bottari-Ticozzi, *Lettere Pittoriche*, vol. VII, 1822, p. 372. Giambattista's Punchinello drawings are discussed by G. Knox in *Interpretazioni Veneziane* (Studies in honour of Michelangelo Muraro), 1984, pp. 439–46.
4. On the question of this 'Gran Ritratto', see M. Levey in *Arte Veneta*, 1978, pp. 420–1.
5. See M. Precerutti Garberi, 'Di alcuni dipinti perduti del Tiepolo', *Commentari*, April-June 1958, pp. 111–12; she also prints Algarotti's 'programme' for the *Timotheus*, drawn from his *Opere*, 1791, vol. XIII, pp. 379–81.
6. Pallucchini, no. 154.
7. Printed by Posse, *loc. cit.*, p. 49, n. 3.
8. Algarotti's will published by G. da Pozzo in *Atti dell'Istituto Veneto . . .*, 1963–64, pp. 181–92.
9. On this subject, see for example M. Santifaller in *Arte Veneta*, 1977, pp. 135–144.
10. For this incident, see Posse, *loc. cit.*, p. 52, n. 2.
11. Knox, *op. cit.*, 1975, no. 329.
12. Posse, *loc. cit.*, p. 64.
13. In a letter of 21 June 1758, reproduced in facsimile, but not transcribed, by L. C. J. Frerichs in *Gazette des Beaux-Arts*, vol. LXXVIII 1971, p. 234.
14. See A. Mariuz, *Giandomenico Tiepolo*, [1971], p. 22.
15. Reproduced in Morassi, *op. cit.*, 1962, fig. 129. For date of delivery of the altarpiece, see F. Zava Bocazzi in *Arte Veneta*, 1976, pp. 232–40. For the related chalk drawings, see G. Knox, *Giambattista and Domenico Tiepolo. A Study and Catalogue raisonné of the Chalk Drawings*, 1980, vol. I, p. 329 (under his ref. X. 11).
16. Pallucchini, no. 242.
17. F. Corner, *Ecclesiae Venetae . . .*, vol. II, 1749, p. 314.
18. The precise member of the Pisani family established by G. Pavanello, when publishing Mengozzi's drawing for the ceiling, in *Bollettino dei Musei Civici Veneziani*, 1979, nos 1–4, pp. 52–9.
19. See M. Levey, 'Two Paintings by Tiepolo from the Algarotti Collection', *Burlington Magazine*, 1960, p. 257.
20. Reasonably good illustrations of the two wall frescoes in Morassi, *op. cit.*, 1962, figs. 318a and b.
21. Fogolari, *loc. cit.*, pp. 36–7.
22. For the complete text, see the exhibition catalogue, *Da Carlevarijs ai Tiepolo . . .*, no. 500.

7. PALAZZO LABIA AND THE THEME OF CLEOPATRA AND ANTONY

1. The fullest documentation, illustration and discussion in T. Pignatti, F. Pedrocco and E. Martinelli Pedrocco, *Palazzo Labia a Venezia*, 1982, with all references and material not otherwise cited below.
2. See *Bergeret et Fragonard: Journal inédit . . .*, ed. M. A. Tornézy, 1895, p. 388.

3. See A. Berti, *Elogio di G. B. Tiepolo*, 1856, p. 20.
4. For these drawings see the discussion in G. Knox, *op. cit.*, 1980, vol. I, pp. 14–18, but see also the caveats in Pignatti *et al.*, *op. cit.*, pp. 79–84.
5. For this see M. Levey, *Tiepolo. Banquet of Cleopatra* (Charlton Lecture), 1965, unpaginated [p. 3].
6. *Ibid.*, n. 23.
7. Reproduced in Pignatti *et al.*, *op. cit.*, pp. 192–3.
8. Haskell, *op. cit.*, 1980, p. 257.
9. For the original Labia collection, see Pignatti *et al.*, *op. cit.*, pp. 163 ff.; their pl. 152 (p. 167) reproduces Tiepolo's altarpiece in colour.
10. Pignatti *et al.*, *op. cit.*, pl. 50 (p. 73).

8. THE YEARS AT WÜRZBURG

1. Pallucchini, nos 190A-E.
2. On this point, see Levey *loc. cit.*, 1978, pp. 418–19.
3. Pallucchini, no. 191. The painting is now in the Australian National Gallery, Canberra.
4. The facts, previously unknown and the subject of confusing hypotheses, established by A. Perez Sanchez, 'Nueva documentación para un Tiepolo problematico', *Archivo Español de Arte*, 1977, pp. 75 ff., leading to re-dating of the painting.
5. Pallucchini, no. 189.
6. For Würzburg and the context for Tiepolo generally, see R. Sedelmaier and R. Pfister, *Die Fürstbischöfliche Residenz zu Würzburg*, 1923, documenting aspects of the building now destroyed; the catalogue of the exhibition, *Tiepolo in Würzburg, 1750–1753*, Würzburg, 1951; M. H. von Freeden and C. Lamb, *Tiepolo. Die Fresken der Würzburger Residenz*, 1956; F. Büttner and W. C. von der Mülbe, *Giovanni Battista Tiepolo. Die Fresken in der Residenz zu Würzburg*, 1980. For the ceiling of the staircase, see particularly M. Ashton, 'Allegory, Fact and Meaning in Giambattista Tiepolo's Four Continents at Würzburg', *Art Bulletin*, March 1978, pp. 109–25.
7. Freeden and Lamb, *op. cit.*, p. 25.
8. See E. Hempel, *Baroque Art and Architecture in Central Europe* (Pelican History of Art), 1965, p. 161.
9. Printed in Freeden and Lamb, *op. cit.*, pp. 107–9.
10. 'gut vorangekommen'; quoted by Freeden and Lamb, *ibid.*, p. 28.
11. See Pallucchini, no. 199, with earlier references.
12. See Knox, *op. cit.*, 1980, pp. 39 ff., for views on Giambattista's activity at Würzburg, and pp. 51 ff., for those on Domenico's.
13. Freeden and Lamb, *op. cit.*, p. 107.
14. L. Münz, *Rembrandt's Etchings*, 1952, vol. I, pls 314–15.
15. Freeden and Lamb, *op. cit.*, p. 29.
16. Reproduced by Freeden and Lamb, *ibid.*, fig 3 and Ashton, *loc. cit.*, p. 122.
17. For this, see Byam Shaw, *op. cit.*, p. 81, no. 45.
18. See, for example, the exhibition catalogue, *Rare Etchings by Giovanni Battista and Domenico Tiepolo*, no. 41.

9. THE LAST YEARS IN ITALY

1. Usefully discussed and illustrated in the exhibition catalogue, *Da Carlevarijs ai Tiepolo* . . ., pp. 225 ff., nos 270–8.
2. See Morassi, *op. cit.*, 1962, p. 235.
3. The documents given in Mariuz, *op. cit.*, 1982, p. 73.

4. *Descrizione di tutte le pubbliche pitture . . . di Venezia*, ed. A. M. Zanetti, 1733, p. 266.
5. In a letter of 10 May 1760: G. Fogolari, 'Lettere inedite di G. B. Tiepolo', *Nuova Antologia*, September 1942, pp. 35–6. A letter of Domenico's, of 1758, already refers to his father suffering severely from gout, *cf.* M. Precerutti Garberi, 'Segnalazioni Tiepoleschi', *Commentari*, 1964, p. 249.
6. On the question of chronology, see the discussion by Russell in the exhibition catalogue, *Rare Etchings* . . ., and by Succi in the catalogue, *Da Carlevarijs ai Tiepolo* . . ., pp. 354 ff., with further references.
7. *Diderot Salons*, ed. J. Seznec and J. Adhémar, vol. III, (1767), 1965, p. 228. For Piazzetta's vignettes, referred to immediately below in the text, see the catalogue by G. Knox of the exhibition, *Piazzetta*, Washington, 1983, nos 100 and 101.
8. For the church and its decoration, including that by Tiepolo, see D. E. Kaley, *The Church of the Pietà*, 1980, utilised for what follows in the text here.
9. Pallucchini, no. 216A.
10. Kaley, *op. cit.*, p. 21.
11. Pallucchini, no. 237.
12. Pallucchini, no. 244.
13. Knox, *op. cit.*, 1980, M.637 and pl. 201.
14. For this see Mariuz, *op. cit.*,]1971], pp. 154–5 and *passim* for further references.
15. See the poem printed by P. L. Sohm, 'Unknown Epithalamia as sources for G. B. Tiepolo's iconography and style', *Arte Veneta*, 1983, p. 143.
16. M. Precerutti Garberi, 'Asterischi sulla attività di Domenico Tiepolo a Würzburg', *Commentari*, 1960, p. 269.
17. Extracts from the documents printed by Morassi, *op. cit.*, 1962, p. 236.
18. Pallucchini, no. 96.
19. Pallucchini, nos 245A and B.
20. Tiepolo's letter, of 16 March 1761, addressed to Algarotti, printed by Fogolari, *loc. cit.*, pp. 36–7.
21. See further Sohm, *loc. cit.*, 1983, pp. 138 ff., for poetic references and what follows in the text.
22. The identity of the commissioner published, along with much useful discussion, by L. Puppi, 'I Tiepolo a Vicenza e le statue dei "Nani" di Villa Valmarana a S. Bastiano', *Atti dell'Istituto Veneto* . . ., 1968, pp. 211–50.
23. Mariuz, *op. cit.*, 1982, no. 154.
24. Pallucchini, no. 112B. For examples in oil, see her nos. 53 and 217.
25. Cited by M. Levey, 'Tiepolo's treatment of classical story at Villa Valmarana', *Journal of the Warburg and Courtauld Institutes*, July–December, 1957, p. 307.
26. For some discussion, see G. Knox, 'The Tasso cycles of Giambattista Tiepolo and Gianantonio Guardi', *Museum Studies* (Art Institute of Chicago), 9, 1978, pp. 49 ff.
27. Pallucchini, nos 236 and 235 respectively.
28. See O. Lavrova, 'Le Tele di Giambattista Tiepolo nel Museo Statale delle Belle Arti A. S. Pushkin (Mosca)', in *Atti del Congresso internazionale di studi sul Tiepolo*, 1970, p. 127 ff.
29. A group of these is in the Victoria & Albert Museum; see Knox, *op. cit.*, 1975, nos 249–60.
30. Mariuz, *op. cit.*, [1971], pp. 138–9 and pls 157–64.
31. Fogolari, *loc. cit.*, p. 37.
32. See the reference to F. M. Tassi, *Vite de'pittori,*

Scultori e Architetti bergamaschi, 1790, vol. I, p. 135 in the exhibition catalogue, *Mostra del Tiepolo, Dipinti*, under no. 70 (p. 138). For the suggestion that Tiepolo's daughters are portrayed, see Precerutti Garberi, *loc. cit.*, 1964, pp. 257 ff.

33. See *Gli Affreschi nelle Ville Venete . . .*, pp. 242–8; to the bibliography there should be added W. Collier, 'The Villa Pisani at Strà', *Italian Studies*, 1962, pp. 35 ff.

34. For this and other references in the text, see Morassi, *op. cit.*, 1962, pp. 236–7.

35. Urbani, *op. cit.*, pp. 62 ff. (Cecilia Tiepolo's will of 1777).

36. See the citation in M. Levey, *Painting in Eighteenth-Century Venice*, 1980 ed., p. 154.

37. Cited by F. Haskell, *op. cit.*, 1980 ed., p. 253, note 2; for Gozzi's comments, see his pp. 323–4.

10. SPAIN: FROM 'GRANDIOSAS IDEAS' TO DEATH

1. Morassi, *op. cit.*, p. 238.

2. For this see Bean and Stampfle, *op. cit.*, no. 150.

3. Urbani, *op. cit.*, p. 49.

4. E. Battisti in *Arte Antica e Moderna*, 1960, pp. 77 ff. for the exchange of letters between Tiepolo and the Spanish ambassador (pp. 80–1 for the ambassador's mention of 'Amigo à Amigo', etc).

5. Morassi, *op. cit.*, 1962, pp. 238–9, for partial publication of the documents; see also F. J. Sánchez Cantón, *J. B. Tiepolo en España*, 1953, though with only brief extracts.

6. H. Swinburne, *Travels through Spain in the years 1775 and 1776*, 1779, p. 337.

7. The imperial ambassador reported in 1764 that 'Le Confesseur est toujours sur le meme pied, quoiqu' il lui arrive quelques fois de ne pas réussir, mais cela n'arrive ordinairement que dans les cas où le Roi a pris sa resolution avant de lui avoir parlé': see letter printed in M. del Carmen Velázquez, *La España de Carlos III de 1764 a 1776 según los embajadores Austriacos*, 1963, p. 19. More generally for the King and the background, see A. H. Hull, *Charles III and the revival of Spain*, 1981.

8. The letter printed in *Opere di Antonio Raffaello Mengs*, ed. G. N. d'Azara and C. Fea, 1787, p. xx, n. b; Mengs added 'tutti due bravi nel fresco . . .'

9. The point seems first made by Knox, *op. cit.*, 1980, p. 75, n. 1.

10. Some conveniently reproduced in the section on Lorenzo in the exhibition catalogue, *Mostra del Tiepolo: Dipinti . . .*, pp. 183 ff.

11. Pallucchini, nos 279D and D¹.

12. Pallucchini, no. 19D.

13. Pallucchini, no. 282.

14. Catalogued by E. Young, *Catalogue of the Spanish and Italian Paintings* (Bowes Museum, Barnard Castle), 1970, pp. 98–100, as pre-Spanish period in date.

15. See the exhibition catalogue, *Da Carlevarijs ai Tiepolo . . .*, no. 538 (the wrong number accompanies the reproduction).

16. Urbani, *op. cit.*, pp. 24–5.

17. The portrait is D. Honisch, *Anton Raphael Mengs*, 1965, p. 104, no. 148.

18. Pallucchini, no. 289.

19. The letter printed in full in G. M. Urbani de Gheltof, *Tiepolo in Ispagna*, 1881, p. 7.

20. The latest and most authoritative discussion, with many new points, by C. Whistler, 'Tiepolo and Charles III: the church of S. Pascual Baylon at Aranjuez', *Apollo*, May 1985, pp. 321 ff.

21. Urbani, *op. cit.*, 1881, p. 9.

22. See the careful discussion by H. Braham in the catalogue of the exhibition, *The Princes Gate Collection*, London, 1981, pp. 75–81, with reproduction of all the modelli. One further as yet little-studied painting of the Spanish period, conceivably related to the S. Pascual Baylon commission, is a *Vision of the Eucharist*, published in the catalogue of the exhibition, *Art–Commerce–Scholarship*, Colnaghi, London, Nov.–Dec. 1984, (no. 32).

23. Pallucchini, no. 108.

24. This is revealed by a recent X-ray, knowledge of which I owe to Helen Braham.

25. Knox, *op. cit.*, 1980, vol. I, p. 328, no. X 7.

26. Urbani, *op. cit.*, 1881, pp. 11–12.

27. Knox, *op. cit.*, 1980, vol. I, p. 328, no. X 4.

28. The paintings are Pallucchini, nos 299D and E.

29. Knox, *op. cit.*, 1980, vol. I, p. 328, no. X 2.

30. Pallucchini, nos 299G and F.

31. Reproduced by Knox, *op. cit.*, 1980, vol. II, pl. 261.

32. The letter cited in note 26 above.

33. Urbani, *op. cit.*, 1881, pp. 14–15.

34. For the commission and the eventual outcome, see P. E. Muller, 'Francisco Bayeu, Tiepolo and the Trinitarian Dome Frescoes of the Colegiata at La Granja', *Pantheon*, 1977, pp. 20–8.

35. See the article by C. Whistler, linking the painting to the La Granja commission, 'A Modello for Tiepolo's Final Commission: The Allegory of the Immaculate Conception', *Apollo*, March 1985, pp. 172 ff.

36. Pallucchini, no. 294.

37. The facts derive from a document printed by Urbani, *op. cit.*, 1879, pp. 47–50.

38. The record of Tiepolo's death printed accurately in M. Agulló y Cobo, *Mas Noticias sobre Pintores Madrileños de los siglos XVI al XVIII*, 1981, pp. 191–2.

39. For this and what follows, see the article cited in note 20 above.

SELECT BIBLIOGRAPHY

THIS BIBLIOGRAPHY omits periodical literature (to which there are numerous references in the Notes) and is deliberately selective in concentrating on the artist himself, along with his sons, and in citing only some important exhibition catalogues and books, among the latter a few more useful for their plates than for their text.

EXHIBITION CATALOGUES

Mostra del Tiepolo, Venice, 1951
Tiepolo in Würzburg, Würzburg, 1951
Disegni del Tiepolo, Udine, 1965
Dal Ricci al Tiepolo, Venice, 1969
Tiepolo, a bicentenary exhibition, Cambridge, Mass., 1970
Tiepolo. Zeichnungen von Giambattista, Domenico und Lorenzo Tiepolo, Stuttgart, 1970
Le Acqueforti del Tiepolo, Udine, 1970
Mostra del Tiepolo: Dipinti; Disegni e Acqueforti, Passariano, 1971
Rare Etchings by Giovanni Battista and Domenico Tiepolo, Washington, 1972
The Tiepolos: Painters to Princes and Prelates, Birmingham, Alabama–Springfield, Mass., 1978
Tiepolo, tecnica e immaginazione, Venice, 1979
Domenico Tiepolo's Punchinello Drawings, Bloomington–Stanford, 1979
Drawings by Tiepolo and Guardi from The Princes Gate Collection, London, 1982
Giambattista Tiepolo, il segno e l'enigma, Gorizia, 1985; Venice, 1986
I Tiepolo: virtuosismo e ironia, Mirano, 1988
I Tiepolo e il Settecento vicentino, Montecchio Maggiore–Vicenza–Bassano del Grappa, 1990
Giambattista Tiepolo, Hanover, 1990
Giambattista Tiepolo. Master of the Oil Sketch, Fort Worth, 1993

BOOKS

P. d'Ancona, *Tiepolo in Milan, the Palazzo Clerici Frescoes*, 1956
W. L. Barcham, *The Religious Paintings of Giambattista Tiepolo*, 1989
W. L. Barcham, *Giambattista Tiepolo*, 1992
G. Brunel, *Tiepolo*, 1991
F. Büttner and W. C. von der Mühlbe, *Giovanni Battista Tiepolo. Die Fresken in der Residenz zu Würzburg*, 1980
J. Byam Shaw, *The Drawings of Domenico Tiepolo*, 1962
H. de Chennevières, *Les Tiepolo*, 1898

M. H. von Freeden and C. Lamb, *Tiepolo. Die Fresken der Würzburger Residenz*, 1956
A. M. Gealt, *Domenico Tiepolo: The Punchinello Drawings*, 1986
D. von Hadeln, *Handzeichnungen von G. B. Tiepolo*, 1927
H. W. Hegemann, *G. B. Tiepolo*, 1940
T. Hetzer, *Die Fresken in der Würzburger Residenz*, 1943
G. Knox, *Catalogue of the Tiepolo Drawings in the Victoria & Albert Museum*, 1960 (second ed., 1975)
——*Domenico Tiepolo. Raccolta di Teste*, 1970
——*Giambattista and Domenico Tiepolo. A Study and Catalogue raisonné of the Chalk Drawings*, 1980
G. Lorenzetti, *Il Quaderno dei Tiepolo al Museo Correr di Venezia*, 1946
A. Mariuz, *Giandomenico Tiepolo*, 1971
G. Mazzariol and T. Pignatti, *Itinerario Tiepolesco*, 1951
G. Molfese and A. Centelli, *Gli Affreschi di G. B. Tiepolo*, 1898
P. Molmenti, Tiepolo. *La Villa Valmarana*, 1880 (second ed., 1928)
——*G. B. Tiepolo*, 1909 (French ed., 1911)
A. Morassi, *G. B. Tiepolo*, 1943
——*G. B. Tiepolo. His life and work*, 1955
——*A Complete catalogue of the paintings of G. B. Tiepolo*, 1962
A. Pallucchini, *L'opera completa di Giambattista Tiepolo*, 1968
R. Pallucchini, *Gli Affreschi di Giambattista e Domenico Tiepolo alla Villa Valmarana*, 1945
——*L'Arte di Giambattista Tiepolo*, pt. I, 1970–71; pt. II, 1971–72
F. Pedrocco, *Disegni di Giandomenico Tiepolo*, 1990
F. Pedrocco and M. Gemin, *Giambattista Tiepolo. I Dipinti. Opera Completa*, 1993
T. Pignatti, *Tiepolo*, 1951
——*Le Aqueforti del Tiepolo*, 1965
T. Pignatti, F. Pedrocco, E. Martinelli Peddrocco, *Palazzo Labia a Venezia*, 1982
A. Rizzi, *The Etchings of the Tiepolos*, 1971
——*Tiepolo a Udine*, 1971 (second ed., 1974)
E. Sack, *G. B. und D. Tiepolo*, 1910
F. J. Sánchez Cantón, *J. B. Tiepolo en España*, 1953
G. M. Urbani de Gheltof, *Tiepolo e la sua famiglia*, 1879
——*Tiepolo in Ispagna*, 1881
G. Vigni, *Disegni del Tiepolo*, 1942 (second ed., 1972)

INDEX OF PERSONS

ILLUSTRATIONS

Figures in **bold type** denote the page number of an illustration. Works are by Giambattista Tiepolo unless otherwise indicated.

PHOTOGRAPHIC ACKNOWLEDGEMENTS

With the exception of those plates listed below, photographs have been supplied by the owners and are reproduced with their kind permission. Special thanks are due to Celia Jones and Helen Braham for their help in the collection of photographs.

Alinari, Florence: 4, 7, 8, 9, 12, 15, 17, 27, 38, 43, 57, 66, 94, 100, 101, 106, 126, 213
Jörg P. Anders, Berlin: 3, 121
Arxiu Mas, Barcelona: 218, 219, 220
Joachim Blauel, Artothek, Munich: 77, 183

Osvaldo Böhm, Venice: 23, 33, 34, 36, 37, 56, 79, 82, 90, 92, 106, 109, 110, 111, 116, 117, 128, 199, 204
Photographie Bulloz, Paris: 119, 131, 134
Christies, London: 225
Foto Elio Ciol, Casarsa: 1, 2, 40, 41, 42, 43, 44, 45, 49, 50, 104, 210, jacket
Foto Costa, Milan: 65, 97
Archivio I.G.D.A., Milan: 72
Bildarchiv Foto Marburg: 149, 156, 157, 186
Wolf-Christian von der Mülbe, Dachau: 158, 159,

161, 162, 170, 175, 178, 179, 180, 181, 182, 187
The National Gallery, London: 117
Phaidon Press, Oxford: 105
Photo Routhier, Paris: 132, 133
Scala, Florence: 21, 84, 102, 103, 107, 135, 136, 137, 140, 151, 153, 200, 201, 202, 203, 206, endpapers
Silvana Editoriale d'Arte, Milan: 203, 204
Foto Riccardo Viola, Mortelgliano, 39, 46, 47, 79